FORMULA ONE

FIA WORLD CHAMPIONSHIP 1988

GRID
PUBLISHING

CONTENTS

PUBLISHER Nick Hervey
EDITOR Bob Constanduros
DEPUTY EDITOR Penny Holme
FEATURES EDITOR Derick Allsop
ART DIRECTOR Nicci Walker
RESULTS & STATISTICS
Mark Flanders
EDITORIAL ASSISTANT
Lorraine Dalgleish
CHIEF PHOTOGRAPHER
John Dunbar
PRODUCTION DIRECTOR
John Petty
PRODUCTION MANAGER
Lauri Brill
SECRETARY Julie Price
EXECUTIVE PUBLISHER
Terry Humphreys

Formula One, FIA Yearbook 1988 is published by Grid Publishing, Greater London House, Hampstead Road, London NW1 7QQ. A subsidiary of Home & Law Publishing.

Printed in the UK by Purnell Book Production Ltd, Paulton, Bristol. Design Consultants, D4, London SW6. Colour origination by Thames Colour Scanning, Acton, London W3. Typesetting by Facet Film Composing Ltd, Leigh-on-Sea, Essex.

Photographs in **Formula One** have been contributed by: John Dunbar, Bryn Williams, David Winter, Bernard Asset, Ferdi Kraling, J-P Froidevaux, Stephen Tee, Keith Sutton, David Phipps, Lukas Gorys, Dave Kennard, Peter Nygaard, Patrick Behar, Mark Newcombe, Jeff Bloxham, Rainer Schlegelmilch, Stephen Davis, Graham Smith, Ercole Colombo, John Blakemore, Peter Gurr, Toshiyuki Kita, Charles Briscoe-Knight, Gerard Petitsean, David Martin.

ACKNOWLEDGEMENTS: The Publisher and Editor would like to thank the following for their assistance in compiling the 1988 FIA Yearbook: Richard West, Creighton Brown, Manfred Oettinger, Kasper Arnet, Derick Allsop, Jackie Stewart, Ann Bradshaw, Hartmut Ganter, David Phipps, Harvey Postlethwaite, Ron Dennis, Agnes Carlier, Peter Windsor, Paul Trenthardt, Frank Dernie, Stuart Sykes, Louise Tingstrom, Tony Jardine, Byron Young, Peter Wright, Ian Phillips, Jackie Oliver, Peter Collins, Danny Hindenhoch, Heini Mader, Derek Moore, Zooom Photographic, Peter Warr, Ken Tyrrell, Venetia Howes, Riccardo Suni, Walt Stannard, David Warren, Mick de Haas, Daniel Beauvois, Lisa Gillson, Michael Holt, John Bisignano, Herbie Blash, Alan Woollard, Sally Shackleton, Antonio Marron, Barry Griffin, Jane Constanduros, Noel Stanbury, Nigel Wollheim, Simon Arkless.

FOREWORD

BERNIE ECCLESTONE

The 1987 season has been another extremely successful year considering that this was the first of the transitional years during which normally aspirated engines take over from turbos. Some teams and drivers were apprehensive about these regulations, but we can see that these fears were not justified.

The racing throughout the field this year was excellent and some of the high spots are recorded in the Formula One Yearbook. Once again over 110,000,000 television viewers in 45 countries were able to follow the FIA Formula One World Championship from its opening in Rio de Janeiro, Brazil, to the close in Adelaide, Australia, as well as nearly 2,000,000 spectators who attended the 16 events. The popularity of the FIA Championship transcends all time and date zones.

In no way did the inclusion of the normally aspirated cars detract from the year's racing. Their own battles for the Jim Clark and Colin Chapman Trophies were just as exciting as those at the front of the field and it proves that we can look forward to even closer racing in the future.

While there has been progress on the track, there have also been developments off the track, and this year the promoters have improved facilities for spectators at many circuits. Furthermore, the promotional possibilities for companies involved in Grand Prix racing have been improved and they are now offered more in terms of exposure and corporate hospitality than ever before.

Progress is what this sport is all about – this year has proved it, and we all look forward to a successful future.

BERNIE ECCLESTONE

5

1987 FIA WORLD CHAMPIONSHIP STATISTICS

Driver	Nat.	Car	Brazil	San Marino	Belgium	Monaco	Detroit	France	Britain	Germany	Hungary	Austria	Italy	Portugal	Spain	Mexico	Japan	Australia	World Championship Points	No. of Grand Prix started	Total Points To Date	No. of Grand Prix Wins	No. of Pole Positions
6 Nelson Piquet	BR	Williams-Honda	2	DNS	R	2	2	2	2	1	1	2	1	3	4	2	15	R	73 (76)	141	378	20	25
5 Nigel Mansell	GB	Williams-Honda	6	1	R	R	5	1	1	R	14	1	3	R	1	1	DNS	–	61	104	202	13	12
12 Ayrton Senna	BR	Lotus-Honda	R	2	R	1	1	4	3	3	2	5	2	7	5	R	2	D	57	62	163	6	15
1 Alain Prost	F	McLaren-TAG	1	R	1	9	3	3	R	7	3	6	15	1	2	R	7	R	46	121	406.5	28	16
28 Gerhard Berger	A	Ferrari	4	R	R	4	4	R	R	R	R	R	4	2	R	R	1	1	36	52	57	3	3
2 Stefan Johansson	S	McLaren-TAG	3	4	2	R	7	8	R	2	R	7	6	5	3	R	3	R	30	57	82	–	–
27 Michele Alboreto	I	Ferrari	8	3	R	3	R	R	R	R	R	R	R	R	15	R	4	2	17	105	147.5	5	2
20 Thierry Boutsen	B	Benetton-Ford	5	R	R	R	R	R	7	R	4	4	5	14	16	R	5	3	15	73	31	–	–
19 Teo Fabi	I	Benetton-Ford	R	R	R	8	R	5	6	R	R	3	7	4	R	5	R	R	12	64	23	–	3
18 Eddie Cheever	USA	Arrows-Megatron	R	R	4	R	6	R	R	R	8	R	R	6	8	4	9	R	8	102	58	–	–
11 Satoru Nakajima	J	Lotus-Honda	7	6	5	10	R	R	4	R	R	13	11	8	9	R	6	R	7	16	7	–	–
3 Jonathan Palmer	GB	Tyrrell-Ford	10	R	DNS	5	11	7	8	5	7	15	14	10	R	7	8	4	7	55	7	–	–
7 Riccardo Patrese	I	Brabham-BMW	R	9	R	R	9	R	R	R	5	R	R	R	13	3	11		6	160	81	2	2
5		Williams-Honda																9					
8 Andrea de Cesaris	I	Brabham-BMW	R	R	3	R	R	R	R	R	R	R	R	R	R	R	R	8	4	104	31	–	1
4 Philippe Streiff	F	Tyrrell-Ford	11	8	9	R	R	6	R	4	9	DNS	12	12	7	8	12	R	4	37	11	–	–
17 Derek Warwick	GB	Arrows-Megatron	R	11	R	R	R	R	5	R	6	R	R	13	10	R	10	R	3	84	40	–	–
30 Philippe Alliot	F	Lola-Ford	–	10	8	R	R	R	R	6	R	12	R	R	6	6	R	R	3	48	4	–	–
9 Martin Brundle	GB	Zakspeed	R	5	R	7	R	R	R	R	R	14	R	R	11	R	R	R	2	47	10	–	–
25 Rene Arnoux	F	Ligier Megatron	–	DNS	6	11	10	R	R	R	R	10	10	R	R	R	R	R	1	126	179	7	18
16 Ivan Capelli	I	March-Ford	DNS	R	R	6	R	R	R	R	10	11	13	9	12	R	R	R	1	19	4	–	–
14 Roberto Moreno	BR	AGS-Ford	–	–	–	–	–	–	–	–	–	–	–	–	–	–	R	6	1	2	1	–	–
29 Yannick Dalmas	F	Lola-Ford	–	–	–	–	–	–	–	–	–	–	–	–	–	9	14	5	0*	3	0	–	–
10 Christian Danner	D	Zakspeed	9	7	R	D	8	R	R	R	R	9	9	DNS	R	R	R	7	0	31	1	–	–
14 Pascal Fabre	F	AGS-Ford	12	13	10	13	12	9	9	R	13	R	DNQ	DNQ	R	DNQ	–	–	0	11	0	–	–
26 Piercarlo Ghinzani	I	Ligier-Megatron	–	R	7	12	R	R	D	R	12	8	8	R	R	R	13	R	0	65	2	–	–
23 Adrian Campos	E	Minardi-Motori Moderni	D	R	R	DNS	R	R	R	R	R	R	R	R	14	R	R	R	0	14	0	–	–
24 Alessandro Nannini	I	Minardi-Motori Moderni	R	R	R	R	R	R	R	R	11	R	16	11	R	R	R	R	0	31	0	–	–
21 Alex Caffi	I	Osella-Alfa Romeo	R	12	R	R	R	R	R	R	R	R	R	R	DNQ	R	R	DNQ	0	15	0	–	–
32 Nicola Larini	I	Coloni-Ford	–	–	–	–	–	–	–	–	–	–	DNQ	–	R	–	–	–	0	1	0	–	–
22 Franco Forini	SW	Osella-Alfa Romeo	–	–	–	–	–	–	–	–	–	–	R	R	DNQ	–	–	–	0	2	0	–	–
22 Gabriele Tarquini	I	Osella-Alfa Romeo	–	R	–	–	–	–	–	–	–	–	–	–	–	–	–	–	0	1	0	–	–
7 Stefano Modena	I	Brabham-BMW	–	–	–	–	–	–	–	–	–	–	–	–	–	–	–	R	0	1	0	–	–

R   Retired
DNS   Did not start
D   Disqualified
DNQ   Did not qualify
*The second Lola wasn't entered in the World Championship at the start of the season, and therefore not eligible for points.

NELSON PIQUET

WORLD CHAMPION

by Bob Constanduros

It was said that he had never won a race in the true sense of the word, that his driving was frivolous, that he was overpaid, that he was lucky and usually out-driven by his own team mate. But Nelson Piquet won the 1987 World Championship in his own indomitable way.

Piquet's third World Championship title came in Japan when team mate and sworn rival Nigel Mansell crashed in the first qualifying session. However tense the relationship with his team mate has seemed over the years, Piquet admitted that, "winning the Championship while seeing someone fly up in the air and get hurt is not good. But the Championship is not this one race," he added, "it is all the races in the year". Statistics show that in the 14 races in which they battled over the World Championship, Nelson out-qualified Nigel four times, he was quicker in the warm-up only once, and he finished ahead of him just three times. But as Nelson pointed out later, there were several times when he drove to take second. This he discussed with Honda engineers beforehand. Austria was one race, for example. That would explain why, when Nigel cleverly used traffic to take the lead, Nelson simply fell away – and finished second.

Italy, on the other hand, was a race that Nelson desperately wanted to win. He'd put in over 4500 miles of testing with the active suspension with only the help of Jean-Louis Schlesser and none from his team mate. Here Piquet felt he would have the advantage and he wanted to use it. He started from pole position and pulled out a 12 second lead before stopping for tyres. Senna didn't stop for tyres and Piquet found himself an equal margin behind his compatriot when he emerged from the pits. Almost instantly

he overheated his tyres as he found himself battling with his own team mate, but he soon began to whittle away Senna's 12 second lead. This was a no-holds-barred contest. Both drivers admitted taking risks that they perhaps hadn't taken in other races. In the end, Senna had less luck than Piquet. The Lotus driver took a risk overtaking Ghinzani and it didn't come off. He spun, Piquet nipped past and Senna rejoined. While Senna took up the role of the chaser, both set their fastest laps on the penultimate lap on tyres that were well past their useful active life.

There was no doubt about the risks taken that day, about the racer in Piquet. People said that Piquet was lucky with his victories. After all, he inherited victory from Prost five laps from the end of the German Grand Prix, inherited victory from Mansell six laps from the end of the Hungarian Grand Prix and that victory in Italy from Senna. His own team counters that 'lucky' claim. The man put himself into that situation of being able to inherit the lead or take six points. How many drivers in Formula One would sniff at six points? The man, it must be remembered, is an out and out racer. He lives for nothing else. With his third title in the bag, he was asked how many more World Championships he would fight for. He admitted, maybe five or six and shrugged, as if to say, who knows? He had no retirement thoughts after three titles. Racing is his life. What

people fail to give Piquet credit for is that he knows the game inside out and backwards after 140 Grand Prix. He hasn't just won the title once. He's known how to win it three times, in different circumstances. After all, his Brabham team mates were never as threatening as Mansell was in 1987. In some ways, this was a new experience. But look how he coped with it.

Piquet only revealed his biggest problem in winning his third World title when he had clinched it in Japan. There he spoke of how he had been ill-prepared for the 1986 season. "In some races I was so tired," he said in Japan. "I could have won Detroit that year so easily, but I came second instead. So then I decided to think about the next year, 1987. I worked a lot over the winter and started this year in very good shape." But then came the Imola accident, when his Williams-Honda suddenly careered off the track at around 180 mph, striking a retaining wall very hard. Although he was not badly injured – testimony itself to his machine – he did receive a bad bang on the head, spent the night in hospital and was not allowed to race on the Sunday. That, he said, was his bad luck for the year. But there was more to that accident than just the race. "It stopped me a lot," continued Nelson. "First I could not continue my physical preparation for a long time. I couldn't go jogging, for instance. But it wasn't only physical, it was mental as well. I couldn't sleep for more than two or three hours at a time. It was very difficult.

"I saw myself as less aggressive. My metabolism had changed. The doctors said that that was normal when you have a bang on the head and that it would take me a long time to recover. I am better, obviously, but I am not like I was before. I used to sleep a lot, ten, eleven hours a night. I can't sleep that much any more and if I have something to read, I lose concentration very easily. In the car I don't feel that way, but I don't feel as I was before in a lot of ways. But for me it was a very, very good year. I have been very consistent, taking very few chances and finishing most of the races. That is why I won the Championship. The engine failed in Belgium, but everywhere else the car was fantastic. If you compare me with Nigel, I think he was more aggressive. He had better results, but he also had the accident with Senna in Belgium."

Nelson still commands huge respect from his mechanics, and that is always an advantage. His biggest fans are probably still Brabham supporters – or even employees. He won the World Championship for Williams in 1987, and his mechanics in that team will always remember the fact, whatever team he drives for in the future.

Previous page: All set and ready to race

Above: Displaying the style and talent that led to his third World Championship

Right: Nelson in pensive mood

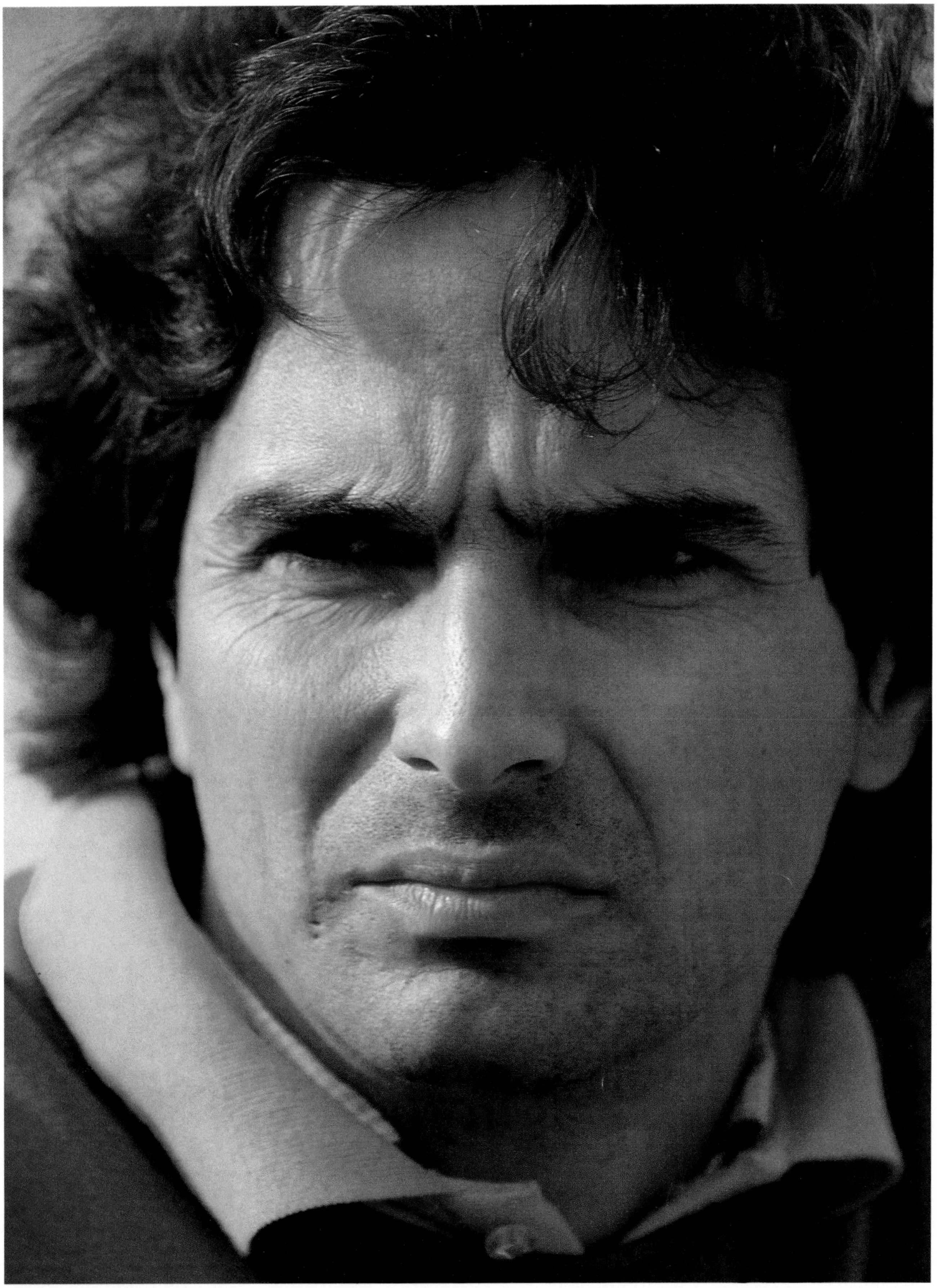

Left: Concentrating on winning

WILLIAMS

FIA CONSTRUCTORS' CHAMPIONS

by Derick Allsop

There can be few sporting teams who have had to contend with the controversy, internal conflict and public examination faced by Williams this past season. Yet in spite of these setbacks, they demolished the opposition in the Constructors' Championship, taking the title with record points.

Midway through the season it was obvious either Piquet or Mansell would become the champion driver and by the final two races, the other two candidates, Ayrton Senna and Alain Prost, had both lost any chance of taking the Drivers' Championship. The outcome brought a wry smile to the face of Frank Williams. "Not such a bad little effort really, is it?" he suggested. It is, in fact, a tribute to Williams and his charges that they have achieved so much success in spite of the extraordinary circumstances. It is an even greater tribute that we expected nothing less. Their expertise, their competitive zeal and their sheer consistency are taken for granted. Such is the burden of true excellence in any walk of life.

But what hurts even a man of Williams' remarkable resilience is a feeling that the endeavours and success of his team have been clouded by the rumblings of discontent and adverse publicity. The smile disappeared when Williams said: "I think it's a little sad that so much rubbish should have been said and written this year when Patrick Head and all the guys here and back at the factory have done such a fantastic job." Talking outside his motorhome hours before yet another triumphant race, Williams hit on a crucial point, revealing much about the man and his philosophy. "I can't praise the team too highly. Everyone has contributed and I believe everyone deserves credit. What makes them such a terrific team is that, without exception, they want to race and they want to win."

The Williams team were comfortable winners of the constructors' title in 1986 and were expected – not least by Honda – to carry off the drivers' crown as well. That was not to be. In Adelaide, Mansell's dramatic blow-out and Piquet's late stop allowed Prost to guide home his McLaren for a second successive Championship. There, insisted the critics, was proof that Williams' policy was wrong. He should, it was said, have restrained Mansell and ensured victory for Piquet, who was, after all, hired as the number one driver. Williams would not, and still does not, agree, "There was only one race last year where team orders would have made a difference, and that was the British Grand Prix at Brands Hatch."

He did not need to say more. You may recall Mansell held off Piquet for lap after lap with no-one else in sight before the Brazilian conceded and Britain celebrated a home success. Imagine the reaction of the 115,000 strong crowd and the millions more watching on television if a British team had instructed a British driver to move over and present the British Grand Prix to his partner. A similar situation arose at Silverstone during the 1987 British round. Piquet had ignited the contest with a few pre-race remarks about Mansell and the team. It was, by then, fairly clear that he would seek pastures new in 1988. Piquet was determined to upstage Mansell this time and won a ferocious scrap for pole position. The duel was resumed on race day and Mansell surged from behind to

claim another magnificent victory. Incredibly, the spectacle and the passion generated in that arena were even greater than at Brands Hatch 12 months earlier. An entire nation was captivated. Well, almost...

Again one or two voices questioned the wisdom of such racing. Couldn't both drivers have been forced off in the heat of the battle? Couldn't either or both have run out of fuel quite needlessly? What it comes down to is how you like your sport. Whether you want people to compete, to stretch their skills and courage to the limit. Williams has no doubt that is what he prefers. "I accept there was a certain element of risk involved that day and I admit I was relieved when it was all over and our drivers came in first and second," said Williams. "But think back very carefully to that day. Everybody, or at least almost everybody, goes on about what a fantastic race it was and how it had them on the edge of their seats. Now, take our two drivers out of that race and what do you have? I'll tell you what you have. You have another boring race. There are enough processions in Formula One without organising them.

"The public and television audiences want to see racing and it's our duty to provide it. If we don't, they won't want to know, and then what do we do? We can't afford to turn them away. I came into racing to race and that's what I intend to go on doing. I'm proud to say that everyone in this team has the same

attitude and that, I'm sure, has been a vital factor in our success." Apart from the ability to fashion a professional team and produce a superb and reliable car, Williams has the fortunate knack of picking up uncut diamonds. Alan Jones and Keke Rosberg exceeded all his expectations to become World Champion in 1980 and 1982 respectively, and Mansell has turned out to be rather more than the 'journeyman' Williams took on at the end of 1984. It might, of course, have been far simpler for Williams had Mansell been no more than a useful second string. But once Mansell's pace and talent became evident, how could they be contained?

McLaren, in 1984, were an example of a team who were lucky in that the Niki Lauda-Alain Prost partnership ran smoothly and effectively. It should also be remembered they had little genuine opposition. In 1985, against many predictions to the contrary, Mansell and Rosberg developed a very good working relationship. The Piquet-Mansell relationship has, alas, been totally different. Piquet, twice World Champion, has

never been used to being a competitive number two. Mansell, fiercely ambitious, has never had such an opportunity to demonstrate his ability. Whatever their opinions of each other at the outset, they soon reached the stage where they simply did not get on.

"We have nothing in common," said Piquet. "He is British, I'm Brazilian. He is Anglo-Saxon, I'm Latin. He sticks to one girl, I like lots of girls." Mansell said, "We have no relationship whatsoever, not even a professional one. He talks only when he wants to. The guy is very good, very quick, but he just can't come to terms with the fact that I'm as good or even better than he is." At various stages during 1987 each driver has complained of the other receiving preferential treatment. Piquet maintained that the car had been built to suit Mansell's requirements and Mansell that he was frequently down on power.

During a Mobil Press conference at Hockenheim Williams drew a few laughs from their rivalry when he said: "It's not true that they don't like each other - they

hate each other." He stuck to his line about healthy competition, although he conceded that he would like them to get on better. "The fact is they don't and this is, after all, motor racing," he concluded. You might expect such turmoil to deflate any team boss's spirit, but when you've gone through the agonies of Williams' recent past you are unlikely to surrender in the face of what amounts to a domestic squabble.

Williams returned to the Grand Prix scene full time at the start of 1987 following his horrific car crash in France on the eve of the previous season. He is confined to a wheelchair and has limited use of his hands. He contends, however, that he is a lucky man. "I could so easily have been killed and yet I wasn't," he reasons. "The trouble was that I could never resist going for a corner. Patrick had told me often enough what would happen to me one day. It was a million per cent inevitable I would go off. I know I should have had a chauffeur for the last three years, but I didn't and sure enough I had my crash. I'll tell you this, though, I'd rather be alive and here, now, like this, than six feet under. I'm lucky. I've got all this, and even though I'm in a wheelchair it's the life and the world I love. It's a fantastic sport, we have a fantastic team and we've had a fantastic season. I don't feel sorry for myself. I count my blessings and look ahead to the next challenge."

Williams looked ahead to the 1987 season with justifiable optimism. Despite ultimate disappointment in the Drivers' Championship, 1986 had been a splendid year and there seemed no reason why the momentum shouldn't be sustained. The Canon Williams-Honda was a formidable car, a near perfect marriage of chassis and engine. Honda had provided the power, and Williams had harnessed it. Williams also had two front-line drivers with the ability to win races and challenge for the Championship, and the boss himself was back in charge. "I thought there had to be some way in which I might help improve things, and that little extra just might make the difference," he said.

The Marlboro McLaren TAG and the Camel Lotus-Honda would clearly present the most serious opposition. In addition Benetton Ford had suggested they were ready to join the elite and

Ferrari are always liable to launch a recovery. In the event Benetton and Ferrari were to come through more forcefully towards the end of the season. The only dangers were Prost's McLaren, Senna's Lotus and, perhaps, the threat of dwindling motivation within the Williams camp itself. "It is difficult to maintain the impetus at this level, but people learn to push themselves one further step ahead," said Williams.

The Williams team knew they had to push a little more when Prost won two of the first three races of the 1987 season – Mansell took the other – and then Senna, with the benefit of active ride suspension, led the way home through the streets of Monaco and Detroit. But Williams, and Mansell in particular, had demonstrated that given a modicum of good fortune the victories would surely begin to flow. The flow, indeed, became a torrent. The Williams pair won in the next six races, Piquet completing the sequence with a triumphant first outing for Williams' version of an 'active' car. Mansell's win in Spain assured Williams

the Constructors' Championship and his success in Mexico reduced the drivers' contest to a purely Williams affair.

That win in Mexico City also served to illustrate the calibre of the Williams team. Mansell's car was damaged in the second of two qualifying crashes, so he had a new one put together the night before the race. "I'd like to pay tribute to my mechanics," said Mansell. "To build a kit car like that and then go out

and win is brilliant." It has, for all the verbal crossfire, been a superb season for Williams and long before the dust had settled on the skirmishes of 1987, they were preparing for 1988. They will have Judd engines next season and the ever-optimistic Williams talks of more success. Restrictions on the turbos will, he argues, narrow the gap. "We'll still be competitive and win races," he predicts. "It could be very open and that's good for the sport."

CHAPMAN/CLARK CHAMPIONSHIPS

BY DERICK ALLSOP

Behind the much publicised turbo battles for the Drivers' Championship and the Constructors' title, the Class Two normally aspirated cars fought another equally important battle – teams competed for the Colin Chapman Trophy, drivers for the Jim Clark Cup.

These competitions mean as much in their own way as the turbo contests, as motor racing begins the countdown to the end of the turbo era. In 1987 there was a mixture of old and new; names from the past and names, possibly, of the future. There was that great motor racing name March, and the Larrousse Lola. There was the French AGS and, late in the season, the Coloni made the grid, and a name for itself. At the top of the list was Tyrrell, a key name in the history of Formula One. With their association with Ford renewed it was, hoped Tyrrell, the beginning of another period of success. With two cars in action all season and so much experience to draw upon, it is scarcely surprising Tyrrell had the Colin Chapman Trophy title secure with almost half the season still to go.

Yet that did not destroy the competitive element in the category and, as the opposition gained knowledge and confidence, so the challenges grew. That keen rivalry was reflected in the Jim Clark Cup. Again, Tyrrell led the way and long before the end of the campaign their pair, Jonathan Palmer and Philippe Streiff, were locked in a duel for the Cup. Eventually it was Jonathan Palmer who came out on top, clinching the championship in Japan by finishing first in the normally aspirated class. For Ken Tyrrell then, two more awards and, more significantly, the impetus he was seeking to carry him into next season and the joust with the big boys.

Tyrrell knows he has to temper celebra-

tions this time, but with greater restrictions on the turbo-charged cars in 1988 he believes the work he put in during this past year will serve him well. As he looked back over the championship Tyrrell admits he would have preferred a bigger entry in the class. "I have to say I was disappointed there weren't more than five cars at the start. Competition is good for everybody and we needed it as much as anyone. Those who were in provided good competition, it's just that we could have done with more of it."

Up against Palmer and Streiff were Frenchmen Philippe Alliot in the Lola and Pascal Fabre in the AGS, and Italian Ivan Capelli in the Leyton House March. Another Italian, Nicola Larini, was to come on to the scene later with the Coloni, as was Frenchman Yannick Dalmas in a second Lola. Tyrrell continues: "Both Lola and March have experience with CART, developing cars, so it is not unexpected that they should have made an impression. They haven't come into this as raw novices. There is a lot of know-how there and we certainly didn't go into the season thinking we would have no opposition."

Going into the second half of the season the closest challenger to the Tyrrell drivers was, in the rankings at least, Fabre in the AGS. But then, as someone once observed, statistics can be a less than true reflection of fact. The AGS was outclassed for much of the season and hauled in the points merely by keeping the wheels turning, even if it was

several laps off the pace. That lack of speed was to catch up with them in the later stages of the competition, when there was no guaranteed place in the race. Fabre failed to qualify in Italy and Portugal, and again in Mexico as the entry increased. The sterner opposition came from the Lola and the March. Both teams were in there to race and both Alliot and Capelli scored significant class successes.

Larini qualified in Spain for the first time, but the Coloni went out with engine trouble on lap nine. Dalmas qualified an impressive 23rd, one place ahead of his partner Alliot, in Mexico. Despite problems he finished ninth, four laps down, on a day when Alliot took a point and top place among the normally aspirated runners. Between the two Lolas in Mexico City were the two Tyrrells. It was perhaps not the best of races for them, but they had more class scores to add to their totals and for both the Clark Cup was the objective. Palmer won the class in Brazil, with Streiff second. In the San Marino Grand Prix Streiff won, while Palmer had a fruitless day. Belgium was to be even more frustrating. Streiff had a big accident and Palmer was unable to avoid the wreckage. Both were unhurt, but the one spare car for the re-start was Streiff's and he picked up a valuable second place.

"What happened at Spa is part of the sport," says Tyrrell. "That's motor racing. You have simply got to learn to put up with that sort of thing." Palmer certainly got over his misfortune and

Previous page: Adding to his Formula Three and Formula Two titles, Jonathan Palmer won the Jim Clark Cup

Right: Ivan Capelli (here overtaking Pascal Fabre's AGS), had a good first season with the re-born March team. Fabre's fortunes on the other hand dwindled to four non-qualifications in a row, and he was replaced by the talented Roberto Moreno

over the following weeks turned the course of the championship in his favour. He won the class and registered his first points with fifth place overall in Monaco, the street circuit that gives the non-turbo a chance to come into its own. He followed up with another first in Detroit, second behind Streiff in France and first at Silverstone in the British Grand Prix. In Germany both were in the points proper, Streiff coming fourth and Palmer fifth. Palmer led the Tyrrell one-two in Hungary to clinch the team prize and establish a vital advantage in the duel for the individual award. Streiff maintained his challenge through the autumn, refusing to concede, ensuring a worthy contest for the Clark Cup – a contest both men enjoyed *and* needed.

"It was important to be recognised as a class," says Palmer, "We had our own race within the race and at Tyrrell we were under instructions to hold our line. The competition was good, really good, because there could be so little difference between the cars. In the end it was down to us two, but the Lola and the March were quick, just as I expected them to be. Philippe and I both wanted that trophy and we both knew we couldn't afford to make mistakes. It has been real racing and there's no question

in my mind that I made the right decision in joining a team with a normally aspirated engine."

Streiff is equally convinced. "It is better to be second in this class than struggling, right out of it, with an uncompetitive turbo. The pit board shows me where I am in my class – that is our race." Palmer chips in, "When they put out the board for you with P1 it means everything. That's what we are racing for – to compete and to win." Tyrrell believes both Palmer and Streiff have learnt from their running battle. Palmer in particular, he suggests, shows the benefit of the constant competition. "No team manager is ever totally happy with the performance of his drivers," declares Tyrrell with a huge grin. "But both have thrived on the situation this season. I'm sure Philippe has surprised Jonathan. It has not been easy for Jonathan to be in command. When you have someone in the same car you have someone to measure yourself against, and that is what concerns drivers. Jonathan has had to maintain his standards but he has responded and he has enjoyed finishing races. Apart from the drivers, the team improves, of course, if the competition is there," adds Tyrrell.

If you picture Ken as some benign old

gent, wallowing in nostalgia and past glories, now content to settle for second best, forget it. What is gone is cherished, but what lies ahead excites him. "People say the game is not like it was but you know what, I think it's exactly as it was," says Tyrrell. "There's so much nonsense talked about how things have supposedly changed. Yes, of course there's more money about. We used to have cups of tea in the pits, now we have our tea in the motorhome. We just spend more money because more money is available. As Colin Chapman used to say, 'the amount of money spent in Formula One is proportionate to the amount you can get'. But the competitive side is still there and it's as good as ever, and I get just the same kick out of it as I ever did."

Much as Tyrrell values the trophies his team have earned this season, it is the points collected in the Championship proper that occupy his attention now. He explains, "The most important thing for us is to assess what progress we have made in terms of our preparations for next year and believe me, I can't wait for 1988. I think a normally aspirated engine will win the Championship next year. When you take into account the boost, fuel and weight regulations, plus the fact that all will have what you might call the

same tyre disadvantage, the gap between the normally aspirated engine and the turbo will be closed. Over 16 races, I back a normally aspirated engine to win. We are one step ahead. We know exactly what gearbox we need and a number of other things. You can only learn by doing it, and we have certainly spent this past year learning."

If Tyrrell are still learning, consider the task confronting March. But they have made steady progress and intend, two years hence, to be competing for the World Championship. Team manager Ian Phillips reveals, "From the start we saw Tyrrell as our target. There's nothing Ken doesn't know. The first

time we were on the grid Ken shook my hand and wished us luck. Mind you, when we were in front of them for the first time he went quiet! We are an all-new team and what we wanted this first season was respectability. We set out with our 'principles of operation'. We made it clear rotten apples didn't stand a chance, all that sort of thing. We felt fairly optimistic, but never expected to really feature in the Championship. Just about everywhere we've been it has taken us until race day to get to grips with things. Our naivety has been exposed at times. We knew we had a lot to learn and hoped to show we'd learned by the second half of the season. Normally aspirated racing is good racing

and we just wanted to win as many points as possible in our class."

True to the Tyrrell guidelines, March have long been planning ahead and next year they will, like Williams, use Judd engines. Phillips says: "We started to look at next year from the middle of this. We have the same engines as Williams next year, we have a second driver next year and our sponsors have been fantastic. We have big team plans and for that you need a big budget. I honestly believe that by 1989 we will be in a position to contest the World Championship. I feel you have got to be aiming and looking ahead all the time, never settling for less. You may not achieve all you aim for, but at least have a go."

Central to those ambitions is Capelli. "He's a great character as well as an outstanding driver," says Phillips. "His personality has kept us going when we've not been too clever." March and Capelli have played their parts in the normally aspirated championship of 1987, but it was the year of the Courtaulds Tyrrell Ford and Uncle Ken's boys. Let's hope that fine scrap between Palmer and Streiff is an indication of what is to come when the turbo finally bows out of Formula One, and the normally aspirated challengers again take centre stage.

Above: Newcomers towards the end of the 1987 season, the Coloni team will contest a full Grand Prix schedule during 1988

Left: Tyrrell were the only team to run two cars in the normally aspirated class, although for the last three Grand Prix, the Larrousse-Lola team ran a second car for Yannick Dalmas

SEASON'S REVIEW

BY BOB CONSTANDUROS

Nelson Piquet, Nigel Mansell, Ayrton Senna and Alain Prost, the gang of four, once again made the running in the 1987 World Championship, although they were joined by Gerhard Berger at season's end. But for most of the year, it looked as though one of the Williams pair would scoop the title, and it was finally decided at 2.40 pm local time on 30th October, when Nigel Mansell crashed and put himself out of the last two races, leaving the unbeatable Nelson Piquet to claim his third World Championship. It was a title that some begrudged three-time winner Piquet. Some said that he hadn't won it in the true sense of the word and that Nigel Mansell, with six wins to his credit, had. But then that's not the way the Championship is structured.

It was a year of transition, the first year that non-turbos had been allowed back in. The pop-off valve was set to four bar to limit power and, for the first time, there was a one-make tyre system in operation, following Pirelli's withdrawal. All this provided initial doubts and worries, but these were forgotten long before mid-season. The regulations, of course, had been formulated during the year to try and cut the phenomenal power that had been wrought from Formula One turbo engines. FISA came up with its own pop-off valve which its engineers would maintain and which would be given out at random prior to each race. Designers said it was the most antiquated part of a Formula One car and there were all kinds of accusations and suggestions flying around in Brazil, as a steady stream of team managers clutching the offending black cylinders marched on Gabriele Cadringher's garage. But that was almost the last that was heard of it. There was the odd mention later and promise of a refined version for 1988, but that was it.

The turbo drivers were afraid of how much they would be held up by the normally aspirated 3.5 litre cars which were bound to be slower than the turbos on certain circuits. Frequently, they had their own, extremely fraught battles: they were much more closely matched than the turbos, but rarely did they actually hinder a lead battle. And how many teams and drivers ended 1987 wishing they'd been running normally

aspirated engines themselves? And then there were the tyres. With Pirelli's retirement from Formula One, only Goodyear was left as a possible supplier and that company did a deal to supply ten sets of tyres per car per meeting, plus rain tyres. They would all be the same, there would be no qualifying tyres, no further development and research and no softer compound for normally aspirated cars. Everyone would use the same tyres. While the negotiation was fraught, the system itself worked superbly. At Imola, the one race where there was the slightest doubt about the product, the company reacted very responsibly and flew in 400 tyres overnight. Otherwise, scarcely a harsh word was said, and at the end of the year, Goodyear celebrated its 200th Grand Prix win. Without Goodyear, there might not have been any Grand Prix racing at all.

The calendar was pretty much as expected, except that a sponsorship and contract squabble over the Canadian Grand Prix eventually cost that country its race, but then there were 17 events on the calendar anyway, thanks to the addition of Japan. It proved a popular move among drivers, who instantly rated the difficult Suzuka circuit one of their favourites. It was also well organised, which is more than could be said for some, and, by the end of the year, several organisers had received fines for late starting practice sessions, including Detroit who disputed their fine. The season nearly didn't get under way at all.

FISA had decided to charge a sliding scale for super licences, and the drivers objected, saying that this could be the start of many charges, and what was to stop FISA charging them twice as much next year? For a while it looked as though the drivers might strike but, in the end, it was discussed amicably and the Brazilian Grand Prix got underway as expected.

In spite of the pop-off valve, there were still cars running out of petrol at Imola, Spa, Detroit, the Hungaroring, Monza, Estoril, Jerez and Suzuka, although they were rarely cars in the top six. And although the first half of the season was a little short in actual racing, the French, British, Austrian, Italian, Portuguese, Spanish and Mexican Grand Prix could all be looked back upon as good races. There were new additions at the beginning of 1987, and farewells at the end of it. The Ford Cosworth engine, of course, returned, and among those who ran it was March, making its return to Grand Prix racing, and Lola, now run by Gerard Larrousse. The rights to the BMW upright engine were bought by Megatron, a division of USF&G and Heini Mader did, after all, look after those engines. Alfa Romeo nearly came back and Italy's Formula Three wizard entrant Enzo Coloni made his Grand Prix debut.

At the end of the year, TAG's turbo engine made its departure after taking Alain Prost to three wins during the season, culminating in a record-breaking 28th in Portugal. Ford's turbo wasn't

WILLIAMS
DOMINANT CHAMPIONS

There can be no denying that Williams dominated the 1987 Championships with their drivers finishing first and second, and the team itself clinching the Constructors' title long before the end of the season. But it was a pity that in not scoring a single point in the last two rounds of the Championship, the team's points score of 137 did not surpass its 1986 points total of 141, nor did it beat McLaren's all-time record of 143.5. Because the team won the Constructors' title, its exploits are recorded elsewhere, so this appraisal deals mainly with the mechanical elements.

The team's weapons for 1987 were based very strongly on the Constructors' winning chassis and engines used in 1986. Indeed, Williams' engineering director Patrick Head considered that there was no point in building a brand new car when first, the current FW11 was winning races and second, a new chassis would be needed for the normally aspirated engine, whenever that was ready, The fact that Honda would not be going normally aspirated immediately in 1988, and that Williams lost Honda was purely coincidental. But the former argument held good anyway. The Williams FW11 was good and the new FW11B, as it was known, was based on that and performed just as well. It featured detail changes including repositioned turbos, revised inlet ducts and a

expected again, nor was the lay down BMW turbo unit. In the words of FISA president Jean-Marie Balestre, "the emphasis in 1987 was on the turbo engine; it will be on the normally aspirated engine in 1988".

stiffer monocoque. "But you would have to look hard to see the changes," said Frank Dernie, the R&D engineer. Although it was probably overtaken by Ferrari by the end of the year, it was probably the best chassis for most of the season. Into the back of it went Honda's all-powerful V6 engine, slightly revised due to a change of regulations which banned mixed intercooling, so that the precise temperature range given by water/air intercoolers in 1986 was replaced by air/air intercoolers in 1987, and although it was at one time suggested that this might make a big difference, that was never apparent. Engine temperature, however, was more crucial in the event.

It was also suggested that development on the engine slowed late in 1986 as Honda's new team, Lotus, didn't want the power unit to change while designers were building around it. During the year, what was known as a stage four engine slid into being, although the Japanese were typically discreet as to

what stage four comprised. Williams's two cars so dominated practice in Brazil that observers genuinely felt that if this was a pointer for the World Championship, it was going to be pretty dull. But then it didn't go that way at all. Both cars overheated due to blocked ducts, Mansell had a puncture, and Mr Sakurai, the Honda motor sport director, blamed Goodyear for supplying tyres which couldn't handle the power. Williams, normally so attentive to blocked radiators, admitted that they hadn't forseen it, and also apologised to Goodyear. The ups and downs of Imola showed up two positive points. The chassis was exceptionally strong, as Piquet found when he crashed heavily, and the team had its first win at Imola.

But Mansell lost a wheel weight, and not for the last time. Belgium wasn't so positive. Mansell is best left unmentioned, but Piquet retired from the lead for the second year running, this time with a turbo boost sensor causing a misfire.

Mansell now dominated practice sessions, and looked as though he might dominate the Monaco race until a turbo wastegate failed, a problem at one time linked with Piquet's retirement in the previous race. The Brazilian, definitely not on form, raced to what was called a lacklustre second place, although this was probably due to the after effects of his Imola accident. Mansell again dominated Detroit qualifying, but complained of cramp on the Saturday and suffered it again in the race. He pitted for tyres when he probably didn't have to and a wheelnut stuck as it is liable to in Detroit. Piquet picked up a puncture, but stormed back to second place. Mansell was fifth.

In France, it was Piquet's turn to have a long stop, when he stalled the engine, while Mansell picked up part of Johansson's front wing which upset the handling. But the pair scored their first one-two of the year, followed a week later by another in Britain. There were more problems, however, for both had dramatic practice and qualifying sessions. Another wheel weight dropped off Mansell's car in the race, and he pitted again for new tyres, whereas Piquet was hoping to go all the way through. But the new tyres proved to be more competitive and Mansell pipped his team mate.

In Germany, Mansell was shadowing Prost when his engine seized, while

Piquet had a dramatic time. The car was jumping about and he lost his fuel read-out, but when it came back, he found he could force the pace and inherited the lead when Prost retired. It was his first win of the year. Two weeks later in Hungary, Mansell seemed to have the race sewn up when his wheelnut came undone, just a few laps from home. Once again, Piquet suffered vibration, but was in the right place to inherit the lead. Just one week later, the pair dominated the Austrian Grand Prix in spite of Mansell's failing clutch at the start which disappeared altogether mid-race. But Piquet was perfectly happy with his second place.

After 4500 miles of testing, mainly by Piquet but also by Jean-Louis Schlesser, Frank Dernie's hydro-pneumatic suspension system was finally allowed its race debut after a particularly successful test at Imola. The system was rather less complicated than Lotus's active, and was more reactive, relying on fewer sensors and less computer power but operated by hydraulic system like Lotus's. Piquet was determined that it should work. His straightline speed depressed Mansell, who described the race as a joke. Lack of fuel economy, bad fuel consumption and vibration were just some of the problems, the engine problems apparently caused by more overheating. While Piquet scored Williams's sixth successive win in a row, Mansell finished third.

Mansell was again wary of his engine's performance in Portugal, and by now had his own 'active' car, although he used a conventional car for the race. But the engine began misfiring, and then stopped altogether when he reacted to Berger pulling away from him. Piquet, meanwhile, damaged his car in a first corner accident, and philosophically accepted that it wouldn't be excellent and finished third. A week later, he finished fourth after a succession of problems and mistakes, but this race was dominated by Mansell and he also dominated the next one in Mexico, once Boutsen and Berger had retired. The Williams pair finished first and second for the fourth time in the year. It was also the team's 21st win in 33 races.

The final two Grand Prix were disastrous for Williams. Mansell crashed in Japan, which gave the title to Piquet. But the Brazilian's car hadn't been returned to qualifying trim for Saturday's timed session and he ended up on row three. The best he could do was race for second and then third, and finally, with rubber clogging the radiator ducts and the engine overheating, it broke altogether. Australia, in Mansell's absence, wasn't much better. Patrese stood in for the injured driver, but he was never in the hunt and retired with a blown engine. Piquet needed new tyres – vibration again – and then suffered both gear selection problems and finally a terminally exploding brake disc.

It wasn't the most appropriate way to celebrate winning both championships, because the team had demonstrated during the season that it was in a class of its own, aided, in no small part, by Honda's reliability. That Honda should then have kicked the team into touch was credible but hard to believe. But then that's another story.

McLAREN
HONDA TROUBLE

If you can't beat 'em, join 'em: that seemed to be McLaren's policy during 1987. Quite simply, TAG's task in trying to take on the unlimited might and resources of Honda was just too much. When there's a problem with a Honda engine, people are brought in until the problem is solved. TAG, operating to a budget, simply had to bow to such might. For McLaren's year was blighted by engine problems. Sometimes – but not often – everything turned out right and then you had races like Belgium, when the team didn't even do that much running during the wet first day and only qualified sixth (Prost) and tenth (Johansson). But they were first and second in the warm-up. And within 17 of what became a very boring 43 lap race, they were running first and second. And although Prost was relying on Johansson's fuel read-outs, since his computer had broken, they cruised in to a crushing one-two. De Cesaris, out of fuel, was a full, 4.3 mile lap behind.

Regrettably, such races were rare, although the year began promisingly in spite of the loss of John Barnard. The team's engineering director announced his intention to work with Ferrari midway during 1986 and was relieved of his post at the Woking factory in September of that year. But Gordon Murray was hired to fill the gap, with Neil Oatley also joining from the defunct Haas-Lola team. However, the new car, a development of the ever faithful MP4, was to be designed by American Steve Nicholls. Ron Dennis had another personnel problem on his hands after

Keke Rosberg announced at the 1986 German Grand Prix that he would quit at the end of the year. Although he tried to persuade him to stay, Dennis had to find a new driver and late in February, it was announced that Stefan Johansson would join the team, although rumours abounded earlier in the year that Rosberg's replacement would be Ayrton Senna. As usual, the team's new car was ready just in time for the Brazilian Grand Prix. To Nicholl's great relief, Prost preferred it in back to back tests with the previous year's championship winning machine. It had more down-force and more grip. The front suspension geometry was slightly different and both front and rear suspensions were structurally different. Nicholls was able to lower the bodywork over the 195 litre fuel tank and there were bigger inter-coolers in lower side pods with bigger intakes. The hubs were improved to facilitate wheel changing.

Prost and Johansson qualified fifth and tenth respectively for the Brazilian Grand Prix and after making only two pit stops for tyres to most people's three, they finished first and third. But if that was good, it all went bad at Imola with three engine breakages due to a wrong chip on the Friday, and another the next day. Prost was looking good in the race until the alternator belt broke early in the race for the first time in years. Johansson finished fourth. The Belgian Grand Prix was probably the highlight of the season apart from Prost's brave and ultimately successful pursuit of Berger in

Portugal. But from Monaco until then, the occasional trouble-free run was interspersed with disappointment and lack of reliability. Prost was heading for third place in Monaco until his smoking engine finally expired three laps from the end. Johansson had already retired with engine problems again, and it was the first time that neither McLaren had finished since Hungary the previous year. It was also the first time that Johansson hadn't been classified in ten races.

In Detroit, they had a rare problem with the chassis in that they couldn't get any temperature in the tyres without three-quarter full fuel tanks. But Prost finished third with a number of problems and went on to finish third again in France. Johansson, after a chapter of incidents, retired at Ricard with another broken alternator belt. Neither car finished in Britain and Prost had the third alternator belt breakage when heading for almost certain victory in Germany. Instead, Johansson picked up a lucky

second place – on three wheels after a last lap puncture. TAG had already promised more reliable engines in Germany and Prost then proceeded to finish third in Hungary, sixth in Austria from the pit lane and then 15th in Italy after a long stop to repair the potentiometer. Johansson, meanwhile, ended a horrific Austrian Grand Prix with seventh, finished sixth in Italy and then fifth in Portugal and third in Spain, reinforcing his reputation as a good, points-winning number two.

Prost, meanwhile, proved that when everything was going well, he could race better than the best of them and scored that elusive 28th win in Portugal after a superb chase which ended with Berger's spin. In Spain, Prost finished second,

after again discovering a phenomenon that he had come across earlier in the year – that his car doesn't react well in close company with other cars. Furthermore, it would take quite a lot of sorting before it was absolutely to Prost's liking. Of course, Goodyear's single compound tyre situation was not entirely to the Frenchman's advantage either.

Before the year was out, McLaren had announced that they would be joining forces with Honda for the 1988 season for an unlimited period, and that Ayrton Senna would be Alain Prost's fourth team mate in as many years. Prost kept in touch with the championship title in 1987, but TAG's problems in the face of Honda's consistent reliability proved too much. It is unlikely to go down as one of the team's greatest years, but with a workforce approaching 150 and a brand new factory, Ron Dennis had to do something to redress the situation and while TAG is still a partner in the team, he has 'joined 'em.'

LOTUS
ACTIVE LEARNING

Considering it was Lotus's first year with active suspension, their engineers can be very proud of what they did with it and the successes gained in 1987. 'Active suspension', to the extent that Lotus have become involved with it, is remarkably complicated engineering. You might even say too complicated for Formula One. But thanks also to Honda engines and Ayrton Senna, Lotus gained considerable success in 1987, remaining in contention for second place in both the Drivers' and Constructors' championships until the very last race in Adelaide. It was a year of changes, not only because of active suspension. The

first change was that both Honda and Japan's first ever full time Formula One driver Satoru Nakajima joined the team. Then some doubts were cast as to whether JPS would continue as sponsors and in early January, it was confirmed

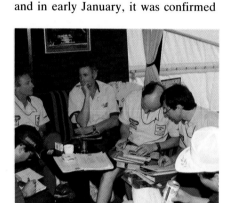

that JPS had indeed taken a back seat. In early February, Lotus's full plans were announced.

It was then that it was confirmed that Camel was taking over as the major sponsor. Rumours that Senna would be joining McLaren were quashed as he stood with Nakajima beside their 1987 mount, the new 99T in its unfamiliar livery. The latest Lotus was a refinement of the previous year's car, said designer Gerard Ducarouge, but the difference was under the skin. There was a new carbon fibre and keylar chassis and new six speed gearbox, fruit of the work done by Johnny Dumfries during the previous year. There were narrower side pods for Honda's revised cooling system, made necessary by the change of intercooling regulations. And a smaller engine cover was used, plus a bigger clutch. The front track was narrower, the rear track wider and the rear suspension was all new – although that would soon become academic, anyway, when, late in February, Lotus brought out their active suspension system. First seen in Rio four years before, it had been shelved after two races in 1983 simply because the banning of ground effect made the initial reason for its development redundant. Now, however, there was great interest from Lotus's road car division and the 1987 push was a joint effort between the team, Lotus Engineering and the Cranfield Institute of Technology.

The purpose of active suspension is to maintain a constant ride height so that the car's aerodynamics can work to maximum efficiency all the time, instead of being subject to such movement, such as roll in corners, diving under braking or being lower when under a high aerodynamic load or on a full fuel load. When the aerodynamics are working efficiently, less wing may be used and therefore the car's straightline speed is greater. Or so the theory goes. Peter Wright, the engineer behind Lotus's active suspension, explained that, "the motivation to use active again in Formula One came because current flat-bottomed cars are difficult to control aerodynamically. They are becoming stiffer and stiffer, making the ride worse and generating handling problems. The other motivation was that there wasn't anything else we could try with the chassis."

Lotus's active suspension worked via a series of 20 sensing systems which told a central computer what the car wanted to do. The computer was programmed to accept just over half-a-billion inputs per lap, and it was programmed to react to certain movements by sending instructions to actuators which moved the suspension by use of a hydraulic pressure system, which in turn had its own radiator, pump and tank. The 1987 Camel Lotus-Honda was a very complicated car, with the myriad of Honda sensors, those of the active suspension and the on-board camera fitted to Nakajima's car. Early testing was sufficiently encouraging for the team to decide to race the active suspension for the entire season. It didn't always work perfectly. Germany was a low spot, when a leak in the hydraulic fluid system resulted in Senna's car running on its underside for many laps. Third place, under those circumstances, was pretty

fortunate. Nakajima had a rear suspension failure in the race, but his car had earlier demonstrated remarkable capability of being able to rise and fall on its suspension on its own in the pits.

But there were high spots too. Monaco was obviously a very encouraging race to win. The active system clearly spared the car's tyres as Senna then demonstrated in the streets of Detroit where he also won, and Monza where he nearly won. He didn't stop for tyres in Spain either, and the car's straightline speed made it almost impossible to overtake, but he eventually finished a lowly fifth. Practice and qualifying sessions were a lot more complicated for the team in 1987, and Senna placed a lot less emphasis on pole position. Not that his car was on a par with the Williams anyway, in spite of using the same power unit. What the 1987 season did prove was that the Renault engine was certainly as good as everyone thought it was, if not better. And what sort of trouble might Lotus have faced if they had not run the reliable Honda engine in 1987? In spite of the frequent and obvious development problems with the active suspension, Senna usually brought the car home in the points, and this showed increased maturity. He had an engine failure in Brazil, tangled with Mansell in Belgium and then finished the next eight races in the points before finishing seventh in Portugal. In Mexico he had a rare spin, but he was obviously learning that to win titles, you need points.

Nakajima had a rather public first season in Formula One, many of his errors, which were faithfully recorded by the on-board camera, were later shown on a huge screen to his local fans as they sat in the main grandstand at Suzuka prior to

the Japanese Grand Prix. He seemed to take much longer than most learning circuits and sometimes seemed out of his depth. But he accepted his role as Lotus number two and happily won his first points at Imola and then Belgium. He overtook his predecessor's 1986 score when he finished fourth at Silverstone and his sixth place at Japan, which was by no means staggering, did involve a fair amount of overtaking and obviously brought great satisfaction.

The 1987 Lotus chassis wasn't the best produced by the team, but Senna and Nakajima did have a lot of factors on their side in 1987. Senna had already decided to leave Lotus when Piquet was announced as his successor in Hungary and the two Brazilian rivals both race different Honda-powered chassis in 1988. Lotus could look back on 1987 as an interim season, considering they had no comparable times for circuits from previous years with active suspension.

FERRARI
A YEAR OF CHANGE

"I'm very happy that Ferrari won here," said Alain Prost in Japan. "A season without Ferrari is not a good season." Ferrari did indeed threaten during the second half of the year, in fact Prost's 28th win nearly didn't happen thanks to a more than threatening Ferrari, and Gerhard Berger was heading for his second Grand Prix victory in Portugal when, under pressure from Prost, he spun off.

A threatening Ferrari, as Prost so succinctly put it, has been a long time coming. It was in Nurburgring in August 1985 that a Ferrari had last taken the chequered flag, and early in the 1987 season the team had the dubious honour of going longer without a win than any previous Ferrari team. They lengthened the record by more than ten races before Berger's long-awaited, and much-deserved win in Japan. The 1987 season started long before the turn of the year with the much-publicised and not entirely popular recruitment of John Barnard from McLaren, while Gerhard Berger was also hired to replace Stefan Johansson in the team before the 1986 season was over. But that wasn't the end of the changes. With an ex-McLaren crew chief, an ex-Renault engineer working on the engines and Austrian

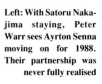

Left: With Satoru Nakajima staying, Peter Warr sees Ayrton Senna moving on for 1988. Their partnership was never fully realised

Right: The 1987 season finally came good for Ferrari, with wins in Japan and Australia

Gustav Brunner designing the car, there wasn't a lot that was Italian about the team. And when the number of mechanics was reduced, the lunches were curtailed and Barnard insisted on there being more feedback between departments, the 'foreigners' became somewhat unpopular.

In the meantime, Ferrari had been arming itself with a new weapon for 1987. The 120 degree V6 turbo engine was replaced by a 90 degree version which, according to Alboreto, had more power and more torque than the old one. He said it was a winner. Testing revealed that the new driver was all too eager to upstage his established team mate. As a young, relatively inexperienced driver, Berger needed the test mileage, but he didn't need to make a competition out of it. He crashed while testing in November, he crashed again at Imola in March, he crashed in Belgium and he crashed in Monaco. At that point, an ex-World Champion pointed out to him that he shouldn't take it all so seriously, it was

still meant to be fun. Although he crashed again in Detroit, Britain and Germany, he ultimately took the advice.

In the meantime, the car had a catalogue of problems. A new, longitudinal six speed gearbox gave trouble, Alboreto's undertray became detached in Brazil, there was a broken driveshaft and a dead engine at Imola. The team made slight aerodynamic changes in Belgium. Berger's engine broke early on, but Alboreto was second, dicing with eventual winner Prost, when he retired. In Monaco, Alboreto crashed with Danner and Berger had his own separate accident. After that, it was a matter of survival and survive they did, Alboreto came third at 'home' and Berger fourth. By now carbon fibre clutches had made

their appearances and the team had the new clutch, various rear wings, a new management system and differential at Detroit. Berger was again fourth. Alboreto had now begun a tedious run of non-finishes. Neither driver finished in France, Britain or Germany. It was a depressing series of races, yet the team was quite optimistic that all that would change. There were a succession of turbo failures caused by overheating. There did appear to be a lack of power, but once all these factors were sorted out, the chassis themselves were handling much better.

Barnard, by this stage, had taken a little more of a back seat, and Brunner had left months ago. Instead, Postlethwaite was 'dusted off' as the Italian press put it, and brought to races. He had been working in the newly commissioned wind tunnel, and it was this work that made the biggest difference during the second half of the season. The team were able to set the cars up for a circuit before they even got to the track, working within a limited range on certain improvements after the bulk of the work had been done back at Maranello. Drivers, engineers, Marco Piccinini *et al* would agree that this accounted for the greatest improvements made during the second half of the season.

The first taste of this improved form came in Hungary, where an unwell Berger put a Ferrari on the front row for the first time in 1987 with Alboreto fifth on what is very definitely a chassis circuit. They were second and third in the warm-up and ran second and third for twelve laps until first Berger and then Alboreto disappeared. The threat continued in Austria and Italy where Alboreto celebrated his hundredth Grand Prix. By now, mechanical reasons such as engine and turbos were causing retirements. In Portugal, Berger started from pole position for the first time in his Grand Prix career, and so nearly won but for that late race spin, no doubt an educational experience. In Spain, the pair were in contention in the queue for second place behind Senna, but both drivers made errors which ultimately caused engine-related retirements. In his 50th Grand Prix in Mexico, Berger again put the Ferrari on the front row and battled with Boutsen, leading again but once more, both drivers retired with engine failure.

The engines, it seemed, weren't entirely consistent. You could get a good one or a bad one, one that kept its edge or went off fairly quickly. It was all a matter of chance intimated Berger after his second pole position of the year at Suzuka. But this time he had a good engine and never really saw much of the opposition after the first lap. He even suggested that the Ferrari didn't have a fuel consumption problem, whereas almost everyone else said that they did. But the Ferrari engine has often appeared more economical than others. So Berger ultimately came up trumps, winning the penultimate round of the series just as he had the previous year.

His team mate, in spite of fluffing the start due to a jammed clutch, was delighted to finish fourth, only the fourth time he had been classified all year. Being outqualified and out-raced by his team mate was beginning to wear his patience if the truth be told, but persistent retirements didn't make matters much easier. So Ferrari finally came good and whether Italy liked it or not, they came good with the help of not only Barnard, but Postlethwaite, Brunner and others. It was the year of change for the team, but it finally reaped success and that, after more than 26 months without a win, was what mattered. After Japan Ferrari showed the fruits of their new form with a one-two in Australia.

BENETTON
RELIABILITY AGAIN

The Benetton team started 1987 as the team considered most likely to ... And that's the way the year ended too, without the team having quite managed that elusive second win. It was, perhaps, the greatest disappointment of the year that Benetton didn't quite do what Ferrari did and challenge the Williams/McLaren/Lotus establishment. But then the fact that they didn't shows just what it takes to get to competitive level.

After just one year, BMW pulled out of their involvement with Benetton and so following the dissolution of the Haas-Lola team, Ford joined forces with Benetton to supply the team's third different engine in as many years. But that wasn't Benetton's only change in 1987. Fabi had already signed for the team during the year, and Thierry Boutsen signed in Adelaide, replacing the departing Gerhard Berger, who had scored the team's first win in Mexico. Australia was also the scene of the team's last race with Pirelli, for whom they had won just two weeks before. So there were several new elements as the Benetton team (rather than Toleman) tackled its second year. One person firmly in place at the head of the design department was Rory Byrne, the team's faithful designer who can, when all else has failed, be relied upon to come up with a good competitive design as he had the previous year.

The Ford engine deal was finally confirmed in December of 1986 and yet Byrne's new B187 appeared just two

months later. It comprised an all-new monocoque with unique pinched-in sides around the driver's knees and a very pinched-in back end. A very low engine cover afforded by the Ford V6 engine made for improved aerodynamics. The chassis itself, in fact, gave few problems. On occasions, it revealed slightly strange traits, such as being particularly sensitive to changing track conditions in Spain and there was a bout of oversteer mid-season. But the car seemed to look after its tyres and although there was one race towards the end of the season when the drivers complained of low straightline speed, if there was any blame to be allotted, it was usually laid on the engine.

In the Ford's second year of competition there was a rash of failures during the first half of the season which proved more than embarrassing. And Cosworth were held largely responsible. Indeed, it seemed that the wrong fuel had been chosen which resulted in one engine

breakage after another, although not necessarily in races. For most of the first half of the season, there were only rare results and few of them points-scoring. Cosworth seemed to be constantly on the verge of solving the problem (with ideas such as turning down the boost), yet never quite did so until some post-Silverstone testing finally produced positive results. A lack of response on tight circuits early in the year was also an embarrassment – although thankfully it was improved for Detroit. The engine's fuel consumption, while not perfect, was not as bad as some. But Cosworth wasn't to blame for everything. There was a rash of gear-linkage trouble, poor brakes and several broken drive-shafts, not to mention problems at the

Brazilian Grand Prix, which was almost totally a waste of time due to overspeeding turbos.

There was a significant improvement mid-way through the season. Boutsen scored the team's best result of the year so far in Hungary, and he started from the second row in Austria where Fabi finished third and Boutsen fourth. But the latter's chapter of incidents (loose gear-linkage, broken undertray stay, broken exhaust) proved that the corner hadn't yet been turned. The undertray again came loose in Italy when Boutsen was running second, and Fabi salvaged fourth in Portugal. Boutsen nearly finished third in Spain but for his late race spin, but the high spot came in Mexico when he again started from the second row, set fastest time in the warm-up and led after two laps. But it only lasted 14 laps until the electrics failed. He had never qualifed higher than he had in Japan and was running second again until the clutch packed up.

But then that was the story of Benetton's 1987 season: hard-luck all the way. After a similar 1986 season, some of those problems should have been avoided. Rory Byrne's chassis certainly deserved a win and the work done by test driver Teo Fabi obviously yielded excellent results in testing. It just failed to materialise in terms of results.

TYRRELL
SUCCESSFUL OPERATION

As winners of both normally aspirated championships, the story of the Tyrrell team's season is told elsewhere, but Ken Tyrrell's aspirations for the 1987 season were certainly fulfilled. He admitted that he didn't have much choice but to go into the normally aspirated class in 1987, but his intention was to win the Colin Chapman and Jim Clark Cups for

constructors and drivers of normally aspirated cars, and win as many World Championship points with a non-turbo engine as he had won the previous year with the Renault turbo unit (11 in all).

He accomplished the former soon after mid-season. His drivers, Jonathan Palmer and Philippe Streiff, were unbeatable by the Spanish Grand Prix and Palmer clinched the Jim Clark Cup in Japan. The 11 points were a little more difficult. The final point needed only came when Senna was disqualified on Sunday evening in Australia. In his three-level quest, he was faithfully supported by sponsors Data General, who were joined on a similar scale by Courtaulds. Both sponsors were very much involved in the design and manufacture of the cars. Tyrrell announced at the start he would be using Ford Cosworth DFZ engines developed by Brian Hart, and no one seemed to get their engines earlier than Hart.

The drivers were in doubt for a while. Martin Brundle decided to plump for a turbo team rather than stay with Tyrrell, although Philippe Streiff decided to stay with the team early on. It was only after Jonathan Palmer qualified first in the normally apirated class and finished in the same position in Brazil that his place for the year was confirmed.

The season wasn't as easy as it might have seemed, however. To begin with, there was a remarkable stuttering misfire that took three races to cure. It was finally traced to a distributor driveshaft vibrating. Then the cars

seemed to suffer from inferior straight-line speed which lasted right the way to the penultimate race when Streiff had to change cars to avoid the problem. The drivers also had to work harder than

some of their competitors to get their cars balanced, although the work usually paid dividends. Finally, it should be said that the drivers were so well matched that they frequently found themselves racing one another, never an exciting prospect for a team manager however much it vindicates his choice of driver! Unfortunately, the Tyrrell drivers found themselves running into one another more than once and Streiff's crashes became rather too frequent. However, a Tyrrell finished every single Grand Prix of the year and the fourth places in Germany (Streiff) and Australia (Palmer) were certainly the highlights.

But whatever the difficulties along the way, they were less than those suffered by other teams, and Ken Tyrrell and his faithful team accomplished what they had set out to do. One suspects that there were quite a few teams that wished they had the strength of mind, conviction and support to take the same route as Tyrrell...

ARROWS
MUCH IMPROVED

One of the pleasant revelations of the 1987 season was the performance of what Jackie Oliver liked to call the 'new Arrows team'. After the disastrous 1986 season when many of the important design staff left, Oliver faced up to reality and decided that he had a major rebuilding job on his hands, if he was to save his team, and he set about restructuring Arrows to become a competitive force again. To the fore-

front in these plans were increased links with the giant American insurance company USF&G. In spite of being wooed elsewhere, the Baltimore-based company gave its go-ahead in late 1986 allowing Oliver and his team to begin their 1987 car in good time. In fact earlier than ever before.

By this time Oliver had found a designer who could pull all his efforts together. Ross Brawn had been one of the Haas-Lola lay-offs, having previously worked at Williams. His speciality was aerodynamics, but he had never designed a whole car before. Not surprisingly, it was on aerodynamics that he concentrated when it came to a successor to the disastrous A9 and the result was the A10, a fairly conventional but neat car with a safe chassis and a fairly low deck. Into the back of this went the familiar turbocharged four cylinder power unit previously known as the BMW. However, BMW had pulled out of everything but its Brabham contract at the end of 1986 and that included

taking back everything with a BMW mark on it from Heini Mader's Gland workshops. But it soon found its way back there again when USF&G bought the rights to the four cylinder 'upright' turbo engine and called it the Megatron after one of the company's divisions. Initially, the engines were to be maintained by John Judd, but they were soon back in Switzerland under Mader's direction.

The only remaining factor in the equation was the drivers. Not surprisingly, American Eddie Cheever featured pretty strongly as a candidate, even though he'd only driven at Detroit in the Haas-Lola in 1986. He already had a Jaguar sports car contract, so it would be a busy year. Although Arrows at one time stated that they would sign up a young driver to run with Cheever, it was the equally experienced Derek Warwick, 32, who finally filled the place, making one of the most popular driver line-ups in current Grand Prix racing. The pair, in fact, worked extremely well together, apart from the occasional hiccup. They were rarely as far apart in qualifying as they were in Brazil where Warwick qualified eighth and Cheever 14th, but then Warwick had spent the latter half of the previous year in Grand Prix racing, whereas Cheever was still getting himself re-acquainted with a modern Formula One car.

Otherwise the two drivers began to settle down somewhere between the lower reaches of the top ten and the latter half of the top 15, and were never far apart (mechanical problems allowing). And in races they never ran far apart either, which led to two of their bigger problems of the year. The first was in Hungary, when an unwell Warwick defended his

seventh place from an eager Cheever, the two collided and both headed for the pits at the same moment with slight damage. There was a similar pit coincidence in Japan, when Cheever misread Warwick's arrow for tyres and came in and pinched his team mate's rubber, refusing to go back out again when Warwick appeared. This was the most unhappy moment of what was otherwise a very positive season.

High spots were Cheever's sixth place in qualifying in Monaco, and his fourths in Belgium and Mexico. Warwick was fifth in Britain and frequently the pair were heading for more points than their final positions in the championship suggested. But it was a year of mechanical problems, which only began to sort

themselves out in the second half of the year. Ligier would have saved themselves some races if they'd paid heed to Arrows' early problems with overheating and there were several engine failures. Megatron recognised this and duly asked Mader to act on it and it was only during the second half of the season that the units became reliable, although these engine problems reappeared with a vengeance in Japan. And the engine still appeared uneconomical. Warwick was in the top six at Imola when he ran out of fuel. Cheever's fourth in Belgium came in spite of having to ease off because of a lack of fuel. He failed to take the chequered flag for his sixth place in Detroit for the same reason. He also dropped a place in Spain, whereas conversely he had fuel to spare when he finished fourth in Mexico because of a lack of boost. Cheever just crossed the line without fuel in Japan.

The cars themselves performed well from the start, although at times the handling was unpredictable. At Silverstone, Warwick complained that the car felt dead to changes, but it was never that way again. It also seemed that the final fine balance was hard to find, and hard to consolidate. But for much of the season the team was knocking on the door of the top six teams and it was just a matter of everyone recognising this and pulling together. The early season retirements were depressing, but the drivers were very economical and rarely damaged their cars. A new chassis had to be built up for the first time all year when Warwick crashed in Mexico, but otherwise the team worked well.

After the disasters of 1986, it was good to see Arrows re-emerge as a force to be reckoned with and Oliver was to be

congratulated in saving his team and giving them a new sense of purpose.

BRABHAM
SURVIVAL

The very existence of the Brabham team seemed somewhat in jeopardy throughout 1987. Its first problem was when BMW stated that they were pulling out of Formula One at the end of the 1986 season. There was just one problem: there was still a year to run in their contract with Brabham and consequently, they honoured that year. But a number of familiar elements in Brabham's team did disappear in 1987. First of all, there was Gordon Murray, whose name had become almost synonymous with Brabham, who was wooed away to McLaren to partially replace John Barnard. Pirelli had also pulled out, of course, but at least a design was on the cards and late in December, Riccardo Patrese was signed as a driver for the forthcoming season.

Patrese occasionally tested one of the previous year's cars during the off-season while David North, Sergio Rhinland, David Baldwin and John Gentry prepared the new BT56 which, when completed, was almost immediately taken to the airport to be transported to Brazil. The factory staff were proud of their 1987 contender, calling it one of the nicest machines they'd produced. With no major sponsor signed and lesser sponsorship from Iceberg and Olivetti again, it hadn't exactly had money lavished on it, but it was more conventional than the super-low but troublesome 1986 Gordon Murray-inspired BT55.

There was some doubt, right up to the final days, just who would drive the second car in Brazil and the race for the seat was like a Grand Prix itself. Emanuele Pirro made the early running and later Michel Ferte and even Hector Rebaque looked favourites. Tomas Kaiser was always waiting in the wings, hoping to get a super-licence, but the failure to do so scuppered his chances. In the end, it looked as if it might go to Mauro Baldi, until Andrea de Cesaris came in with a late run to scoop the drive. And all that was before the start of the season!

The cars had a number of Achilles heels throughout the season, although they

Left: Both Eddie Cheever and Derek Warwick ran well in their first season with the revitalised Arrows team

started very promisingly. Admittedly, they weren't very quick in Brazil qualifying, but they were fairly reliable, although de Cesaris was rather frequently out of shape. Both were steadily moving up the field until Patrese went out with a loose battery and de Cesaris's transmission broke.

The team then entered probably its best era during the year. Using a mechanical fuel pump, Patrese qualified ninth, but moved up tremendously during the race, running second to Mansell until an electrical problem slowed him during the closing stages. He deserved better than ninth at his favourite circuit. But a race later, team mate de Cesaris was on the rostrum. He was lucky, for in the first start he damaged the car, but was able to take the second start and gently moved up the order, claiming third even though he did run out of petrol on the last lap. But several weaknesses had already been exposed. The engines didn't like being over-revved and, not surprisingly, tended to break when they were. Equally unsurprising was the fact that the front uprights took objection to hitting solid objects and the gearbox proved somewhat fragile as it had the previous year.

Away from the track, the team was obviously still for sale and no major sponsor was forthcoming, although the size of Olivetti identification did vary from race to race. David North and John Gentry both left before mid-season to go to Ralt and Benetton respectively, leaving Baldwin and Rhinland to hold the reins. Mid-season, the team was

almost more famous for its spectacular fires in France and Britain than for fiery performances on the track. After his disappointing ninth at Imola, Patrese finished ninth again in Detroit but fifth

in Hungary. De Cesaris had a good race in Portugal, but two pit stops and a broken injector pipe inevitably meant that he didn't finish.

Brabham was back on the rostrum again in Mexico when Patrese avoided the carnage and gently moved up the order, racing particularly sensibly in the second half of the race to claim third overall behind the Williams duo. He was classified again in Japan in spite of an engine problem, while de Cesaris was also classified in Australia despite two excursions, including a spin on the last lap caused by the loss of a front nose wing which he'd knocked off some laps previously. The Brabhams were generally reliable midfield runners in 1987, closing in on the top three occasionally. Patrese and de Cesaris shared their best

qualifying position, seventh. It was tempting to suggest that Brabham's problems generated from BMW's lack of development, but that wouldn't be entirely true, although the high pressure fuel pumps used after Monaco lacked the development of the low pressure pumps used previously for fuel consumption purposes. By the end of the year, the team's future was again being discussed, with two programmes on the drawing table.

LOLA
PROMISING DEBUT

Even as the Haas-Lola effort was winding down after Adelaide in 1986, plans were afoot for the Huntingdon company to be represented in Formula One by a new team based in France and run by Gerard Larrousse. Philippe Alliot would follow Larrousse from Ligier to do the driving. And as he celebrated the ten years since he arrived at Silverstone with the first Renault turbo Formula One car, it was amusing to reflect that having built both engine and chassis at Renault, then only the chassis at Ligier, Larrousse was now going for a combination of engine and chassis that were both bought in. And there was no chance that he might go back on his decision. The contract was with Lola for two years, with an option on a third.

Larrousse's partner in the new team was Didier Calmels, who brought together a formidable array of sponsors to support the venture. The team's 'Club F1' broke new ground in promotional terms, and the sponsors were most professionally serviced. On several occasions, government ministers attended races, and the team did a deal with its local 'department' in France to represent it in exchange for a grant for a factory. Larrousse's original idea had been to go into Formula 3000, finally shaking off the turbo image with which he had so long been associated, but with the establishment of a new normally aspirated class, plans changed and he went into Formula One with a modified version of Ralph Bellamy's F3000 Lola chassis, fitted with the inevitable Ford Cosworth DFZ engine, in this instance serviced by Heini Mader. Later the team would switch to Magnetti Marelli ignition, but otherwise it was a fairly standard power plant.

The team suffered delays with the supply of engines like a number of others, partially due to a lack of cylinder heads. And this, coupled with general unreadiness, caused them to miss the Brazilian Grand Prix for which they received a $50,000 fine. Instead the attractive blue car made its debut at Imola, where it ran reliably, qualifying second in class and running third until Fabre spun in front of his compatriot and Alliot went off too, recovering to finish second in class after two pit stops. One race later, Alliot won the normally aspirated class in spite of running out of brakes, having a spin and then pushing his own car off the kerbs before rejoining.

These incidents, unfortunately, tended to characterise an otherwise excellent debut season for the team. The car was always competitive in qualifying, apart from Mexico, where Alliot was a relatively lowly fourth in class after mechanical problems. But he was rather 'incident-prone'. After his spins at Imola and Spa, he tangled with Nakajima at Ste Devote at Monaco, crashed with Arnoux in Detroit, had a collision with Campos at Silverstone, but ended the first half of the season with sixth place overall on the Hockenheim power circuit. Alliot followed that up with sixth place in Spain and Mexico, but there was still a fair sprinkling of incidents during the second half of the season. Regrettably, he has suffered such problems during most of his motor racing career.

This young team then chose to run a second car for F3000 winner and Formula One newcomer, Yannick Dal-

mas, from Toulon, running him in the last three Grand Prix. He proved to be thoroughly competitive and generally speaking, kept his nose clean. He almost looked as though he might win the class in Japan, until he suffered brake problems and then he had trouble with the engine and its electrics. All in all, however, Larrousse and Calmels had reason to be proud of their new team and the choice they made in its equipment. The Lola, with Bellamy usually in attendance, proved a more than adequate weapon against the more specialist Tyrrells and March and the team proved perfectly capable of extending itself to run two cars at the end of the season.

ZAKSPEED
PROGRESS

Zakspeed won its first World Championship points in 1987 and that, in itself, is progress. The West-sponsored team no doubt saw a number of occasions

when it might have scored more than the two points that Martin Brundle won at Imola. There were three seventh places, for instance. At the end of the year, West had confirmed their continued support, so they, at least, were satisfied. At the same time, an expatriot asked why the team didn't have the support of Germany's industry and Erich Zakowski had to admit that he didn't know. His was still one of the smallest teams in Formula One and, with 50 people, certainly the smallest building both engine and chassis, naturally with inherent problems!

The team's facilities were certainly enough to impress Martin Brundle, who decided that he didn't want to go normally aspirated with Ken Tyrrell, hoped to get the McLaren drive, but ultimately went for Zakspeed. By the end of February, he and Christian Danner were confirmed as Zakspeed's two drivers. The team, meanwhile, was

working on its new 871, but considerable testing had been done with the four cylinder turbo engine which now boasted an up-to-date Bosch management system and quite a lot of items that some teams had been using for several years. The two drivers started the season in 861s, but Brundle got his Chris Murphy-designed 871 for Imola, and Danner got his a race later in Belgium.

It took just one race for Brundle to win those first points for the team, although he won no more. The cars were reasonably reliable in Brazil and Danner finished ninth, although Brundle retired. Brundle found the new car reliable in Imola and just decided to try and get to the end. He decided not to stop for new tyres, as he had neither the brakes nor the fuel to use the tyres – and two points was the reward. A milestone was reached. Furthermore, Danner finished seventh in the old 861. The cars weren't reliable in Belgium and Danner crashed due to a lack of brakes. His trouble continued when he was excluded from the Monaco Grand Prix after his accident with Alboreto which even the Italian considered to be a harsh decision. Brundle, meanwhile, was becoming a little frustrated but drove as best as he could to finish seventh behind two normally aspirated cars.

The Detroit Grand Prix saw a fairly dramatic two days of qualifying, with more brake problems for Brundle when they locked up and he hit a wall, continuing the weekend in the spare car. He retired from the race with a blown turbo, while Danner finished eighth with a full hiccup problem. Back at Ricard for the French Grand Prix, Brundle admitted that he felt that the team was up against a bit of a barrier. They were trying to take off wing for straightline speed, but then would find that they didn't have the grip in the corners. He lost a wheel in the race, while Danner's engine overheated. The British Grand Prix was just as dramatic although it did see a change in the team's internal organisation which would mean a better finishing record in the second half of the year, if no points. Brundle wasn't classified in Britain after a change of black box, while Danner was a retirement. It was the same story in Germany where Brundle was again not classified and the chassis obviously wasn't suited to the Hungaroring, where both cars again had to retire.

Austria, a week later, saw an upturn in fortunes although, for a while, you wouldn't have thought so, when Brundle's car suddenly veered off into the barrier at the start for no apparent reason. This caused the first race stoppage. They were both involved in the next shunt too and neither car handled the same again, yet both finished – with Danner ninth and Brundle 14th. At Monza, the pair ran well and looked as though they might both finish again, until Brundle had more gearbox trouble but Danner finished ninth. Both cars were involved in the first corner accident in Portugal as well, and Danner failed to take the restart, but Brundle was in the top ten when he retired. The twisty circuit of

Jerez again didn't suit them and although Brundle never really featured, he did finally finish eleventh.

The Mexican Grand Prix was the team's 30th and at one time had the potential to be one of their best. Brundle was 10th in the first practice session and moved up a place the next morning, eventually qualifying 13th. But neither car lasted more than three laps. As usual, they qualified around the 15 mark in Japan, only to retire again. In Australia, Danner looked to be heading for points, but his brake problems reappeared and he slipped back to be classified a disappointing seventh. The team was at least finishing, unlike some others, but the situation of the under-financed turbo team is certainly not enviable. But it is Zakspeed's engine, and the team is committed to it. It has no normally aspirated experience and, consequently, the team will be continuing with their unit in 1988.

MARCH
INSTANT
RECOGNITION

March's forays into Grand Prix racing have never appeared particularly convincing and have not lasted long. They've usually ended with a sell-out of the company's FOCA membership to someone else, hence ATS and the John MacDonald March operation. But in late 1986, a number of elements came together which persuaded March to come back into the Grand Prix arena. The company had just won the F3000

championship with a car entered by Genoa Racing, a private team run by Cesare Gariboldi, whose driver, Ivan Capelli was now champion. Capelli then had a couple of runs in Japan's similar series with sponsorship from real estate company Leyton House. Gariboldi cleverly brought March, Capelli and Leyton House together to form a one car Formula One team with normally aspirated engines for the 1987 season. Rumours that it would include a second Italian driver were discounted.

It had been ten years since Robin Herd and Max Mosley sold their works Formula One operation to ATS, and eleven years since Ronnie Peterson gave March their last Formula One win with victory in the 1976 Italian Grand Prix. But re-entering Grand Prix racing would bring a useful spin-off for March. The company was about to be listed on the stock market, and this would doubtless give them added kudos. The project engineer for the car, to be known as an 871, was Gordon Coppuck, working under Robin Herd, while Tim Holloway would be race engineer. Established mechanics were hired and from a personnel point of view, it was a very strong team.

The car, however, would not be ready until the San Marino Grand Prix, but pressure was brought to bear on team manager Ian Phillips to take a machine to Brazil for the first Grand Prix. The team had a converted F3000 car variously known as the 871P, the 87B/B or 87P with which initial testing had been

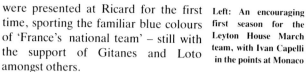

carried out, and once Mader was finally supplied with his Cosworth engines, it was shipped to Brazil although it had such reduced tankage that everyone knew it would never be able to finish the race. In the event, it didn't need to. After two blown engines and constant misfiring, the car was withdrawn from the race, but on its one good lap, it ran only a few mph slower than the Tyrrells on the straight. The team's neat 871 was finally ready during the San Marino Grand Prix, but then the team discovered a succession of mechanical problems. The rotor arm broke at Imola, in Belgium there were electrical problems, and then Capelli was leading the class until the oil pressure disappeared. There were more electrical problems in Monaco, but they were cured before the race, when Capelli had his first finish and gained a World Championship point for the team with sixth place. There was an electrical misfire in Detroit and in spite of more electrical problems, Capelli qualified first in France. He was leading the class when the engine broke. There were more engine problems at Silverstone, including trouble with the fuel system, but Capelli retired when he spun and damaged the gearbox on a kerb.

But now came the turning point. It seemed that Cosworth had modified their electrical mapping system and not told Mader. Consequently, the team had wasted the entire first half of the season, working to an outdated set of rules. But Capelli then finished the next five races, winning Jim Clark Cup and Colin Chapman Cup points in every one, with class wins in both Austria and Portugal. The car was clearly capable of more than challenging the others in the class and during his first full season, Capelli made fewer mistakes than some more experienced drivers. The team quickly became part of the establishment and is clearly in Formula One racing to stay. Indeed, halfway through the 1987 season, March was already making plans for a two car team in 1988 and those plans were well advanced, even to the extent of testing the new Judd V8 engine, when the curtain fell on the team's first full season.

LIGIER
A SURVIVAL YEAR

How are the mighty fallen? The Ligier team was a pale shadow of its former self in 1987, and those involved found they had to lay the blame fairly and squarely at the door of Alfa Romeo. The deal for Alfa Romeo to supply the team with a brand new turbo power unit was done long before the end of the previous season. Renault was quitting Formula One (how many teams regretted not signing for the French company for 1987?), so a new power unit had to be found. But the Italian connection was weakened by Pirelli's withdrawal. Not only did Ligier lose Pirelli and Renault, but they also lost team manager Gerard Larrousse, who had always been keen to form his own team and now did so. Rene Arnoux was confirmed as one driver before the end of the year and early in January, the first engine was ready. Early in February, engine and chassis were presented at Ricard for the first time, sporting the familiar blue colours of 'France's national team' – still with the support of Gitanes and Loto amongst others.

The chassis was designed by former Renault man Michel Tetu and his team, and was a totally new car retaining only the front wheel hubs, some sections of the uprights and the gearbox internals of the JS27. Otherwise, the team had pulled out all the stops to produce a new car. The chassis was built by Advanced Composites, whose quality control was sadly not perfect, while the front springs were mounted on top of the chassis for increased safety for the driver's legs in the event of an accident. This proved to be extremely fortuitous when Arnoux lost his brakes going into the first corner at Jerez in testing. But it was also the front suspension that cost the team their first race at Imola ... Alfa·Romeo's engineers were somewhat taken aback by the intercooler rule change and spent a month of development coming up with twin, side-by-side turbos on the left hand side. Pipework and bodywork also had to be altered. The engine was tested for 3600 kilometres in an old Euro-racing chassis at Alfa's test track at Balocco before it appeared in the Ligier JS29. The engine weighed 15 kilos less than Renault's V6, but the engine/transmission system weighed considerably more in spite of a compact six speed gearbox designed by Michel Beaujon and Glaenzer Spicer.

While the car was making all-too-brief forays onto the circuit, the possible candidature of either Jacques Laffite or Didier Pironi as second driver was being considered. Laffite drove a Formula Renault and then a Formula Three car, but in the end, Piercarlo Ghinzani was hired, a very popular and deserving choice. Then it all began to go wrong. Late in March, a succession of Garrett turbo failures forced the team to scrub its plans to go to Brazil. But only two days later, Arnoux spoke his mind about the slow response of the engine to three Italian TV stations, and Alfa Romeo immediately pulled out of what was to be a three year programme. The team was instantly deprived of its engines.

Ligier were left without a power unit only days from the start of the season. Megatron offered them the former BMW engine, the four cylinder now

exclusively offered by the division of USF&G and serviced and maintained by Heini Mader in Gland, Switzerland. Ligier, frankly, had little choice. Not surprisingly, they went for it, but at what cost? First, the weight penalty of adapting what now became the JS29B to the new power unit, cost the team the whole of the first half of the season. Indeed, Ligier really only joined the field in Belgium if the truth be told, after the front suspension failures at Imola. Yet it was at Spa that Arnoux scored the team's only point. Although there were troubles adapting to the engine, the team was by no means exclusively stuck with these. While overheating featured prominently with Megatron users, the Ligier also had its own causes for retirement. There were electrical problems, holed radiators and broken exhausts, but more familiarly, the cars ran out of fuel and the ignition pick-up gave problems.

The Ligier team also had its own problems with the chassis. The change of power unit meant a change of rear bodywork which upset the aerodynamics. It was only when Arnoux got a new rear bodywork in France that things improved. This meant a smaller intercooler, lower siting of the rear extractors, new rear bodywork and underwing. The JS29C as it now became, felt less heavy, said Arnoux on his 39th birthday. He was keeping up with the Ferraris until his exhaust began to break up. But then a new problem reared its head. The team's engine deal did not include sufficient engine rebuilds. The engine installation, hurried as it obviously was, hadn't been the best, and it had cost them dearly in terms of reliability. The team began to feel the pinch in Italy, there might not be enough power units with which to finish the season.

From then on, the team cut out practice sessions, did as few laps as possible in qualifying and took things relatively easy – although Arnoux on 4.2 bar boost, after knocking off both Alliot and Capelli in Japan, ran contrary to this policy. He ran out of fuel seven laps from the end. But then as a driver he doesn't seem to have matured. He still makes remarkable mistakes which escape penalties by the governing body. Everyone was upset that Ghinzani, who finally looked to have an ideal drive, was robbed of his chances and found himself back running alongside his former mount, the paler blue car of Osella. It was not a successful season and Ligier tried to do the best thing possible – forget 1987 and start planning for 1988 by fixing up a good engine deal early for the new year.

AGS
RELIABLE BUT...

After its brief two race debut with Motori Moderni power in 1986, the small AGS team from just north of Toulon in France returned for a full season in 1987. Their equipment was, in some ways, almost unchanged. The big bulky chassis was still based on a two-year-old Renault, but now the car would be powered by a Cosworth DFZ engine and the team would be contesting the Colin Chapman Cup along with the likes of Tyrrell, March and Lola. El Charro remained the faithful sponsors of Henri Julien's team again, but with Ivan

Capelli going off to March, a new driver had to be found. In the end, Pascal Fabre, a Formula 3000 winner, signed for the French team, although not until February, as he had been hoping for a Ligier ride. If that was one delay, the other was that Heini Mader was unable to supply engines early, because of Cosworth's development problems and also a lack of cylinder heads.

The team's philosophy for its first full year in Formula One was simply that reliability was everything and that the car must finish. This they proceeded to prove with a magnificent run of seven finishes, but they just failed to complete the half season, as the engine broke in Germany. By this stage, the car and driver were acquiring something of a reputation for continually being at the back and occasionally being in the way. While it looked smart and well presented, it was quite obviously not quick and didn't respond to basic changes to make it quicker. And Fabre didn't

always keep the car on the track. There were mechanical failures as well, but they were never serious and not usually at bad times. However, warning bells sounded during the second half of the season. Fabre was regularly around 1.5 seconds off the pace, and in Austria, that rose to over 5 seconds. If there were 27 cars or even 28 as was threatened by the arrival in Italy of another Osella, another Lola, Middlebridge's Benetton-BMW and the Coloni, then the AGS's chances of qualifying looked slim.

By this stage, F3000 star Roberto Moreno was involved with the team and might have raced a second car (which the team could ill-afford) in Italy, but for Fabre's spectacular involvement in the start line crash in Austria which meant

that there wasn't a car for the Brazilian. After non-classification in Austria, and non-qualification in Italy, the team felt themselves forced to make improvements to their existing chassis and aerodynamics – and possibly into changing their driver. Moreno did the testing and set the fastest ever normally aspirated time around Ricard's short circuit. Some of these modifications were subsequently incorporated into the car, but first Fabre failed to qualify in Portugal, although he was lucky to get on the grid in Spain. Benetton refused to sign a waiver allowing 27 cars to start the final three Grand Prix, and when Fabre failed to qualify in Mexico, the writing was on the wall. Moreno, who had been waiting eagerly in the wings, was nominated for Japan and was lucky that Mansell withdrew, otherwise he would have been out of a race as he was still slowest. At least, he pointed out, the car was now only half-a-second slower than the one in front.

At Adelaide, however, he showed renewed form, and Moreno battled constantly and on even terms with the Lolas and no one begrudged him his point, although there were plenty of turbo teams who would have loved it.

Although they didn't exactly cover themselves in glory, the team's early season reliability was a point in its favour and with a new car on the drawing board from designer Christian Vanderpleyn, more could be expected in 1988.

COLONI
BRIEF DEBUT

Enzo Coloni made the big step from Formula Three into Formula One with a brief if reasonably promising debut in the normally aspirated class. Coloni had been the man to beat in the Italian F3 championship ever since the days of Euro-racing, although he wasn't always popular. In 1986, he fielded two Marches in the Formula 3000 championship and began tentative development of those cars, which no doubt encouraged him to go into Formula One. As is often common with such exploits, everyone was rather surprised when the pale yellow car duly turned up at Monza, complete with support from Q8 oil and fuel and Renzacci.

The car, in fact, was fairly straightforward and simple, with the usual Ford Cosworth DFZ in the back. In spite of a couple of test sessions, however, there proved to be a major problem with the clutch and driver Nicola Larini joined Fabre (who was slower) as a non-qualifier. The team's other outing was in Spain after giving Portugal a miss due to prior commitments. This outing was much more promising and the car ran reliably, pipping both Osellas to the final spot on the grid. Larini was 1.9 seconds slower than Ghinzani's Ligier, 1.4 seconds slower than local boy Campos's Minardi, and 0.5 seconds slower than Fabre's AGS – although he had been quicker than Fabre's eventual qualifying time in an unofficial session. All of this pointed to a promising debut, but it

lasted no more than eight laps before he had to retire. The programme was simply a toe-in-the-water exercise for a more extensive and serious outing in 1988, but it provided interest and novelty mid-season.

OSELLA
STILL A STRUGGLE

There may be few high points in the life of Enzo Osella, but one of them must have been during the 1987 Monaco Grand Prix when his car and driver battled briefly with Teo Fabi's Benetton and led Stefan Johansson's admittedly sick McLaren until the Osella fell back after 31 laps. Two cars that were behind it at that moment then went on to score points! But such happy moments were rare for the Osella team in 1987 – although to see the team at work you would never believe that the cheerful Italians were the slightest bit pessimistic. When Osella ran two cars at Jerez, neither of them made the cut, but that was a rare occurrence.

Osella was encouraged to stay in Formula One due to the re-admittance of normally aspirated engines, but in the end, he stuck with the old Alfa Romeo V8 engines that are now getting very long in the tooth. Indeed, by the end of the season, even Alfa Romeo were disowning them. Osella requested that they should not be referred to as Alfa Romeos and no name appeared on the cam covers. Meanwhile Landis and Gyr continued their financial support as sponsors for most of the year until

Stievani electrical goods stepped in to support the team. By the end of the season Osella was already saying that he had a sponsor prepared to finance development on the still thirsty V8 turbo

engine that the team intended to use in 1988. As for cars, a new FA1I appeared, although it was the use of carbon fibre that made it different from the previous model. And in spite of the use of lighter

material, it was still very heavy at over 600 kilos.

The man hired to drive this machine was Alex Caffi, the little Italian who drove for the team the previous year at Monza. Generally speaking, he did a workmanlike job in a difficult car. Every now and then, number 21 would suddenly appear higher up on the lap chart than usual, but

unfortunately it rarely lasted. His best grid position for most of the season was 16th in Monaco – ironic when you consider that this year 26 cars were allowed to start. When only 20 were allowed to start, only twice in the history of the Monaco Grand Prix and Osella, one of the Italian cars qualified. If the car did get to the end of a race, it invariably ran out of fuel, as it did when Caffi was classified 12th at Imola. That was his best result all year. He had been 13th in the warm-up. In Hungary and Japan, he wasn't classified – no retirement, but no fuel either. Unfortunately, mechanical bothers frequently sidelined the pale blue car. There was a succession of turbo failures, engine failures and even gearbox failures. In Austria the electrics were to blame and only in Italy, where rear suspension caused his retirement, was it anything other than mechanical. Rarely, too, did the driver cause retirement. In Brazil he was exhausted by the heat, but otherwise he

emulated his predecessor, Ghinzani, by doing a difficult job well.

On four occasions, this little overworked team chose to run two cars, for financial reasons – why else? Formula 3000 driver Tarquini made his Grand Prix debut at Imola (thanks to the withdrawal of Piquet's Williams) and Switzerland's formula F3 champion;

Franco Forini, drove in Italy and Spain, but joined Caffi in the grandstands in Jerez after failing to qualify.

One couldn't help asking if Osella would not have been much better off going the normally aspirated Cosworth route and at least having a reliable power unit with which to race. Perhaps the heavy chassis needed the equally heavy turbo power, but it seems a waste of time going racing when, if mechanical bothers don't get you, fuel consumption will. Yet the team works hard and happily.

MINARDI
GRADUAL IMPROVEMENT

The Minardi team is still a relatively young one in Formula One racing, but one can't help thinking that they would have been better off in the normally aspirated class in 1987. Their lack of reliability can't be entirely attributed to engine problems and there were a fair number of turbo failures, but the drivers saw the chequered flag just once each in 1987, although Nannini was classified twice more – but out of fuel. The team did attempt to improve its Caliri-designed chassis in 1987. It spent two months in the Fiat wind tunnel, which resulted in revised rear end aerodynamics, including repositioned radiators and intercoolers – plus a new exhaust system. There was new suspension and a six-speed gearbox. The team used the Marelli Weber electronic fuel management system instead of the three-year-old system previously used.

The cars were ready in good time for Alessandro Nannini and new driver Adrian Campos to go testing before the start of the season, but it didn't do them much good. The material, quite simply, wasn't reliable. Nannini, however, gradually pulled the Minardis, with their Motori Moderni engines, further and further up the grid. By the end of the year, he was regularly qualifying around the 14th mark with a best of 13th in Australia and Monaco. It was ironic that one of his worst qualifying performances came in Hungary – a circuit not ideally suited to the chassis. Yet this was the one race in which Nannini saw the chequered flag, finishing 11th. In the meantime, there was a string of retirements caused by a broken hub in Brazil, engine in Imola, turbo failure in Belgium, electrics in Monaco, gearbox problems in Detroit

Nannini's only finish was the 11th place already mentioned in Hungary, but he was also classified in Italy, out of fuel, slipping from 11th to 16th. The same thing happened three weeks later in

Portugal where he was heading for ninth, eventually ending up 11th. So the Minardi could be reliable, if not very consistently. The driver himself was generally thought to be better than his material and showed maturity. His early exit from the final race of the year was uncharacteristic. By the end of the year, Nannini was, unsurprisingly, being courted elsewhere. His team mate was, however, a different kettle of fish. Andrea de Cesaris, having called the team, "a Mickey Mouse outfit" and considering that he was worthy of better, departed, leaving his vacant seat to be filled by Spain's Adrian Campos, who brought Lois Jeans sponsorship. Campos had considerable trouble getting his season started. There was a $3000 fine for missing a weigh-in in Brazil and then a black flag for making up grid positions on the final parade lap. He raced in Imola before the frequent gearbox problem which also cost him his race in Belgium when he stripped first gear at the start. He crashed in practice at Monaco, and wasn't allowed to race, and retired on the first lap after a shunt with Nakajima in Detroit. He finally got going in France and briefly showed eighth in Germany. He was tough on the gearbox, while his only finish of the year, 14th at home in Spain, was more good luck than judgement, for he twice left the road in the race. Like a number of others, his best grid position, 16th, was in the first race of the year.

It wasn't a good year for Minardi, but they kept up appearances and the preparation of the cars was good, even if the results weren't. But there is still room for improvement.

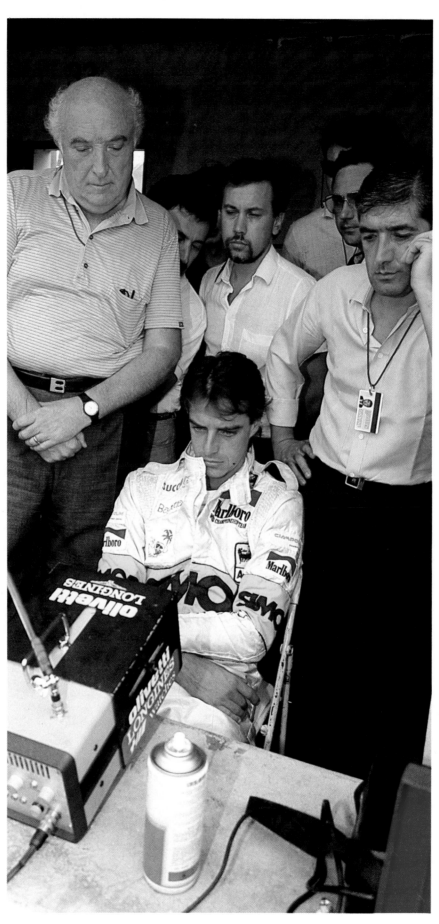

Left: A mixed first season for Campos

Right: A season of total unreliability hindered Alessandro Nannini's obvious talent

ALAIN PROST

BY JACKIE STEWART

Jackie Stewart appraises the man who beat his 14-year-old record of 27 Grand Prix wins, and compares their different eras . . .

There was a time when it was perfectly feasible that Alain Prost might not beat my record in 1987. It was unlikely but feasible. The only reason it was feasible was the obvious superiority of the Honda engine. But Alain Prost is into winning races. If he's on the third row of the grid he can still win a race. You never know just when he's going to do it, but he has the confidence that he doesn't have to be on pole position to win. It's not arrogance, it's not overconfidence, it's just a depth of knowledge and that's what makes Alain Prost, in my mind, the best driver in the world at this time. It's for that reason that when he won his 28th Grand Prix victory I didn't at all mind handing over a baton which has been in the hands of at least two of the people that I've worshipped in racing: Juan Manuel Fangio and Jim Clark.

I would be a hypocrite if I didn't say that it's been a very nice record to have held since I won my 26th race 14 years ago. It's a wonderful thing to be able to stand up and be introduced as the driver who has won more Grand Prix races than any other man in the history of motor sport. I can still claim to have won 27 Grand Prix but I will no longer be able to claim the record. It's gone as it clearly was going to one day. But it's very good to know that it's going to the man who I would wish to be like if I were driving today. His skills and the way he does his business are very commendable. He's been a good World Champion. He represents the sport well, he speaks well, he projects well, he has a recognisable presence. He knows and accepts his responsibilities. All of those things are ingredients that make up the big cake and right now he's definitely the best cake.

I first recognised his talent when he was driving for Renault. It was clear that he had a very unique skill, but I would be hypocritical if I claimed that I said then: "There's the driver of the decade or of the period". His team had an almost unfair advantage with the TAG Porsche engine when he raced for McLaren early on. It would have been very difficult for Alain and Niki not to have won races that year, in the same way as Nelson and Nigel have in 1987. You would have had to be a very poor performer to let opportunities like that slip by without winning. So his real skill for me only came into its own when he was driving faster than Niki. I respected Niki even if he was coming back after retirement. He was driving a car that was miles superior to anybody else's. It was a wonderful way to come back. His timing and understanding of when to come back was very astute, and that I respected.

But Alain was clearly better than Niki. He started to threaten him seriously in that final year when he lost the Championship by half a point. Alain knew he was better, and he was satisfied to have won seven Grand Prix in a year even though he did not win the Championship. He was disappointed to lose the Championship but he knew he was going to win it one day. That knowledge was there, and I certainly knew it was there. I don't think I was any visionary to see it. But you never know with people. Racing drivers can slip on a banana skin any day and it can affect their approach to racing and their dedication to it.

Alain emerged as the best driver in the world halfway through 1986 as far as I was concerned. Although he had won the World Championship convincingly prior to that, I thought he was still slightly behind Nelson Piquet until that point. Then suddenly he made that final stride when all of the little elements came together to produce the big picture. He had the skill and natural ability. He had the experience and the knowledge of winning. Suddenly he attained maturity. Not everyone who has experience and knowledge gains maturity. But it's what makes the difference to an intelligent sportsman. At the end of the day there is an abundance of natural skill and God-given talent within many of the people who make up a starting grid. They've all come up through the normal channels and formulae leading to this golden pot at the end of the rainbow. Most have been champions in Formula Ford, Formula Three or whatever. But there are only those rare few who are capable of going further, and what makes the difference is intelligence. It's the mind, it's not the body. It's not a driver's ability to press his hands on the steering wheel at the right time and the right place. It's the way he channels his resources most positively – it's his mind.

Prost has a mind which has matured to a level now where he knows when it's possible to do something and when it's not correct to make the extra effort. That may sound almost a defeatist's statement, but it's not. In my book, *The Principles of Performance Driving*, I wrote that there's no point in driving your pack of huskies abnormally hard, to beat another man across the Arctic ice pack to the North pole, if they are never going to be able to get you back again.

You've got to go home and there is no way home other than on those sledges pulled by huskies. Alain Prost now recognises that on some days there is no point in pushing his racing car, his tyres or himself to a level which would be unrealistic. He appreciates that he has to finish a race to collect enough points to be within the parameters of a chance of the Championship.

When there is a chance to win a race however, he recognises it. He knows when to go, how to do it and how to pace himself. Now that is maturity and that's what marks the great champions. That's why Fangio was able to go and win at the Nurburgring in 1957 when he drove that Maserati to beat Collins and Hawthorn. On that day he did the right thing and drove out of his skin. Similarly, it would have been foolish for me to have overdriven the Nurburgring in the rain in 1968. I had to drive as hard as I did to win and it would have been wrong for me not to make an effort that day. I had a similar situation at Monza when I had a puncture. I knew that maybe I could finish fourth. It was a bit of a dream but it was achievable and that's how I clinched the Championship in 1973.

There were races when Niki Lauda did exactly the same thing and there would have been races when Jim Clark saw his chance and so did Stirling Moss. These are people who have marked themselves out in history, in the annals of motor racing and in my mind, at the present time, Alain Prost is the Jim Clark of his day. Some people say it was easier in my era for me to win 27 Grand Prix than it has been for Alain Prost in his era. But I think it's all relative. It's very difficult to make such comparisons. One could have said it was easier for Fangio because he was only ever the real number one in any of his teams, whether it was Maserati, Ferrari or Mercedes Benz. But I don't think it mattered. I think if Ascari, Villoresi, Taruffi, Fagioli and Farina had all been driving against Fangio, he still would have won, even if they had all been in Mercedes Benz, Maseratis or Ferraris. At that time he was the man.

They say Jim Clark never had to race anybody. He didn't because he was so good that he was able to take advantage of people without racing them. Of course, Jim Clark was driving a Lotus created by Colin Chapman, in my mind

the greatest creator of racing cars in the history of motor sport. I drove a Lotus Formula One car maybe only twice but I raced against Clark many times and in the Tasman Championship I raced against him a lot. The Lotus had grip. The centre of gravity of that car was six inches below the ground. The car almost destroyed the tarmacadam because of the enormous depth of its grip. I was driving a BRM at that time and the centre of gravity was six inches above the ground. The car was slipping on top of the road surface in a way you couldn't believe.

Jim Clark was better and it didn't matter what he was driving. It just so happened he was driving a Colin Chapman car. I was part of his period and I took my hat off to him. He was the master. I was able to develop my skill as I went along and how long could Jim Clark have been the master? Would Jochen Rindt have unsettled him; would Niki Lauda have passed him had they overlapped? Who knows? But we do know that Fangio became the master. We know that Stirling Moss then took over the role. Jim Clark then took the mantle and maybe I took the role. Niki Lauda certainly became the master and, following Niki Lauda, Alain Prost has taken it. There have been people between but as real masters those drivers will all go down in history.

I don't know if it was easier for me. How can one say it was easier when one thinks of what Alain had in the McLaren-TAG when there was nobody to compete with those two cars. But Fangio had a Mercedes Benz in the mid-1950s as did Stirling Moss. I'm sure the Matra MS80 was one of the best cars ever created but so too was the Lotus 49 at the same time. My race with Jochen Rindt in the 1969 British Grand Prix at Silverstone was one of the great classics of that period because there were two great cars being driven very well on that particular day by two very clean drivers. But these two cars used the same power plants and it was very difficult to get any advantage. Your advantage had to come in other ways.

I have never said nor thought that I was better during the period of my success than one of my predecessors because it was more difficult in my day. It just isn't like that. Times do change but superior talent doesn't. Alain was the dominant individual for the first third of the 1987 season until the Williams-Honda destroyed that situation. But he was clearly the identifiable leader of the pack. Nobody quite knew whether Nelson Piquet or Nigel Mansell was faster or better. But nobody questioned that Alain Prost was the best, so the pack had acknowledged its leader. This is something that happens not by planning, not

by a PR man, nor by marketing. It comes about by respect and by acknowledgement. Of his challengers, Ayrton Senna is still learning. He is 27 years of age and hasn't yet had the confidence of knowing that he is the best. He has still got to consolidate the skill that has already been accepted by others. Nelson Piquet had an injection of much needed adrenalin from what I would have called a passive first two thirds of the year. He's got the skill God gave him and he's used it in a frivolous fashion without actually having to work at it. He is so good that he can still drive and perform and do wonderful things. Nigel is still so hungry to prove that he can be the World Champion that he is still maybe just a little bit impetuous with it all. He's very forceful, very skilled, very determined, single minded but for the moment he just hasn't got the rounded edges of Mr Prost.

So how does Alain round the edges? He does it in the classic way that has marked all of the Champions of that thin-air group. It is the smoothness, delicacy and gentleness in a motor car which appears to the spectator as an unhurried, docile performance, yet all the time he is driving the car to the ultimate ability, not only of the chassis, but of the tyres and the engine, keeping in mind all of the necessities of durability. During practice in Belgium I was able to go out to watch at quite a few corners. At La Source hairpin you see lots of little things. It's a slow corner and because there is a very good viewpoint for the privileged few who can walk that close to the corner, you see the little subtleties that make big differences. When he arrives at La Source hairpin, the brakes are clearly on deep in the corner, but then you get the feeling that for the last ten metres the brakes are no longer on because he has had the time to ease them off so smoothly. It's where you take the brakes off going into a corner that's far more important than where you put them on.

When he turns the steering wheel it's not a sharp movement, it's a slow, very gentle turn to the right. There's no sudden movement as though he's saying 'Oh my goodness I'm at the apex, I've got to turn'. With Alain there's no rush. I must have watched this demonstration for 20 or 30 laps. I try to suggest this technique at some of the driving days I do with the press for the Ford Motor Company. I try to show them how to do it and try to make them feel it. But people say, "Well, yes, that's OK but we were doing it in a 4×4 Sierra. If we were doing it now in a Formula Ford, Formula Three or Formula One car, clearly we wouldn't have the time to do that. We would all be going into the corner at the same time and there just isn't enough space available in the milliseconds allowed". So how does he cope so beautifully with those corners? It is difficult to comprehend when you're on the absolute limit of your own and of the car's ability that you would still have time in those milliseconds to conduct those subtleties of movement. But it's like anything else. If your mind is capable of synchronising with the elements that you are competing against by producing a slow motion effect on everything that you do, there is plenty of time to turn in. Now many of the 26 Grand Prix drivers who have risen to the heady heights from winning Formula Ford and Formula Three races never find that space in time, and I have difficulty telling them that this can be done. But I remember when I discovered it and suddenly there was all the time in the world when there hadn't been before. Prost has that time and if I said to certain drivers, 'Look how Prost's doing it' they wouldn't see it. It's not that they are unintelligent. It is just that they have not got the capacity to execute it. Ivan Lendl has that capacity, I'm sure. Becker has it, Borg certainly had it and Mohammed Ali had it in boxing – all the time in the world. He saw the punch coming from the ankles to the knees to the thighs to the waist, before the arm was even set in motion. It was as though he could see the tissues starting to move. Everybody who has excelled in his or her speed sport has it.

Equally important is the ability to consume information at the same time. That's why Prost today is a very good test driver, and I think that is why he is pleased Ayrton Senna is coming to contribute to the McLaren team when he moves in 1988. I think Prost believes that Senna has that kind of skill and two being able to test and provide information is going to be far better than one very tired man. As I write this, we're three-quarters of the way through the season and Alain Prost is too tired a man to give of his best. He's washed out. He's done too many races, too many aeroplanes, too many hotels, too many trips, too much testing. McLaren needs the information that only Alain Prost can get. No disrespect to Stefan Johansson but he cannot give it to them in the same way. Senna, I believe, can give that information. When he brakes into La Source, he has all the time to turn into that corner but he also has the ability to register whether the springs are wrong, the ride height's wrong, the roll stiffness is wrong, the camber's wrong, or whatever else is wrong, and what is needed to improve matters.

There is time to consume information as well as deliver instructions to the car. It's those elements that mark a man of that skill and that talent at a time when he has three serious competitors who are obviously all quite fast enough to take the World Championship: Nelson Piquet, Nigel Mansell and Ayrton Senna. But at the moment he's got the grasp of it more completely than any of those three. (And he has Berger to deal with as well.) Part of the picture of the total racing driver is to do wonderful things consistently without making unforced errors. But a driver must also generate enthusiasm in his team and demand that the team give of its best in every little avenue. It's not being able to go out and set pole position in an extraordinary way as Piquet did in Monza. It's motivation of people, it's management of people, it's the politics of having people do things for you that they would not normally do.

Prost gets that and the respect of his team to produce these kind of performances. He's never had any real bad times or any real accidents, so he's conducted his business in a very satisfactory way. It's important that he hasn't had any accidents because accidents quite often are created by people who are not thinkers. They generally happen through lapses of concentration. The mechanical reliability that prevents accidents is part of the motivation that a driver produces within a team to ensure that a wheel isn't loose, that there isn't a spanner in a footwell, or the rear wing is about to fall off. That's part of the overall package. I'm not saying that it isn't the responsibility of Ron Dennis and his merry men, because it is. But the motivation that Prost provides and the respect that his dedicated mechanics have for him makes the difference, the attention to the minute detail in the car's preparation. If you go round the car and kick the tyres and jump in and drive it and don't acknowledge anybody, sooner or later it has an effect on people's attention to detail and the seriousness with which they take their responsibilities. It isn't just lucky that he hasn't had accidents: it's because of very solid preparation which arises from the

considerable respect of those involved in that preparation.

Which brings me to another quality which I respect and I think is of immense importance particularly when driving a racing car, but also in almost any avenue of life. Alain has the ability to control emotion. Emotion is the most dangerous thing that exists. How many times have you got angry, said or done things that later in the cold light of day you have regretted. You are sorry you ever uttered the words and you are desperately annoyed that you did such a thing in a moment of anger. A moment of anger is a loss of emotional balance. You do things that are irrational and that usually get you in trouble. If you've had a rush of success and you become a little flippant, it is again a reflection of emotion. Your effervescence is causing you to be less than very serious and you get careless. Carelessness produces potential trouble and that again is emotion. Prost has been very good at controlling all these things. I found out how to control emotion on my own. I found it out in the same way as most people discover it, and when they do so, it just emerges. You're not

conscious of it to begin with but it's only when you've got time to think about it that you realise that that control of emotional balance is one of the major ingredients of allowing you to take advantage of other people's inability to do the same under the same circumstances, and I think Prost uses it, perhaps not even consciously.

I remember my most balanced state with regards to being behind a steering wheel. Yet at that time I was being pressured very heavily in other areas because I was by far the highest paid driver of the time. I had lots of different demands on my time. I was going through the whole safety thing which was often last minute and highly emotional. Tremendously emotional people were frantic about the element of safety, never mind the application required at the eleventh hour for something to be done or changed. I'm sure I allowed my emotions to show through then because of annoyance or anger but then it was not the area in which I was most skilled. My forte was driving cars. It was frustrating to work under pressure and the demands on my time were irritating as I'm sure they are to Alain. How many times have I gone to Alain Prost and said 'Alain, I've got to do an interview for the American ESPN TV station'. Now he knows I understand. My God, I've been through it every bit as much as he has, but I have still got to do my job. Now he's trying to do something else. He's trying to be somewhere else, he's trying to carry out all his other obligations and he sees me and says, 'Oh God. I've got to do Jackie's interview'. Sometimes you get ragged and then someone is bound to say, 'He's got so big time he's become difficult'.

These are part of the pressures Prost has and the media pressure today is much more than I ever had, but I know what it's like. I know the problems from both sides of the fence which of course helps me to understand. I think he copes with that side very well and that is part of the overall Prost picture. However talented and skilled he is at the present time, he will not be as introspective today as he will be in three years, and then he will see things that he is doing today that he never realised he was doing. It will

explain a lot of things to him, things that I am now capable of seeing. I don't drive many competition cars, but I am still driving a lot and I can see things now that I never saw before. I'm looking at it from a distance. I'm now seeing every individual tree whereas before I couldn't see the trees for the woods.

Alain Prost, driving a less powerful car than his rivals, has a different situation which he has dealt with superbly. It's difficult to analyse when you are coming through from behind as Alain has done so many times because his car hasn't necessarily been on the front two rows of the grid. I would suspect that Alain, maybe not today but in future, will think back and recognise a period, a race or a time when he suddenly grew older and saw something that opened up with clarity. He'll realise that before he had been an express train running through a tunnel of trees and suddenly the trees became recognisable as chestnuts and oaks.

In 1988, Alain will form the most powerful team with Senna, McLaren,

Left: With Jackie Stewart, the man whose record he beat, at the Portuguese Grand Prix

Below: Perfect driving skill from the man whom contemporaries consider to be the best

Honda and Goodyear since Mercedes Benz. For me he is the best. He will not remain the best because nobody does. It remains to be seen how long he is prepared to be the best and how he handles the upthrust of future contenders for that position. That will affect how long he stays in racing and only he can decide that. But I suspect he will be intelligent enough to decide when it is no longer appropriate. He has views of other things that life has to offer, other than steering a car, and the time will come when I hope Alain will remove himself from the sport as a matter of choice.

JOHN BARNARD

BY MIKE DOODSON

"To turn Ferrari's fortunes around involves far more than just designing them a good car. They don't have a management structure, they have a political structure, and I have severe reservations about whether anyone who doesn't speak Modenese Italian, and doesn't have an in-depth understanding of how Italians work, could ever penetrate this political structure. But I really wish him all the best. If he does it, it will be an incredible feat. And that is the motivation that he's now got: to show the world that he can turn Ferrari round."

– Ron Dennis, October 1986.

John Barnard's record as a racing car designer is the most illustrious of the past seven years – which is as long as he's been in Formula One. The basic McLaren MP4 which he designed back in 1980/81 has been the second most successful car of the 1987 season. Yet the doubt remains. Can this 41-year-old Londoner, the engineer whose Chaparral 2K was an instant trend-setter at Indianapolis, do for Ferrari what he did for McLaren?

The signs are that he can. In spite of being 'keel-hauled' by the Italian press, who find him rude and arrogant (the feeling is mutual), Ferrari has turned a corner this year. Since JB's appointment as Technical Director in October 1986, Ferrari has turned from being something of a bad joke to being a team that can seriously think of beating Williams and Honda. But Barnard himself knows that the difficult part is still to come. "At the beginning there were a lot of people saying, 'you'll never do it, you'll never get them up and running.' I suppose I felt much the same. I had to ask myself if I was talking about something that was possible. I came in there trying ... not just to do technical things, but to reorganise the way things functioned. I couldn't understand how the race team operated, so I wanted to re-structure it in a way that I could understand."

Barnard is not the first Englishman to have enjoyed the trust and confidence of Enzo Ferrari. That distinction also belongs to the late Mike Parkes, the ex-Rootes production engineer and racing driver who went to Maranello in 1962 as a development engineer and, later, as a member of the Ferrari sports car and F1 teams. In 1972/73, Ferrari contracted British specialist John Thompson to design and make the very first true monocoque Ferrari F1 chassis. And since 1982, Dr Harvey Postlethwaite has had an important role in the team's swing to composite materials in the construction of its cars.

Barnard, however, is much more than a specialist engineer or a sub-contractor. His three-year Ferrari appointment as the Scuderia's Technical Director, began in October 1986 with virtually unlimited powers. He refused to disrupt his family, insisting from the outset on being allowed to stay in Britain. Having set up the appropriately-named autonomous GTO division (Guildford Technical Office), he now operates with a staff of 20 from its Surrey offices, where the workshop has its own 40-ton autoclave and other machinery.

Traditionalists have been scandalised. Many of them regarded Ferrari as a sacred institution with its roots, like the Vatican's, to be forever nourished on Italian soil. Only six months after the Englishman's appointment, the great but eccentric Mauro Forghieri left the company to which he had dedicated 24 years of his life, muttering that Ferrari was not what it used to be.

The reality, which Enzo Ferrari and his trusted henchman Marco Piccinini faced squarely in 1986, was that the Scuderia and its byzantine method of working could never be great again without sweeping modernisaion. The F1 programme had gone into a technical slump immediately after Michele Alboreto's victory in the 1985 German Grand Prix. Since then the red cars had been humiliated by the supremely efficient technocrats of Porsche and Honda, who had established themselves in the position which Ferrari had for long believed was its own – F1 racing's leading engine makers.

The constructors' titles of 1982 and 1983 already seemed a long time ago, and Jody Scheckter's 1979 world drivers' championship even more distant. Fiat's Vittorio Ghidella, who represents his company's 51 per cent financial interest in Ferrari, let it be known that the Scuderia's artisan approach to racing would have to be relinquished in favour of a technocracy more in line with the 20th century. The time had come for a change – if not for a revolution. The answer, concluded Messrs Ferrari and Piccinini, would be to recruit a current designer with known abilities. In mid-

1986 they had approached the French designer Gérard Ducarouge, who had briefly been employed at Alfa Romeo and was known to enjoy working in Italy. Ducarouge was ready to talk, but soon afterwards the 'poachers' were warned off by Lotus.

At the time, Barnard was a director of McLaren International, which was hugely successful and as secure as it's possible to be in the mercurial racing business. There were reports, though, that he had disposed of the shares which he had once owned in the company – now a valuable commodity. More significantly, his renowned fits of perfectionist rage were said to be directed, increasingly, against Ron Dennis, the management brains behind the McLaren successes. Although Dennis went out of his way to let Barnard publicly share the McLaren limelight, stories continued to circulate that the trained engineer resented the power and glory acquired by Dennis, whose career had started with a spanner in his hand. When Piccinini approached Barnard, he got a cautious but favourable response. By the middle of 1986 the likelihood of a Ferrari/Barnard liaison had become more than press gossip. At races Barnard was openly consorting with Piccinini. In August, Dennis' sense of loyalty was so outraged that he demanded Barnard's resignation.

After less than a year with Ferrari, Barnard has yet to prove that he is the right man to lead the revolution that Ghidella has demanded. But he has not hesitated to impose his will where he sees a need to do so, including a shake-up of the racing team under an ex-McLaren mechanic, the multi-lingual Spaniard, Joan Villadelprat. With a determined Englishman coming into such a hidebound Italian team, perhaps an 'us and them' was inevitable. Among the team gripes have been a ban on long lunches, his clashes with Michele Alboreto and a wary approach to Postlethwaite. Barnard comments: "All the stories of banning Lambrusco ... well, I never really did that. It was a simple request. I said, 'look, instead of sitting down to a big meal in the middle of the day, can we do it in the evening?' That way we were able to get through the majority of the work during the day and not have to hang around late at night. With the sit-down meal moved back, the Lambrusco got moved to later on. In

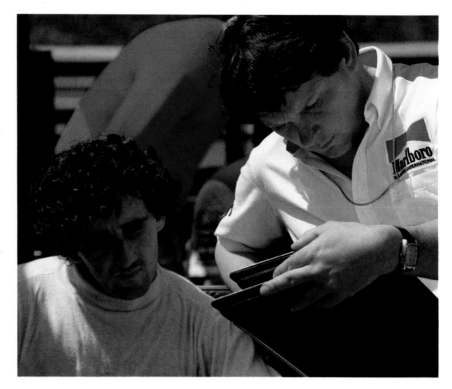

fact, I don't think they do take wine now, most of them stick to Coke or water. But nobody's moaning about it, because most of them seem to find it easier to work like that."

The relationship with Alboreto has been ticklish. Barnard is regarded as a 'Berger man', and the Italian driver has been quoted as saying that this year's improvement is entirely the work of Postlethwaite. "It's not been easy with Michele. Although he speaks good English, I think he feels that in an Italian team he shouldn't be speaking English. I also don't think he's the kind of person who likes to spend hours talking about the car. In the briefings that I've had with him, he tends to want to get it over and done with fairly quickly. I can't always do that. But Gerhard is the other way. He spends a long time, or even sometimes goes away and comes back later on, to digest the whole thing. Very often, after several hours, you've got another question that you want to put to the driver. With Gerhard, it is possible to do that."

With Postlethwaite, there is what appears to be an uneasy truce. Barnard insists that the work which bore fruit after he stopped going to races in August had been done earlier. Ferrari's dramatically improved qualifying performances, he says, were due more to being able to run to maximum boost than to any superior input from Postlethwaite. But the two men are undoubtedly incompatible personality-wise, and both seem much happier to be collaborating (if that's the right word) from a distance of several hundred miles.

River House, on a smart industrial estate overlooking the River Wey near Godalming, is the headquarters Barnard chose for Ferrari's English home. It is an elegant red-brick building with such distinctive glazed gable-ends that they already feature in the cartoons to be found in *Autosprint*, the weekly motorsports magazine. Indeed, when the facility was still new and only partly occupied, an *Autosprint* photographer got in by pretending to be measuring up the offices for carpets. His photographs, mainly of the toilet area, were published in full colour ...

GTO is now up and running in an orderly fashion. It has been supplying certain parts to Maranello, mainly suspension components, since the beginning of the 1987 season, and the arrival of the autoclave at the end of the summer gives the well-equipped factory the capacity to make an entire chassis. To supervise the day-to-day management, Barnard has appointed his old friend Peter Reinhardt, a German with a business background. They met in 1979, when Reinhardt was managing Mexican Hector Rebaque's short-lived season as a

privateer with a Lotus 79 lookalike on which Barnard had helped with some of the details.

Administration, Barnard admits, is not his scene. There is a drawing board just out of sight in an alcove adjoining his tastefully carpeted office, and he has spent many creative hours in front of it during 1987. "At the moment, I see my job as producing a new car, and that is the most important thing. I don't want any new car to come out that I haven't given my best to. If it's necessary for the administration to fall down a little bit, I won't mind because I've got to get the car right. It is, after all, something that's going to be around for a long time."

Just as it was at McLaren, his working pattern is to create the initial basic layouts or schemes, and to pass them on to others to develop. "If it's a new part, even a small one, I may detail it quite closely on the layout, just to get the part the way I want it." He is currently hard at work on a chassis to accept the 65-degree 3.5-litre V12 engine which Ferrari is developing for the normally-aspirated F1 rules which become universal in 1989. There's a project brewing to build a semi-automatic gearbox, an idea which Barnard has been pursuing since early McLaren days. He's passed it on to Ing De Silvestri (the wizard behind this year's longitudinal gearbox) to look

after at Maranello.

Barnard has not been to a race since August, and stayed away from Maranello for many weeks, a situation which he agrees may have undone some of his innovations. "I think one of the problems in me having pulled out halfway through the season was that I wasn't able to entrench the changes and make everything run automatically. So there may be some wobbling. But what's happened is that a lot of people have said to me that now they're beginning to realise that some of those changes were a good thing, and have led to the team working in a better way."

While he insists that he takes no interest in the press and its comments, he is still aware of everything that has been written about him. "I seem to have had this black image built up for me by the press, over the years, as a person who's hard to talk to ... who has to have his way. The Italian press was waiting around for me to grab somebody by the collar or to start shouting at the mechanics. And if there was any hint of controversy, they were on to it so fast."

When suspicion fell on GTO's British-built suspension parts after a number of mid-season incidents, Barnard's refusal to admit any responsibility earned him even more vitriol in the Italian papers. At Hockenheim, though, photos clearly

showed bent front suspension was responsible for a big 'off' by Berger in qualifying, and that night Barnard was to be seen reinforcing the suspect parts by wrapping them in carbon fibre in the Ferrari pit. "The thing that really bothered me is that I still can't figure out why it bent," he insists. "I still don't believe that the loads themselves caused it to buckle. To be honest with you, wrapping the suspension with carbon was a wonderful solution. I may even use it in the new designs for the 1988 car!"

Mr Ferrari was less than thrilled with an article printed in the *Sunday Times* in which JB was rash enough to criticise his road car, a Ferrari Mondial, for its lack of an ABS system. Because the piece was written by an Englishman, it generated enormous interest among Italian pressmen who feel that they are victimised by Barnard. "There was a lot of the *Sunday Times* article which was perfectly correct. But I think that most of the reaction was because the piece got taken to Italy, translated by – how shall I say? – bloodthirsty Italian journalists in such a way that certain things that were said as a joke found their way into the headlines. They came out as statements of fact in giant letters." The Mondial, incidentally, was parked outside. Its owner swears he drives it every day, "but not when I need to use the multi-storey car park, because a Ferrari isn't built for that kind of thing!"

To restore himself in the affections both of Mr Ferrari and the inevitable Italian pressmen, John Barnard now needs to produce a winning F1 racing car. After some highly promising tests with the 1988-spec, low-boost version of the 1987 V6 engine however, the Scuderia looked as though it would start the new season with a modified version of the 1987 engine and chassis. Barnard's project is exclusively for the V12.

Switching from one design to the other in mid-season is a nightmare for any team. "Having said that, there still may come a time when we have to do it," confesses Barnard, who wants to have his own car racing as soon as possible. Both his enemies and his friends may therefore have a longer wait than they expected before they see what he has achieved under the Ferrari regime. A great engineer's reputation will hang on this one car. John Barnard is confident that he's going to stand the test.

BRAZILIAN

GRAND PRIX

The result of the 1987 Brazilian Grand Prix gave many a sense of *déjà vu*. For at Adelaide, six months previously, Nigel Mansell had suffered a punctured rear left tyre and Alain Prost had won. The same happened at Jacarepagua, but with less drastic results, since it was the opening race of the season, rather than the deciding race of the championship.

Naturally, this opening race of the year answered lots of questions, but begged even more. There were numerous changes: John Barnard and Gerhard Berger to Ferrari; Gordon Murray, Neil Oatley and Stefan Johansson to McLaren; Ford engines and Thierry Boutsen to Benetton; Andrea de Cesaris in at sponsorless Brabham: Camel, Satoru Nakajima and Honda new to Lotus and everyone on Goodyear tyres – ten sets per car and no qualifiers. Some things, at least, were more simple than before. Normally aspirated engines were back with Ford Cosworth DFZs in the back of Tyrrells, and a lone AGS and March, who were making their own reappearance. Absent from this first race, after an unfortunate power loss a few weeks from the start of the season, was the Ligier team. Rene Arnoux had had a few brutally honest words to say about the new Alfa Romeo four-cylinder turbo engine, and Alfa had promptly cancelled the contract to supply the team for the next three years. The new Larrousse/Calmels team weren't ready to come to Brazil anyway at that point.

But as the new season-opener approached, there were doubts and question marks hanging over one or two matters. Just a few weeks before the race, the governing body revealed that it would be charging drivers 5000 French francs for a super licence, plus 1000 francs for each point gained in the previous year's championship. As the opening race loomed, drivers met –

upset and worried that this could lead to even bigger charges in the future. Diplomatically, Alain Prost became their spokesman and went so far as to say that there would be no strike as there was in Kyalami a few years previously. Even so, the media, eager for a story, seemed to blow the episode out of proportion. Eventually the drivers did pay up on the promise of a meeting with FISA and no escalation of charges higher than the cost-of-living, The governing body was quick to claim victory and blame journalist Johnny Rives of *L'Equipe* for stirring up the situation.

If this worry was eventually dispelled, there was another in the form of FISA's effort to limit power – the pop-off valve. This was to be attached to all turbo engines, set to limit turbo's contribution to four bar boost which would principally affect qualifying as no one used more than four bar in the race anyway. However, in testing, teams found that it could cut in earlier and one manager described this CART-derived device as the crudest bit of engineering on a Formula One car. The path from the pits to FISA's garage during practice confirmed everyone's worst fears.

By the time practice and qualifying had begun, everyone should have had a nice tan. Teams had been scheduled to test most of the previous week, but had been seriously disrupted by rain. Prost confessed that he and his team weren't as ready as he would have liked prior to

qualifying, and to some extent it showed. It wouldn't have made much difference in any other team than McLaren, but they followed their usual style of finishing their new Steve Nicholls-designed MP4/3 very late in the day. Prost would have very little time in the new car, team mate Stefan Johansson none at all. Someone else who clocked in late was Nigel Mansell, badly delayed by a tardy Varig flight, and practice itself was delayed due to lack of transport for firemen (an instant $15000 fine).

Meanwhile, Brazil itself was working up to a frenzy of excitement as the race approached. The Piquet and Senna factions were hard at work, angling for their men, but the drive from the airport suggested there was a lot more support for Senna – the 'Nacional Kid' adorned numerous posters. In the end, this local support had a rather drastic effect, but it was certainly a remarkable boost for the gate. There were five new grandstands and those, plus the huge grandstand that lines the main straight, were packed to capacity. Such was the support that the crowded roads almost made the man himself late for Sunday's warm-up.

If the Senna faction outnumbered the Piquet fan club, the latter still had plenty to lift his spirits as they took their places some five hours before the start of the race on Sunday morning. For up there on the front row were the two Williams, quickest in qualifying by a phenomenal two seconds. Despite his late arrival,

Right: The season gets underway with Piquet leading Senna and the two Benettons

Below: Pop-off valves were the talk of the Brazilian Grand Prix

Nigel Mansell made a good battle of it as the two Williams men sparred for the honour of starting from pole position. Apart from a water pump problem, the Williams-Hondas were as reliable as they could be, allowing their drivers to trade pole on the two days. Ultimately, said the drivers, it would come down to pop-off valves and traffic.

Goodyear's race tyres allowed them to do many more qualifying laps than the qualifying tyres used previously, which meant all the cars were on the track that much longer, and Mansell was especially critical of traffic on Friday. On Saturday, he was again involved in traffic, but found some clear laps even if one lap was upset by his own team mate tangling with Nannini's Minardi. First blood, then, to Mansell, with Piquet alongside him. Best of the rest was Senna in the yellow Lotus with its new active suspension in which he very firmly believed. Engineer Peter Wright had gone back to England to write a new programme for the computer-controlled suspension, but it transpired that it was better suited to the Safari rally, so Peter Warr said. From then on, Senna made progress, but team mate Satoru Nakajima unfortunately suffered a computer failure.

As expected, the Benetton-Fords were well up, with Fabi fourth and Boutsen sixth, but they were also pop-off valve victims, this in turn made their turbos over-speed, and both drivers had turbo-charger failure. Prost would later say that he and his team were relatively unprepared for the opening of the season, due to the rain-interrupted test days. Ferrari weren't in as good a shape as one might have expected, and on-lookers suggested that the Gustav Brunner-designed chassis was not as efficient as it might have been, although

the drivers were complimentary about the power from the new engine. Berger qualified quicker than Alboreto. There was good news and bad news at Arrows. There was delight at Warwick's eighth on the grid, although he had had a spin when going for the top six time. But Cheever wasn't so happy, with a burnt out wiring loom, a misfire and fuel pump problem, plus perennial pop-off valve problems. Brabham weren't that unhappy. The chassis was supposedly the best that had ever left the factory, although the engine, according to Patrese, was no better than it had been. De Cesaris had several gyrations getting used to the new mount. Nannini wasn't much quicker than team mate Campos, although the latter would be relieved of $3000 for missing a weigh-in! Danner was the quicker of the Zakspeed runners, Brundle being even slower than his Tyrrell replacement using a DFZ engine, Jonathan Palmer.

But the normally aspirated drivers weren't happy. Streiff was dogged by a curious, stuttering misfire in both his race car and the spare. Caffi was the final turbo runner, in the FA1I which he twice parked out on the circuit. Newcomer Fabre's El Charro AGS looked big, but Capelli's under-tanked March consistently suffered engine trouble, and blew

one during second qualifying. When it did the same during the warm-up, the entry was withdrawn, leaving 22 starters. The turbo-engined cars looked positively reliable in comparison to the new generation of normally aspirated cars, which were not nearly as reliable as their similarly powered F3000 counterparts.

As Brazilians streamed into the circuit, the Sunday morning warm-up suggested that the Williams superiority would by no means be as clear-cut as suggested by practice. That familiar name, Prost, was quickest, followed by Alboreto, then Senna, Mansell and Piquet, all these virtually covered by a second. The newcomers had not behaved particularly well during practice – they received a collective slapped wrist from Nigel Mansell after practice – but Nakajima was hauled before the clerk of the course for overtaking under the yellow flag. Campos not only lost $3000 but was then disqualified for leaving the dummy grid late and then taking up his place on the grid, and Fabre's manoeuvres as he struggled in the race with a recalcitrant gearbox upset the organisers.

With the stands full to capacity, there were great cheers as Piquet was followed by Senna into the first corner. Mansell experienced too much wheelspin and dropped back to fifth behind the Benettons, determined to get through the first lap which he had failed to do in the past two years. But Mansell soon made up time, shooting through from fifth to third in double quick time, chased by Prost. But at lap six, when the order was Piquet, then Senna, Mansell, Fabi and Prost within seconds, trouble struck. Waste paper, no doubt some of it posters for the Brazilian heroes, covered the track. Piquet, as leader, picked up some of it. So did Senna in second place, So did Mansell, as he swerved off line to overtake the Benettons.

Piquet was the first to suffer, into the pits on lap seven, the Williams mechanics scooping rubbish out of the cooling inlets, at the same time giving the leader a new set of tyres. That left a three-strong battle for the lead: Senna, Mansell and Prost gaining. But then it was Mansell's turn in the pit, the Williams men again clearing the cooling inlets as well as giving him new tyres. Senna was in a couple of laps later for the same reason. Prost now led by 5.2 seconds from Boutsen (Fabi had retired, with engine misfire), Berger, Piquet and Johansson. Frankly, the pits were busier than the track.

It was not, in this instance, a tyre race. After their initial stops, it seemed that the Honda-powered front runners had done irreparable damage to their power units. Mansell would report having to lap so slowly that the temperatures would never come down to less than 15 degrees above normal. To the spectators, it seemed as though there was nothing but tyre trouble, but the tyre changes were merely coincidental to the increased engine temperatures. Mansell later said he might have gone the whole distance on one set. Piquet claimed to be happy with his tyres. Williams apologised to Goodyear for making it seem that the tyres weren't up to the job, while Senna was told off for rubbishing the tyres and a Honda representative claimed that the tyres couldn't take Honda's power.

Whatever, as leader Prost was making his second stop for tyres, Piquet was making his third. Prost stayed in the lead by 23 seconds. Piquet dropped to fourth. But after a third pit stop, Senna retired when the engine began to make ominous noises. Piquet had already gradually overtaken Johansson in the second McLaren to claim second place. These three would mount the rostrum.

Mansell had usually been fourth or thereabouts, but then a tyre blow-out relegated him to ninth behind both Ferraris and Boutsen. Senna's retirement elevated them all, and then came a great battle between the Ferraris, with Prost in the middle of the two of them. Prost, not surprisingly, let them get on with it, and had an eye witness view of Alboreto's underbody collapsing on the main straight, which sent sparks showering into Berger's face. Happily, Alboreto didn't lift off, and the Austrian nipped round to move up to fourth. Alboreto spun off less than a lap later, deprived of downforce. A lap down were Boutsen and Mansell, both the victims of punctures, while Nakajima finished his first Grand Prix seventh, in spite of his water-cooled skull cap exploding – a memorable occasion for everyone. Neither Zakspeed shone, Palmer took the normally aspirated class although Streiff was unwell and the Arrows were both engine replacements, in spite of showing well. Brabham performed similarly, but their retirements were non-engine related.

So Prost had won his fourth Brazilian Grand Prix, McLaren had performed well again and Williams hadn't been as dominant as in practice. Were Lotus disadvantaged by innovation again? Benetton showed promise, so did Arrows, Ferrari less so. Only time could tell who would come out on top at the end of the season.

Left: Mansell, six-wheeled, as he overtakes Streiff

Right: Senna's first race with Honda ended in engine failure when he was second

Far right: Nannini lost a wheel when a hub broke

Centre left: Mansell finished sixth, delayed not only by this puncture, but also overheating

Centre right: Berger qualified ahead of team mate Alboreto – despite the distractions

Below: Prost began 1987 as he ended 1986 – with a win

Left: Behind Senna,
Mansell leads Boutsen,
Prost, Berger and
Alboreto after 10 laps

Prost was only sixth
when he led the Ferraris
on the first lap

Right: The crowd celebrates the first lap led by Brazilians, but their ticker-tape welcome proved fatal for the Williams-Honda

Far left: Piquet scored the first of his many second places – note his front left tyre

Left: Warwick's race ended in engine failure

Centre, far left: Alain Prost wins his fourth Brazilian Grand Prix

Below: Berger finished fourth in his first race for Ferrari

BRAZILIAN GRAND PRIX · April 12

Entries and Practice Times

Cos=Cosworth
Ch=Champion
Win=Wintershall
McL=McLaren
Mar=Marelli
Bra=Brabham
Bre=Brembo
Bil=Bilstein
L/A=Lotus Active
Marz=Marzocchi

Driver	Nat.	Car	Practice 1	Practice 2	Warm Up	Engine	Turbos	Electrics/Plugs	Fuel/Oil	Brake Discs/Calipers	Shocks
1 Alain Prost	F	Marlboro McLaren MP4/3	1m29.522s	**1m29.175s**	1m33.161s	1.5t TAG V6	KKK	Bosch	Shell	SEP/McL	Bil
2 Stefan Johansson	S	Marlboro McLaren MP4/3	1m31.343s	**1m30.476s**	1m36.468s	1.5t TAG V6	KKK	Bosch	Shell	SEP/McL	Bil
3 Jonathan Palmer	GB	Data General/Courtaulds Tyrrell DG/016	1m37.488s	**1m36.091s**	1m41.529s	3.5 Ford Cosworth DFZ V8		Cos/Ch	Elf	AP	Koni
4 Philippe Streiff	F	Data General/Courtaulds Tyrrell DG/016	1m38.822s	**1m36.274s**	1m44.308s	3.5 Ford Cosworth DFZ V8		Cos/Ch	Elf	AP	Koni
5 Nigel Mansell	GB	Canon Williams FW11B	1m27.901s	**1m26.128s**	1m33.595s	1.5t Honda V6	IHI	Honda/NGK	Mobil	SEP/AP	Showa
6 Nelson Piquet	BR	Canon Williams FW11B	1m27.822s	**1m26.567s**	1m34.126s	1.5t Honda V6	IHI	Honda/NGK	Mobil	SEP/AP	Showa
7 Riccardo Patrese	I	Brabham BT56	1m32.001s	**1m31.179s**	1m35.780s	1.5t BMW S4	Garrett	Bosch/Ch	Win/Castrol	SEP/Bra	Koni
8 Andrea de Cesaris	I	Brabham BT56	**1m32.402s**	1m34.115s	1m35.816s	1.5t BMW S4	Garrett	Bosch/Ch	Win/Castrol	SEP/Bra	Koni
9 Martin Brundle	GB	West Zakspeed 861	1m37.235s	**1m36.160s**	1m39.438s	1.5t Zakspeed S4	Garrett	Bosch/Ch	Win/Castrol	AP	Sachs
10 Christian Danner	D	West Zakspeed 861	1m36.178s	**1m35.212s**	1m40.046s	1.5t Zakspeed S4	Garrett	Bosch/Ch	Win/Castrol	AP	Sachs
11 Satoru Nakajima	J	Camel Lotus 99T	1m34.445s	**1m32.276s**	1m37.435s	1.5t Honda V6	IHI	Honda/NGK	Elf	SEP/Bre	L/A
12 Ayrton Senna	BR	Camel Lotus 99T	1m29.002s	**1m28.408s**	1m33.547s	1.5t Honda V6	IHI	Honda/NGK	Elf	SEP/Bre	L/A
14 Pascal Fabre	F	El Charro AGS JH22C	1m44.126s	**1m39.816s**	1m43.442s	3.5 Ford Cosworth DFZ V8		Cos/Ch	Acto	SEP/AGS	Koni
16 Ivan Capelli	I	Leyton House March 871B	**1m43.580s**	2m02.966s	1m43.474s	3.5 Ford Cosworth DFZ V8		Cos/Ch	BP	AP	Koni
17 Derek Warwick	GB	USF&G Arrows A10	1m32.531s	**1m30.467s**	1m35.030s	1.5t Megatron S4	Garrett	Bosch/Ch	Win/Castrol	AP	Koni
18 Eddie Cheever	USA	USF&G Arrows A10	1m33.084s	**1m32.769s**	1m38.302s	1.5t Megatron S4	Garrett	Bosch/Ch	Win/Castrol	AP	Koni
19 Teo Fabi	I	Benetton B187	1m30.439s	**1m28.417s**	1m34.615s	1.5t Ford V6	Garrett	Ford EED/Ch	Mobil	SEP/AP	Koni
20 Thierry Boutsen	B	Benetton B187	1m30.166s	**1m29.450s**	1m35.424s	1.5t Ford V6	Garrett	Ford EED/Ch	Mobil	SEP/AP	Koni
21 Alex Caffi	I	Landis & Gyr Osella FA1I	1m39.931s	**1m38.770s**	1m41.093s	1.5t Alfa Romeo V8	KKK	Mar/Ch	Agip	Bre	Koni
23 Adrian Campos	E	Minardi M186		**1m33.825s**	1m40.667s	1.5t Motori Moderni V6	KKK	Mar/Ch	Agip	Bre	Koni
24 Alessandro Nannini	I	Minardi M186	1m33.980s	**1m33.729s**		1.5t Motori Moderni V6	KKK	Mar/Ch	Agip	SEP	Koni
27 Michele Alboreto	I	Ferrari F187	1m31.218s	**1m30.468s**	1m33.432s	1.5t Ferrari V6	Garrett	Mar-Weber/Ch	Agip	SEP/Bre	Marz
28 Gerhard Berger	A	Ferrari F187	1m31.444s	**1m30.357s**	1m35.639s	1.5t Ferrari V6	Garrett	Mar-Weber/Ch	Agip	SEP/Bre	Marz

April 10 Hot/dry/humid   April 11 Hot/dry/humid   April 12 Hot/dry/humid

Starting Grid

	5 Mansell
Piquet 6	
	12 Senna
Fabi 19	
	1 Prost
Boutsen 20	
	28 Berger
Warwick 17	
	27 Alboreto
Johansson 2	
	7 Patrese
Nakajima 11	
	8 de Cesaris
Cheever 18	
	24 Nannini
Campos 23	
	10 Danner
Palmer 3	
	9 Brundle
Streiff 4	
	21 Caffi
Fabre 14	
	16 Capelli

Results, Retirements and Fastest Laps

Place	Driver	Car	Laps	Time/Retirement	Fastest Lap No./Time	
1	Alain Prost	1.5t McLaren-TAG MP4/3	61	1h39m 45.141s	45	1m35.811s
2	Nelson Piquet	1.5t Williams-Honda FW11B	61	1h40m25.688s	42	1m33.861s
3	Stefan Johansson	1.5t McLaren-TAG MP4/3	61	1h40m41.899s	43	1m35.299s
4	Gerhard Berger	1.5t Ferrari-Spa F187	61	1h41m24.376s	54	1m35.769s
5	Thierry Boutsen	1.5t Benetton-Ford B187	60	1h40m29.148s	50	1m35.737s
6	Nigel Mansell	1.5t Williams-Honda FW11B	60	1h41m23.874s	49	1m34.602s
7	Satoru Nakajima	1.5t Lotus-Honda 99T	59	1h41m26.362s	40	1m38.482s
8	Michele Alboreto	1.5t Ferrari-Spa F187	58	1h36m31.385s Underbody Collapsed	37	1m35.773s
9	Christian Danner	1.5t Zakspeed 861	58	1h41m09.369s	38	1m40.112s
10	Jonathan Palmer	3.5 Tyrrell-Ford DG/016	58	1h41m34.177s	26	1m41.495s
11	Philippe Streiff	3.5 Tyrrell-Ford DG/016	57	1h41m15.688s	23	1m43.049s
12	Pascal Fabre	3.5 AGS-Ford JH22C	55	1h40m54.893s	27	1m43.129s
	Eddie Cheever	1.5t Arrows-Megatron A10	52	Engine	48	1m33.978s
	Ayrton Senna	1.5t Lotus-Honda 99T	50	Oil system/engine	48	1m35.312s
	Riccardo Patrese	1.5t Brabham-BMW BT56	48	Electrics	44	1m36.846s
	Andrea de Cesaris	1.5t Brabham-BMW BT56	21	Gearbox	19	1m38.194s
	Derek Warwick	1.5t Arrows-Megatron A10	20	Overheating	18	1m36.553s
	Alex Caffi	1.5t Osella-Alfa Romeo FA1I	20	Driver exhaustion	3	1m44.130s
	Alessandro Nannini	1.5t Minardi-Motori Moderni M186	17	Rear suspension	16	1m39.108s
	Martin Brundle	1.5t Zakspeed 861	15	Overheated engine	4	1m40.683s
	Teo Fabi	1.5t Benetton-Ford B187	9	Engine misfire	5	1m36.511s
	Adrian Campos	1.5t Minardi-Motori Moderni M186	3	Disqualified	2	1m40.714s
	Ivan Capelli	3.5 March-Ford 871B	0	Did not start		

Average Speed of Winner: 184.592 km/h, 114.699 mph
Fastest Lap: Nelson Piquet on lap 42, 1m33.861s, 192.962 km/h, 119.901 mph
Lap Record: Nelson Piquet (1.5t Williams-Honda FW11), 1m33.546s, 193.612 km/h, 120.305 mph

Circuit Data

Brazilian Grand Prix, Jacarepagua, Rio de Janeiro

Circuit Length: 5.013 km/3.126 miles
Race Distance: 61 laps, 306.891 km/190.693 miles
Race Weather: Hot/dry

Past Winners

Year	Driver	Nat.	Car	Circuit	Distance miles/km	Speed mph/km/h
1977	Carlos Reutemann	RA	3.0 Ferrari 312T-2/77	Interlagos	197.85/318.42	112.92/181.73
1978	Carlos Reutemann	RA	3.0 Ferrari 312T-2/78	Rio de Janeiro	196.95/316.95	107.43/172.89
1979	Jacques Laffite	F	3.0 Ligier-Ford JS11	Interlagos	197.85/318.42	117.23/188.67
1980	Rene Arnoux	F	1.5 Renault RS t/c	Interlagos	195.70/314.95	117.40/188.93
1981	Carlos Reutemann	RA	3.0 Williams-Ford FWO7C	Rio de Janeiro	193.82/311.92	96.59/155.45
1982	Alain Prost	F	1.5 Renault RE t/c	Rio de Janeiro	196.95/316.95	112.97/181.80
1983	Nelson Piquet	BR	1.5 Brabham-BMW BT52 t/c	Rio de Janeiro	196.95/316.95	108.93/175.30
1984	Alain Prost	F	1.5 McLaren-TAG MP4/2 t/c	Rio de Janeiro	190.69/306.89	111.54/179.51
1985	Alain Prost	F	1.5 McLaren-TAG MP4/2B t/c	Rio de Janeiro	190.69/306.89	112.79/181.53
1986	Nelson Piquet	BR	1.5 Williams-Honda FW11 t/c	Rio de Janeiro	190.69/306.89	114.94/184.98

Lap Chart

Grid Order — laps 1–61, finishing position at right:

Grid Order	Lap sequence (1→61)	Pos
5 Nigel Mansell	6 6 6 6 6 6 6 12 12 12 12 12 1 1 1 1 6 6 6 6 1 1 1 1 1 1 1 1 1 1 1 1 1 1 1 1 1 1 1 1 1 1 1 1 1 1 1 1 1 1 1 1 1 1 1 1 1 1 1 1 1	1
6 Nelson Piquet	12 12 12 12 12 12 5 5 5 1 1 12 20 20 20 20 20 5 5 12 12 12 12 12 2 2 2 2 2 2 6 6 6 6 12 12 12 12 12 6 6 6 6 6 6 6 6 6 6 6 6 6 6 6 6 6 6 6 6 6 6	2
12 Ayrton Senna	19 19 5 5 5 5 5 1 1 1 5 20 20 28 6 6 5 5 5 1 12 5 2 2 2 2 2 6 6 6 6 6 6 2 12 12 12 2 2 2 2 2 2 2 2 2 2 2 2 2 2 2 2 2 2 2 2 2 2 2 2	3
19 Teo Fabi	20 5 19 19 19 19 19 20 20 20 28 28 6 28 28 28 1 1 12 2 6 6 6 6 12 5 12 12 12 12 5 2 2 6 6 6 6 12 12 12 12 12 12 27 27 27 27 27 28 28 28 28	4
1 Alain Prost	5 20 1 1 1 1 1 20 19 28 28 2 2 2 5 5 1 12 12 20 6 6 5 5 5 5 5 5 12 12 5 5 5 5 2 5 5 5 5 5 5 5 28 28 28 27 27 28 28 28 28 28 28	5
20 Thierry Boutsen	1 1 20 20 20 20 20 28 28 27 27 6 6 5 17 12 12 28 2 2 28 28 28 28 28 28 28 28 28 28 18 18 28 28 28 28 28 28 27 27 28 28 20 20 20 20 20 20 5 5	6
28 Gerhard Berger	28 28 28 28 28 28 28 27 27 2 2 27 5 17 12 17 18 2 28 28 7 7 7 7 7 7 7 7 7 7 18 18 28 28 18 27 27 27 27 7 7 7 20 20 5 5 5 5 5 5 5 5 5 11	7
17 Derek Warwick	27 27 27 27 27 27 27 2 2 7 6 17 17 12 18 18 2 18 7 7 27 27 27 27 27 27 27 18 7 27 27 27 7 7 7 7 7 20 20 20 20 5 5 11 11 11 11 11 11 11 11	8
27 Michele Alboreto	7 7 7 7 7 2 2 7 7 6 17 5 18 18 2 2 7 27 20 20 20 20 20 18 18 18 18 27 27 27 7 7 20 20 20 20 5 5 5 11 10 10 10 10 10 10 10 10	9
2 Stefan Johansson	2 2 17 2 2 7 7 17 17 17 18 8 8 8 7 27 17 18 18 18 18 18 18 18 20 20 20 20 20 20 20 20 20 18 18 18 18 18 11 11 11 10 10 3 3 3 3 3 3 3 3	10
7 Riccardo Patrese	17 17 2 17 17 17 18 18 18 7 24 7 7 27 17 17 18 7 11 11 11 11 11 11 11 11 11 11 11 11 11 11 11 11 11 11 11 11 3 10 3 4 4 4 4 4 4 4	11
11 Satoru Nakajima	18 18 18 18 18 18 6 6 24 24 8 7 27 27 8 24 8 8 11 3 3 10 10 10 10 10 10 10 10 10 10 3 3 3 3 3 3 3 3 10 10 3 4 14 14 14 14	12
8 Andrea de Cesaris	24 24 24 24 24 24 24 11 8 7 27 24 11 24 11 11 3 10 3 3 3 3 3 3 3 3 3 10 10 10 10 10 10 10 10 4 4 4 14 14 18 18	13
18 Eddie Cheever	11 11 11 11 11 11 11 11 8 11 11 11 11 11 9 3 3 3 10 14 14 14 4 4 4 4 4 4 4 4 4 4 4 4 4 4 4 14 14 14 18 18	14
24 Alessandro Nannini	23 23 9 9 8 8 8 8 9 9 9 9 24 11 10 10 10 4 4 4 14 14 14 14 14 14 14 14 14 14 14 14 14 14 14 14 14 18 18 18	15
23 Adrian Campos	9 9 3 8 8 9 9 9 9 10 10 10 3 3 3 4 10 4 4 4 14	16
10 Christian Danner	3 3 8 3 10 10 10 10 10 3 3 3 10 4 10 4 14 14 14	17
3 Jonathan Palmer	4 10 10 10 3 3 3 3 3 21 21 4 14 14 14 14 21 21 21	18
9 Martin Brundle	21 21 21 21 21 21 21 21 4 4 21 21 10 21 21	19
4 Philippe Streiff	8 8 23 4 4 4 4 4 14 14 14 14 10 21	20
21 Alex Caffi	10 4 4 14 14 14 14 14 14	21
14 Pascal Fabre	14 14 14	22
16 Ivan Capelli		23

Championship Points

Drivers			Constructors		
1	Alain Prost	9 pts	1	McLaren	13 pts
2	Nelson Piquet	6 pts	2	Williams	7 pts
3	Stefan Johansson	4 pts	3	Ferrari	3 pts
4	Gerhard Berger	3 pts	4	Benetton	2 pts
5	Thierry Boutsen	2 pts			
6	Nigel Mansell	1 pt			

Jim Clark Cup			Colin Chapman Cup		
1	Jonathan Palmer	9 pts	1	Tyrrell	15 pts
2	Philippe Streiff	6 pts	2	AGS	4 pts
3	Pascal Fabre	4 pts			

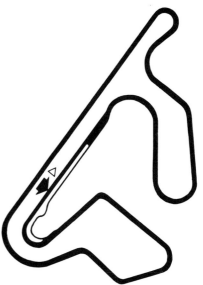

SAN MARINO

GRAND PRIX

There was an air of frustration as Grand Prix teams, drivers and spectators left Imola after the seventh San Marino Grand Prix. It wasn't just the traffic jams. The Grand Prix dashed hopes of both the drivers and the spectators.

Worst affected was Nelson Piquet who had viewed the whole race as an unhappy and mainly silent guest commentator for Italian television. He watched unsmiling, as World Championship points slipped away. Nelson's frustration had been apparent from Saturday morning. The previous afternoon, he'd just set the fastest lap of the first qualifying session when he crashed at the 180 mph Tamburello corner just after the start/finish line. No one knows what exactly happened, but according to Adrian Campos who was following him, the Williams-Honda suddenly snapped out of line, spun round once and crashed sideways into a huge concrete wall. It bounced back onto the grass and harmlessly spun further down the circuit. Marshals lifted Piquet from the car and laid him gently on the grass. Needless to say, the worst was feared. Professor Sid Watkins was quickly on the scene and within a few minutes Piquet was transported to the medical centre. "He's knocked about a bit and has concussion, but otherwise he's OK, no broken bones", reported the doctor soon after.

It was all swiftly and undramatically dealt with. Piquet was then taken to Bellaria hospital for a brain scan and next morning he was back at the circuit, desperately trying to persuade doctors to allow him to take part in the practice and race. Not surprisingly, the doctors were adamant that he should not. Those with longer memories remembered Nigel Mansell after his accident at the Signes corner at Ricard two years earlier. Nigel hadn't entirely recovered from concus-

sion two weeks later. Eventually Nelson capitulated. He would withdraw from the race. His Williams had stood up extremely well to such an incredible impact. There was a long gash in the front left-hand side of the monocoque, but otherwise it was in very good shape. A new car was built up from a spare monocoque, and Williams were back up to strength. But it wasn't needed.

Piquet's withdrawal robbed the race of one of its major participants. Another went after 20 minutes of the race – it had been a frustrating weekend for Alain Prost anyway. On Friday, a new microchip caused McLaren's TAG engines to run too lean. By the end of the qualifying session, the three in the McLarens were all broken, and for another reason, a fourth was damaged the next morning. It left Prost badly behind on race preparation, although he had been testing at the circuit a few days before. However, Prost had crossed the finishing line first for the past three years, so he knew what was required of this circuit with its straights and tight chicanes, so demanding on fuel consumption. And his recent praise of the work that Porsche's engineers had done on the TAG engine indicated that he reckoned to be just as competitive as before – if not more so. After fifth on the grid in Rio, he was third at San Marino once Piquet's Williams-Honda had been withdrawn. Less than a second covered the first three on the grid. Fabi, in fourth, was another second behind.

In Sunday morning's warm-up, Prost was thrust back to third by quick laps late

in the session by both Fabi and, in particular, Mansell. But again, there was only 0.2 seconds between the three of them. Senna, meanwhile, was seventh. Prost tried to get his Marlboro McLaren in front right from the word go. But while being squeezed out by Mansell and Senna, he could see that there were one or two other things to be sorted out first and he hung back and let the pair of them battle it out. Mansell rushed by Senna at the end of the straight on lap two and by the end of the lap the Englishman already had a one second lead.

Prost, meanwhile, was briefly embroiled in a four-car battle, with the two Ferraris behind, and Senna's Lotus ahead. But on lap five, he got by the yellow Lotus and took stock of his situation. While he'd been struggling with the rest, Mansell had pulled out a lead of a second a lap. It was now up to five seconds. Prost, however, was in stunning form. He had pulled 2.5 seconds ahead of Senna by the next lap, and 4.4 seconds ahead of him a lap later. Furthermore, he was whittling away that lead of Mansell's: 4.7s, 4.1s, 3.8s, 3.6s and then 2.7s. By lap 13, it was down to a second, but when he reappeared on lap 14, it was 2.1 seconds and Prost was slowing. His alternator belt had broken and he would do no more laps. A frustrated Prost walked to the pits. The brakes, engine, tyres, balance – everything had been superb. All he could do now was serve notice on the Williams camp and wait until Belgium.

Ayrton Senna hid his lesser frustration. Lotus' active suspension was still very

much in the throes of development – a development which has already taken years and could take months more. But partially thanks to the somewhat depleted opposition, Senna had started from pole position for the third time running at Imola, so clearly the active suspension was working well enough. Come the race, however, there was nothing he could do about Prost overtaking, and when Mansell was left with an 11.2 seconds lead after Prost retired, there was little Senna could do about that either. It was the first time that the active suspension would complete race distance and it was, dare he say it, not entirely consistent. Just before Prost retired, Senna was overtaken by both Ferraris on the same lap and was briefly back in fifth place although Berger slowed almost immediately as he lost power. Senna was soon back up to third when Prost retired, and then spent most of the rest of the race battling with Alboreto and some pretty mean dicing there was too. Alboreto overtook Senna at Aqua Minerale with a ruthless move, daring Senna to come back across and have an accident. But Senna got his own back later with a rush that took the Italian by surprise and took the edge out of the fight. Senna's second place was safe – albeit 27 seconds behind Mansell.

Ferrari's frustration was deep. There was inevitably great encouragement

from the locals in Imola, but they were ignoring history. In their droves, they flocked to the Circuito Dino Ferrari to idolise their beloved red cars, but Ferrari were about to break one of their own records, and not one to be proud of either. When they arrived, they had gone 24 races without a win, equal to the previous longest lean spell in their history: France 1968 to Austria 1970. When they left, that unenviable record had been surpassed. Undaunted, the locals cheered and waved their flags, and there was something to cheer about. Berger's retirement with a broken black box had been signalled by a low moan throughout the circuit, but the Senna versus Alboreto battle was keenly followed. Although Alboreto was the loser of that particular duel, it was his best result for six races.

Equally deserving of the crowd's praise that day was Riccardo Patrese, who showed renewed form in the Brabham-BMW, now sporting a couple of stickers from Olivetti. Qualifying had already revealed that the Brabham had benefited from extensive testing since Rio. Patrese soon latched onto the Ferraris behind Senna and then fought off Stefan Johansson's McLaren. When Mansell became the first to pit for new tyres, Patrese had been fourth. Mansell rejoined behind him, passed him and when Senna and Alboreto also stopped

for new rubber, Mansell found himself back in the lead with a margin of just over three seconds on Patrese. Patrese, of course, would have to stop for tyres – or would he? It wasn't a question of wear at Imola. The tyres would last race distance, but they would get slower, which encouraged everyone to change tyres. Patrese, however, was not following that scenario. He was never more than three seconds behind Mansell, and sometimes half that. But on lap 37, he dived for the pits and new tyres.

But Patrese still featured as a front runner. When he re-emerged, he first of all fought off Johansson again, and then advanced on Senna and Alboreto. It took Patrese just two laps to dispose of the two of them, but he never really gained on Mansell. And then a few laps later, the Brabham's engine suddenly began to lose power and drop back. With ten laps to go, the Senna/Alboreto duo was gaining and steadily the unfortunate Patrese dropped back, seeing one point after another slip away. He finally wound up ninth, but it was a very unsatisfactory result considering the second place he held ten laps from the end. Even as Patrese was beginning to struggle, there were two eager Benettons hungry for points. They had both quietly moved up in the order, although Fabi had been delayed by losing his wing end plate to Cheever and that had been replaced at the mid-race tyre stop. With eleven laps to go, Boutsen was fifth and Fabi sixth. But even at that juncture, Boutsen was heading for the pits. Quite suddenly, the engine stopped. Fuel had been no problem, reported the driver. One Benetton was out. At least Fabi was there to take his place but three laps later he too headed, frustrated, for the pits – his car also had a broken engine.

Johansson was the man who took over fourth place, but he'd already suffered his frustration. He'd made his first pit stop for new tyres from fifth place on lap 24. He'd battled with Patrese after his pit stop, but was still in fifth place on lap 43 when he had to have another stop, this time for a new front wing end plate, and now he was down in eighth place. But disposing of Derek Warwick, Patrese's delay and the retirements of the two Benettons elevated Johansson to fourth place at the end. Warwick might have finished fifth. He and Cheever had had a weekend of ups and downs with reliability problems, and the two had run close together during the opening stages, sandwiching Boutsen's Benetton. But with only 11 laps to go, they were lying eighth and ninth. Then Cheever's engine overheated leaving Warwick to steadily move up as retirements took place ahead

of him. But he too became a statistic when Imola's thirsty nature claimed him and his Arrows without fuel, although Derek swore he had enough left.

Fortunately, not everyone was frustrated. Martin Brundle, for instance, was delighted to slot into fifth place in his first run with the latest Zakspeed, even if he and the team did feel that they needed testing. He didn't make a tyre stop either, because problems with the brakes meant that he had neither the brakes nor the fuel to use the tyres to their best advantage. Zakspeed were naturally delighted with their first-ever championship points. Satoru Nakajima was truly delighted to score Japan's first-ever World Championship point with sixth place, even though he'd missed the start altogether when his battery had short-circuited and he had then suffered a puncture. Eventually, he raced in a spare car to sixth place.

Behind Christian Danner's seventh-placed Zakspeed, there had been a very fraught battle for the normally aspirated class. Palmer had led this for much of the distance, with team mate Streiff right behind him and Alliot making a magnificent debut in the Larrousse Lola.

Unfortunately, the latter was delayed when Fabre spun in front of him and then Palmer found his car sinking lower and lower. He thought it was just the underbody, but in fact it turned out to be a puncture. Ten laps from the end, Palmer lost the clutch, and the engine stopped due to an electrical failure, leaving Streiff to claim the class win from the recovered Alliot. Capelli's recently completed March 871 had suffered a broken rotor arm earlier in the race after a promising debut. Caffi had put on a good show in the Osella, holding eighth place until it inevitably ran out of fuel, while Gabriele Tarquini made an inauspicious debut in a second car. Minardi had a miserable weekend with turbos and engines going pop.

Finally, Ligier were welcomed back, two chassis fitted with Megatron engines for Arnoux and Ghinzani. But the Italian had a front suspension mounting collapse on the Friday and the same thing happened to Arnoux on Sunday. Ghinzani's suspension mounting was strengthened for the race, and Arnoux's withdrawn, but the Frenchman only lasted a few laps before retiring. Mansell was left the delighted winner, but most of the rest of the field could only hope that their day would come in Belgium.

Left: Ligier withdrew Arnoux after his car suffered front suspension failure. Ghinzani was withdrawn after a few laps for exactly the same reason

Right: Fabi spins off ahead of Palmer, Streiff and Alliott, who was also delayed

Far left: Brundle (left) with team mate Danner. The Englishman scored Zakspeed's first ever World Championship points

Left: Fabi leads Alboreto's Ferrari, but the Benetton retired with turbo failure

Below left: Warwick (ninth) leads Boutsen, Cheever, Brundle, Nannini and Caffi in the early stages

Below right: The wreckage after Piquet's 180mph accident is returned to the pits. The car stood up to the impact remarkably well

Streiff bounces over the curbs towards eighth place and nine points in the Jim Clark Cup

Right: Ferrari – at home

Far right: Michele Alboreto was a very popular third

Centre, far right: As usual Riccardo Patrese went superbly at Imola and deserved better than the ninth place he eventually won having lost turbo boost

Below: Prost comes up to lap Nakajima who scored Japan's first ever World Championship point with sixth place

SAN MARINO GRAND PRIX · May 3

Entries and Practice Times

Cos=Cosworth
Ch=Champion
Win=Wintershall
McL=McLaren
Mar=Marelli
Bra=Brabham
Bre=Brembo
Bil=Bilstein
L/A=Lotus Active
Marz=Marzocchi

Driver	Nat.	Car	Practice 1	Practice 2	Warm Up	Engine	Turbos	Electrics/Plugs	Fuel/Oil	Brake Discs/ Calipers	Shocks
1 Alain Prost	F	Marlboro McLaren MP4/3	1m29.317s	1m26.135s	1m30.853s	1.5t TAG V6	KKK	Bosch	Shell	SEP/McL	Bil
2 Stefan Johansson	S	Marlboro McLaren MP4/3	1m30.416s	1m28.708s	1m31.535s	1.5t TAG V6	KKK	Bosch	Shell	SEP/McL	Bil
3 Jonathan Palmer	GB	Data General/Courtaulds Tyrrell DG/016	1m34.632s	1m36.127s	1m36.422s	3.5 Ford Cosworth DFZ V8		Cos/Ch	Elf	AP	Koni
4 Philippe Streiff	F	Data General/Courtaulds Tyrrell DG/016	1m35.001s	1m33.155s	1m36.483s	3.5 Ford Cosworth DFZ V8		Cos/Ch	Elf	AP	Koni
5 Nigel Mansell	GB	Canon Williams FW11B	1m26.204s	1m25.946s	1m30.605s	1.5t Honda V6	IHI	Honda/NGK	Mobil	SEP/AP	Showa
6 Nelson Piquet	BR	Canon Williams FW11B	1m25.997s*			1.5t Honda V6	IHI	Honda/NGK	Mobil	SEP/AP	Showa
7 Riccardo Patrese	I	Brabham BT56	1m28.447s	1m28.421s	1m33.855s	1.5t BMW S4	Garrett	Bosch/Ch	Win/Castrol	SEP/Bra	Koni
8 Andrea de Cesaris	I	Brabham BT56	1m30.627s	1m30.382s	1m33.450s	1.5t BMW S4	Garrett	Bosch/Ch	Win/Castrol	SEP/Bra	Koni
9 Martin Brundle	GB	West Zakspeed 871	1m31.931s	1m31.094s	1m35.277s	1.5t Zakspeed S4	Garrett	Bosch/Ch	Win/Castrol	AP	Sachs
10 Christian Danner	D	West Zakspeed 861	1m32.977s	1m31.903s	1m34.542s	1.5t Zakspeed S4	Garrett	Bosch/Ch	Win/Castrol	AP	Sachs
11 Satoru Nakajima	J	Camel Lotus 99T	1m29.579s	1m30.545s	1m33.567s	1.5t Honda V6	IHI	Honda/NGK	Elf	SEP/Bre	L/A
12 Ayrton Senna	BR	Camel Lotus 99T	1m27.543s	1m25.826s	1m32.416s	1.5t Honda V6	IHI	Honda/NGK	Elf	SEP/Bre	L/A
14 Pascal Fabre	F	El Charro AGS JH22C	1m39.747s	1m36.159s	1m38.515s	3.5 Ford Cosworth DFZ V8		Cos/Ch	Acto	SEP/AGS	Koni
16 Ivan Capelli	I	Leyton House March 871	1m37.463s	1m33.872s	1m37.320s	3.5 Ford Cosworth DFZ V8		Cos/Ch	BP	AP	Koni
17 Derek Warwick	GB	USF&G Arrows A10	1m28.887s	1m29.236s	1m33.662s	1.5t Megatron S4	Garrett	Bosch/Ch	Win/Castrol	AP	Koni
18 Eddie Cheever	USA	USF&G Arrows A10	1m30.379s	1m28.848s	8m59.511s	1.5t Megatron S4	Garrett	Bosch/Ch	Win/Castrol	AP	Koni
19 Teo Fabi	I	Benetton B187	1m27.801s	1m27.270s	1m30.634s	1.5t Ford V6	Garrett	Ford EED/Ch	Mobil	SEP/AP	Koni
20 Thierry Boutsen	B	Benetton B187	1m28.929s	1m28.908s	1m31.984s	1.5t Ford V6	Garrett	Ford EED/Ch	Mobil	SEP/AP	Koni
21 Alex Caffi	I	Landis & Gyr Osella FA1I	1m32.308s	1m33.298s	1m34.421s	1.5t Alfa Romeo V8	KKK	Mar/Ch	Agip	Bre	Koni
22 Gabriele Tarquini	I	Landis & Gyr Osella FA1H†	1m43.446s		1m41.415s	1.5t Alfa Romeo V8	KKK	Mar/Ch	Agip	Bre	Koni
23 Adrian Campos	E	Minardi M186	1m41.520s	1m31.818s	20m41.214s	1.5t Motori Moderni V6	KKK	Mar/Ch	Agip	Bre	Koni
24 Alessandro Nannini	I	Minardi M186	1m31.789s		8m22.515s	1.5t Motori Moderni V6	KKK	Mar/Ch	Agip	Bre	Koni
25 Rene Arnoux	F	Loto Ligier JS29B	1m31.078s	1m29.861s	1m36.491s	1.5t Megatron S4	Garrett	Bosch/Ch	Win/Castrol	SEP/Bre	Koni
26 Piercarlo Ghinzani	I	Loto Ligier JS29B	1m32.873s	1m32.248s	1m35.788s	1.5t Megatron S4	Garrett	Bosch/Ch	Win/Castrol	SEP/Bre	Koni
27 Michele Alboreto	I	Ferrari F187	1m29.653s	1m28.074s	1m32.477s	1.5t Ferrari V6	Garrett	Mar-Weber/Ch	Agip	SEP/Bre	Marz
28 Gerhard Berger	A	Ferrari F187	1m28.229s	1m27.280s	1m31.551s	1.5t Ferrari V6	Garrett	Mar-Weber/Ch	Agip	SEP/Bre	Marz
30 Philippe Alliott	F	Larrousse Lola LC87	1m34.458s	1m33.846s	1m36.368s	3.5 Ford Cosworth DFZ V8		Cos-Mar/Ch	BP	SEP/AP	Koni

*Piquet withdrew from entire race after crashing in practice on May 1
†Tarquini practised in car FA1F and raced in FA1H

May 1 Warm/overcast
May 2 Sunny/warm
May 3 Sunny/warm

Starting Grid

Senna **12**			
Prost **1**	**5**	Mansell	
	19	Fabi	
Berger **28**			
	27	Alboreto	
Patrese **7**			
	2	Johansson	
Cheever **18**			
	17	Warwick	
Boutsen **20**			
	11	Nakajima	
Arnoux **25**			
	8	de Cesaris	
Brundle **9**			
	24	Nannini	
Campos **23**			
	10	Danner	
Ghinzani **26**			
	21	Caffi	
Streiff **4**			
	30	Alliot	
Capelli **16**			
	3	Palmer	
Fabre **14**			
	22	Tarquini	

Results, Retirements and Fastest Laps

Place	Driver	Car	Laps	Time/Retirement	Fastest Lap No./Time
1	Nigel Mansell	1.5t Williams-Honda FW11B	59	1h31m24.076s	56 1m30.771s
2	Ayrton Senna	1.5t Lotus-Honda 99T	59	1h31m51.621s	53 1m30.851s
3	Michele Alboreto	1.5t Ferrari-Spa F187	59	1h32m03.220s	32 1m31.054s
4	Stefan Johansson	1.5t McLaren-TAG MP4/3	59	1h32m24.664s	54 1m29.543s
5	Martin Brundle	1.5t Zakspeed 871	57	1h31m30.235s	44 1m34.573s
6	Satoru Nakajima	1.5t Lotus-Honda 99T	57	1h31m31.203s	57 1m31.891s
7	Christian Danner	1.5t Zakspeed 861	57	1h32m19.109s	31 1m34.996s
8	Philippe Streiff	3.5 Tyrrell-Ford DG/016	57	1h32m50.146s	49 1m35.406s
9	Riccardo Patrese	1.5t Brabham-BMW BT56	57	1h33m27.029s	46 1m31.564s
10	Philippe Alliot	3.5 Lolal-Ford LC87	56	1h32m39.468s	53 1m33.668s
11	Derek Warwick	1.5t Arrows-Megatron A10	55	1h27m22.118s out of fuel	22 1m31.582s
12	Alex Caffi	1.5t Osella-Alfa Romeo FA1I	54	1h27m14.535s out of fuel	31 1m34.506s
13	Pascal Fabre	3.5 AGS-Ford JH22C	53	1h32m51.943s	6 1m38.543s
	Teo Fabi	1.5t Benetton-Ford B187	51	Engine	51 1m29.246s
	Thierry Boutsen	1.5t Benetton-Ford B187	48	Engine	35 1m31.586s
	Eddie Cheever	1.5t Arrows-Megatron A10	48	Overheating engine	21 1m32.262s
	Jonathan Palmer	3.5 Tyrrell-Ford DG/016	48	Electrics	17 1m36.182s
	Andrea de Cesaris	1.5t Brabham-BMW BT56	39	Spin	37 1m31.160s
	Adrian Campos	1.5t Minardi-Motori Moderni M186	30	Gearbox	20 1m34.709s
	Gabriele Tarquini	1.5t Osella-Alfa Romeo FA1H	26	Electrics	5 1m40.126s
	Alessandro Nannini	1.5t Minardi-Motori Moderni M186	25	Engine	14 1m34.036s
	Ivan Capelli	3.5 March-Ford 871	18	Rotor arm	14 1m37.839s
	Gerhard Berger	1.5t Ferrari-Spa F187	16	Black box	4 1m32.929s
	Alain Prost	1.5t McLaren-TAG MP4/3	15	Alternator belt	11 1m31.409s
	Piercarlo Ghinzani	1.5t Ligier -Megatron JS29B	7	Withdrew	4 1m34.817s

Average Speed of Winner: 193.807 km/h, 120.437 mph
Fastest lap: Teo Fabi on Lap 51, 1m29.246s, 201.851 km/h, 125.435 mph
Lap Record: Nelson Piquet (Williams-Honda FW11), 1m28.667s, 204.631 km/h, 127.152 mph (1986)

Circuit Data

San Marino Grand Prix, Imola, Italy

Circuit Length: 5.040 km/ 3.132 miles
Race Distance: 295.236 km/ 184.788 miles
Race Weather: Hazy/breezy

Past Winners

Year	Driver	Nat.	Car	Circuit	Distance miles/km	Speed mph/km/h
1981	Nelson Piquet	BR	3.0 Brabham-Ford BT49C	Imola	187.90/302.40	101.20/162.87
1982	Didier Pironi	F	1.5 Ferrari 126C2 t/c	Imola	187.90/302.40	116.63/187.70
1983	Patrick Tambay	F	1.5 Ferrari 126C2/B t/c	Imola	187.90/302.40	115.25/185.48
1984	Alain Prost	F	1.5 McLaren-TAG MP4/2 t/c	Imola	187.90/302.40	116.35/187.25
1985	Elio de Angelis	I	1.5 Lotus-Renault 97T t/c	Imola	187.90/302.40	119.17/191.79
1986	Alain Prost	F	1.5 McLaren-TAG MP4/2C t/c	Imola	187.90/302.40	121.92/196.21

Grid Order	1	2	3	4	5	6	7	8	9	10	11	12	13	14	15	16	17	18	19	20	21	22	23	24	25	26	27	28	29	30	31	32	33	34	35	36	37	38	39	40	41	42	43	44	45	46	47	48	49	50	51	52	53	54	55	56	57	58	59	Pos
12 Ayrton Senna	12	5	5	5	5	5	5	5	5	5	5	5	5	5	5	5	5	5	5	5	5	5	27	27	27	12	5	5	5	5	5	5	5	5	5	5	5	5	5	5	5	5	5	5	5	5	5	5	5	5	5	5	5	5	5	5	5	5	5	1
5 Nigel Mansell	5	12	12	12	1	1	1	1	1	1	1	1	1	1	27	27	27	27	27	27	12	12	5	5	7	7	7	7	7	7	7	7	7	7	7	12	12	12	12	12	27	7	7	7	7	7	7	12	12	12	12	12	12	12	12	12	12	12	12	2
1 Alain Prost	1	1	1	1	12	12	12	12	12	12	12	27	12	12	12	12	12	12	7	7	7	7	12	12	12	5	12	12	12	27	27	27	27	27	27	7	27	27	27	27	7	27	27	27	27	27	27	27	27	27	27	27	27	27	27	27	27	27	27	3
19 Teo Fabi	27	27	27	27	27	27	27	27	27	27	27	12	7	7	7	7	7	5	2	5	17	27	27	27	27	27	27	27	27	7	7	7	7	7	7	12	12	12	12	12	27	19	2	2	2	2	2	2	2	2										4
28 Gerhard Berger	28	28	28	28	28	28	28	28	28	28	28	28	2	2	2	2	2	2	5	17	27	2	2	2	2	2	2	2	2	2	2	2	2	2	2	2	2	20	20	20	20	20	20	19	19	7	7	17	17	17	9	9								5
27 Michele Alboreto	7	7	7	7	7	7	7	7	7	7	7	7	28	19	20	20	20	17	17	20	2	17	17	17	17	17	17	17	20	20	20	20	20	20	20	19	19	19	19	19	2	2	2	17	7	7	9	11	11											6
7 Riccardo Patrese	2	19	19	19	19	19	19	19	2	2	2	2	19	19	20	17	17	17	20	2	20	20	20	20	20	20	20	17	8	8	8	8	17	17	17	17	17	17	17	17	17	2	17	17	9	9	9	11	10	10										7
2 Stefan Johansson	19	2	2	2	2	2	2	2	19	19	19	19	20	17	18	18	18	18	18	18	18	8	8	8	8	8	8	8	17	17	17	19	19	19	19	2	2	2	2	2	17	9	9	9	11	11	11	7	7	4										8
18 Eddie Cheever	17	17	17	17	17	17	17	17	17	20	20	17	18	8	8	8	8	8	8	8	18	18	18	18	18	19	19	19	19	19	19	8	18	18	18	18	18	18	18	21	21	21	21	21	21	10	4	7											9
17 Derek Warwick	18	20	20	20	20	20	20	20	20	20	17	17	18	8	9	9	9	9	9	9	9	19	19	19	19	18	18	18	18	18	18	9	9	9	9	9	9	11	11	11	10	10	10	4	30													10
20 Thierry Boutsen	20	18	18	18	18	18	18	18	18	18	18	9	9	21	21	21	21	21	21	19	19	9	9	9	9	9	9	21	21	21	21	21	21	21	21	10	10	10	4	4	4	30																	11
11 Satoru Nakajima	9	9	9	9	9	9	9	9	9	8	9	9	8	21	19	19	19	19	19	21	21	21	21	21	21	21	21	10	10	10	10	10	10	10	11	4	4	4	30	30	30																		12
25 Rene Arnoux	24	24	24	26	26	26	8	8	8	8	9	8	21	10	10	10	10	10	10	10	10	10	10	10	10	10	10	3	11	11	11	11	11	11	11	11	11	10	30	30	14	14																	13
8 Andre de Cesaris	26	26	26	24	24	24	24	21	21	21	21	21	23	10	3	3	3	3	3	3	3	3	3	3	3	3	3	11	3	3	3	3	3	4	4	4	4																						14
9 Martin Brundle	21	21	21	21	21	8	24	24	23	23	23	23	10	3	4	4	4	4	4	4	4	4	4	4	4	4	4	4	4	4	4	4	4	4	3	3																							15
24 Alessandro Nannini	23	8	8	8	8	8	21	23	10	10	10	10	3	4	30	30	30	30	30	30	30	30	30	30	30	1	11	11	11	11	11	11	11	30	30	30	30	30	30	30	30																		16
23 Adrian Campos	8	23	23	23	23	23	10	10	3	3	3	3	4	30	24	24	24	24	24	11	11	11	11	11	11	11	11	30	30	30	30	30	30	14	14	14	14	14	14	14																			17
10 Christian Danner	4	10	10	4	10	10	10	11	11	4	4	4	4	30	24	16	11	11	11	11	14	14	14	14	14	14	30	14	14	14	14	14	14																									18
26 Piercarlo Ghinzani	10	4	4	10	4	11	3	3	30	30	30	30	30	16	11	11	14	14	14	23	23	23	23	23	23	23																																	19
21 Alex Caffi	16	16	16	16	3	11	4	4	4	16	16	16	16	24	11	14	14	23	23	23	23	24	24	24	22																																	20
4 Philippe Streiff	30	30	30	3	11	3	3	30	30	24	14	24	24	24	11	14	23	23	22	22	22	22	22	22	22																																	21
30 Philippe Alliot	14	3	3	30	16	30	30	16	16	14	24	14	14	11	14	22	22	22																																								23
16 Ivan Capelli	3	14	14	11	30	16	16	14	14	11	11	11	14	22	23																																											24
3 Jonathan Palmer	22	11	11	14	14	14	14	22	22	22	22	22	22	22																																												25
14 Pascal Fabre	11	22	22	22	22	22	22																																																			26
22 Gabriele Tarquini																																																									27

Championship Points

Drivers			Constructors		
1	Nigel Mansell	10 pts	1=	McLaren	16 pts
2	Alain Prost	9 pts	1=	Williams	16 pts
3	Stefan Johansson	7 pts	3=	Lotus-Honda	7 pts
4=	Ayrton Senna	6 pts	3=	Ferrari	7 pts
4=	Nelson Piquet	6 pts	5=	Zakspeed	2 pts
6	Michele Alboreto	4 pts	5=	Benetton	2 pts
7	Gerhard Berger	3 pts			
8=	Thierry Boutsen	2 pts			
8=	Martin Brundle	2 pts			
10	Satoru Nakajima	1 pt			

Jim Clark Cup			Colin Chapman Cup		
1	Philippe Streiff	15 pts	1	Tyrrell	24 pts
2	Jonathan Palmer	9 pts	2	AGS	8 pts
3	Pascal Fabre	8 pts	3	Lola	6 pts
4	Philippe Alliot	6 pts			

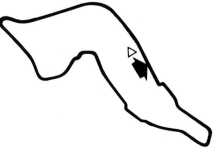

BELGIAN

GRAND PRIX

The unfortunate Belgians had endured two days of typical Ardennes weather, with only a scrap of excitement during the wet qualifying sessions, making it all a lottery. But the banks around one of Formula One's most popular tracks were crowded. The Belgians had returned to Grand Prix racing with a vengeance.

The locals did get the bonus of two starts – but both were costly. On the first lap of the first start, they lost local hero Thierry Boutsen and Friday's provisional poleman, Gerhard Berger. Both returned for the second start, but then they lost potential winners Ayrton Senna and 1986 winner Nigel Mansell on the first lap. In the meantime, Philippe Streiff had a terrifying accident at the top of the infamous Eau Rouge, and Jonathan Palmer ploughed into the wreckage. The race was stopped and Palmer didn't take part in the new race. If that wasn't enough excitement for the day, something was to happen later that would again get the Grand Prix into the headlines – but for more unsavoury reasons. There were also statistics which were milestones in the sport: Alain Prost equalled Jackie Stewart's 27 wins with an almost unrivalled display, and Ferrari recorded their 26th Grand Prix without a win, a less distinguished record.

Spa is becoming *the* cosmopolitan race, which used to be epitomised by the Austrian Grand Prix. The car parks are as full of German, British, Dutch and French cars as they are of Belgian. But if this is the home race of any team, it must be Zakspeed – whose home base is around two hours away. Any team that tests at the Nurburgring as often as Zakspeed must be prepared for the showers experienced on 300 out of 365 days a year at Spa. It produces lush greenery and a feeling of relief when the sun shines, but it also makes for practice

and qualifying sessions which are consistently described as a lottery. Indeed, the term could even be used to describe the race itself for there's no private pre-race testing at Spa. But there can't be anything more challenging, nor more exhilarating, than dashing down the hill into Eau Rouge and then trying to keep the car straight as it skids up through the Raidillon, right and then left. Combine this with the ball of spray that's the car in front and things are even more unpredictable. Both Arrows drivers knew what it was like to get unstuck there!

On Friday, Derek Warwick came up against a problem – but didn't mention it to his pit afterwards. "Good driving and a lot of luck got me out of that", he eventually conceded. Cheever's car, meanwhile, returned on the back of a breakdown truck. "My Dad once said that you don't run those in the wet", said Cheever, pointing to his slicks. It was typical of the weekend's problems. On both afternoons it was sheer chance if you were out on the right tyres at the right time with the right amount of fuel. Cheever was out on his slicks with the right amount of fuel. Only problem was, it had just started raining. Fortunately, his Arrows wasn't badly damaged. There were others with similar problems. Mansell got a wheel onto the wet and had a wild spin, Later, he and Capelli had a near miss and broken bolts were found in the transmission after the Williams-Honda had been forced off the circuit. But Mansell was in pole position

with a time that was substantially quicker than Piquet's in 1986, despite pop-off valves (remember them?) and the weather. Mansell was nearly 1.4 seconds faster than his own team mate, 1986 poleman Nelson Piquet, now almost completely recovered from his Imola shunt. The two Williams-Hondas pushed Ayrton Senna back to third fastest, the Lotus active suspension slightly confused by the new dimension of rain – the Brazilian complained of slight instability and a misfire at crucial moments in the weather.

Little by little, things were coming right at Ferrari. Berger had been quickest in Friday's session and, although he and Alboreto were pushed down to fourth and fifth on the grid, a Ferrari hadn't been as high as fourth on the grid for exactly a year. Sixth was where one would expect to find Alain Prost, although the team had been cautious about its Friday laps due to a limited supply of Goodyear's wet tyres. Not surprisingly, the team felt that they were a little behind with their set-up but then they had been behind the previous two races as well. Thierry Boutsen kept local interest alive at seventh on the grid, although his chance of success was still subject to engine problems, and the computer not keeping up with temperature changes. Both Thierry and team mate Fabi suffered engine breakages on Saturday which naturally upset their set-up programme. Riccardo Patrese, the Grand Old Man of the Belgian

Previous page: Gerhard
Berger at La Source

Right: Arnoux was
lucky to finish sixth in
the spare Ligier after
crashing his own car at
the first start

Grand Prix with 11 participations, was eighth on the grid and optimistic after his performance at Imola, although he and de Cesaris had differing fuel injection systems. Stefan Johansson was just 1.6 seconds slower than team mate Prost, while the Arrows had a relatively problem-free weekend – apart from those already mentioned. Behind de Cesaris came Alessandro Nannini in the Minardi, again more reliable and promising than in recent races, as was team mate Campos. Nakajima suffered from the weather – it was the active suspension's first wet weather experience in qualifying – and a flat battery.

Ligier had three reinforced cars for Spa but the strengthening process that took place back in England was expensive in terms of weight, resulting in cars which were around 50 kilos overweight. The Zakspeed duo both had engine failures which cost them time at a crucial juncture. In the normally aspirated class, Ivan Capelli's March 871 came out tops (21st overall) after a promising test session at Silverstone. The big airbox had proved to be beneficial in terms of revs (300 rpm more) but not so in terms of buffeting. In the end it was discarded. Second fastest was Alliot in the Lola from the two Tyrrells, once again suffering from the dreaded misfire which, at various times during the weekend, the team thought they had finally lost.

After all the complaints about wet practice and qualifying, the weather had almost cleared for race day. This state of affairs was greeted with relief by most drivers, but was met by the furrowed brow of Alain Prost as he mentally tried to set up his car. Advancing clouds compounded his worry. Inclement weather didn't worry the locals, who flocked to the circuit in unprecedented numbers. Apart from a delayed first session on Friday morning which cost the organisers the usual dollar fine, the organisation had generally been good. Prost's brow cleared after the warm-up when he and Johansson set fastest time from Berger, Mansell, Boutsen and Alboreto. Senna was some way behind, complaining of lack of straight line speed while Capelli's March stopped on the circuit with dead electrics.

After the parade lap Roland Brunseraede, here on home ground and acting clerk of the course, flashed the lights to

green and 24 cars were on their way. The hundred-yard blast to the first corner had been feared by everyone, but it went fairly well for most of the front runners. Although Senna tried to slot himself between the two Williams, Mansell got himself ahead while Piquet was alongside the Lotus driver. As the leaders blasted down the hill to Eau Rouge, Arnoux ran into the back of de Cesaris. Arnoux soon pulled off while de Cesaris drove slowly to the pits with a disintegrating tyre. Mansell had a 1.6 second lead over Senna at the end of that first lap. Behind Piquet, Berger hit the barrier coming out of the Bus Stop chicane and also collected Boutsen. The crowd groaned.

At the start of the second lap, Streiff's Tyrrell suddenly got away from him going up the hill out of Eau Rouge. The car crashed into the barrier on both sides of the track and ended up in two pieces – rear suspension and engine in one spot, Streiff in a two-wheeled monocoque in another. In all the dust, Palmer had little chance of avoiding the wreckage. Mercifully, neither of them were hurt. The race was red-flagged, and after

they'd driven back to the pits in a course car, Streiff calmly climbed into the spare car which was set up for him. Palmer, unfortunately, wouldn't race.

Stopping the race benefited several drivers; Arnoux's car was repaired, de Cesaris made the restart, and Berger took the team's spare car, as did Boutsen. The restart was less fortunate for Mansell who had enjoyed a relatively good lead at the end of that first lap. Now he had to go over it all again, and Prost, already nervous after his contretemps the previous year, wasn't entirely happy either. At the restart, Senna made it between the Williams this time, while Piquet made a bad start again and came round third, behind Mansell. Alboreto, Prost (after a hairy moment beside Berger) and Boutsen followed.

At the back of the circuit where there's a quick right/left, Mansell thought Senna braked early, nipped out from behind him and came down on the left-hand and outside line. As they turned in, Senna braked hard and hit the kerb on the inside. Mansell, meanwhile, was ahead but not using all the road because of the left-hander that followed. Senna's Lotus, unsettled, slid into the Williams and the two spun in perfect unison, ending up on the outside of the corner as the field, now led by Piquet, steamed through. Senna's Lotus stuck hard in the gravel trap – where it would remain for the rest of the day. Mansell eventually rubbed his Williams back over the kerbs and rejoined the race.

Piquet led lap one from Alboreto, Prost, Boutsen, Berger, Fabi, Patrese, Johansson and the rest. Berger blew up at the end of lap two and Patrese's clutch went soon after. Piquet, meanwhile, wasn't drawing away from Alboreto and Prost, battling over second place. Boutsen lost fourth place to Fabi on lap six as his engine went down on power and Johansson followed the Italian through soon after. On lap 10 of the 43, the race became virtually cut and dried. Piquet pitted with a broken turbo sensor which was causing a misfire – he was out. Alboreto also pitted with broken transmission. He was out too. It left Prost with a 3.1 second lead which became 5.1s within four laps and 11.9s within another three. The man in second place had been Fabi but Johansson left Boutsen behind,

soon to retire with a faulty wheel-bearing, and closed on the Italian, taking second place on lap 17. A lap later, the leader pitted for new tyres but still kept the lead. When Johansson and Fabi both pitted, Prost was left with a 15.4s lead which soon became 20.5s. But there was still half the race to go...

In the second half, Prost set fastest race lap and suffered a broken computer. "I didn't know my fuel figures, temperatures – nothing, so I radioed to the pits and they radioed to Stefan who told me what to do", said the Frenchman. It worked perfectly. Prost scored his 27th and surely his easiest win. He was thronged by photographers who had been waiting at the rostrum since half distance – there hadn't been much else to photograph. Johansson set second quickest lap and finished 24.5 seconds behind, the tenth time he'd been classified in as many races. The Benetton challenge had faded when Fabi's exhaust had broken on lap 27 and then the engine had broken with eight laps to go. Fabi had already been pushed down to fourth by de Cesaris who had earlier overtaken Cheever. Both were in trouble with fuel consumption: de

Cesaris ran out on the last lap; while Cheever had been conducting useful testing with Megatron engineers trying various ways of saving fuel. They finished third and fourth.

Potential early points scorers were Warwick, who lost his water hose, and there was a good battle between Arnoux, Brundle and Nakajima. Nakajima finished a happy fifth, Arnoux came home sixth having been alarmed by his fuel read-out, while Brundle's engine broke. Piercarlo Ghinzani, seventh, was nearly caught by Alliot until the Frenchman had two spins due to lack of brakes. He narrowly missed Prost in the first and had to push himself off the kerbs after the second, but he still won the normally aspirated class after Capelli's oil pressure plummeted. Streiff's misfire returned but he managed to come through in second place.

It certainly wasn't the most notable Belgian Grand Prix, and the crowd deserved better. But regrettably the headlines were reserved for the physical altercation between Mansell and Senna in the pits after the Englishman retired and continued the dispute over whose line it had been.

Left: Action in the rain

The race was stopped when Streiff lost control of his Tyrrell in the Raidillon and the wreckage was hit by team mate Palmer. In spite of Streiff's car being cut in half, he was uninjured and started in the spare car. Palmer, however, did not race

Right: The field, led by
Teo Fabi, go out for
qualifying

Left: Berger blew up on lap two

Centre left: The Williams team seemed to have trouble with Senna in Belgium

Centre right: De Cesaris ran out of fuel on the last lap, but still finished third

Below: Cheever hit the barrier when he slid off the wet track while using slicks

Cheever finished fourth
in the Arrows

Right: Prost scored win number 27 in Belgium

Far right: Johansson and de Cesaris spray Champagne with Prost

Below: Mansell leads Senna and Piquet at the start

83

Entries and Practice Times

	Driver	Nat.	Car	Practice 1	Practice 2	Warm Up	Engine	Turbos	Electrics/Plugs	Fuel/Oil	Brake Discs/Calipers	Shocks
1	Alain Prost	F	Marlboro McLaren MP4/3	2m11.203s	1m54.186s	1m58.278s	1.5t TAG V6	KKK	Bosch	Shell	SEP/McL	Bil
2	Stefan Johansson	S	Marlboro McLaren MP4/3	2m12.063s	1m55.781s	1m59.705s	1.5t TAG V6	KKK	Bosch	Shell	SEP/McL	Bil
3	Jonathan Palmer	GB	Data General/Courtaulds Tyrrell DG/016	2m14.931s	2m04.677s	2m07.794s	3.5 Ford Cosworth DFZ V8		Cos/Ch	Elf	AP	Koni
4	Philippe Streiff	F	Data General/Courtaulds Tyrrell DG/016	2m18.900s	2m03.098s	2m07.320s	3.5 Ford Cosworth DFZ V8		Cos/Ch	Elf	AP	Koni
5	Nigel Mansell	GB	Canon Williams FW11B	2m06.965s	1m52.026s	1m59.909s	1.5t Honda V6	IHI	Honda/NGK	Mobil	SEP/AP	Showa
6	Nelson Piquet	BR	Canon Williams FW11B	2m08.143s	1m53.416s	2m00.693s	1.5t Honda V6	IHI	Honda/NGK	Mobil	SEP/AP	Showa
7	Riccardo Patrese	I	Brabham BT56	2m12.914s	1m55.064s	2m01.612s	1.5t BMW S4	Garrett	Bosch/Ch	Win/Castrol	SEP/Bra	Koni
8	Andrea de Cesaris	I	Brabham BT56	2m13.871s	1m57.101s	2m01.762s	1.5t BMW S4	Garrett	Bosch/Ch	Win/Castrol	SEP/Bra	Koni
9	Martin Brundle	GB	West Zakspeed 871	2m14.432s	2m00.433s	2m02.870s	1.5t Zakspeed S4	Garrett	Bosch/Ch	Win/Castrol	AP	Sachs
10	Christian Danner	D	West Zakspeed 871	2m20.610s	2m01.072s	2m05.295s	1.5t Zakspeed S4	Garrett	Bosch/Ch	Win/Castrol	AP	Sachs
11	Satoru Nakajima	J	Camel Lotus 99T	2m11.441s	1m58.649s	2m05.371s	1.5t Honda V6	IHI	Honda/NGK	Elf	SEP/Bre	L/A
12	Ayrton Senna	BR	Camel Lotus 99T	2m08.450s	1m53.426s	2m02.000s	1.5t Honda V6	IHI	Honda/NGK	Elf	SEP/Bre	L/A
14	Pascal Fabre	F	El Charro AGS JH22C	2m26.498s	2m07.361s	2m11.657s	3.5 Ford Cosworth DFZ V8		Cos/Ch	Acto	SEP/AGS	Koni
16	Ivan Capelli	I	Leyton House March 871	2m13.355s	2m02.036s	2m15.345s	3.5 Ford Cosworth DFZ V8		Cos/Ch	BP	AP	Koni
17	Derek Warwick	GB	USF&G Arrows A10	2m10.946s	1m56.359s	2m01.466s	1.5t Megatron S4	Garrett	Bosch/Ch	Win/Castrol	AP	Koni
18	Eddie Cheever	USA	USF&G Arrows A10	2m15.321s	1m55.899s	2m02.503s	1.5t Megatron S4	Garrett	Bosch/Ch	Win/Castrol	AP	Koni
19	Teo Fabi	I	Benetton B187	2m12.358s	1m55.339s	2m01.165s	1.5t Ford V6	Garrett	Ford EED/Ch	Mobil	SEP/AP	Koni
20	Thierry Boutsen	B	Benetton B187	2m08.752s	1m54.300s	2m00.354s	1.5t Ford V6	Garrett	Ford EED/Ch	Mobil	SEP/AP	Koni
21	Alex Caffi	I	Landis & Gyr Osella FA1I	2m16.268s	2m12.086s	2m06.559s	1.5t Alfa Romeo V8	KKK	Mar/Ch	Agip	Bre	Koni
23	Adrian Campos	E	Minardi M186	2m14.945s	2m00.763s	2m06.350s	1.5t Motori Moderni V6	KKK	Mar/Ch	Agip	Bre	Koni
24	Alessandro Nannini	I	Minardi M186	2m09.650s	1m58.132s	2m05.300s	1.5t Motori Moderni V6	KKK	Mar/Ch	Agip	Bre	Koni
25	Rene Arnoux	F	Loto Ligier JS29B	2m15.012s	1m59.117s	2m02.518s	1.5t Megatron S4	Garrett	Bosch/Ch	Win/Castrol	SEP/Bre	Koni
26	Piercarlo Ghinzani	I	Loto Ligier JS29B	2m15.329s	1m59.291s	2m05.077s	1.5t Megatron S4	Garrett	Bosch/Ch	Win/Castrol	SEP/Bre	Koni
27	Michele Alboreto	I	Ferrari F187	2m07.459s	1m53.511s	2m00.463s	1.5t Ferrari V6	Garrett	Mar-Weber/Ch	Agip	SEP/Bre	Marz
28	Gerhard Berger	A	Ferrari F187	2m06.216s	1m53.451s	1m59.859s	1.5t Ferrari V6	Garrett	Mar-Weber/Ch	Agip	SEP/Bre	Marz
30	Philippe Alliot	F	Larrousse Lola LC87	2m13.082s	2m02.347s	2m05.779s	3.5 Ford Cosworth DFZ V8		Cos-Mar/Ch	BP	SEP/AP	Koni

Cos=Cosworth
Ch=Champion
Win=Wintershall
McL=McLaren
Mar=Marelli
Bra=Brabham
Bre=Brembo
Bil=Bilstein
L/A=Lotus Active
Marz=Marzocchi

May 15	May 16	May 17
Wet	Drying	Sunny/cool

Starting Grid

Piquet	6	5	Mansell
Berger	28	12	Senna
Prost	1	27	Alboreto
Patrese	7	20	Boutsen
Johansson	2	19	Fabi
Warwick	17	18	Cheever
Nannini	24	8	de Cesaris
Arnoux	25	11	Nakajima
Brundle	9	26	Ghinzani
Danner	10	23	Campos
Alliot	30	16	Capelli
Palmer	3	4	Streiff
Caffi	21	14	Fabre

Results, Retirements and Fastest Laps

Place	Driver	Car	Laps	Time/Retirement	Fastest Lap No./Time
1	Alain Prost	1.5t McLaren-TAG MP4/3	43	1h27m03.217s	26	1m57.153s
2	Stefan Johansson	1.5t McLaren-TAG MP4/3	43	1h27m27.981s	33	1m59.015s
3	Andrea de Cesaris	1.5t Brabham-BMW BT56	42	1h26m10.046s Out Of Fuel	33	2m00.154s
4	Eddie Cheever	1.5t Arrows-Megatron A10	42	1h28m21.788s	29	2m02.706s
5	Satoru Nakajima	1.5t Lotus-Honda 99T	42	1h28m22.923s	34	2m03.091s
6	Rene Arnoux	1.5t Ligier-Megatron JS29B	41	1h27m44.166s	15	2m04.471s
7	Piercarlo Ghinzani	1.5t Ligier-Megatron JS29B	40	1h25m28.345s Out Of Fuel	13	2m04.691s
8	Philippe Alliot	3.5 Lola-Ford LC87	40	1h27m48.192s	16	2m05.456s
9	Philippe Streiff	3.5 Tyrrell-Ford DG/016	39	1h29m39.718s	19	2m09.872s
10	Pascal Fabre	3.5 AGS-Ford JH22C	38	1h23m46.508s Electrics	15	2m09.977s
	Teo Fabi	1.5t Benetton-BMW B187	34	Engine	8	1m59.927s
	Martin Brundle	1.5t Zakspeed 871	19	Engine	16	2m04.227s
	Thierry Boutsen	1.5t Benetton-BMW B187	18	Wheel Bearing	4	2m01.020s
	Nigel Mansell	1.5t Williams-Honda FW11B	17	Underbody Damage	12	1m59.651s
	Ivan Capelli	3.5 March-Ford 871	14	Oil Pressure	13	2m06.011s
	Nelson Piquet	1.5t Williams-Honda FW11B	11	Turbo Sensor	8	1m59.572s
	Alex Caffi	1.5t Osella-Alfa Romeo FA1I	11	Engine	6	2m05.825s
	Michele Alboreto	1.5t Ferrari-Spa F187	9	Transmission	7	2m00.017s
	Christian Danner	1.5t Zakspeed 871	9	Brakes	8	2m05.247s
	Derek Warwick	1.5t Arrows-Megatron A10	8	Water Hose	6	2m03.843s
	Riccardo Patrese	1.5t Brabham-BMW BT56	5	Clutch	2	2m05.206s
	Gerhard Berger	1.5t Ferrari-Spa F187	2	Engine	2	2m09.474s
	Alessandro Nannini	1.5t Minardi-Motori Moderni M186	1	Engine	1	2m17.571s
	Ayrton Senna	1.5t Lotus-Honda 99T	0	Collision/Mansell		
	Adrian Campos	1.5t Minardi-Motori Moderni M186	0	Gearbox		
	Jonathan Palmer	3.5 Tyrrell-Ford DG/016	–	Accident Damage at First Start		

Average Speed of Winner: 205.680 km/h, 127.803 mph
Fastest Lap: Alain Prost on Lap 26, 1m57.153s, 213.260 km/h, 132.513 mph (record)
Previous Lap Record: Alain Prost (McLaren-TAG MP4/2C), 1m59.282s, 209.453 km/h, 130.148 mph (1986)

Circuit Data

Belgian Grand Prix, Spa, Belgium

Circuit Length: 6.940 km/4.312 miles
Race Distance: 43 laps, 298.420 km/185.429 miles
Race Weather: Dry/sunny

Past Winners

Year	Driver	Nat.	Car	Circuit	Distance miles/km	Speed mph/km/h
1979	Jody Scheckter	ZA	3.0 Ferrari 312T-4	Zolder	185.38/298.34	111.24/179.02
1980	Didier Pironi	F	3.0 Ligier-Ford JS11/15	Zolder	190.66/306.86	115.82/186.40
1981	Carlos Reutemann	RA	3.0 Williams-Ford FWO7C	Zolder	143.01/230.15	112.12/180.44
1982	John Watson	GB	3.0 McLaren-Ford MP4B	Zolder	185.38/298.34	116.19/187.00
1983	Alain Prost	F	1.5 Renault RE40 t/c	Francorchamps	173.13/278.62	119.14/191.73
1984	Michele Alboreto	I	1.5 Ferrari 126C4 t/c	Zolder	185.38/298.34	115.22/185.43
1985	Ayrton Senna	BR	1.5 Lotus-Renault 97T t/c	Francorchamps	185.67/298.81	117.94/189.81
1986	Nigel Mansell	GB	1.5 Williams-Honda FW11 t/c	Spa	185.43/298.42	126.48/203.55

Grid Order	1	2	3	4	5	6	7	8	9	10	11	12	13	14	15	16	17	18	19	20	21	22	23	24	25	26	27	28	29	30	31	32	33	34	35	36	37	38	39	40	41	42	43	
5 Nigel Mansell	6	6	6	6	6	6	6	6	6	1	1	1	1	1	1	1	1	1	1	1	1	1	1	1	1	1	1	1	1	1	1	1	1	1	1	1	1	1	1	1	1	1	1	1
6 Nelson Piquet	27	27	27	27	27	27	27	27	27	19	19	19	19	19	19	19	2	2	2	19	2	2	2	2	2	2	2	2	2	2	2	2	2	2	2	2	2	2	2	2	2	2	2	2
12 Ayrton Senna	1	1	1	1	1	1	1	1	1	1	2	2	2	2	2	2	2	19	19	19	19	2	19	19	19	19	19	19	19	8	8	8	8	8	8	8	8	8	8	8	8	8	8	3
28 Gerhard Berger	20	20	20	20	20	19	19	19	19	20	20	20	20	20	20	20	8	8	8	8	8	8	8	8	8	8	8	8	8	19	19	19	19	19	18	18	18	18	18	18	18	18		4
27 Michele Alboreto	28	19	19	19	19	20	2	2	2	8	8	8	8	8	8	8	20	18	18	18	18	18	18	18	18	18	18	18	18	18	18	18	18	18	11	11	11	11	11	11	11	11	11	5
1 Alain Prost	19	7	2	2	2	2	20	20	20	18	18	18	18	18	18	18	18	25	25	11	26	26	26	11	11	11	11	11	11	11	11	11	11	11	25	25	25	25	25	25	25			6
20 Thierry Boutsen	7	2	7	18	18	8	8	8	8	25	25	25	25	25	25	25	25	11	11	25	11	11	11	26	26	26	26	25	25	25	25	25	25	25	30	30	26	26	26	26				7
7 Riccardo Patrese	2	18	18	8	8	18	18	18	18	9	9	9	9	9	9	9	9	9	26	26	25	25	25	25	25	25	26	26	26	26	26	26	30	26	26	30	30	30	30					8
19 Teo Fabi	18	17	17	17	17	17	17	25	25	11	11	11	11	11	11	11	11	26	30	30	30	30	30	30	30	30	30	30	30	30	30	30	26	14	14	14	14	4						9
2 Stefan Johansson	17	8	8	25	25	25	25	9	9	26	26	26	26	26	26	26	26	30	9	4	4	4	4	4	4	14	14	14	14	14	14	14	14	4	4	4	4							10
18 Eddie Cheever	8	28	25	7	9	9	9	11	11	16	16	16	16	16	30	30	30	20	4	14	14	14	14	14	14	4	4	4	4	4	4	4	4											11
17 Derek Warwick	24	25	9	9	11	11	11	26	26	30	30	30	30	30	5	5	5	4	14																									12
8 Andrea de Cesaris	11	9	11	11	26	26	26	10	10	6	5	5	5	5	5	4	4	4	14																									13
24 Alessandro Nannini	25	11	26	26	10	10	10	16	16	5	4	4	4	4	14	14	14																											14
11 Satoru Nakajima	9	26	10	10	16	21	21	30	30	4	14	14	14	14																														15
25 Rene Arnoux	26	10	16	16	21	16	16	5	5	14	6																																	16
26 Piercarlo Ghinzani	10	16	30	30	30	30	30	21	4	21	21																																	17
9 Martin Brundle	16	30	21	21	7	5	5	4	14																																			18
23 Adrian Campos	30	21	14	14	14	4	4	14	21																																			19
10 Christian Danner	21	14	4	4	4	14	14	17																																				20
16 Ivan Capelli	14	4	5	5	5																																							21
30 Philippe Alliot	4	5																																										22
4 Philippe Streiff	5																																											23
3 Jonathan Palmer																																												24
14 Pascal Fabre																																												25
21 Alex Caffi																																												26

Championship Points

Drivers				Constructors		
1	Alain Prost	18 pts		1	McLaren	31 pts
2	Stefan Johansson	13 pts		2	Williams	16 pts
3	Nigel Mansell	10 pts		3	Lotus	9 pts
4=	Ayrton Senna	6 pts		4	Ferrari	7 pts
4=	Nelson Piquet	6 pts		5	Brabham	4 pts
6=	Michele Alboreto	4 pts		6	Arrows	3 pts
6=	Andrea de Cesaris	4 pts		7=	Zakspeed	2 pts
8=	Gerhard Berger	3 pts		7=	Benetton	2 pts
8=	Eddie Cheever	3 pts		9	Ligier	1 pt
8=	Satoru Nakajima	3 pts				
11=	Thierry Boutsen	2 pts				
11=	Martin Brundle	2 pts				
13	Rene Arnoux	1 pt				

Jim Clark Cup				Colin Chapman Cup		
1	Philippe Streiff	21 pts		1	Tyrrell	30 pts
2	Philippe Alliot	15 pts		2	Lola	15 pts
3	Pascal Fabre	12 pts		3	AGS	12 pts
4	Jonathan Palmer	9 pts				

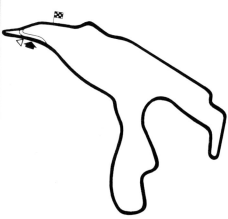

MONACO

GRAND PRIX

The 45th Monaco Grand Prix did little to modify the World Championship table. For several drivers there was deep disappointment, although Ayrton Senna did score the fifth Grand Prix victory of his 50 race GP career and Lotus' 78th.

Among those drivers facing disappointment was Stefan Johansson, who failed to be classified for the first time since the British Grand Prix the previous year. Nigel Mansell dominated qualifying and the early stages of the race, but retired before half distance. Alain Prost didn't score his 28th Grand Prix victory and poor Christian Danner didn't get to race at all, nor did Adrian Campos after collapsing, following a crash in practice. But Ayrton Senna's victory was the first with the revolutionary new active suspension, and if it could work well enough for Prost to beat Piquet's Williams by more than half a minute over the bumps of Monaco, then what could it do elsewhere?

Piquet was probably the most miserable of the top six finishers, physically suffering from the 78 laps of this street circuit, as did Alboreto in third. Happiest driver of all must have been Jonathan Palmer who really enjoyed flinging the Tyrrell around the principality's streets and came home a fine fifth to score his first ever World Championship points. His performance, and that of Ivan Capelli in the sixth-placed March, confirmed Ken Tyrrell's feeling that a normally aspirated car could score points in Monaco. Apart from the odd drop of rain on Friday afternoon, the weather was mainly good and the anticipated Mistral gave way to warm sun on Saturday and Sunday. Probably the worst thing about the race was actually getting to Monaco. Nice airport had just recovered from the influx of the Cannes Film Festival traffic and there had been intermittent strikes for several weeks. The place just isn't designed for heavy traffic! If the lure of the Tip Top and Rosie's tended to dull one's responses to the on-track features it was hard to ignore the excitement on the other side of the barrier. It was almost as though Nigel Mansell had decided that the best PR operation he could mount to erase the memories of Belgium was to simply annihilate the opposition.

On the first day of practice, he set four laps which were quicker than anyone else's best. And on the Saturday, he again set four laps which would have been good enough for pole. Mansell was going for it all the time, and by the end of Saturday he was exhausted. But he accomplished what he set out to achieve: pole position, the fourth time in succession that he would start from the front row of the grid in Monaco. His only problem was that he wasn't quite as quick as he would have liked in race form. Team mate Nelson Piquet wasn't so happy, having damaged an engine and not really enjoying his home streets of Monaco as a racing circuit. Even so, he started from third on the grid. Most drivers reported a certain curiosity as to what would happen when Mansell and fellow front row man Ayrton Senna tried to funnel into the first corner together. Following their altercation two weeks previously there were some unkind jokes at their expense.

Information from the active suspension tests was beginning to fall into a pattern which meant that although there was still a lot to be established, engineer Peter Wright and his team could fall back on previous information. Even so, Senna was still utterly committed to the suspension and felt that the team was working in the right direction. "The more laps we do, the more we learn," said Wright. Senna's team mate Nakajima pounded round and round, learning the circuit. Alain Prost always said that it would be dangerous to make this race an exception, just because it might provide his 28th Grand Prix win. But he was still the favourite having won the last three Monaco Grand Prix. After practice, however, he was not pleased. He went quicker on Saturday morning than on Saturday afternoon and finally his engine broke. The perfectionist was not his usual happy self.

Ferrari's weekend had begun disastrously. Everyone had feared that with 26 cars on the track, there would be endless problems with traffic. In fact there were relatively few, but when Michele Alboreto ran over the front wheel of Christian Danner's slower Zakspeed on the way up the hill, everyone felt that their worst fears had been confirmed. The Ferrari launched into the air and came crashing down against the barriers. There was debris everywhere and the Ferrari was so badly damaged that Michele joked that it had been sent back to Maranello in a bag, although initially he was furious with the German driver. The incident then became the subject of a stewards' meeting, and after hearing evidence from marshals and the two drivers, Danner was excluded from the meeting for dangerous driving. However, he had several independent witnesses who claimed he wasn't to

Previous page: First lap at the Loews. Mansell leads Senna, Piquet, Alboreto, Prost, Cheever, Berger, Boutsen and Johansson

Right: Campos collapsed after crashing in practice and was not able to start

blame and he felt that he had become a scapegoat so that there would be fewer than 26 starters. Even Alboreto eventually admitted that the penalty of exclusion was too harsh but that the organisers were trying to prove that they were doing everything they could to make the starting situation safer.

Meanwhile Ferrari had damaged another car when Berger crashed later in the afternoon, so two more Ferraris were found and Berger's repaired as a spare. But Alboreto's fifth on the grid and Berger's eighth were good placings under the circumstances, although Alboreto was suffering from one or two pulls and strains. Although Eddie Cheever put his Arrows into an excellent sixth place on the grid, his head gasket blew as he did it. Team mate Warwick's engine also stopped in qualifying, but the Arrows drivers were looking forward to racing with no fuel consumption worries. Benetton thought that this would be their worst race of the year, handicapped by turbo lag, while Thierry Boutsen also suffered down-on-power engines on two days. His Italian team mate, Teo Fabi doesn't like Monaco

anyway, so the Benetton duo were predictably disappointing.

Brabham had curious problems – first of all a welter of gearbox trouble and then a lack of turbo boost. Nannini was consistently well up in the Minardi, although he had two broken driveshafts in the warm-up. Team mate Campos crashed at Casino Square on Saturday morning, walked down the hill to the pits and then collapsed. On recovering, he didn't remember his walk at all, and was promptly taken to hospital. The doctors took this opportunity to insist that he take no further part in the weekend. He had only completed 30 laps racing in the four races held so far in 1987. Now there were 24 runners. Brundle was 14th in the lone Zakspeed, just ahead of the first normally aspirated car, Jonathan Palmer's Tyrrell. Testing prior to the Grand Prix, the team had thankfully found and cured the misfire that had plagued them so far this season. Alliot was second in that class in the Lola while Capelli suffered electrical problems.

The Ligiers found that their new engine cover was affecting their aerodynamics

and had to change it, while their extra weight was also costing them performance. But Caffi in the Osella was consistently competitive, and Osella would certainly get their second race at the circuit since 1980. Local driver Didier Artzet won the 29th Monaco Formula Three race from Jean Alesi and Johnny Herbert on the Saturday, and the fact that he'd been second on the grid in 1986 and started from pole to win in 1987 pointed to an analogy with Nigel Mansell's position. He had also been second on the grid in 1986 (and 1985 and 1984) and was on pole now; could he win the Formula One Grand Prix?

The huge crowd on the grassy slopes in front of the castle whistled and cheered as the 24 cars took up their positions in front of the Royal Family. When the light turned green, Mansell shot off, engraving two heavy black lines and quickly making sure that Senna was behind him. Round the first corner behind Mansell crowded Senna, Piquet and Alboreto – Alliot and Nakajima both had to go wide when they found themselves three abreast with Capelli, and the Ligiers both pitted at the end of the lap after first lap troubles. Mansell, meanwhile, was streaking away from his pursuers. Even at the end of lap one, he had a two second lead. By lap 15, it was 10 seconds, and there it remained, dipping as low as 7.8s during the next 10 laps. Then Mansell put in what turned out to be second quickest lap of the race and soon the gap was back up to 10.2s. But on the next lap, Mansell lost boost, and cruised into the pits with a broken exhaust. The Williams-Honda was out. But he'd made his point.

Senna had run to his own pace during those opening laps, and once he had wanted to, he had been able to limit the lead gap to around 10 seconds. No-one could say whether he would have won if Mansell hadn't retired, but by the time Senna inherited the lead he was around 17 seconds ahead of fellow Brazilian Nelson Piquet, and that gap got bigger and bigger. Only when Senna eased up at the end did the lead gap fall from 40 seconds to 33. Senna's nine points put him second in the Championship to Prost, while Piquet went into fourth ahead of Mansell. The Brazilian hadn't been happy throughout the race, and was suffering physically. He didn't look the slightest bit happy with his second place and, privately, some of the Williams team thought his performance was decidedly lack-lustre.

Alain Prost probably thought that his race was the toughest for some time. He became caught up in a big battle for fourth place with the Ferraris, Arrows and also Patrese at one time. Boutsen dropped out of this battle early on with a broken constant velocity joint. On lap eight, Prost was challenging Alboreto for fourth place and, apart from the occasional let-up, that challenge continued right up until Alboreto's pit stop on lap 34. Prost would complain of being held up by Alboreto, but the Ferrari driver insisted that only Prost's traction out of slow corners was superior. The Ferrari had superior top speed. Prost stopped for tyres a lap after the Ferrari, his stop was much quicker but then he found himself behind Cheever's Arrows which had yet to stop. For five laps he tried to get past the Arrows until it, too, came into the pits for tyres and battled with Berger thereafter.

Prost now found himself third, and although he began to catch Piquet, he was in trouble and knew it. The car had been smoking since lap 20 and the oil pressure began to fall. Only three laps from the end, the car stopped altogether: no points for Prost, and McLaren's disappointment was compounded by Johansson's retirement after a race of intermittent misfires. Rarely is a McLaren seen struggling to overtake an Osella. So third was a happy Alboreto, suffering from a sore neck, hand and foot, while Gerhard Berger salvaged fourth place. He had battled with both Arrows, but around the 60 lap mark, they disappeared. Cheever suf-

fered overheating and Warwick went out with a broken gearbox selector finger.

That promoted a thrilled Jonathan Palmer to fifth place and his first ever World Championship points. Although he had led the class throughout, he had been challenged by Capelli's March which overcame its electrical problems to finish a fine sixth and score points in what was only the team's third race of the year. Martin Brundle could have been forgiven for thinking that such points might have been his, but a sticking clutch dropped him several places at the start, and he found the Zakspeed's steering heavy. The Ligiers finished after a miserable race, as did Fabi who was held up by a long stop for new tyres. Brabham, too, might have thought themselves worthy of points, particularly with Patrese battling with Warwick early on, but Patrese's engine went when the electronics failed. De Cesaris, on his 28th birthday, damaged a front upright as at Imola. The top three, all residents of Monaco, indulged in a champagne battle on the royal rostrum, which was brought to a halt by local officials.

Ayrton Senna, meanwhile, was saying that he was quietly confident about Detroit. The active suspension was obviously working well. Early the next morning he was stopped by the police for not wearing a crash helmet on a moped on his way to a team celebration. But the police mainly wanted his autograph.

Left: Palmer passes Streiff's crashed Tyrrell in practice. The Englishman finished fifth but Streiff crashed again in the race

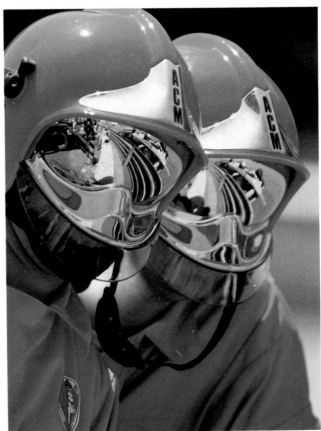

Left: Senna scored Lotus' first win with active suspension

Magnificent Monaco on race day

Right: Mansell dominated the race before his wastegate broke

Left: Senna douses team manager Peter Warr and the Royal Family with the traditional champagne

Far left: Nannini retired with broken electrics

Centre left: First lap at Ste Devote: Capelli muscles through on the inside, Nakajima and Alliott have to take avoiding action

Below left: Monegasque resident Boutsen rushes past the Hotel de Paris

Below right: Caffi got up to 10th place before retiring the Osella

Left: Boutsen qualified ninth and retired with broken transmission

MONACO GRAND PRIX · May 30

Entries and Practice Times

Cos=Cosworth
Ch=Champion
Win=Wintershall
McL=McLaren
Mar=Marelli
Bra=Brabham
Bre=Brembo
Bil=Bilstein
L/A=Lotus Active
Marz=Marzocchi

Driver	Nat.	Car	Practice 1	Practice 2	Warm Up	Engine	Turbos	Electrics/Plugs	Fuel/Oil	Brake Discs/Calipers	Shocks
1 Alain Prost	F	Marlboro McLaren MP4/3	1m25.574s	1m25.083s	1m29.169s	1.5t TAG V6	KKK	Bosch	Shell	SEP/McL	Bil
2 Stefan Johansson	S	Marlboro McLaren MP4/3	1m27.701s	1m26.317s	1m30.500s	1.5t TAG V6	KKK	Bosch	Shell	SEP/McL	Bil
3 Jonathan Palmer	GB	Data General/Courtaulds Tyrrell DG/016	1m30.307s	1m28.088s	1m32.305s	3.5 Ford Cosworth DFZ V8		Cos/Ch	Elf	AP	Koni
4 Philippe Streiff	F	Data General/Courtaulds Tyrrell DG/016	1m30.765s	1m30.143s	1m33.034s	3.5 Ford Cosworth DFZ V8		Cos/Ch	Elf	AP	Koni
5 Nigel Mansell	GB	Canon Williams FW11B	1m24.514s	1m23.039s	1m27.617s	1.5t Honda V6	IHI	Honda/NGK	Mobil	SEP/AP	Showa
6 Nelson Piquet	BR	Canon Williams FW11B	1m25.917s	1m24.755s	1m29.676s	1.5t Honda V6	IHI	Honda/NGK	Mobil	SEP/AP	Showa
7 Riccardo Patrese	I	Brabham BT56	1m26.957s	1m26.763s	1m31.878s	1.5t BMW S4	Garrett	Bosch/Ch	Win/Castrol	SEP/Bra	Koni
8 Andrea de Cesaris	I	Brabham BT56	1m32.643s	1m29.827s	1m34.677s	1.5t BMW S4	Garrett	Bosch/Ch	Win/Castrol	SEP/Bra	Koni
9 Martin Brundle	GB	West Zakspeed 871	1m29.801s	1m27.894s	1m30.432s	1.5t Zakspeed S4	Garrett	Bosch/Ch	Win/Castrol	AP	Sachs
10 Christian Danner	D	West Zakspeed 871*				1.5t Zakspeed S4	Garrett	Bosch/Ch	Win/Castrol	AP	Sachs
11 Satoru Nakajima	J	Camel Lotus 99T	1m30.606s	1m28.890s	1m34.003s	1.5t Honda V6	IHI	Honda/NGK	Elf	SEP/Bre	L/A
12 Ayrton Senna	BR	Camel Lotus 99T	1m25.255s	1m23.711s	1m26.796s	1.5t Honda V6	IHI	Honda/NGK	Elf	SEP/Bre	L/A
14 Pascal Fabre	F	El Charro AGS JH22C	1m35.179s	1m31.667s	1m34.985s	3.5 Ford Cosworth DFZ V8		Cos/Ch	Acto	SEP/AGS	Koni
16 Ivan Capelli	I	Leyton House March 871	1m31.589s	1m29.147s	2m05.477s	3.5 Ford Cosworth DFZ V8		Cos/Ch	BP	AP	Koni
17 Derek Warwick	GB	USF&G Arrows A10	1m27.685s	1m27.294s	1m29.615s	1.5t Megatron S4	Garrett	Bosch/Ch	Win/Castrol	AP	Koni
18 Eddie Cheever	USA	USF&G Arrows A10	1m27.716s	1m26.175s	1m31.011s	1.5t Megatron S4	Garrett	Bosch/Ch.	Win/Castrol	AP	Koni
19 Teo Fabi	I	Benetton B187	1m29.264s	1m27.622s	1m30.772s	1.5t Ford V6	Garrett	Ford EED/Ch	Mobil	SEP/AP	Koni
20 Thierry Boutsen	B	Benetton B187	1m27.082s	1m26.630s	1m29.123s	1.5t Ford V6	Garrett	Ford EED/Ch	Mobil	SEP/AP	Koni
21 Alex Caffi	I	Landis & Gyr Osella FA11	1m36.267s	1m28.233s	1m32.178s	1.5t Alfa Romeo V8	KKK	Mar/Ch	Agip	Bre	Koni
23 Adrian Campos	E	Minardi M186	1m30.805s†			1.5t Motori Moderni V6	KKK	Mar/Ch	Agip	Bre	Koni
24 Alessandro Nannini	I	Minardi M186	1m28.517s	1m27.731s	1m38.023s	1.5t Motori Moderni V6	KKK	Mar/Ch	Agip	Bre	Koni
25 Rene Arnoux	F	Loto Ligier JS29B	1m31.270s	1m30.000s	1m32.767s	1.5t Megatron S4	Garrett	Bosch/Ch	Win/Castrol	SEP/Bre	Koni
26 Piercarlo Ghinzani	I	Loto Ligier JS29B	1m31.098s	1m29.258s	1m32.875s	1.5t Megatron S4	Garrett	Bosch/Ch	Win/Castrol	SEP/Bre	Koni
27 Michele Alboreto	I	Ferrari F187	1m27.017s	1m26.102s	1m30.056s	1.5t Ferrari V6	Garrett	Mar-Weber/Ch	Agip	SEP/Bre	Marz
28 Gerhard Berger	A	Ferrari F187	1m29.281s	1m26.323s	1m29.486s	1.5t Ferrari V6	Garrett	Mar-Weber/Ch	Agip	SEP/Bre	Marz
30 Philippe Alliot	F	Larrousse Lola LC87	1m29.114s	1m29.459s	1m30.990s	3.5 Ford Cosworth DFZ V8		Cos-Mar/Ch	BP	SEP/AP	Koni

*Danner was excluded from the meeting and did not set a qualifying lap at all.
†Adrian Campos set a qualifying lap on the Thursday but later crashed and did not set a lap on the Saturday and did not race.

May 27	May 29	May 30
Cloudy	Warm/sunny	Warm/sunny

Starting Grid

		5	Mansell
Senna	12	6	Piquet
Prost	1	27	Alboreto
Cheever	18	2	Johansson
Berger	28	20	Boutsen
Patrese	7	17	Warwick
Fabi	19	24	Nannini
Brundle	9	3	Palmer
Caffi	21	11	Nakajima
Alliot	30	16	Capelli
Ghinzani	26	8	de Cesaris
Arnoux	25	4	Streiff
Campos	23	14	Fabre

Results, Retirements and Fastest Laps

Place	Driver	Car	Laps	Time/Retirement		Fastest Lap No./Time
1	Ayrton Senna	1.5t Lotus-Honda 99T	78	1h57m54.085s	72	1m27.685s
2	Nelson Piquet	1.5t Williams-Honda FW11B	78	1h58m27.297s	49	1m28.642s
3	Michele Alboreto	1.5t Ferrari-Spa F187	78	1h59m06.924s	58	1m28.914s
4	Gerhard Berger	1.5t Ferrari-Spa F187	77	1h57m57.226s	51	1m29.220s
5	Jonathan Palmer	3.5 Tyrrell-Ford DG/016	76	1h57m54.207s	20	1m30.817s
6	Ivan Capelli	3.5 March-Ford 871	76	1h58m21.402s	48	1m30.502s
7	Martin Brundle	1.5t Zakspeed 871	76	1h58m52.282s	44	1m31.619s
8	Teo Fabi	1.5t Benetton-Ford B187	76	1h59m21.092s	22	1m31.207s
9	Alain Prost	1.5t McLaren-TAG MP4/3	75	1h54m04.621s Engine	39	1m28.891s
10	Satoru Nakajima	1.5t Lotus-Honda 99T	75	1h58m32.081s	61	1m32.265s
11	Rene Arnoux	1.5t Ligier -Megatron JS29B	74	1h58m14.833s	47	1m32.417s
12	Piercarlo Ghinzani	1.5t Ligier -Megatron JS29B	74	1h58m18.059s	47	1m32.389s
13	Pascal Fabre	3.5 AGS-Ford JH22C	71	1h59m15.352s	8	1m35.699s
	Eddie Cheever	1.5t Arrows-Megatron A10	59	Overheating	21	1m29.905s
	Derek Warwick	1.5t Arrows-Megatron A10	58	Gear Selector Finger	57	1m29.048s
	Stefan Johansson	1.5t McLaren-TAG MP4/3	57	Engine	38	1m29.758s
	Philippe Alliot	3.5 Lola -Ford LC87	42	Engine	19	1m31.271s
	Riccardo Patrese	1.5t Brabham-BMW BT56	41	Electrics	39	1m30.077s
	Alex Caffi	1.5t Osella-Alfa Romeo FA11	39	Electrics	16	1m31.474s
	Andrea de Cesaris	1.5t Brabham-BMW BT56	38	Broken Upright	16	1m31.511s
	Nigel Mansell	1.5t Williams-Honda FW11B	29	Exhaust Wastegate	26	1m28.049s
	Alessandro Nannini	1.5t Minardi-Motori Moderni M186	21	Electrics	10	1m31.393s
	Philippe Streiff	3.5 Tyrrell-Ford DG/016	9	Accident/brakes	8	1m32.715s
	Thierry Boutsen	1.5t Benetton-Ford B187	5	CV Joint	4	1m31.300s

Average Speed of Winner: 132.102 km/h, 82.084 mph
Fastest Lap: Ayrton Senna on lap 72, 1m27.685s, 136.635 km/h, 84.901 mph
Lap Record: Alain Prost (McLaren-TAG MP4/2C), 1m26.607s, 138.335 km/h, 85.957 mph (1986)

Circuit Data

Monaco Grand Prix, Monaco

Circuit Length: 3.328 km/ 2.068 miles

Race Distance: 259.584 km/ 161.298 miles

Race Weather: Sunny/hot

Past Winners

Year	Driver	Nat.	Car	Circuit	Distance miles/km	Speed mph/km/h
1978	Patrick Depailler	F	3.0 Tyrrell-Ford 008	Monte Carlo	154.35/248.40	80.36/129.33
1979	Jody Scheckter	ZA	3.0 Ferrari 312T-4	Monte Carlo	156.41/251.71	81.34/130.90
1980	Carlos Reutemann	RA	3.0 Williams-Ford FWO7B	Monte Carlo	156.41/251.71	81.20/130.68
1981	Gilles Villeneuve	CDN	1.5 Ferrari 126CK	Monte Carlo	156.41/251.71	82.04/132.03
1982	Riccardo Patrese	I	3.0 Brabham-Ford BT49D	Monte Carlo	156.41/251.71	82.21/132.30
1983	Keke Rosberg	SF	3.0 Williams-Ford FW08C	Monte Carlo	156.41/251.71	80.52/129.59
1984	Alain Prost	F	1.5 McLaren-TAG MP4/2 t/c	Monte Carlo	63.80/102.67	62.62/100.77
1985	Alain Prost	F	1.5 McLaren-TAG MP4/2B t/c	Monte Carlo	160.52/258.34	86.02/138.30
1986	Alain Prost	F	1.5 McLaren-TAG MP4/2C t/c	Monte Carlo	160.52/258.34	83.66/134.63

Grid Order	Laps 1–61 →	Pos
5 Nigel Mansell	5 5 5 5 5 5 5 5 5 5 5 5 5 5 5 5 5 5 5 5 5 5 5 5 5 5 5 5 5 5 5 5 5 5 5 5 5 5 5 5 12 12 12 12 12 12 12 12 12 12 12 12 12 12 12 12 12 12 12 12 12	1
12 Ayrton Senna	12 12 12 12 12 12 12 12 12 12 12 12 12 12 12 12 12 12 12 12 12 12 12 12 12 12 6 6 6 6 6 6 6 6 6 6 6 6 6 6 6 6 6 6 6 6 6 6 6 6 6 6 6 6 6 6 6	2
6 Nelson Piquet	6 6 6 6 6 6 6 6 6 6 6 6 6 6 6 6 6 6 6 6 6 6 6 6 6 6 27 27 27 1 18 18 18 18 18 18 18 18 18 18 18 18 18 18 18 18 18 18 1 1 1 1 1 1 1 1 1 1 1 1 1	3
1 Alain Prost	27 27 27 27 27 27 27 27 27 27 27 27 27 27 27 27 27 27 27 27 27 27 27 27 27 27 1 1 1 18 1 1 1 1 1 1 1 1 1 1 1 1 1 1 1 1 1 1 27 27 27 27 27 27 27 27 27 27 27 27 24	4
27 Michele Alboreto	1 1 1 1 1 1 1 1 1 1 1 1 1 1 1 1 1 1 1 1 1 1 1 1 1 1 18 18 18 18 17 17 17 17 17 17 17 17 17 17 17 17 17 18 18 18 18 18 18 18 18 28 28	5
18 Eddie Cheever	18 18 18 18 18 18 18 18 18 18 18 18 18 18 18 18 18 18 18 18 18 18 17 17 28 28 28 27 17 17 17 17 28 28 28 28 28 28 28 28 28 28 28 28 3 3 6	6
2 Stefan Johansson	28 28 28 28 28 28 28 28 28 28 28 28 28 28 28 28 28 28 28 28 28 28 28 28 28 28 28 28 17 17 17 17 17 17 17 17 17 3 16 16 7	7
28 Gerhard Berger	20 20 20 20 20 17 17 17 17 17 17 17 17 17 17 17 17 17 17 17 17 7 7 19 19 19 19 19 19 19 19 3 3 3 3 3 3 3 3 3 3 3 3 3 16 9 9 8	8
20 Thierry Boutsen	17 17 17 17 7 7 7 7 7 7 7 7 7 7 7 7 7 7 7 7 7 7 7 7 7 19 19 3 3 3 3 3 3 16 16 16 16 16 16 16 16 16 16 16 16 9 19 19 9	9
7 Riccardo Patrese	7 7 7 7 19 19 19 19 19 19 19 19 19 19 19 19 19 19 19 19 19 19 19 19 21 21 16 16 16 16 16 16 9 9 9 9 9 9 2 2 2 2 9 9 9 9 9 19 11 11 10	10
17 Derek Warwick	19 19 19 19 21 21 21 21 21 21 21 21 21 21 21 21 21 21 21 21 21 21 21 3 3 9 9 9 9 9 9 9 2 2 2 2 2 9 9 9 9 2 2 2 2 2 19 11 25 25 11	11
19 Teo Fabi	21 21 21 21 2 2 24 24 24 24 24 24 24 24 24 24 24 24 24 3 3 3 3 3 3 16 2 2 2 2 2 2 19 19 19 19 19 19 19 19 19 19 19 19 19 19 11 25 26 26	12
24 Alessandro Nannini	2 2 2 2 24 24 3 3 3 3 3 3 3 3 2 3 3 3 16 16 16 16 16 9 9 9 8 8 8 8 8 8 11 11 11 11 11 11 11 11 11 11 11 11 11 25 26 14 14	13
9 Martin Brundle	24 24 24 24 3 3 16 16 16 16 16 2 2 2 3 16 16 16 9 9 9 9 9 2 2 11 11 11 11 11 30 30 30 25 25 25 25 25 25 25 25 25 25 25 25 26 14	14
3 Jonathan Palmer	3 3 3 16 16 16 2 2 2 2 2 16 16 16 9 9 9 8 8 8 8 2 8 30 30 30 30 30 25 25 26 26 26 26 26 26 26 26 26 26 26 14	15
21 Alex Caffi	16 16 16 16 9 9 9 9 9 9 9 9 9 9 9 8 8 8 2 2 2 2 8 8 11 11 25 25 25 26 26 26 14 14 14 14 14 14 14 14 14 14	16
11 Satoru Nakajima	9 9 9 9 8 8 8 8 8 8 8 8 8 8 2 2 2 1 11 11 11 11 11 11 25 25 26 26 26 26 26 14 14 14	17
30 Philippe Alliot	8 8 8 8 4 4 4 4 30 30 30 11 11 11 11 11 11 11 25 25 25 25 25 25 30 30 14 14 14 14 14 21 7 7	18
16 Ivan Capelli	4 4 4 4 30 30 30 30 11 11 11 11 14 14 14 14 26 25 25 26 30 30 30 26 26 26 21 21 21 21 21 7	19
26 Piercarlo Ghinzani	14 14 14 30 30 14 14 14 11 14 14 14 26 26 26 26 14 25 26 30 30 30 26 26 26 14 14 7 7 7 7 7	20
8 Andrea de Cesaris	30 30 30 14 14 11 11 11 11 11 26 26 26 26 25 25 25 25 14 30 14 14 14 14 14 14 14	21
25 Rene Arnoux	11 11 11 11 11 26 26 26 26 25 25 25 30 30 30 30 30 30 14	22
4 Philippe Streiff	26 26 26 26 25 25 25 25	23
23 Adrian Campos	25 25 25 25 25	24
14 Pascal Fabre		25

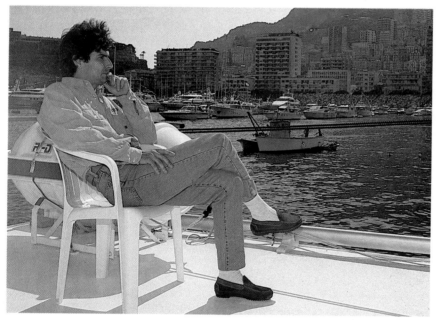

Lap Chart continued

Laps 62–78 →	Pos
12 12 12 12 12 12 12 12 12 12 12 12 12 12 12 12 12	1
6 6 6 6 6 6 6 6 6 6 6 6 6 6 6 6 6	2
1 1 1 1 1 1 1 1 1 1 1 1 1 1 27 27 27	3
27 27 27 27 27 27 27 27 27 27 27 27 27 27 28 28	4
28 28 28 28 28 28 28 28 28 28 28 28 28 3	5
3 3 3 3 3 3 3 3 3 3 3 3 3 16	6
16 16 16 16 16 16 16 16 16 16 16 16 16 9	7
9 9 9 9 9 9 9 9 9 9 9 9 9 19	8
19 19 19 19 19 19 19 19 19 19 19 19 19	9
11 11 11 11 11 11 11 11 11 11 11 11 11 11	10
25 25 25 25 25 25 25 25 25 25 25 25	11
26 26 26 26 26 26 26 26 26 26 26 26	12
14 14 14 14 14 14 14 14 14 14	13

Championship Points

	Drivers			Constructors	
1	Alain Prost	18 pts	1	McLaren	31 pts
2	Ayrton Senna	15 pts	2	Williams	22 pts
3	Stefan Johansson	13 pts	3	Lotus	18 pts
4	Nelson Piquet	12 pts	4	Ferrari	14 pts
5	Nigel Mansell	10 pts	5	Brabham	4 pts
6	Michele Alboreto	8 pts	6	Arrows	3 pts
7	Gerhard Berger	6 pts	7=	Zakspeed	2 pts
8	Andrea de Cesaris	4 pts	7=	Tyrrell	2 pts
9=	Satoru Nakajima	3 pts	7=	Benetton	2 pts
9=	Eddie Cheever	3 pts	10=	March	1 pt
11=	Thierry Boutsen	2 pts	10=	Ligier	1 pt
11=	Martin Brundle	2 pts			
11=	Jonathan Palmer	2 pts			
14=	Rene Arnoux	1 pt			
14=	Ivan Capelli	1 pt			

	Jim Clark Cup			Colin Chapman Cup	
1	Philippe Streiff	21 pts	1	Tyrrell	39 pts
2	Jonathan Palmer	18 pts	2	AGS	16 pts
3	Pascal Fabre	16 pts	3	Lola	15 pts
4	Philippe Alliot	15 pts	4	March	6 pts
5	Ivan Capelli	6 pts			

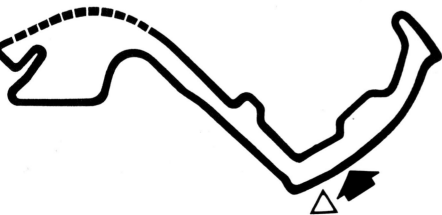

DETROIT
GRAND PRIX

They were waiting in the pits – waiting for Ayrton Senna to make his pit stop. The other drivers had made their tyre stops, where was Senna? Slowly the Lotus mechanics relaxed. Senna never came in. He didn't need new tyres and in retrospect, neither did several others who did stop.

The fifth round of the World Championship should have taken place across the Detroit river, in Canada, but problems arose when rival brewers Molsons and Labbatts disputed a contract that existed with the organisers, and it finally transpired that the actual cancellation of the Canadian race also owed a certain amount to its low standard of facilities. Its replacement, the Detroit Grand Prix, also had somewhat temporary facilities, but since the Australian Grand Prix at Adelaide had set such a high standard as a temporary race circuit, there seemed no reason why facilities shouldn't be as good if not better at the North American circuits. One argument that is frequently put forward is that America must be able to do better than a round-the-houses concrete course which is bumpy and featureless, but Alain Prost was strong in his condemnation of Motown's circuit, although Nigel Mansell decided to praise it and win a few friends.

It isn't just the circuit that's unpopular. The Westin Hotel in the Renaissance Centre and the lack of reasonable restaurants both came in for a hammering. There were various predictions for the weekend's weather, but it started off well enough with a lovely day for first qualifying. This day is free to spectators and excellent promotion for the race, although ultimately, crowd figures were slightly down for the weekend. Lousy race day weather could be blamed for some of that. Saturday started off wet and damp, and it looked unlikely that

Friday's times would be beaten. However it dried up enough for all the fast times to be set on Saturday afternoon.

Detroit was a mirror image of Monaco in many ways. Just as Nigel Mansell dominated Monaco at various junctures, so he also dominated Detroit. Of the five practice and qualifying sessions prior to the race, he was quickest in four of them and that included the all-important Saturday afternoon timed session which gave him his fourth pole position in five races. Although he was complimentary about the track, the Williams-Honda team did run the car so low that it ripped its bottom on a manhole cover in one session, and in the vital qualifying session, the car broke fifth gear on a bump. Mansell was effusive in his praise for the marshals when he had a spin in another session and they got him going again. A private worry on Saturday night was that he had had a cramp in one leg during the day. "Must be a salt deficiency", he told himself. Mansell was surprised that he had quite such a margin over his nearest challenger, Ayrton Senna. After all, there was 1.4 seconds between Williams-Honda and Lotus-Honda in qualifying. Senna, of course, was winner of the last Detroit Grand Prix – never twice won by the same manufacturer – and winner of the previous Grand Prix in Monaco – the man was on form.

Interestingly, Senna's main pre-occupation was with the physical demands of

the Detroit race in a heat of up to 90°F. When he discovered heat coming into his race car, that was a worry. Senna was quickest in the one session in which Mansell wasn't top. Nelson Piquet maintained the Brazilian and Honda challenge in third spot on the grid, but lost a nose section out on the track. He also had problems with third gear, although he finally found some reasonable grip. But he didn't share his team mate's enthusiasm for the circuit. Detroit was as bad as Monaco as far as Piquet was concerned, and the sooner the two of them were out of the way the better. For Thierry Boutsen, Detroit was very different from Monaco which is, of course, his own base, Detroit was the base of his engine suppliers, Ford, and there was plenty of socialising, including a press party at Ford's superb museum, and a rather more private but equally good party at Ford competitions director, Mike Kranefuss', house. But there was another reason for the difference. Since Monaco, Cosworth had found a means of drastically limiting the previously disastrous turbo lag. Boutsen was generous in his praise of the new turbo set-up and it got him onto fourth spot on the grid. A broken driveshaft on Saturday morning proved a worry but the vital qualifying session was more perturbing – he had a bad misfire and missed four shifts on his quick lap due to a recalcitrant gearbox and there was a problem with the turbo regulator. What he could have done without his problems!

Indeed what could Alain Prost have done with different tyres? His weren't warming up sufficiently, and the World Champion's weekend of misery was compounded by positions of seventh, ninth and seventh prior to final qualifying. But with around 150 litres of fuel on board (most others used about 40), he finally got his temperatures and qualified fifth.

If Benetton-Ford felt at home in America, so too did the Arrows team, for their sponsors USF&G come from Detroit. Eddie Cheever brought a smile to their faces with sixth spot on the grid, although he didn't achieve it without problems either. The Ferraris had a fair following in Detroit and had developed their management systems and differentials. But their qualifying was dramatic; with a five cylinder engine for Alboreto and a brush with the wall for Berger. On Friday they were fifth and eighth. On Sunday they were seventh and twelfth. Behind Fabi, unwell on Friday and not a street circuit enthusiast, came Patrese, keeping up his team's sense of humour which was wearing a little thin as they dealt with a succession of motor cars broken by his team mate. Derek

Warwick was another who was unwell, although he achieved sixth in poor health, and only tenth in good. Johansson suffered the McLaren malaise while the Tyrrell duo were looking forward to a final move on World Championship points before the faster circuits in theory confined their sights to Clark and Chapman Cup battles.

The Zakspeed duo also had their problems, Brundle suffered an engine fire before hitting the wall, and needed the spare 861 for the rest of the weekend. Behind de Cesaris, Nannini had been going well until the final session when both he and team mate Campos suffered gearbox trouble. Alex Caffi also had an engine fire in the Osella, while Philippe Alliot shunted on cold tyres. The Ligiers were in disastrous shape in spite of new rear bodywork and Capelli suffered with an overheated engine. Nakajima never really got into the swing of things, and Pascal Fabre brought up the tail end of the grid as usual, although he hit the barrier in the warm-up. And race day's warm-up was miserable. Even the top of the sixty-floor RenCen was in cloud. Everyone was pleased when it cleared up for the race itself, although it was still

warm and muggy and there was only a brief respite from the rain.

Once again, the race was a Mansell/Senna benefit. They had already opened up a gap from the rest within a couple of laps, and indeed, even Mansell was drawing away from Senna at the rate of a second a lap. By lap six, they were more than 15 seconds ahead of the third man. But while Mansell and Senna were drawing away from the rest at a prodigious rate, this was no battle for the lead. Mansell was once more in a class of his own. He had pulled out a lead of more than 18 seconds by lap 17. There was good reason for this, Senna had found he had a soft brake pedal a few laps in and that brought back memories of hitting the wall. So he cut his pace to get the brakes back. Just after the 20 lap mark, with a lighter fuel load, Senna was able to force the pace again. On lap 23, the gap was 22 seconds, on lap 25, it was down to 16.7s. In five laps or so, the tyre stops would begin. In fact the first of the front runners to pit was Berger, holding fourth, and a lap later Mansell was in for new tyres. Three wheels were changed in immaculate order but the rear right picked up a thread and 18 seconds had elapsed before the Williams-Honda screamed back into the race.

Mansell was now in third, behind Senna and Prost, but he caught Prost up on his new tyres on lap 37. Even so, Mansell was some 23 seconds behind Senna. But even as Prost pitted for new tyres, Senna was posting quicker times on his old tyres than Mansell was on his new tyres. Prost hadn't wanted to come in for new tyres, and thought that his team management must have misunderstood him, when they called him in anyway. Senna's pit crew relaxed when they realised he wasn't coming in. "We were scheduled to stop," he said later, "but when it was obvious that we were running at just as good a pace as the others, we decided against it. It was a gamble. Furthermore, my brake problems had caused me to ease up early on and that meant that I'd conserved my tyres. My only worry was lack of rubber, but in the end there was nothing to worry about."

The yellow Camel Lotus-Honda cruised home to a good, relaxed win, some 33 seconds ahead of the next man. With Mansell stopping for tyres, and most of the other front runners too, suddenly second place was more competitive. Behind the first two, there had been a huge battle for third place in the early stages: Piquet leading Cheever, Fabi, Alboreto, Prost, Boutsen, Berger, Warwick, Johansson and then a gap to Palmer, Patrese and the rest. Cheever's pressure then caused Piquet to run wide on lap three and he picked up a puncture requiring a quick stop. Piquet rejoined 18th. Cheever now led the pack disputing third, but then Fabi tried to get by in turn three. Too late he realised that he hadn't quite made it, and locked his brakes. Cheever came across on the line and wiped off the Benetton nose section, at the same time puncturing a tyre on the Arrows. Both headed for the pits where Fabi retired as a new nose couldn't be made to fit, and Cheever rejoined 19th.

Now Alboreto was in third, challenged by Boutsen, while Prost and Berger watched, as did Johansson. Warwick had been involved too but slid wide and thumped a wall. Damage to the driveshaft resulted in retirement. Johansson was also delayed with a misfire. A lengthy pit stop saw his management system replaced but it cost him dearly. Boutsen's challenge of Alboreto lasted until lap 14 before he found his place threatened by Prost and Berger who were coming up behind. The Belgian's Benetton was badly afflicted: he had lost his brakes, but he struggled

on, then the gear linkage came loose when he was in fifth gear, he lost his clutch and eventually a brake disc exploded. By lap 22, he was out of the running for third place. Alboreto, challenged by Prost, was also in gearbox trouble and he had slipped behind both Prost and Berger by lap 25, retiring one lap later. Prost held third place and was pulling away from Berger.

Who should now re-emerge but Piquet, driving hard and well through the field and finding himself ahead of Berger and lying fourth when the Austrian pitted for new tyres? After Prost pitted, the three found themselves running nose to tail. While Senna had pulled away to score his second victory, Mansell's lap times suddenly became more erratic, varying by some six seconds. The man himself was suffering from cramp again in his right leg. Every time he passed the pits, he wanted to come in, but his typical gritty willpower dictated that he stay out. However, on lap 52, he was caught by Piquet and Prost and suddenly Mansell was knocked down to fourth place. Berger got by three laps later, and now Mansell was fifth. His team mate, meanwhile, was cruising to an excellent second place after his earlier hitches. Prost admitted that he might have had a go at Piquet, but for difficulty with his gear shifts from third to fourth and fourth to fifth, and the fact that he was

feeling tired. Berger was the last man on the same lap.

Behind them came Mansell, a lap down, and Cheever, out of fuel and two more laps down, but still the final point-winner. Johansson was out of the points as were Danner, Patrese and the still troubled Ligier team. Best of the normally aspirated bunch was Jonathan Palmer, even though he had to have a front link replaced after a spinning Patrese had knocked into him. Everyone was pleased to leave Detroit with whatever points they could get, and there weren't too many damaged cars either. After it was all over, a tornado struck the outlying area, and the rain bucketed down. The most irritating effect of this was that the London flight had to wait on the tarmac for two hours before it was safe to leave.

Right: Practice in down-
town Detroit, not the
most popular of Grand
Prix circuits but still
providing spectacle

Left: Prost in concrete. In spite of gear selection problems he finished a contented third: "now for the Championship"

Centre left: Piquet looks pensive as team mate Mansell passes

Centre right: Philippe Alliot was battling with Arnoux when he hit the wall and retired

Below: When it rains it pours: Brundle prepares to go out onto Detroit's soaking streets

Senna and Boutsen: varying fortunes. Senna didn't make a pit stop and won. Boutsen made two and retired with an exploded brake disc

107

108

Left: Senna and Mr Senna Senior discuss tactics

Far left: The Lotus lads had a quiet race – Senna didn't stop for tyres

Below left: Alboreto leads the battle for fifth place in the early stages, ahead of Prost, Boutsen, Berger, Warwick and Johansson

Below right: Cheever finished sixth for Arrows in his 'home' Grand Prix

DETROIT GRAND PRIX · June 21

Entries and Practice Times

Cos=Cosworth
Ch=Champion
Win=Wintershall
McL=McLaren
Mar=Marelli
Bra=Brabham
Bre=Brembo
Bil=Bilstein
L/A=Lotus Active
Marz=Marzocchi

Driver	Nat.	Car	Practice 1	Practice 2	Warm Up	Engine	Turbos	Electrics/Plugs	Fuel/Oil	Brake Discs/Calipers	Shocks
1 Alain Prost	F	Marlboro McLaren MP4/3	1m46.042s	**1m42.357s**	2m11.004s	1.5t TAG V6	KKK	Bosch	Shell	SEP/McL	Bil
2 Stefan Johansson	S	Marlboro McLaren MP4/3	1m46.623s	**1m43.797s**	2m14.108s	1.5t TAG V6	KKK	Bosch	Shell	SEP/McL	Bil
3 Jonathan Palmer	GB	Data General/Courtaulds Tyrrell DG/016	1m47.010s	**1m44.350s**	2m10.875s	3.5 Ford Cosworth DFZ V8		Cos/Ch	Elf	AP	Koni
4 Philippe Streiff	F	Data General/Courtaulds Tyrrell DG/016	1m47.963s	**1m45.037s**	2m14.048s	3.5 Ford Cosworth DFZ V8		Cos/Ch	Elf	AP	Koni
5 Nigel Mansell	GB	Canon Williams FW11B	1m42.223s	**1m39.264s**	2m08.593s	1.5t Honda V6	IHI	Honda/NGK	Mobil	SEP/AP	Showa
6 Nelson Piquet	BR	Canon Williams FW11B	1m43.152s	**1m40.942s**	2m10.638s	1.5t Honda V6	IHI	Honda/NGK	Mobil	SEP/AP	Showa
7 Riccardo Patrese	I	Brabham BT56	1m46.932s	**1m43.479s**	2m17.850s	1.5t BMW S4	Garrett	Bosch/Ch	Win/Castrol	SEP/Bra	Koni
8 Andrea de Cesaris	I	Brabham BT56	1m47.670s	**1m46.046s**	2m15.931s	1.5t BMW S4	Garrett	Bosch/Ch	Win/Castrol	SEP/Bra	Koni
9 Martin Brundle	GB	West Zakspeed 861*	1m48.932s	**1m45.291s**	2m12.441s	1.5t Zakspeed S4	Garrett	Bosch/Ch	Win/Castrol	AP	Sachs
10 Christian Danner	D	West Zakspeed 871	1m48.867s	**1m45.740s**	2m23.912s	1.5t Zakspeed S4	Garrett	Bosch/Ch	Win/Castrol	AP	Sachs
11 Satoru Nakajima	J	Camel Lotus 99T	1m51.355s	**1m48.801s**	2m12.402s	1.5t Honda V6	IHI	Honda/NGK	Elf	SEP/Bre	L/A
12 Ayrton Senna	BR	Camel Lotus 99T	1m42.985s	**1m40.607s**	2m12.734s	1.5t Honda V6	IHI	Honda/NGK	Elf	SEP/Bre	L/A
14 Pascal Fabre	F	El Charro AGS JH22C	1m57.475s	**1m53.644s**	2m26.634s	3.5 Ford Cosworth DFZ V8		Cos/Ch	Acto	SEP/AGS	Koni
16 Ivan Capelli	I	Leyton House March 871	1m49.969s	**1m46.269s**	2m13.914s	3.5 Ford Cosworth DFZ V8		Cos/Ch	BP	AP	Koni
17 Derek Warwick	GB	USF&G Arrows A10	1m45.234s	**1m43.541s**	2m10.231s	1.5t Megatron S4	Garrett	Bosch/Ch	Win/Castrol	AP	Koni
18 Eddie Cheever	USA	USF&G Arrows A10	1m45.296s	**1m42.361s**	2m13.647s	1.5t Megatron S4	Garrett	Bosch/Ch	Win/Castrol	AP	Koni
19 Teo Fabi	I	Benetton B187	1m47.064s	**1m42.918s**	2m17.446s	1.5t Ford V6	Garrett	Ford EED/Ch	Mobil	SEP/AP	Koni
20 Thierry Boutsen	B	Benetton B187	1m44.686s	**1m42.050s**	2m12.476s	1.5t Ford V6	Garrett	Ford EED/Ch	Mobil	SEP/AP	Koni
21 Alex Caffi	I	Landis & Gyr Osella FA1I	1m55.787s	**1m46.124s**	†	1.5t Alfa Romeo V8	KKK	Mar/Ch	Agip	Bre	Koni
23 Adrian Campos	E	Minardi M186	**1m50.495s**	3m26.319s	2m19.299s	1.5t Motori Moderni V6	KKK	Mar/Ch	Agip	Bre	Koni
24 Alessandro Nannini	I	Minardi M186	1m46.449s	**1m46.083s**	2m11.514s	1.5t Motori Moderni V6	KKK	Mar/Ch	Agip	Bre	Koni
25 Rene Arnoux	F	Loto Ligier JS29B	1m48.338s	**1m46.211s**	2m14.375s	1.5t Megatron S4	Garrett	Bosch/Ch	Win/Castrol	SEP/Bre	Koni
26 Piercarlo Ghinzani	I	Loto Ligier JS29B	1m48.661s	**1m47.471s**	2m13.648s	1.5t Megatron S4	Garrett	Bosch/Ch	Win/Castrol	SEP/Bre	Koni
27 Michele Alboreto	I	Ferrari F187	1m45.437s	**1m42.684s**	2m13.334s	1.5t Ferrari V6	Garrett	Mar-Weber/Ch	Agip	SEP/Bre	Marz
28 Gerhard Berger	A	Ferrari F187	1m45.054s	**1m43.816s**	2m11.344s	1.5t Ferrari V6	Garrett	Mar-Weber/Ch	Agip	SEP/Bre	Marz
30 Philippe Alliot	F	Larrousse Lola LC87	1m47.470s	**1m46.194s**	2m11.606s	3.5 Ford Cosworth DFZ V8		Cos-Mar/Ch	BP	SEP/AP	Koni

*Note: Brundle raced in car 861, although he practised in 871.
†Caffi did not warm up on day of race.

June 19	June 20	June 21
Sunny/hot	Dry/overcast	Damp

Starting Grid

Mansell	5	12	Senna
Piquet	6	20	Boutsen
Prost	1	18	Cheever
Alboreto	27	19	Fabi
Patrese	7	17	Warwick
Johansson	2	28	Berger
Palmer	3	4	Streiff
Brundle	9	10	Danner
de Cesaris	8	24	Nannini
Caffi	21	30	Alliot
Arnoux	25	16	Capelli
Ghinzani	26	11	Nakajima
Campos	23	14	Fabre

Results, Retirements and Fastest Laps

Place	Driver	Car	Laps	Time/Retirement	Fastest Lap No./Time	
1	Ayrton Senna	1.5t Lotus-Honda 99T	63	1h50m16.358s	39	1m40.464s
2	Nelson Piquet	1.5t Williams-Honda FW11B	63	1h50m50.177s	57	1m41.196s
3	Alain Prost	1.5t McLaren-TAG MP4/3	63	1h51m01.685s	56	1m41.340s
4	Gerhard Berger	1.5t Ferrari-Spa F187	63	1h51m18.959s	46	1m42.238s
5	Nigel Mansell	1.5t Williams-Honda FW11B	62	1h50m34.832s	36	1m40.535s
6	Eddie Cheever	1.5t Arrows-Megatron A10	60	1h48m58.338s Out of Fuel	35	1m43.951s
7	Stefan Johansson	1.5t McLaren-TAG MP4/3	60	1h50m16.597s	53	1m42.332s
8	Christian Danner	1.5t Zakspeed 871	60	1h50m40.144s	38	1m47.532s
9	Riccardo Patrese	1.5t Brabham-BMW BT56	60	1h50m57.292s	46	1m44.255s
10	Rene Arnoux	1.5t Ligier-Megatron JS29B	60	1h51m08.353s	38	1m46.937s
11	Jonathan Palmer	3.5 Tyrrell-Ford DG/016	60	1h51m27.149s	41	1m44.048s
12	Pascal Fabre	3.5 AGS-Ford JH22C	58	1h50m43.574s	32	1m50.309s
	Thierry Boutsen	1.5t Benetton-Ford B187	52	Brake Disc	41	1m42.252s
	Piercarlo Ghinzani	1.5t Ligier-Megatron JS29B	51	Not classified	21	1m47.477s
	Philippe Streiff	3.5 Tyrrell-Ford DG/016	44	Lost Wheel/sheered wheel nuts	35	1m46.048s
	Philippe Alliot	3.5 Lola LC87	38	Accident	33	1m45.869s
	Michele Alboreto	1.5t Ferrari-Spa F187	25	Gearbox	19	1m45.016s
	Alessandro Nannini	1.5t Minardi-Motori Moderni M186	22	Engine	13	1m47.069s
	Martin Brundle	1.5t Zakspeed 861	16	Turbo	14	1m48.744s
	Derek Warwick	1.5t Arrows-Megatron A10	12	Accident	11	1m47.260s
	Ivan Capelli	3.5 March-Ford 871	9	Electrical misfire	5	1m49.341s
	Teo Fabi	1.5t Benetton-Ford B187	6	Collision/Cheever	4	1m48.325s
	Alex Caffi	1.5t Osella-Alfa Romeo FA1I	3	Gearbox	2	1m53.496s
	Andrea de Cesaris	1.5t Brabham-BMW BT56	2	Gearbox	2	1m53.860s
	Adrian Campos	1.5t Minardi-Motori Moderni M186	1	Collision/Nakajima	1	2m16.237s
	Satoru Nakajima	1.5t Lotus-Honda 99T	0	Accident/Campos	–	–

Average Speed of Winner: 137.912 km/h, 85.697 mph
Fastest Lap: Ayrton Senna on Lap 39, 1m40.464s, 144.167 km/h, 89.584 mph (record)
Previous Lap Record: Nelson Piquet (1.5t Williams-Honda FW11), 1m41.233s, 143.077 km/h, 88.904 mph (1986)

Circuit Data

Detroit Grand Prix, Detroit, USA
Circuit Length: 4.023 km/2.5 miles
Race Distance: 63 laps, 253.472 km/157.500 miles
Race Weather: Warm/muggy

Past Winners

Year	Driver	Nat.	Car	Circuit	Distance miles/km	Speed mph/km/h
1982	John Watson	GB	3.0 McLaren-Ford MP4B	Detroit	154.57/248.75	78.20/128.85
1983	Michele Alboreto	I	3.0 Tyrrell-Ford 011	Detroit	150.00/241.40	81.16/130.61
1984	Nelson Piquet	BR	1.5 Brabham/BMW BT53 t/c	Detroit	157.50/253.47	81.68/131.45
1985	Keke Rosberg	SF	1.5 Williams-Honda FW10 t/c	Detroit	157.50/253.47	81.70/131.48
1986	Ayrton Senna	BR	1.5 Lotus Renault 98T	Detroit	157.50/253.47	84.97/136.75

Grid Order	1	2	3	4	5	6	7	8	9	10	11	12	13	14	15	16	17	18	19	20	21	22	23	24	25	26	27	28	29	30	31	32	33	34	35	36	37	38	39	40	41	42	43	44	45	46	47	48	49	50	51	52	53	Pos
5 Nigel Mansell	5	5	5	5	5	5	5	5	5	5	5	5	5	5	5	5	5	5	5	5	5	5	5	5	5	5	5	5	5	5	5	5	5	5	12	12	12	12	12	12	12	12	12	12	12	12	12	12	12	12	12	12	12	1
12 Ayrton Senna	12	12	12	12	12	12	12	12	12	12	12	12	12	12	12	12	12	12	12	12	12	12	12	12	12	5	1	1	5	5	5	5	5	5	5	5	5	5	5	5	5	5	5	5	5	5	5	5	5	5	5	5	6	2
6 Nelson Piquet	6	6	18	18	18	18	27	27	27	27	27	27	27	27	27	27	27	27	27	27	27	1	1	1	1	1	1	1	1	1	1	1	1	5	5	1	1	1	1	1	1	6	6	6	6	6	6	6	6	6	6	6	1	3
20 Thierry Boutsen	18	18	19	19	19	19	20	20	20	20	20	20	20	20	20	20	20	1	1	1	1	1	1	28	28	28	28	28	28	28	28	6	6	6	6	6	6	6	6	6	6	6	1	1	1	1	1	1	1	1	1	1	5	4
1 Alain Prost	19	19	27	27	27	27	1	1	1	1	1	1	1	1	1	1	1	1	20	20	28	28	28	28	28	27	20	6	6	6	6	6	6	28	28	28	28	28	28	28	28	28	28	28	28	28	28	28	28	28	28	28	28	5
18 Eddie Cheever	27	27	1	1	1	1	28	28	28	28	28	28	28	28	28	28	28	28	20	20	20	20	6	20	20	20	20	20	20	20	20	20	20	20	20	20	20	20	20	20	4	18	18	18	18	18	18	18	18	18	18	18	18	6
27 Michele Alboreto	1	1	20	20	20	20	17	2	2	2	2	2	2	2	2	2	6	6	6	6	6	6	6	6	7	7	7	7	4	4	4	4	4	4	4	4	4	4	4	4	4	4	18	4	20	20	20	20	20	20	20	20	10	7
19 Teo Fabi	20	20	28	28	28	28	2	17	17	17	7	7	7	7	7	7	7	7	7	7	7	7	7	4	4	4	7	7	7	7	18	18	18	18	18	18	18	20	20	10	10	10	10	10	10	10	10	10	7					8
7 Riccardo Patrese	28	28	17	17	17	17	7	7	7	7	6	6	6	6	24	4	4	4	4	4	4	4	10	10	10	18	18	18	10	10	10	10	10	10	10	10	10	10	25	25	25	25	25	25	25	25	7	25	9					9
17 Derek Warwick	17	17	2	2	2	2	9	9	24	6	24	24	24	24	4	24	10	10	10	10	10	10	10	18	18	18	18	10	10	10	25	25	25	25	25	25	25	25	7	7	7	7	7	7	7	25	2							10
2 Stefan Johansson	2	2	7	7	3	7	4	24	24	4	24	4	4	4	4	10	10	24	24	24	25	25	18	18	25	25	25	25	25	25	30	30	30	30	30	7	7	7	7	7	2	2	2	2	2	2	2	3						11
28 Gerhard Berger	3	3	3	3	7	9	24	4	4	6	4	9	9	9	9	10	25	25	25	25	25	30	18	25	25	30	30	30	30	30	30	30	30	30	7	7	7	7	7	2	2	2	2	2	3	3	3	3	3	3	3	14		12
3 Jonathan Palmer	7	7	9	9	9	4	10	6	6	9	9	10	10	10	10	25	30	30	30	30	30	18	30	30	30	14	14	14	14	14	14	14	14	14	2	2	2	3	3	3	3	3	3	14	14	14	14	14	14	14	14			13
4 Philippe Streiff	9	9	4	4	4	24	6	10	10	10	10	25	25	25	25	30	18	18	18	18	18	24	14	14	14	2	2	2	2	2	2	2	2	2	3	3	3	14	14	14	14	14	26	26	26	26	26	26						14
9 Martin Brundle	4	4	24	24	24	10	25	25	25	25	30	30	30	30	18	14	14	14	14	14	3	2	2	3	3	3	3	3	3	3	3	3	14	14	14	26	26	26	26	26														15
10 Christian Danner	8	8	25	25	25	25	30	30	30	30	14	14	18	18	14	2	3	3	3	3	2	3	26	26	26	26	26	26	26	26	26	26	26	26																				16
8 Andrea de Cesaris	24	24	10	10	10	30	16	16	14	14	14	18	18	14	14	9	3	2	2	2	2	2	26	26	26																													17
24 Alessandro Nannini	10	10	6	30	30	6	14	14	16	18	18	3	3	3	3	26	26	26	26	26																																		18
21 Alex Caffi	25	25	26	16	16	16	18	18	18	3	3	26	26	26	26	26																																						19
30 Philippe Alliot	26	26	30	26	6	14	26	26	26	26	26	17																																									20
25 Rene Arnoux	30	30	16	6	14	26	3	3	3																																													21
16 Ivan Capelli	16	16	21	14	26	3																																																22
26 Piercarlo Ghinzani	21	21	14																																																			23
11 Satoru Nakajima	14	14																																																				24
23 Adrian Campos	23																																																					25
14 Pascal Fabre																																																						26

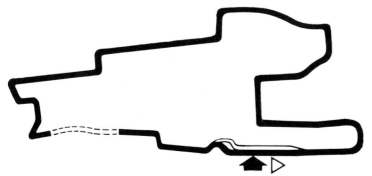

Lap Chart continued

	54	55	56	57	58	59	60	61	62	63	Pos
	12	12	12	12	12	12	12	12	12	12	1
	6	6	6	6	6	6	6	6	6		2
	1	1	1	1	1	1	1	1	1	1	3
	5	5	28	28	28	28	28	28	28		4
	28	28	5	5	5	5	5	5			5
	18	18	18	18	18	18	18				6
	10	10	10	10	2	2	2				7
	2	2	2	2	10	10	10				8
	7	7	7	7	7	7					9
	25	25	25	25	25	25	25				10
	3	3	3	3	3	3					11
	14	14	14	14	14						12

Championship Points

	Drivers			Constructors	
1	Ayrton Senna	24 pts	1	McLaren	35 pts
2	Alain Prost	22 pts	2	Williams	30 pts
3	Nelson Piquet	18 pts	3	Lotus	27 pts
4	Stefan Johansson	13 pts	4	Ferrari	17 pts
5	Nigel Mansell	12 pts	5=	Arrows	4 pts
6	Gerhard Berger	9 pts	5=	Brabham	4 pts
7	Michele Alboreto	8 pts	7=	Zakspeed	2 pts
8=	Andrea de Cesaris	4 pts	7=	Tyrrell	2 pts
8=	Eddie Cheever	4 pts	7=	Benetton	2 pts
10	Satoru Nakajima	3 pts	10=	March	1 pt
11=	Thierry Boutsen	2 pts	10=	Ligier	1 pt
11=	Martin Brundle	2 pts			
11=	Jonathan Palmer	2 pts			
14=	Rene Arnoux	1 pt			
14=	Ivan Capelli	1 pt			

	Jim Clark Cup			Colin Chapman Cup	
1	Philippe Streiff	21 pts	1	Tyrrell	39 pts
2=	Jonathan Palmer	18 pts	2	AGS	18 pts
2=	Pascal Fabre	18 pts	3	Lola	15 pts
4	Philippe Alliot	15 pts			

FRENCH

GRAND PRIX

The result of the excellent French Grand Prix made the World Championship even more closely contested. Winner Nigel Mansell moved up from fifth to fourth, Nelson Piquet narrowed the gap with the leading pair to take third place, and Alain Prost moved a point nearer to series leader Ayrton Senna.

Everyone was looking forward to the French Grand Prix, particularly the reigning World Champion Prost who said after the Detroit Grand Prix, "now the Championship can really begin". He then had the pleasant surprise of starting on the front row of the grid for the first time in seven races, alongside Nigel Mansell. But while Prost was able to hang onto the two Williamses ahead of him for much of the first half of the race, he was already a worried man. His car had been misfiring. Now it began to lose power. Prost turned down the boost and settled for third place, unhappy that his car had been unreliable. The fact that team mate Stefan Johansson had retired with a broken alternator belt compounded his worry. With five races in seven weeks to come, this was not the time to hit problems. Prost hoped that the French Grand Prix would not be a pointer for the next races.

Ayrton Senna simply hadn't been able to hang on to Prost at all. He'd been third on the grid and found himself in fourth spot as Piquet charged up to second place on the first lap. The Lotus driver remained part of the leading bunch until they began to lap slower cars. Then he and Boutsen became detached from the trio of the Williamses and Prost. Senna was left to struggle with the Benetton driver as the Williamses and McLaren pulled away. Lotus active suspension, it seemed, didn't work as well on these conventional circuits as it did in the streets, and it wasn't a good stage in the

season to discover that. Regrettably, there were other difficulties to confront. Even though Teo Fabi finished fifth for Benetton, the lack of Benetton reliability was still apparent as Teo's car limped round the final lap with broken transmission. Boutsen's had been more competitive but he had to retire with broken electrics, and practice had been "busy" as one team member put it, adding, "at least the hire car's OK at the moment!"

Similarly, Arrows were competitive once more, but again suffered the odd problem although Cheever's retirement with electrical failure couldn't be blamed on the team. However, the team had worked on its fuel consumption in testing and one engineer reported, "We learned an incredible amount here." Both Tyrrell and Zakspeed found that their cars were slow in a straight line. "We've come up against a bit of a barrier," said Martin Brundle. "Other cars are coming past us as though we're on our slowing down lap and it's not as though we're bundles quicker than them in the corners. This is where you really find out where your underbody works. When you take a wing off to reduce drag, you shouldn't have to trade off handling if it works well." In the normally aspirated Jim Clark Cup, the Tyrrells were outclassed due to their low straightline speed. Capelli's March looked the best almost throughout, although Alliot's Lola was also on form. March lost their spare chassis when the quick-lift jack broke on Friday evening

and the car crashed to the ground, fortunately without injuring anyone. Luckily they didn't need the spare for the rest of the weekend.

Added to these various problems was an abrasive surface, and the weather provided variety as well. After two days of gorgeous weather leading up to the first day of qualifying, it was overcast as the cars went out onto the track. In fact the clouds turned away and although there were one or two improvements later in the session, everyone said that next day the track would be quicker. It was for a few but not for many. In Nigel Mansell's case, his opening quick lap on Friday turned out to be good enough for pole position. Thereafter, he'd gone race testing, putting in a valuable half hour on full tanks.

Prost was happy to be back at home, where his career really started when he won the Volant Elf back in 1975. He felt that he had a better race chassis than Mansell, and Mansell agreed. But Prost had a problem with one chassis in Friday's timed practice when a brake locked, and he quickly hopped into the second car to set his time. Eventually, it was Senna who put his Lotus third on the grid, although he and team mate Satoru Nakajima did have various problems – the Japanese driver only making progress during the final qualifying session which he ended in 16th spot. Senna, meanwhile, was delayed by a transmission check, and later by an engine that misfired so drastically that he actually switched it off. Piquet and Senna shared row two to make it an all-Brazil row, both set their times in the slower session.

Boutsen and Fabi lined up behind Mansell and Senna on the third and fourth rows, both setting their times on the Friday. But it was a fairly dramatic two days for both Benetton-Ford drivers, with a variety of engine, transmission and turbo problems. Opposite the Benetton men were the two Ferraris of Berger and Alboreto, the Austrian complaining of the dreaded understeer which many drivers suffered, partially because of the surface, partially because Goodyear had produced some very efficient new rears which tended to 'push' the fronts. Johansson and Warwick completed the top ten, the Arrows driver having set a quicker time in unofficial practice. Both he and team mate Cheever suffered a variety of niggling problems, the two of them sandwiching the Brabham-BMW pair of de Cesaris and Patrese and Rene Arnoux's Ligier. De Cesaris had his usual share of incidents, while Patrese had one or two problems as he celebrated his 150th Grand Prix. Much improved was Rene Arnoux's Ligier with its new rear bodywork, which the Frenchman said felt less heavy.

It took three hours for spectators to get into the circuit on Sunday, and they were still arriving as the cars formed up on the grid for the relatively early 1.30 pm start. One or two people admitted that there would, almost certainly, be a bigger crowd than ever, although it felt like a club meeting in the paddock during practice. And when it was all over, the traffic arrangements were superb. But in between, there was a great French Grand Prix. Like every session of practice and qualifying, and the warm-up, it was dominated by one man, Nigel Mansell. In spite of already being in pole position, Mansell went out during the second, slower qualifying session and was the only man to lap in the 1m 0.6s bracket. Then he was quickest in the warm-up too. And when the lights turned green on the sunny Sunday, it was Mansell who scorched into the lead. Piquet rapidly pushed Prost back to third and Senna quickly slotted into fourth place ahead of the Benetton duo Boutsen and Fabi and then the two Brabhams. Berger made an appalling start, while Alboreto found himself battling with Patrese, Arnoux and Warwick. Nannini was doing a good job of sticking with them. Cheever was soon out and so was de Cesaris. First of all he ran over Johansson's front wing at the first corner which necessitated an early

stop for the Swede, and then a piece came out of the Brabham-BMW's engine. All the oil spilled out and ignited a very lively conflagration.

At first the lead group comprised Mansell, Piquet, Prost, Senna, Boutsen and Fabi, but when they started lapping, Senna and the Benettons began to drop away. Mansell was never able to pull away much, however. He'd picked up a bit of Johansson's front wing on his, and it was causing pretty nasty understeer. Mansell wanted to pit, but knew that if he did so, he would have to pit again later for new tyres, so he just hung on grimly. Consequently, his lead gap was never much more than the 2.7s that he had on lap 10 out of the scheduled 80. Piquet and Prost shadowed him, and things didn't change when the Brazilian half spun at the first corner and Prost nipped into second place on lap 19. Now it was Piquet's turn to sit back and watch the fun as Prost pressured the Englishman. Right up to lap 30, the three of them were rarely more than three seconds apart.

They rapidly opened up a big gap to Senna who still had Boutsen just behind, but Fabi had dropped away. Then there was the big gap to Alboreto who had been penalised a minute for a jumped start. Berger had caught up to eighth,

Previous page: The face of the exhausted winner

Right: After the mid-race pit stops, the two Ferraris found themselves running together in fifth and sixth, until Berger pulled ahead

ahead of the battling duo of Warwick and Arnoux. Nannini and Ghinzani had both retired, Brundle had lost a wheel on the first corner after a tyre stop, so Capelli was next, easily ahead of his normally aspirated rivals after finally managing to get past Danner's Zakspeed. After Mansell's winning two-stop formula the previous year, most people's attitude to the number of tyre stops was, 'wait and see' in 1987. But on lap 30, Piquet made the first scheduled stop and as it was well before half distance, it appeared that he would be making two stops, and as it turned out, that was his strategy. Senna stopped two laps later, Boutsen retired and then Prost came in for a super-quick stop on lap 34. Mansell's was two seconds longer as they flicked away the errant piece of Johansson's wing. Fabi stopped at the same time.

The order was now Piquet, Prost, Mansell. Piquet had managed to lap well with new tyres, when the others were slowing on their fading old tyres and he was almost four seconds ahead of Prost who was quickly being hauled in by Mansell. On lap 38, the Englishman overtook the World Champion and within two laps, was 2.2 seconds in front. Prost faded badly, his engine had been misfiring in the warm-up, and misfired during the opening stages of the race, but now it began to lose power as well. Within another six laps, Mansell had caught Piquet and was sitting on his tail. Then Piquet made his second mistake of the race, running wide in the double

right-hander after Signes, which let Mansell through in a flash. But Piquet latched onto the Englishman's tail and for the next 15 laps, Mansell had no respite from his team mate.

On lap 64, Piquet dived for the pits for his second set of tyres, but this stop was a tardy 15 second effort as the Brazilian stalled the engine. He was now 23 seconds behind his team mate, whose gearknob had come unscrewed. In the final 17 laps, Piquet reduced that lead to 7.7 seconds on his new tyres. One could only speculate on what might have been if he hadn't stalled the engine during the pit stop. The winner was exhausted having been under pressure the whole time. He'd broken his run of bad luck and had won, as he said, at the slowest possible pace, even if that did mean being under pressure for all but the final 17 laps of the race. Williams were delighted with this 1-2 in France, particularly as the very unhappy Prost had turned down his turbo boost and settled for third place. Senna was a disappointed fourth, a lap behind. Berger and Alboreto both passed Fabi when the Benetton driver had to complete one slow lap with a puncture. But then Alboreto went out under pressure from Fabi when his engine gave out. 12 laps from the end, Berger went out when his suspension collapsed.

Fabi was then cruising in for his first points of the Championship when another driveshaft broke. He was able to limp round to cross the start/finish line,

although he wasn't credited with the final lap. Sixth, in these closing stages, was none other than Johansson, having had two more pit stops after replacing his damaged wing, one for a wayward brake duct and the third for new tyres. He inherited sixth place when Berger retired, but with six laps to go, Johansson pulled off with a broken alternator belt. Neither McLaren driver was a happy man after the race. Derek Warwick might have picked up his first point of the season, but his turbo set itself to four bar boost (the maximum allowed by FISA's pop-off valve) and even that proved too much for the turbo which then blew up.

Ivan Capelli had been master of the normally aspirated field in the March but then his engine went, leaving the class to be fought out by the two Tyrrells and Alliot's Lola. The latter disappeared on lap 59 leaving the Tyrrells to fight their own very close battle. But Palmer had worked out a suspension set-up which proved costly to his tyres and it was Streiff who won the normally aspirated class and took the final point for sixth place. Who said normally aspirated cars could only score on street circuits?

The French Grand Prix was the most closely fought of the season so far, with a great battle between the Williams drivers and Prost. But if anyone else was going to get a look-in, they were going to have to work hard. The way the Williamses were going in France was a worry for most of the field.

Right: Fabi struggled
home to finish fifth in
the Benetton in spite of a
broken driveshaft

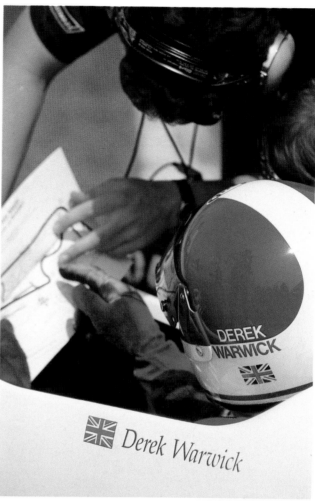

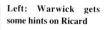

Left: Warwick gets some hints on Ricard

Far left: Piquet slides wide at the first corner. Prost nips up into second place

Centre left: Fabi locks up overtaking Capelli

Below: Warwick looked a potential points winner until retirement 18 laps from the end

Mansell smokes his tyres off the grid ahead of Prost, Senna, Piquet, Boutsen, Berger and Alboreto, who had jumped the start due to a dragging clutch

Left: Mansell, Piquet, Prost: the order for much of the race, but from lap 12 to 17 the first three ran this close. Note the piece of Johansson's wing on Mansell's front wing

Centre: Johansson collided with Campos in practice, damaging the McLaren's front left wheel. Prost looks on disapprovingly

Below: The Tyrrell duet: they were never far apart for most of the race

FRENCH GRAND PRIX · July 5

Entries and Practice Times

Cos=Cosworth
Ch=Champion
Win=Wintershall
McL=McLaren
Mar=Marelli
Bra=Brabham
Bre=Brembo
Bil=Bilstein
L/A=Lotus Active
Marz=Marzocchi

Driver	Nat.	Car	Practice 1	Practice 2	Warm Up	Engine	Turbos	Electrics/Plugs	Fuel/Oil	Brake Discs/Calipers	Shocks
1 Alain Prost	F	Marlboro McLaren MP4/3	1m06.877s	1m07.843s	1m11.075s	1.5t TAG V6	KKK	Bosch	Shell	SEP/McL	Bil
2 Stefan Johansson	S	Marlboro McLaren MP4/3	1m08.577s	1m09.095s	1m11.963s	1.5t TAG V6	KKK	Bosch	Shell	SEP/McL	Bil
3 Jonathan Palmer	GB	Data General/Courtaulds Tyrrell DG/016	1m13.443s	1m13.474s	1m16.393s	3.5 Ford Cosworth DFZ V8		Cos/Ch	Elf	AP	Koni
4 Philippe Streiff	F	Data General/Courtaulds Tyrrell DG/016	1m13.553s	1m13.525s	1m16.641s	3.5 Ford Cosworth DFZ V8		Cos/Ch	Elf	AP	Koni
5 Nigel Mansell	GB	Canon Williams FW11B	1m06.454s	1m06.705s	1m10.224s	1.5t Honda V6	IHI	Honda/NGK	Mobil	SEP/AP	Showa
6 Nelson Piquet	BR	Canon Williams FW11B	1m07.270s	1m07.140s	1m10.689s	1.5t Honda V6	IHI	Honda/NGK	Mobil	SEP/AP	Showa
7 Riccardo Patrese	I	Brabham BT56	1m09.458s	1m08.993s	1m12.226s	1.5t BMW S4	Garrett	Bosch/Ch	Win/Castrol	SEP/Bra	Koni
8 Andrea de Cesaris	I	Brabham BT56	1m09.499s	1m08.949s	1m12.602s	1.5t BMW S4	Garrett	Bosch/Ch	Win/Castrol	SEP/Bra	Koni
9 Martin Brundle	GB	West Zakspeed 871	1m11.451s	1m11.170s	1m13.318s	1.5t Zakspeed S4	Garrett	Bosch/Ch	Win/Castrol	AP	Sachs
10 Christian Danner	D	West Zakspeed 871	1m11.456s	1m11.389s	1m14.769s	1.5t Zakspeed S4	Garrett	Bosch/Ch	Win/Castrol	AP	Sachs
11 Satoru Nakajima	J	Camel Lotus 99T	1m12.268s	1m10.652s	1m13.354s	1.5t Honda V6	IHI	Honda/NGK	Elf	SEP/Bre	L/A
12 Ayrton Senna	BR	Camel Lotus 99T	1m07.303s	1m07.024s	1m10.797s	1.5t Honda V6	IHI	Honda/NGK	Elf	SEP/Bre	L/A
14 Pascal Fabre	F	El Charro AGS JH22C	1m14.699s	1m14.787s	1m17.034s	3.5 Ford Cosworth DFZ V8		Cos/Ch	Acto	SEP/AGS	Koni
16 Ivan Capelli	I	Leyton House March 871	1m13.204s	1m12.654s	1m15.077s	3.5 Ford Cosworth DFZ V8		Cos/Ch	BP	AP	Koni
17 Derek Warwick	GB	USF&G Arrows A10	1m09.256s	1m08.800s	1m12.679s	1.5t Megatron S4	Garrett	Bosch/Ch	Win/Castrol	AP	Koni
18 Eddie Cheever	USA	USF&G Arrows A10	1m09.828s	1m09.869s	1m13.276s	1.5t Megatron S4	Garrett	Bosch/Ch	Win/Castrol	AP	Koni
19 Teo Fabi	I	Benetton B187	1m08.293s	1m11.815s	1m11.369s	1.5t Ford V6	Garrett	Ford EED/Ch	Mobil	SEP/AP	Koni
20 Thierry Boutsen	B	Benetton B187	1m08.077s	1m08.176s	1m11.328s	1.5t Ford V6	Garrett	Ford EED/Ch	Mobil	SEP/AP	Koni
21 Alex Caffi	I	Landis & Gyr Osella FA1I	1m12.167s	1m12.555s	1m16.427s	1.5t Alfa Romeo V8	KKK	Mar/Ch	Agip	Bre	Koni
23 Adrian Campos	E	Minardi M186	1m13.145s	1m12.551s	1m56.068s	1.5t Motori Moderni V6	KKK	Mar/Ch	Agip	Bre	Koni
24 Alessandro Nannini	I	Minardi M186	1m10.388s	1m09.868s	1m14.518s	1.5t Motori Moderni V6	KKK	Mar/Ch	Agip	SEP/Bre	Koni
25 Rene Arnoux	F	Loto Ligier JS29C	1m09.430s	1m09.970s	1m12.478s	1.5t Megatron S4	Garrett	Bosch/Ch	Win/Castrol	SEP/Bre	Koni
26 Piercarlo Ghinzani	I	Loto Ligier JS29C	1m10.798s	1m10.900s	1m14.187s	1.5t Megatron S4	Garrett	Bosch/Ch	Win/Castrol	SEP/Bre	Koni
27 Michele Alboreto	I	Ferrari F187	1m08.390s	1m08.916s	1m11.717s	1.5t Ferrari V6	Garrett	Mar-Weber/Ch	Agip	SEP/Bre	Marz
28 Gerhard Berger	A	Ferrari F187	1m08.198s	1m08.335s	1m11.994s	1.5t Ferrari V6	Garrett	Mar-Weber/Ch	Agip	SEP/Bre	Marz
30 Philippe Alliot	F	Larrousse Lola LC87	1m13.026s	1m14.422s	1m15.382s	3.5 Ford Cosworth DFZ V8		Cos-Mar/Ch	BP	SEP/AP	Koni

July 3
Overcast/warm

July 4
Sunny/hot

July 5
Sunny/warm

Starting Grid

Prost	1	5	Mansell
Piquet	6	12	Senna
Berger	28	20	Boutsen
Alboreto	27	19	Fabi
Warwick	17	2	Johansson
Patrese	7	8	de Cesaris
Cheever	18	25	Arnoux
Nakajima	11	24	Nannini
Brundle	9	26	Ghinzani
Caffi	21	10	Danner
Capelli	16	23	Campos
Palmer	3	30	Alliot
Fabre	14	4	Streiff

Results, Retirements and Fastest Laps

Place	Driver	Car	Laps	Time/Retirement	Fastest Lap No./Time	
1	Nigel Mansell	1.5t Williams-Honda FW11B	80	1h37m03.839s	42	1m10.405s
2	Nelson Piquet	1.5t Williams-Honda FW11B	80	1h37m11.550s	68	1m09.548s
3	Alain Prost	1.5t McLaren-TAG MP4/3	80	1h37m59.094s	44	1m11.324s
4	Ayrton Senna	1.5t Lotus-Honda 99T	79	1h37m22.323s	47	1m12.231s
5	Teo Fabi	1.5t Benetton-Ford B187	77	1h35m46.386s Driveshaft*	57	1m12.101s
6	Philippe Streiff	3.5 Tyrrell-Ford DG/016	76	1h38m15.054s	56	1m16.433s
7	Jonathan Palmer	3.5 Tyrrell-Ford DG/016	76	1h38m21.802s	47	1m16.256s
8	Stefan Johansson	1.5t McLaren-TAG MP4/3	74	1h33m53.211s Alternator Belt	39	1m11.874s
9	Pascal Fabre	3.5 AGS-Ford JH22C	74	1h37m55.651s	3	1m17.499s
	Gerhard Berger	1.5t Ferrari-Spa F187	71	Suspension	42	1m11.675s
	Satoru Nakajima	1.5t Lotus-Honda 99T	71	Not Classified	36	1m14.524s
	Michele Alboreto	1.5t Ferrari-Spa F187	64	Engine	57	1m12.457s
	Derek Warwick	1.5t Arrows-Megatron A10	62	Turbo	45	1m13.245s
	Philippe Alliot	3.5 Lola -Ford LC87	57	Transmission	41	1m15.984s
	Ivan Capelli	3.5 March-Ford 871	52	Engine	5	1m16.290s
	Adrian Campos	1.5t Minardi-Motori Moderni M186	52	Turbo	22	1m17.836s
	Rene Arnoux	1.5t Ligier-Megatron JS29C	33	Exhaust	5	1m13.845s
	Thierry Boutsen	1.5t Benetton-Ford B187	31	Engine	5	1m12.567s
	Christian Danner	1.5t Zakspeed 871	26	Overheating	3	1m16.133s
	Piercarlo Ghinzani	1.5t Ligier -Megatron JS29C	24	Engine	6	1m15.367s
	Alessandro Nannini	1.5t Minardi-Motori Moderni M186	23	Turbo	7	1m14.248s
	Riccardo Patrese	1.5t Brabham-BMW BT56	19	Differential	5	1m13.984s
	Martin Brundle	1.5t Zakspeed 871	18	Lost Wheel	7	1m15.549s
	Alex Caffi	1.5t Osella-Alfa Romeo FA1I	11	Gearbox	3	1m19.147s
	Andrea de Cesaris	1.5t Brabham-BMW BT56	2	Oil Leak/Fire	2	1m14.098s
	Eddie Cheever	1.5t Arrows-Megatron A10	–	Master Switch		

*Fabi's final lap was over time allowed
Average Speed of Winner: 188.560 km/h, 117.165 mph
Fastest Lap: Nelson Piquet on Lap 68, 1m09.548s, 197.372 km/h, 122.641 mph (record)
Previous Lap Record: Nigel Mansell (1.5t Williams-Honda FW11), 1m09.993s, 196.117 km/h, 121.861 mph (1986)

Circuit Data

French Grand Prix
Circuit: Paul Ricard, France
Circuit Length: 3.813 km/2.369 miles
Race Distance: 80 laps, 305.040 km/189.543 miles
Race Weather: Hot/sunny

Past Winners

Year	Driver	Nat.	Car	Circuit	Distance miles/km	Speed mph/km/h
1981	Alain Prost	F	1.5 Renault RE t/c	Dijon-Prenois	188.88/304.00	118.30/190.39
1982	Rene Arnoux	F	1.5 Renault RE t/c	Paul Ricard	194.95/313.74	125.02/201.20
1983	Alain Prost	F	1.5 Renault RE t/c	Paul Ricard	194.95/313.74	124.19/199.87
1984	Niki Lauda	A	1.5 McLaren-TAG MP4/2 t/c	Dijon-Prenois	186.53/300.20	125.53/202.02
1985	Nelson Piquet	BR	1.5 Brabham-BMW BT54 t/c	Paul Ricard	191.34/307.93	125.09/201.32
1986	Nigel Mansell	GB	1.5 Williams-Honda FW11	Paul Ricard	189.54/305.04	116.86/188.06

Lap Chart

Grid Order	1	2	3	4	5	6	7	8	9	10	11	12	13	14	15	16	17	18	19	20	21	22	23	24	25	26	27	28	29	30	31	32	33	34	35	36	37	38	39	40	41	42	43	44	45	46	47	48	49	50	51	52	53	54	55	56	57	58	59	60	
5 Nigel Mansell	5	5	5	5	5	5	5	5	5	5	5	5	5	5	5	5	5	5	5	5	5	5	5	5	5	5	5	5	5	5	5	5	5	5	5	5	5	5	6	6	6	6	6	6	6	6	6	6	6	6	5	5	5	5	5	5	5	5	5	5	1
1 Alain Prost	6	6	6	6	6	6	6	6	6	6	6	6	6	6	6	6	6	6	1	1	1	1	1	1	1	1	1	1	1	1	1	1	1	1	1	1	1	1	1	6	1	1	5	5	5	5	5	5	5	5	6	6	6	6	6	6	6	6	6	6	2
12 Ayrton Senna	1	1	1	1	1	1	1	1	1	1	1	1	1	1	1	1	1	1	6	6	6	6	6	6	6	6	6	6	6	6	6	12	6	6	6	1	5	5	1	1	1	1	1	1	1	1	1	1	1	1	1	1	1	1	1	1	1	1	1	1	3
6 Nelson Piquet	12	12	12	12	12	12	12	12	12	12	12	12	12	12	12	12	12	12	12	12	12	20	19	19	19	12	12	12	12	12	12	12	12	12	12	12	12	12	12	12	12	12	12	12	12	12	12	12	12	12	12	12	12	12	12	12	12	12	12	12	4
20 Thierry Boutsen	20	20	20	20	20	20	20	20	20	20	20	20	20	20	20	20	20	20	20	20	20	6	19	12	12	28	27	28	28	28	28	28	28	28	28	28	28	28	28	28	28	28	28	28	28	28	28	28	28	28	28	28	28	28	28	28	28	28	28	28	5
28 Gerhard Berger	19	19	19	19	19	19	19	19	19	19	19	19	19	19	19	19	19	19	19	19	19	19	28	28	28	27	28	27	27	27	27	27	27	27	27	27	27	27	27	27	27	27	27	27	27	27	27	27	27	27	27	27	27	27	27	27	27	27	27	26	6
19 Teo Fabi	8	8	7	7	7	7	7	7	7	7	7	7	27	27	27	27	27	27	27	27	27	27	27	27	28	28	28	17	17	27	27	19	19	19	19	19	19	19	19	19	19	19	19	19	19	19	19	19	19	19	19	19	19	19	19	19	19	19	19	19	7
27 Michele Alboreto	7	7	27	27	27	27	27	27	27	27	27	27	25	25	25	25	28	28	28	28	28	28	28	28	17	17	17	27	27	17	17	17	17	17	17	17	17	17	17	17	17	17	17	17	17	17	17	17	17	17	17	17	17	17	17	17	17	17	17	17	8
2 Stefan Johansson	27	27	25	25	25	25	25	25	25	25	25	25	7	17	28	28	28	25	25	17	17	17	17	17	17	25	25	27	27	16	16	16	16	16	16	16	16	16	16	16	16	16	16	16	16	16	16	2	2	2	2	2	2	2	2	2	2	2	2	2	9
17 Derek Warwick	25	25	17	17	17	17	17	17	17	17	17	17	28	17	17	17	17	17	17	25	25	25	25	25	27	27	27	16	4	4	4	4	4	4	4	4	4	3	3	3	3	3	3	2	16	3	3	3	3	3	3	3	3	3	3	3	3	3	3	3	10
8 Andrea de Cesaris	24	24	24	24	24	24	24	24	24	24	28	28	8	7	24	24	24	24	24	24	24	26	16	16	16	16	16	4	3	3	3	3	3	3	3	3	3	4	4	4	4	3	3	3	3	4	4	4	4	4	4	4	4	4	4	4	4	4	4	4	11
7 Riccardo Patrese	17	17	9	9	28	28	28	28	28	28	24	24	24	26	26	26	26	26	26	26	26	16	10	4	4	4	4	3	30	30	30	30	30	30	30	30	30	30	30	2	4	4	4	30	30	30	30	30	14	14	14	12
25 Rene Arnoux	9	9	11	28	9	9	9	9	9	9	9	9	9	9	9	9	9	9	9	10	10	10	10	10	3	4	3	3	3	3	30	30	23	2	2	2	2	2	2	2	2	2	2	2	30	30	30	30	14	14	14	14	11	11	11	13
18 Eddie Cheever	11	11	28	11	26	26	26	26	26	26	26	26	26	10	10	16	16	16	16	16	3	4	3	30	30	30	30	2	2	14	2	23	23	23	23	23	23	23	14	14	14	14	14	14	11	11	11	11	14
24 Alessandro Nannini	26	28	26	26	11	11	10	10	10	10	10	10	10	16	16	16	3	3	3	3	4	30	30	2	2	2	2	23	23	2	14	14	14	14	14	14	14	23	23	23	23	23	23	15
11 Satoru Nakajima	2	26	10	10	10	10	16	16	16	16	16	16	16	3	3	3	4	4	4	4	30	23	23	23	23	23	14	11	11	11	11	11	11	11	11	11	11	11	11	11	11	11	11	11	11	11	11	16
26 Piercarlo Ghinzani	16	10	16	16	16	16	3	3	3	3	3	3	3	4	4	4	30	30	30	30	2	14	2	14	14	14	14	14	11	11	17
9 Martin Brundle	10	16	3	3	3	3	4	4	4	4	4	4	4	30	30	30	23	2	2	2	23	2	14	11	11	11	11	11	18
10 Christian Danner	28	3	23	4	4	4	23	23	2	2	2	30	30	30	30	23	23	14	23	23	23	14	11	11	19
21 Alex Caffi	3	23	4	23	23	23	30	30	30	30	30	2	23	23	14	14	14	2	14	14	14	14	11	20
23 Adrian Campos	23	4	14	14	14	30	14	2	23	23	23	14	14	14	7	7	2	11	11	11	11	11	21
16 Ivan Capelli	4	14	30	30	30	14	2	14	14	14	14	2	2	2	2	2	7	7	22
30 Philippe Alliot	21	30	21	21	21	21	21	21	11	11	11	11	11	11	11	11	11	11	23
3 Jonathan Palmer	14	21	2	2	2	2	11	11	21	21	21	24
4 Philippe Streiff	30	2	25
14 Pascal Fabre	26

Lap Chart continued

	61	62	63	64	65	66	67	68	69	70	71	72	73	74	75	76	77	78	79	80	
	5	5	5	5	5	5	5	5	5	5	5	5	5	5	5	5	5	5	5	5	1
	6	6	6	1	1	6	6	6	6	6	6	6	6	6	6	6	6	6	6	2	2
	1	1	1	6	6	1	1	1	1	1	1	1	1	1	1	1	1	1	1	1	3
	12	12	12	12	12	12	12	12	12	12	12	12	12	12	12	12	12				4
	28	28	28	28	28	28	28	19	19	19	19	19	19	19	19	19	19	19			5
	27	27	27	27	19	19	19	28	2	2	2	2	2	2	4	4					6
	19	19	19	19	2	2	2	2	4	4	4	4	4	3	3						7
	17	17	2	2	4	4	4	3	3	3	3	3	3								8
	2	2	3	4	3	3	3	3	28	28	28	14	14	14							9
	3	3	4	3	14	14	14	14	14	14	14										10
	4	4	14	14	11	11	11	11	11	11	11										11
	14	14	11	11																	12
	11	11																			13

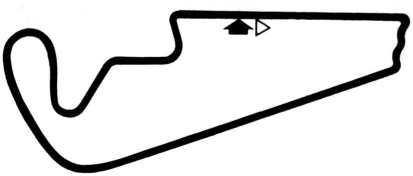

Championship Points

	Drivers				Constructors	
1	Ayrton Senna	27 pts	1		Williams	45 pts
2	Alain Prost	26 pts	2		McLaren	39 pts
3	Nelson Piquet	24 pts	3		Lotus	30 pts
4	Nigel Mansell	21 pts	4		Ferrari	17 pts
5	Stefan Johansson	13 pts	5=		Arrows	4 pts
6	Gerhard Berger	9 pts	5=		Brabham	4 pts
7	Michele Alboreto	8 pts	5=		Benetton	4 pts
8=	Andrea de Cesaris	4 pts	8		Tyrrell	3 pts
8=	Eddie Cheever	4 pts	9		Zakspeed	2 pts
10	Satoru Nakajima	3 pts	10=		March	1 pt
11=	Thierry Boutsen	2 pts	10=		Ligier	1 pt
11=	Teo Fabi	2 pts				
11=	Martin Brundle	2 pts				
11=	Jonathan Palmer	2 pts				
15=	Rene Arnoux	1 pt				
15=	Ivan Capelli	1 pt				
15=	Philippe Streiff	1 pt				

	Jim Clark Cup			Colin Chapman Cup	
1	Jonathan Palmer	33 pts	1	Tyrrell	63 pts
2	Philippe Streiff	30 pts	2	AGS	26 pts
3	Pascal Fabre	26 pts	3	Lola	15 pts
4	Philippe Alliot	15 pts	4	March	6 pts
5	Ivan Capelli	6 pts			

BRITISH

GRAND PRIX

Nigel Mansell's victory at Silverstone must have been the most popular of the year. The papers had been full of him and he faced great pressure to win at home. All the elements had come together for Nelson Piquet to mount a strong challenge, but Mansell was able to pip the Brazilian with just a lap or two to go.

It was brilliant stuff and when Mansell's fuel-less Williams-Honda ground to a halt on his slowing down lap, he was surrounded by a sea of excited and delighted fans. Only Alboreto winning in Italy would be rewarded by such scenes. There's something about the British Grand Prix which makes it unusual. A week previously, the paddock felt as empty as a club race, but Silverstone suddenly became one of the biggest towns in Northamptonshire. By the time practice started, the interior of the circuit was packed with caravans and motor-homes, and there was row upon row of caravans outside the circuit too. Villages of tents reflected the growing attraction for corporate hospitality.

The true race fans, however, made their way to spectator banks around the circuit – there were a recorded 180,000 spectators over the three days. What did come as a surprise to everyone was how Nelson Piquet grabbed the opportunity to rival his own team mate. What wasn't a surprise was that the two Williams-Hondas were head and shoulders above everyone else. The team battle held the crowd spellbound from first practice on Friday to the chequered flag – and beyond – on Sunday. Both Williams-Honda drivers had two cars at their disposal throughout the weekend. At first Piquet had one in short wheelbase form, one in long wheelbase. But while he found the former easier to drive, the latter had more downforce and finally all four cars were in the same long wheelbase specification.

Mansell claimed first blood on Friday with the fastest time in the unofficial session, but that afternoon, with the weather overcast, he encountered what he called, "the full range of elements in motor racing... It was one of those sessions," continued Mansell. "The first set of tyres was out of balance and then I had a rear tyre deflate going into Becketts. It was a huge moment. You should see the skid marks. I can't tell you what I thought. It wasn't a very fruitful session." Later Mansell flipped up a piece of metal debris which scythed into Ayrton Senna's front wing, but it didn't really affect his own time. Mansell was just pleased to get into the 1 minute 7 seconds bracket.

Piquet, meanwhile, had gone quicker with 1 minute 07.596 seconds and when he was fastest again the next morning, it was obvious that he was determined to bring to an end a run of three successive second places and that he intended to end all this talk (which he claimed to ignore) about how he was less competitive than Mansell. Piquet declared that the elements were now in place for him to counter his team mate's domination. Yet the final qualifying session was an odd hour. First of all, both drivers went out in their cars and had to promptly change machines. They had forgotten to alter Piquet's packers after he'd been running on full tanks during the morning. "I was fighting the car all over the place," reported the Brazilian, "and then I realised that the packers were still in." It was then that he improved his

time, although not before a spin which neatly flat-spotted his tyres.

Now Mansell had to try again and depose his team mate. He was already on used tyres. Whether he was quicker up to the new Woodcote or not remained a matter of conjecture, but there he spun after locking up a brake. "We took off the ducts, and I lost the fine edge to them," said Nigel after successfully rescuing his car from the gravel trap. He would start from the front row of the grid, but he wasn't too worried – he had started there all that season. That afternoon, he sneaked off for a quick round of golf – beating his pal Greg Norman! Both drivers had their problems during the pre-race warm-up on Sunday morning. While race day traffic filled Northamptonshire's leafy lanes, Piquet was put off the road by Jonathan Palmer and slightly damaged his car's underbody. Mansell was now worried: his clutch had broken and he could not relax until it was put right.

Finally the cars were on the grid, and with no further delay the lights turned to green and they were on their way. In the battle to the first corner, Piquet and Mansell were so busy watching one another that they almost failed to notice the red and white car of the the World Champion making a great start and coming down the outside to snatch the lead going into Copse for the first time. Prost then led until just before Becketts where Piquet got ahead with team mate Mansell following through a few seconds later. Within a lap, they had created a gap from the rest and very rapidly it became a matter of which Williams driver would win. Early on, Piquet eased away to a 3.1 second lead. By lap eight it was 2.6 seconds going up to 3.5 seconds as they approached the 15 lap mark out of the projected 65. By lap 20, with Mansell using traffic to his advantage, the gap had been cut to 1.6 seconds – and then it began to rise again. By lap 25, Mansell was 4.5 seconds down in second place.

After about 10 laps, Mansell had felt a vibration beginning to build up and he was worried that it could have a lasting effect on his tyres. He reckoned it was a wheel weight, and now he was in a quandary – should he stop for new tyres, or continue according to plan? Piquet and various others were convinced that they wouldn't have to stop for new tyres at all in this race. The obvious solution for Mansell was to stop for tyres. In heavy traffic, he closed up on his team mate as they came up to the 30 lap mark, and it looked as if his problem had cleared up. But then, he rushed into the pits at the end of lap 35 for a super-quick 9.2 second stop for new tyres.

Mansell rejoined nearly half a minute behind Piquet. Could he now catch the Brazilian? There was no guarantee that he would now be quicker. He hadn't been quicker than Senna on new tyres in

Detroit, and Prost, who had stopped on lap 29, hadn't been any quicker or slower on new tyres. But within a lap, Mansell had set up a new lap record and there were plenty more to come, although not before Piquet had replied with his own fastest lap. Mansell's task now was to reduce his own team mate's lead of 28.3s in 30 laps. With 20 laps to go, it was down to 20 seconds. After another fastest lap, it was down to less than 9 seconds and with the crowd willing him ("that alone was an extra 5 seconds in my pocket"), the seconds were whittled away until, with five laps to go, the two Williams-Hondas were nearly nose to tail.

In fairness, no one would blame Piquet if he tried some blocking tactics. He did make an effort to keep his team mate's faster Williams-Honda behind him on lap 63, but there were still two and a half laps to go and Mansell was plainly quicker. Piquet blocked Mansell's first move, and his second, but he'd left a gap and Mansell went for it. The Englishman emerged in the lead to ecstatic cheers from the crowd. But Piquet wasn't finished yet. He kept up the pressure and he was right to. Mansell was using his last drops of petrol. "We have a built-in margin to our fuel gauges," explained Frank Williams afterwards. "Nigel knew what that margin was, and he used it. He took a gamble and it paid off."

Mansell's car ran out of fuel on the last lap going out of Maggotts, but the car picked up again and finally ran out of fuel on the slowing down lap. An unhappy Piquet had finished second again, for the fourth race in succession. The obligatory tyre change had been fortuitous for Mansell. Piquet was surprised just how badly his tyres went off in the last ten laps. There were other cars and drivers in the British Grand Prix, but all admitted that the Williamses were in a class of their own. In the second division were probably the Lotuses and McLarens – their team leaders on a par. Ron Dennis admitted that the Honda engine was stronger in acceleration than the TAG, but that the two engines' terminal speed was similar. Twice his drivers suffered down-on-power engines during qualifying, but Prost started fourth and was second quickest in the morning warm-up.

Senna proved that it didn't just take a Honda engine to get on the front row, although he wasn't unhappy with his third fastest grid placing. He was having trouble with two corners on the circuit, although they were sorted out by second qualifying. After Prost's electrifying start, he was not only passed by the Williams cars but also, briefly, by Senna. But as Alboreto's fifth-placed Ferrari closed on him, Prost fought back and

Previous page: The Benettons of Fabi and Boutsen, Alboreto and Johansson give chase on lap one, behind the two Williams and Senna

Right: Derek Warwick's Arrows-Megatron is lit up by well-used brake discs and flame-out on his way to fifth place and his first points of the year

Left: While the Williams drivers covered one another's moves at the start, Alain Prost nipped into the lead

moved back up to third on lap five, rapidly pulling away from Senna and Alboreto. Twelve laps later, it seemed as if he was pulling in the leading pair, but they remained around 12 seconds in front, the Frenchman being careful to keep an eye on his fuel gauge as his consumption was dangerously high.

After his tyre stop on lap 29, Prost fell back behind both Senna and Alboreto, overtaking the Ferrari driver soon after and being lapped by the Williamses a couple of laps after the Ferrari's rear suspension failed. Prost still wasn't making much impression on Senna due to a faulty clutch which suddenly caused his engine to cut out altogether, and his race was over with only ten laps to go. Senna, then, was a lapped and resigned third, admitting that there wasn't a lot he could do about it, and his fuel consumption was high as well. "We'll just have to keep trying and keep fighting", he said.

Making it a clear sweep for Honda was Satoru Nakajima in the second Lotus. After an oil leak had delayed his practice, he was soon up to ninth from 12th on the grid and although Johansson swept by, he picked up a place when de Cesaris' Brabham burst into flames for the second race running. Then the Japanese driver began to catch Boutsen's Benetton, but, although Nakajima overtook the Belgian, Patrese got by Nakajima as well. From there on, Nakajima had a lonely race, but kept his nose clean, taking advantage of the retirements of Alboreto and Patrese, moving from sixth place to end in fourth – his best ever Grand Prix result.

Both Arrows and Benetton found the improved reliability that they were desperately seeking, although it was fairly well disguised. Cheever had a problem with his fuel system, then suffered a gearbox oil leak and then a hole appeared in his undertray. In final qualifying, engine problems delayed both Arrows cars, while Warwick suffered a fuel leak and then found his car's handling 'dead'. But even though they started on the seventh row of the grid, four rows behind the two Benettons, the four cars were to be found battling it out just before the 20 lap mark. The Arrows pair were soon pulling away, but then Cheever's head gasket blew and he headed for the pits. Fortunately, Warwick continued, in spite of suffering from vibration, and the Englishman scored a popular fifth place, even finding much improved fuel consumption.

Benetton tried to scupper recent unreliability by turning down the boost, but both Fabi and Boutsen still suffered engine problems. But when they did go well they were very competitive, as their third row grid positions testified. But Boutsen had another dramatic race, the wrong front wing end plates caused understeer, a wheel weight came off, the throttle stuck and he had punctured the right rear tyre. That put him back in seventh place, one place behind team mate Fabi, who at least scored a point even if he was watching his fuel gauge like a hawk. Leading home the normally aspirated brigade was Jonathan Palmer after a long battle with his own team

mate Philippe Streiff. Both had been out-qualified by the Lola of Philippe Alliot. Joint team owner Gerard Larrousse was celebrating 10 years of Grand Prix racing at Silverstone. But Alliot was soon out of the race with gearbox problems. Capelli's gearbox casing split when he thumped over a kerb, which left the Tyrrells racing together, Streiff leading, as Palmer coped with a handling problem. But the Frenchman's engine was badly sick and Palmer came home first in the class, with the ever reliable Fabre second again.

Of the rest, Gerhard Berger departed the scene early on when he had a fast spin into the barrier at Abbey and both Zakspeeds had a dramatic time. Both lost bodywork in practice and both also had engine problems, while Brundle's rear suspension also broke. Danner went out early while Brundle came in to have his black box replaced, which cost him so much time that he wasn't classified. Ligier also had a miserable weekend – Arnoux going out with electrical problems early in the race and Ghinzani being totally excluded from the meeting for refuelling out on the circuit on the Friday. It's fair to say that most people left the circuit happy. As the helicopters queued up to take out some 12,000 passengers, and cars filled the lanes of Northamptonshire again, spectators reflected that Nigel Mansell's third consecutive victory in Britain had been superb. It was also the first time that Frank Williams' team had won at Silverstone since his first ever Grand Prix victory, eight years before.

Right: Berger laps
Palmer in the Tyrrell on
the way up from Abbey

Left: Ghinzani is rescued from the trackside by his Ligier mechanics after running out of fuel. It was to earn him disqualification from the meeting

Far left: On lap three, Johansson moves into ninth place ahead of Nakajima, Warwick and Cheever

Centre: Lap one, with the field heading towards Maggotts Curve, led by Prost's McLaren

Below left: Capelli's weekend was dominated by problems with the fuel system until he damaged his gearbox on a kerb during the race

Below right: Picking up a few tips on his latest love, photography, was 1981 British Grand Prix winner, John Watson

Andrea de Cesaris retired in flames for the second weekend running. This time it was caused by a fractured fuel pipe

131

Right: Mansell pitted for new tyres on lap 35 after a wheel weight had come adrift. It allowed him to attack team mate Piquet – who didn't stop

Far right: Nigel's fans came in all shapes, sizes and styles!

Centre: Mansell's weekend included this harmless spin at Woodcote, there was also a flat tyre at Becketts

Below: The two Williamses accelerate off the line, Piquet watches Mansell. The pair came this close again, three laps from home, when Mansell took the lead from Piquet

Left: Mansell was the centre of attraction before and after the race

Below: It was Nigel's day: Rosanne, Chloe and Leo all agreed

BRITISH GRAND PRIX · July 12

Entries and Practice Times

Cos=Cosworth
Ch=Champion
Win=Wintershall
McL=McLaren
Mar=Marelli
Bra=Brabham
Bre=Brembo
Bil=Bilstein
L/A=Lotus Active
Marz=Marzocchi

Driver	Nat.	Car	Practice 1	Practice 2	Warm Up	Engine	Turbos	Electrics/Plugs	Fuel/Oil	Brake Discs/Calipers	Shocks
1 Alain Prost	F	Marlboro McLaren MP4/3	1m08.577s	1m09.492s	1m12.598s	1.5t TAG V6	KKK	Bosch	Shell	SEP/McL	Bil
2 Stefan Johansson	S	Marlboro McLaren MP4/3	1m10.242s	1m09.541s	1m13.063s	1.5t TAG V6	KKK	Bosch	Shell	SEP/McL	Bil
3 Jonathan Palmer	GB	Data General/Courtaulds Tyrrell DG/016	1m16.644s	1m17.105s	1m18.517s	3.5 Ford Cosworth DFZ V8		Cos/Ch	Elf	AP	Koni
4 Philippe Streiff	F	Data General/Courtaulds Tyrrell DG/016	1m17.208s	1m16.524s	1m18.956s	3.5 Ford Cosworth DFZ V8		Cos/Ch	Elf	AP	Koni
5 Nigel Mansell	GB	Canon Williams FW11B	1m07.725s	1m07.180s	1m12.889s	1.5t Honda V6	IHI	Honda/NGK	Mobil	SEP/AP	Showa
6 Nelson Piquet	BR	Canon Williams FW11B	1m07.596s	1m07.110s	1m12.190s	1.5t Honda V6	IHI	Honda/NGK	Mobil	SEP/AP	Showa
7 Riccardo Patrese	I	Brabham BT56	1m10.012s	1m10.020s	1m14.117s	1.5t BMW S4	Garrett	Bosch/Ch	Win/Castrol	SEP/Bra	Koni
8 Andrea de Cesaris	I	Brabham BT56	1m10.787s	1m09.475s	1m14.096s	1.5t BMW S4	Garrett	Bosch/Ch	Win/Castrol	SEP/Bra	Koni
9 Martin Brundle	GB	West Zakspeed 871	1m12.852s	1m12.632s	1m16.127s	1.5t Zakspeed S4	Garrett	Bosch/Ch	Win/Castrol	AP	Sachs
10 Christian Danner	D	West Zakspeed 871	1m15.833s	1m13.337s	1m16.660s	1.5t Zakspeed S4	Garrett	Bosch/Ch	Win/Castrol	AP	Sachs
11 Satoru Nakajima	J	Camel Lotus 99T	1m10.619s	1m10.998s	1m13.852s	1.5t Honda V6	IHI	Honda/NGK	Elf	SEP/Bre	L/A
12 Ayrton Senna	BR	Camel Lotus 99T	1m09.255s	1m08.181s	1m13.450s	1.5t Honda V6	IHI	Honda/NGK	Elf	SEP/Bre	L/A
14 Pascal Fabre	F	El Charro AGS JH22C	1m19.163s	1m18.237s	1m20.234s	3.5 Ford Cosworth DFZ V8		Cos/Ch	Acto	SEP/AGS	Koni
16 Ivan Capelli	I	Leyton House March 871	1m17.122s	1m16.692s	1m19.483s	3.5 Ford Cosworth DFZ V8		Cos/Ch	BP	AP	Koni
17 Derek Warwick	GB	USF&G Arrows A10	1m10.654s	1m10.781s	1m14.752s	1.5t Megatron S4	Garrett	Bosch/Ch	Win/Castrol	AP	Koni
18 Eddie Cheever	USA	USF&G Arrows A10	1m11.053s	1m11.310s	1m14.499s	1.5t Megatron S4	Garrett	Bosch/Ch	Win/Castrol	AP	Koni
19 Teo Fabi	I	Benetton B187	1m10.264s	1m09.246s	1m14.672s	1.5t Ford V6	Garrett	Ford EED/Ch	Mobil	SEP/AP	Koni
20 Thierry Boutsen	B	Benetton B187	1m09.724s	1m08.972s	1m14.412s	1.5t Ford V6	Garrett	Ford EED/Ch	Mobil	SEP/AP	Koni
21 Alex Caffi	I	Landis & Gyr Osella FA1I	1m18.495s	1m15.558s	1m17.003s	1.5t Alfa Romeo V8	KKK	Mar/Ch	Agip	Bre	Koni
23 Adrian Campos	E	Minardi M186	1m15.719s	1m13.793s	1m18.170s	1.5t Motori Moderni V6	KKK	Mar/Ch	Agip	Bre	Koni
24 Alessandro Nannini	I	Minardi M186	1m13.737s	1m12.293s	1m16.385s	1.5t Motori Moderni V6	KKK	Mar/Ch	Agip	SEP/Bre	Koni
25 Rene Arnoux	F	Loto Ligier JS29C	1m12.503s	1m12.402s	1m15.781s	1.5t Megatron S4	Garrett	Bosch/Ch	Win/Castrol	SEP/Bre	Koni
26 Piercarlo Ghinzani	I	Loto Ligier JS29C*	–	–	–	1.5t Megatron S4	Garrett	Bosch/Ch	Win/Castrol	SEP/Bre	Koni
27 Michele Alboreto	I	Ferrari F187	1m10.441s	1m09.274s	1m13.212s	1.5t Ferrari V6	Garrett	Mar-Weber/Ch	Agip	SEP/Bre	Marz
28 Gerhard Berger	A	Ferrari F187	1m10.328s	1m09.408s	1m13.448s	1.5t Ferrari V6	Garrett	Mar-Weber/Ch	Agip	SEP/Bre	Marz
30 Philippe Alliot	F	Larrousse Lola LC87	1m16.770s	1m15.868s	1m18.016s	3.5 Lola LC87		Cos-Mar/Ch	BP	SEP/AP	Koni

*Note: Ghinzani was excluded from the meeting after setting a time of 1m13.381s in the first qualifying session

July 10 Overcast/warm July 11 Sunny/warm July 12 Overcast/warm

Starting Grid

Mansell **5**		**6** Piquet	
Prost **1**		**12** Senna	
Fabi **19**		**20** Boutsen	
Berger **28**		**27** Alboreto	
Johansson **2**		**8** de Cesaris	
Nakajima **11**		**7** Patrese	
Cheever **18**		**17** Warwick	
Arnoux **25**		**24** Nannini	
Danner **10**		**9** Brundle	
Caffi **21**		**23** Campos	
Streiff **4**		**30** Alliot	
Capelli **16**		**3** Palmer	
		14 Fabre	

Results, Retirements and Fastest Laps

Place	Driver	Car	Laps	Time/Retirement	Fastest Lap No./Time
1	Nigel Mansell	1.5t Williams-Honda FW11B	65	1h19m11.780s	58 1m09.832s
2	Nelson Piquet	1.5t Williams-Honda FW11B	65	1h19m13.698s	62 1m10.632s
3	Ayrton Senna	1.5t Lotus-Honda 99T	64	1h19m20.600s	60 1m11.605s
4	Satoru Nakajima	1.5t Lotus-Honda 99T	63	1hr19m34.322s	61 1m13.780s
5	Derek Warwick	1.5t Arrows-Megatron A10	63	1h19m48.012s	53 1m14.210s
6	Teo Fabi	1.5t Benetton-Ford B187	63	1h20m09.905s	51 1m13.885s
7	Thierry Boutsen	1.5t Benetton-Ford B187	62	1h19m22.661s	54 1m14.162s
8	Jonathan Palmer	3.5 Tyrrell-Ford DG/016	60	1h20m01.827s	33 1m18.543s
9	Pascal Fabre	3.5 AGS-Ford JH22C	59	1h20m18.077s	55 1m19.784s
	Philippe Streiff	3.5 Tyrrell-Ford DG/016	57	Engine	38 1m18.745s
	Martin Brundle	1.5t Zakspeed 871	54	Not classified	43 1m14.102s
	Alain Prost	1.5t McLaren-TAG MP4/3	53	Clutch/engine	47 1m13.346s
	Michele Alboreto	1.5t Ferrari-Spa F187	52	Rear suspension	49 1m12.846s
	Eddie Cheever	1.5t Arrows-Megatron A10	45	Overheating	42 1m14.346s
	Adrian Campos	1.5t Minardi-Motori Moderni M186	34	Electrics/fuel pump	32 1m18.859s
	Alex Caffi	1.5t Osella-Alfa Romeo FA1I	32	Turbo	28 1m17.347s
	Christian Danner	1.5t Zakspeed 871	32	Gearbox	28 1m19.848s
	Riccardo Patrese	1.5t Brabham-BMW BT56	28	Metering unit	17 1m14.814s
	Stefan Johansson	1.5t McLaren-TAG MP4/3	18	Engine	14 1m14.380s
	Alessandro Nannini	1.5t Minardi-Motori Moderni M186	10	Engine	8 1m17.383s
	Andrea de Cesaris	1.5t Brabham-BMW BT56	8	Fuel pipe/fire	7 1m15.401s
	Gerhard Berger	1.5t Ferrari-Spa F187	7	Accident	7 1m14.879s
	Philippe Alliot	3.5 Lola -Ford LC87	7	Gearbox	7 1m18.924s
	Rene Arnoux	1.5t Ligier -Megatron JS29C	3	Electrics	3 1m17.552s
	Ivan Capelli	3.5 March-Ford 871	3	Accident	3 1m18.999s

Average Speed of Winner: 235.292 km/h, 146.208 mph
Fastest Lap: Nigel Mansell on Lap 58, 1m09.832s, 246.318 km/h, 153.059 mph (record)
Previous Lap Record: Jacques Laffite (1.5t Ligier-Renault JS25), 1m11.526s, 211.735 km/h, 131.566 mph (1985)

Circuit Data

British Grand Prix

Circuit: Silverstone, England
Circuit Length: 4.778 km/ 2.969 miles
Race Distance: 65 Laps, 310.571 km/192.985 miles
Race Weather: Sunny with clouds/ warm

Past Winners

Year	Driver	Nat.	Car	Circuit	Distance miles/km	Speed mph/km/h
1977	James Hunt	GB	3.0 McLaren-Ford M26	Silverstone	199.38/320.88	130.36/209.79
1978	Carlos Reutemann	RA	3.0 Ferrari-3/78 312T	Brands Hatch	198.63/319.67	116.61/187.66
1979	Clay Regazzoni	CH	3.0 Williams-Ford FW07	Silverstone	199.38/320.88	138.80/223.37
1980	Alan Jones	AUS	3.0 Williams-Ford FW07B	Brands Hatch	198.63/319.67	125.69/202.28
1981	John Watson	GB	3.0 McLaren-Ford MP4	Silverstone	199.38/320.88	137.64/221.51
1982	Niki Lauda	A	3.0 McLaren-Ford MP4B	Brands Hatch	198.63/319.67	124.70/222.68
1983	Alain Prost	F	1.5 Renault RE40 t/c	Silverstone	195.44/316.17	139.22/224.05
1984	Niki Lauda	A	3.5 McLaren-TAG MP4/2 t/c	Brands Hatch	185.57/298.64	124.41/200.21
1985	Alain Prost	F	1.5 McLaren-TAG MP4/2B	Silverstone	190.58/306.71	146.27/235.40
1986	Nigel Mansell	GB	1.5 Williams-Honda FW11	Brands Hatch	196.05/315.51	129.78/208.86

134

Lap Chart

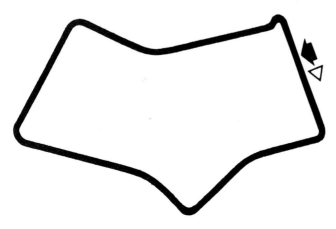

Grid Order	1	2	3	4	5	6	7	8	9	10	11	12	13	14	15	16	17	18	19	20	21	22	23	24	25	26	27	28	29	30	31	32	33	34	35	36	37	38	39	40	41	42	43	44	45	46	47	48	49	50	51	52	53	54	55	
6 Nelson Piquet	6	6	6	6	6	6	6	6	6	6	6	6	6	6	6	6	6	6	6	6	6	6	6	6	6	6	6	6	6	6	6	6	6	6	6	6	6	6	6	6	6	6	6	6	6	6	6	6	6	6	6	6	6	6	6	1
5 Nigel Mansell	5	5	5	5	5	5	5	5	5	5	5	5	5	5	5	5	5	5	5	5	5	5	5	5	5	5	5	5	5	5	5	5	5	5	5	5	5	5	5	5	5	5	5	5	5	5	5	5	5	5	5	5	5	5	5	2
12 Ayrton Senna	1	12	12	12	1	1	1	1	1	1	1	1	1	1	1	1	1	1	1	1	1	1	1	1	1	1	1	1	1	1	1	1	1	12	12	12	12	12	12	12	12	12	12	12	12	12	12	12	12	12	12	12	12	12	12	3
1 Alain Prost	12	1	1	1	12	12	12	12	12	12	12	12	12	12	12	12	12	12	12	12	12	12	12	12	12	27	27	1	1	1	1	1	1	1	1	1	1	1	1	1	1	1	1	1	1	1	1	1	1	1	1	1	11	11		4
20 Thierry Boutsen	20	20	27	27	27	27	27	27	27	27	27	27	27	27	27	27	27	27	27	27	27	27	1	1	27	27	27	27	27	27	27	27	27	27	27	27	27	27	27	11	11	11	11	11	11	11	11	17	17							5
19 Teo Fabi	27	27	20	20	20	20	20	2	2	2	2	2	2	2	2	2	2	2	7	7	7	7	7	7	7	7	7	7	7	11	11	11	11	11	11	11	11	11	11	11	11	11	11	11	11	11	11	11	11	11	11	11	19	19	19	6
27 Michele Alboreto	19	19	19	8	2	2	2	20	20	20	20	20	20	20	11	7	7	11	11	11	11	11	17	17	17	17	17	17	17	17	17	17	17	17	17	17	17	17	17	17	17	17	17	17	17	17	27	20	20	20	19	19	20	20	20	7
28 Gerhard Berger	8	8	8	2	8	8	8	11	11	11	11	11	7	11	11	11	7	11	11	20	17	17	17	17	17	18	18	18	18	18	18	18	18	18	18	18	18	18	18	18	18	18	20	20	19	27	20	20	20	27	20	3	3	8
8 Andrea de Cesaris	11	11	2	11	11	11	11	11	17	17	17	17	17	7	20	20	20	17	18	18	18	18	18	18	18	20	20	20	20	20	20	20	20	20	20	20	20	20	20	19	19	27	27	27	27	27	20	3	4	4	9
2 Stefan Johansson	2	2	11	19	17	28	28	17	18	18	7	7	7	17	17	17	17	18	20	20	20	20	20	20	20	19	19	19	19	19	19	19	19	19	19	19	19	19	19	18	3	3	3	3	3	3	4	14	14	10
7 Riccardo Patrese	17	17	17	17	28	17	17	18	7	7	18	18	18	18	18	18	18	19	19	19	19	19	19	9	9	9	9	9	9	9	9	9	9	9	9	4	4	4	4	3	4	4	4	4	4	4	14	9	11
11 Satoru Nakajima	28	18	18	28	18	18	18	7	19	19	19	19	19	19	19	19	9	9	9	9	9	9	9	9	9	21	21	21	21	23	4	4	4	4	3	3	3	3	3	4	14	14	14	14	14	14	9	12
17 Derek Warwick	18	28	28	18	7	7	7	19	9	9	9	9	9	9	9	9	21	21	21	21	21	21	21	23	23	23	23	3	4	3	3	3	3	3	14	14	14	14	14	9	9	9	9	9	13
18 Eddie Cheever	7	7	7	7	19	19	19	9	21	21	21	21	21	21	21	21	21	23	23	23	23	23	23	4	4	4	3	23	14	14	14	14	9	9	9	9	9	14
24 Alessandro Nannini	9	9	9	9	9	9	9	21	23	23	23	23	23	23	23	23	4	4	4	4	4	4	4	3	3	3	3	14	14	15
25 Rene Arnoux	25	25	25	21	21	21	21	23	3	3	3	4	4	4	4	4	4	3	3	3	3	3	3	3	3	10	10	10	14	16
9 Martin Brundle	21	21	21	30	30	30	30	4	4	4	3	3	3	3	3	3	10	10	10	10	10	10	10	10	10	14	14	14	10	17
10 Christian Danner	16	16	16	23	23	23	23	4	10	10	10	10	10	10	10	10	10	14	14	14	14	14	14	14	14	14	18
23 Adrian Campos	30	30	30	3	3	3	3	10	14	14	14	14	14	14	14	14	19
21 Alex Caffi	23	23	23	4	4	4	4	14	24	24	20
30 Philippe Alliot	3	10	10	10	10	10	10	24	21
4 Philippe Streiff	10	3	3	14	14	14	14	22
3 Jonathan Palmer	4	4	4	24	24	24	24	23
16 Ivan Capelli	14	14	14	24
14 Pascal Fabre	24	24	24	25

Lap Chart continued

	56	57	58	59	60	61	62	63	64	65	
	6	6	6	6	6	6	6	5	5	5	1
	5	5	5	5	5	5	5	6	6	6	2
	12	12	12	12	12	12	12	12			3
	11	11	11	11	11	11	11	11	11		4
	17	17	17	17	17	17	17	17			5
	19	19	19	19	19	19	19	19			6
	20	20	20	20	20	20	20				7
	3	3	3	3	3						8
	4	14	14	14							9
	14	4									10

Championship Points

	Drivers			Constructors	
1	Ayrton Senna	31 pts	1	Williams	60 pts
2=	Nigel Mansell	30 pts	2	McLaren	39 pts
2=	Nelson Piquet	30 pts	3	Lotus	37 pts
4	Alain Prost	26 pts	4	Ferrari	17 pts
5	Stefan Johansson	13 pts	5	Arrows	6 pts
6	Gerhard Berger	9 pts	6	Benetton	5 pts
7	Michele Alboreto	8 pts	7	Brabham	4 pts
8	Satoru Nakajima	6 pts	8	Tyrrell	3 pts
9=	Andrea de Cesaris	4 pts	9	Zakspeed	2 pts
9=	Eddie Cheever	4 pts	10=	March	1 pt
11	Teo Fabi	3 pts	10=	Ligier	1 pt
12=	Thierry Boutsen	2 pts			
12=	Martin Brundle	2 pts			
12=	Jonathan Palmer	2 pts			
16=	Rene Arnoux	1 pt			
16=	Ivan Capelli	1 pt			
16=	Philippe Streiff	1 pt			

	Jim Clark Cup			Colin Chapman Cup	
1	Jonathan Palmer	42 pts	1	Tyrrell	72 pts
2	Pascal Fabre	32 pts	2	AGS	32 pts
3	Philippe Streiff	20 pts	3	Lola	15 pts
4	Philippe Alliot	15 pts	4	March	6 pts
5	Ivan Capelli	6 pts			

GERMAN

GRAND PRIX

Spectators who braved the bad weather to attend the eighth round of the World Championship came away disappointed. Bad weather reduced practice and qualifying by half, and the race itself eventually petered out into near farce, with only seven runners and seven classified finishers.

In the end, history repeated itself. Nelson Piquet won the German Grand Prix for the second year running, equalling the 1987 Canon Williams-Honda hat trick. In spite of a visit to Frank Williams the day after the British Grand Prix, Piquet's luck didn't turn in Hockenheim until the final four laps of the 44 circuit race. Until then, as he himself admitted, he wasn't really in the race. In the first session on Friday morning, even team mate Nigel Mansell admitted that the Williams-Honda team had taken a wrong turning. Piquet's car was bottoming, although the team did admit that they had probably saved themselves some time. That afternoon, Piquet did one slow lap and then spent most of his time in the pits again. A turbo clip had broken, and it took several long minutes to replace. His car oversteered as well, and he, like many others, was looking forward to a better, more constructive day on Saturday.

Mansell, meanwhile, was provisionally in pole position, but admitted that he didn't particularly like the circuit, the pace was too jerky; down into second gear for the first two chicanes and then right up through the gears to sixth, racing through the tall pines to the next chicane. It was too erratic in terms of car set-up too: take off a wing for straightline speed, put it back on again for the downforce and grip in the chicanes and the stadium area. Then there was the race pattern itself – take off a wing again to overtake down the straights, but then there were problems

with slowing in the tight corners. Mansell's fastest lap on Friday certainly hadn't been perfect. He had to overtake four cars along the way and had missed an apex by about a yard, which probably meant that he was one or maybe two tenths of a second slower than he should have been. But at 1 minute 42.616 seconds, Mansell was pretty close to Keke Rosberg's pole of the previous year, 1 minute 42.013 seconds, and that, said Mansell, had been set with five bar boost and qualifying tyres, so he wasn't too dissatisfied.

Saturday morning was initially overcast and damp, although it began to dry out. Piquet still wasn't happy with his car but Mansell had improved his effectively. Everything was looking good for an excellent show-down in the race for pole position. But, sadly, rain prior to the second qualifying session scuppered that. However Mansell was looking happy – he was in his sixth pole position of the year. He went out to check where the puddles were and wound up two seconds quicker than anyone else. But no-one enjoyed it. Drivers commented that, "the visibility was really dreadful."

Piquet's misery continued into Sunday. His underbody dropped onto the track within minutes of the start of the warm-up session, and he only had a couple of laps in his race car. Even at the start of the race, he complained that his car was going up and down like a ping-pong ball, and it was soon clear that

while it was superior to the Lotus of compatriot Ayrton Senna in fourth place, there was a duel taking place out in front, which was outclassing Piquet's Williams-Honda. Mansell and Prost had steadily eased away, Prost overtaking the Englishman on lap eight, but Mansell shadowed his every move, even to the extent of suggesting that he was actually saving petrol by slip-streaming the World Champion. Just before the 20 lap mark, the cars started to stop for new tyres; sixth-placed Johansson was the first as early as lap 17, so that he wouldn't be clogging up valuable road when his more competitive team mate came in for rubber.

When Prost did come in on lap 19, it was a super-quick stop, but then Ron Dennis took away the 'brake' sign a fraction early and Prost let out the clutch, jamming the front jack under the McLaren's nose. It took a second or two to sort out, and any advantage had gone. Piquet was in a lap later for an 8.4 second stop. Mansell, hopping over the pit lane kerbs, came in two laps after that for a 9.1 second stop. He was 4.5 seconds behind Prost when he rejoined. Prost set his fastest lap of the race a lap later, on his 24th, but then Mansell went more than a second quicker, also setting the fastest lap of the race on his 24th and cutting the gap to 3.4 seconds. Now the race could really begin. As soon as we had that thought Mansell was parking his Williams-Honda on the outside of the Sach's Curve. The engine had seized, his race was over.

Prost was now 37 seconds ahead of the second-placed Piquet, but while the Frenchman matched his on-board readouts, so Nelson matched his. Up until the moment that he had pulled out of the pits after his tyre change, his read-outs had been blank. Now he had something to read, and it was very encouraging. He had fuel in hand, and he set off, determined to use it. While the lead gap hovered around the 37 second mark for some laps, it suddenly took a dive to three seconds a lap. With nine laps to go, Nelson was 30 seconds behind. At that rate, he wouldn't catch Prost by the end, although spectators couldn't calculate what problems Prost might face. But Piquet closed the gap at a prodigious rate. Perhaps Prost knew he was closing but knew that he had time in hand. By lap 37 (seven to go) the gap was down to 24 seconds. It was 21 seconds a lap later and 17.2 seconds the lap after that. Then suddenly the red and white car was pulling off the track. Prost, just four laps from that record-breaking 28th win, had to retire. Once again his alternator belt had broken, as it had in Imola and as had happened to Johansson at Ricard. As Prost pondered his problems under the pines, Piquet reeled off the laps.

That's all that Piquet had to do. His nearest challenger, Johansson, was many seconds behind. And in the end, the Williams-Honda crossed the line nearly one hundred seconds ahead of his nearest challenger. "I guess today was my lucky day," said the Brazilian, "after such a bad weekend, I count myself lucky. Furthermore, I've never led the championship so early in the season, I usually come from behind." With both Mansell and Prost out, one would expect Piquet's nearest rival to be Ayrton Senna, but this was a disastrous race for the man who had finished second the previous year. He had two 'moments' in qualifying, one where he ran out of road and went bumping across the grass when his car jumped out of second gear. That damaged the undertray, and his race car was bottoming too. He wasn't happy with either engine or handling in the warm-up, and there were Camel Lotuses at either end of the grid as they lined up, Senna was still unsure of which car he would be using.

When the race did get underway, Senna made a great start to lead the first lap, but he was pretty depressed by his lack of straightline speed when he was shunted back to third on lap two and to fourth (challenged by Alboreto) on lap three. Alboreto soon dropped back and was a retirement at the 10 lap mark with a blown turbo. His successor, Thierry Boutsen, chipped away at the gap between his Benetton-Ford and the Lotus-Honda – Senna was unable to turn up the boost any more. Boutsen pitted first for new tyres, a lap ahead of Senna and when they rejoined, the two were inches apart. But Senna was back into the pits again a lap later to have his suspension checked and back in again a lap after that to have his nose section replaced after it had been broken by the turbulence in the battle with Boutsen. Even as Senna drove out of the pits, he left a trail of hydraulic fluid from his suspension. For the rest of the race, Senna drove a sledge which bottomed almost everywhere. And it wasn't Boutsen who picked up third place. In spite of supposedly more reliable engines, both he and team mate Fabi went out with engine problems in the watershed around the 27th lap.

The man to pick up the pieces was Stefan Johansson who had been pushing Boutsen, just ahead of the Berger/Fabi duo. Berger, like team mate Alboreto, went out with turbo failure. But as cars pulled off to left, right and centre with 14 laps to go, Johansson sailed serenely on. He hadn't been pleased with his straightline speed, since in the warm-up, and after his tyre stop, the engine had made a nasty noise, so he was literally trying to save the engine in the final stages. He was delighted when third became second, even if it was to the disadvantage of his team mate. But as he set out on his final lap, his front right tyre exploded. Undaunted, Johansson continued at near racing speed. Perhaps the experience of driving a hire car with four flat tyres from the Jacarepagua circuit in Brazil to his hotel the previous year would come in useful after all. By the time he crossed the finishing line second

for the fourth time in his career, there was precious little left of the tyre, and the suspension was scarcely attached to the car either.

Behind the similarly hobbled Senna, virtually anyone could have taken points, for the drop out rate was exceptional. Hockenheim's long straights had a lot to do with it, the turbo cars seemed incapable of holding together – and that in relatively low temperatures. The Arrows went out with turbo and throttle cable-related failures, Warwick making a particularly fiery exit. The Brabhams' departures were also mechanical, while Nakajima's weekend was almost as exciting as Senna's, with his suspension sometimes being extremely active with remarkable effect. Ultimately, it caused the Japanese driver's second retirement of the year. At half way, the Minardis were very much in touch, with Nannini eighth and Campos tenth behind Ghinzani who had just made a pit stop. But neither of the Italian cars were destined to finish. Nannini actually rose to sixth just before his retirement with an engine complaint and Campos wasn't long in following him. Ghinzani looked as though he might have brought a miserable season and weekend to a halt when he was lying fifth with 12 laps to go, but then his

succession of engine failures continued. Team mate Arnoux went out with an incurable electrical misfire. As for the Zakspeeds, they didn't have a happy time on home ground in spite of new rear suspension, and although Brundle was still running, he was too far behind to be classified after a succession of pit stops. All of which left the way open for the normally aspirated cars to top up the top six. Tyrrells, March, Lola and AGS were not meant to take points on ultra-fast circuits. But in Germany, Streiff was fourth, Palmer fifth and Alliot in the Lola sixth. The racing amongst the 'atmos' had always been good and close, even if spectators' attention had to be specifically drawn to it. Capelli had had a last minute panic when his black box failed out on the circuit. Willed on by spectators, he made it back to the pits, but started from the pit lane. He was soon out with a broken rotor arm, and just when the AGS team had decided to try and be more competitive, they had their first retirement of the year with a broken valve in the engine.

This left a fine tussle for much of the race between the Tyrrells and Alliot's Lola. The Lola led the class for much of the first half but then an electrical problem cut the Lola's revs, and the Tyrrell duo took over, alternately leading one

another until Palmer hit Warwick's oil and half spun, allowing Streiff to lead the class and steadily notch up places. At half distance, they were eleventh and twelfth, but the rash of retirements soon after saw them sixth and seventh at two thirds distance. By now Palmer had closed on Streiff again, but team orders said 'stay' and Palmer thought that he had better do so. They were still only a lap down on the leader at the end, and on the same lap as Senna's Lotus-Honda. "We'll be on the rostrum at the Oesterreichring," joked Tyrrell after the race. And Alliot scored the Larrousse Lola team's first point with sixth place. Alain Prost was the last driver to be classified and take points.

So at half distance in the championship, Nelson Piquet found himself the series leader, four points ahead of compatriot Senna. Mansell was another five behind, and Prost another four. Johansson was only seven points behind his team mate, but the rest were 10 points further back. McLaren and Lotus were still in touch with constructors' leader Williams. Palmer had a nine point lead in the Jim Clark Cup, ahead of his own team mate Philippe Streiff, while Tyrrell were untouchable in the Colin Chapman Cup. Everyone was looking forward to the second half of the series.

Walking home: The high retirement rate in the German Grand Prix meant a long walk home for many drivers: Warwick (right), Cheever (centre), Ghinzani (far right), Mansell (below left) and de Cesaris (below right)

Right: Approaching the Onko Kurve on the first lap, led by Nelson Piquet who is hidden behind the blue barrier

Left: Gerhard Berger crashed his Ferrari at the first corner after front suspension failure and ended up tenth on the grid

Patrese turns to the
timing screens for his
excitement

143

Right: Another lap and Johansson wouldn't have claimed second place. He had a puncture on the last lap but kept going to the flag. By the time he crossed the line, there was almost nothing left of his right front tyre

144

Left: Senna finished a lucky third in the Lotus-Honda which spent much of the race on its belly after an active suspension failure

Centre left: Piercarlo Ghinzani looked as though he might finally score some points, until his Ligier's engine stopped when he was fifth

Centre right: Jonathan Palmer, Ken Tyrrell and the team had lots to laugh about: team mate Streiff finished fourth overall and Palmer (under team orders) finished fifth

Below: The end for Nigel Mansell when his engine seizes. Piquet prepares to take over the lead

GERMAN GRAND PRIX · July 26

Entries and Practice Times

Cos=Cosworth
Ch=Champion
Win=Wintershall
McL=McLaren
Mar=Marelli
Bra=Brabham
Bre=Brembo
Bil=Bilstein
L/A=Lotus Active
Marz=Marzocchi

Driver	Nat.	Car	Practice 1	Practice 2	Warm Up	Engine	Turbos	Electrics/Plugs	Fuel/Oil	Brake Discs/Calipers	Shocks
1 Alain Prost	F	Marlboro McLaren MP4/3	1m43.202s		1m48.207s	1.5t TAG V6	KKK	Bosch	Shell	SEP/McL	Bil
2 Stefan Johansson	S	Marlboro McLaren MP4/3	1m45.428s		1m50.021s	1.5t TAG V6	KKK	Bosch	Shell	SEP/McL	Bil
3 Jonathan Palmer	GB	Data General/Courtaulds Tyrrell DG/016	1m54.491s	2m06.769s	1m55.637s	3.5 Ford Cosworth DFZ V8		Cos/Ch	Elf	AP	Koni
4 Philippe Streiff	F	Data General/Courtaulds Tyrrell DG/016	1m53.528s	2m10.404s	1m56.000s	3.5 Ford Cosworth DFZ V8		Cos/Ch	Elf	AP	Koni
5 Nigel Mansell	GB	Canon Williams FW11B	1m42.616s	2m00.832s	1m48.216s	1.5t Honda V6	IHI	Honda/NGK	Mobil	SEP/AP	Showa
6 Nelson Piquet	BR	Canon Williams FW11B	1m43.705s		1m49.038s	1.5t Honda V6	IHI	Honda/NGK	Mobil	SEP/AP	Showa
7 Riccardo Patrese	I	Brabham BT56	1m46.096s		1m50.347s	1.5t BMW S4	Garrett	Bosch/Ch	Win/Castrol	SEP/Bra	Koni
8 Andrea de Cesaris	I	Brabham BT56	1m45.411s		1m50.417s	1.5t BMW S4	Garrett	Bosch/Ch	Win/Castrol	SEP/Bra	Koni
9 Martin Brundle	GB	West Zakspeed 871	1m51.062s	2m12.913s	1m53.142s	1.5t Zakspeed S4	Garrett	Bosch/Ch	Win/Castrol	AP	Sachs
10 Christian Danner	D	West Zakspeed 871	1m51.448s	2m11.115s	1m53.434s	1.5t Zakspeed S4	Garrett	Bosch/Ch	Win/Castrol	AP	Sachs
11 Satoru Nakajima	J	Camel Lotus 99T	1m46.760s		1m50.702s	1.5t Honda V6	IHI	Honda/NGK	Elf	SEP/Bre	L/A
12 Ayrton Senna	BR	Camel Lotus 99T	1m42.873s	1m19.245s	1m49.718s	1.5t Honda V6	IHI	Honda/NGK	Elf	SEP/Bre	L/A
14 Pascal Fabre	F	El Charro AGS JH22C	1m54.997s	1m57.975s	3.5 Ford Cosworth DFZ V8		Cos/Ch	Acto	SEP/AGS	Koni
16 Ivan Capelli	I	Leyton House March 871	1m54.616s	2m09.992s	1m57.126s	3.5 Ford Cosworth DFZ V8		Cos/Ch	BP	AP	Koni
17 Derek Warwick	GB	USF&G Arrows A10	1m46.525s		1m50.561s	1.5t Megatron S4	Garrett	Bosch/Ch	Win/Castrol	AP	Koni
18 Eddie Cheever	USA	USF&G Arrows A10	1m47.780s	2m04.003s	1m50.646s	1.5t Megatron S4	Garrett	Bosch/Ch	Win/Castrol	AP	Koni
19 Teo Fabi	I	Benetton B187	1m45.497s	2m06.857s	1m49.047s	1.5t Ford V6	Garrett	Ford EED/Ch	Mobil	SEP/AP	Koni
20 Thierry Boutsen	B	Benetton B187	1m45.066s	2m02.981s	1m49.484s	1.5t Ford V6	Garrett	Ford EED/Ch	Mobil	SEP/AP	Koni
21 Alex Caffi	I	Landis & Gyr Osella FA1I	6m04.561s	2m07.753s	2m07.093s	1.5t Alfa Romeo V8	KKK	Mar/Ch	Agip	Bre	Koni
23 Adrian Campos	E	Minardi M186	1m49.668s	1m56.020s	1.5t Motori Moderni V6	KKK	Mar/Ch	Agip	Bre	Koni
24 Alessandro Nannini	I	Minardi M186	1m47.887s	1m52.299s	1.5t Motori Moderni V6	KKK	Mar/Ch	Agip	SEP/Bre	Koni
25 Rene Arnoux	F	Loto Ligier JS29C	1m46.323s		1m50.135s	1.5t Megatron S4	Garrett	Bosch/Ch	Win/Castrol	SEP/Bre	Koni
26 Piercarlo Ghinzani	I	Loto Ligier JS29C	1m49.236s	2m09.440s	1m51.796s	1.5t Megatron S4	Garrett	Bosch/Ch	Win/Castrol	SEP/Bre	Koni
27 Michele Alboreto	I	Ferrari F187	1m43.921s	2m05.139s	1m48.851s	1.5t Ferrari V6	Garrett	Mar-Weber/Ch	Agip	SEP/Bre	Marz
28 Gerhard Berger	A	Ferrari F187	1m45.902s	2m03.172s	1m49.838s	1.5t Ferrari V6	Garrett	Mar-Weber/Ch	Agip	SEP/Bre	Marz
30 Philippe Alliot	F	Larrousse Lola LC87	1m52.760s	2m11.588s	1m54.574s	3.5 Ford Cosworth DFZ V8		Cos-Mar/Ch	BP	SEP/AP	Koni

July 24 — Warm/dry
July 25 — Wet/overcast
July 26 — Cool/dry

Starting Grid

Senna 12		5	Mansell
Piquet 6		1	Prost
Boutsen 20		27	Alboreto
Johansson 2		8	de Cesaris
Berger 28		19	Fabi
Arnoux 25		7	Patrese
Nakajima 11		17	Warwick
Nannini 24		18	Cheever
Campos 23		26	Ghinzani
Danner 10		9	Brundle
Streiff 4		30	Alliot
Capelli 16		3	Palmer
Caffi 21		14	Fabre

Results, Retirements and Fastest Laps

Place	Driver	Car	Laps	Time/Retirement	Fastest Lap No./Time
1	Nelson Piquet	1.5t Williams-Honda FW11B	44	1h21m 25.091s	39 1m47.517s
2	Stefan Johansson	1.5t McLaren-TAG MP4/3	44	1h23m04.682s	22 1m49.778s
3	Ayrton Senna	1.5t Lotus 99T	43	1h22m52.066s	5 1m49.187s
4	Philippe Streiff	3.5 Tyrrell-Ford DG/016	43	1h23m05.134s	20 1m54.228s
5	Jonathan Palmer	3.5 Tyrrell-Ford DG/016	43	1h23m06.022s	20 1m54.294s
6	Philippe Alliot	3.5 Lola -Ford LC87	42	1h23m17.334s	7 1m54.771s
7	Alain Prost	1.5t McLaren-TAG MP4/3	39	1h11m33.332 s alternator belt	24 1m46.807s
	Martin Brundle	1.5t Zakspeed 871	34	Not classified	34 1m49.742s
	Piercarlo Ghinzani	1.5t Ligier -Megatron JS29C	32	Engine	5 1m52.512s
	Adrian Campos	1.5t Minardi-Motori Moderni M186	28	Engine	23 1m54.705s
	Thierry Boutsen	1.5t Benetton-Ford B187	26	Engine	4 1m49.864s
	Nigel Mansell	1.5t Williams-Honda FW11B	25	Seized engine	24 1m45.716s
	Alessandro Nannini	1.5t Minardi-Motori Moderni M186	25	Engine	6 1m52.382s
	Derek Warwick	1.5t Arrows-Megatron A10	23	Turbo	17 1m50.608s
	Christian Danner	1.5t Zakspeed 871	21	Input shaft	7 1m54.464s
	Gerhard Berger	1.5t Ferrari-Spa F187	19	Turbo	6 1m50.667s
	Teo Fabi	1.5t Benetton-Ford B187	18	Engine	8 1m50.758s
	Alex Caffi	1.5t Osella-Alfa Romeo FA1I	17	Turbo	5 1m55.549s
	Andrea de Cesaris	1.5t Brabham-BMW BT56	12	Engine	7 1m50.436s
	Michele Alboreto	1.5t Ferrari-Spa F187	10	Turbo	5 1m49.509s
	Pascal Fabre	3.5 AGS-Ford JH22C	10	Valve	2 1m58.770s
	Eddie Cheever	1.5t Arrows-Megatron A10	9	Turbo	8 1m51.014s
	Satoru Nakajima	1.5t Lotus-Honda 99T	9	Suspension	6 1m51.054s
	Ivan Capelli	3.5 March-Lotus 871	7	Rotor arm	6 1m57.292s
	Rene Arnoux	1.5t Ligier -Megatron JS29C	6	Electrical misfire	2 1m53.433s
	Riccardo Patrese	1.5t Brabham-BMW BT56	5	Ignition pick-up	3 1m53.002s

Average Speed of Winner: 220.394 km/h, 136.946 mph
Fastest Lap: Nigel Mansell on lap 24, 1m45.716s, 231.462 km/h, 143.823 mph (record)
Previous Lap Record: Gerhard Berger (1.5t Benetton-BMW B186), 1m46.604s, 229.534 km/h, 142.626 mph (1986)

Circuit Data

**German Grand Prix,
Hockenheim,
West Germany**
Circuit Length: 6.797 km/ 4.223 miles
Race Distance: 299.068 km/ 185.832 miles
Race Weather: Overcast/cool

Past Winners

Year	Driver	Nat.	Car	Circuit	Distance miles/km	Speed mph/km/h
1979	Alan Jones	AUS	3.0 Williams-Ford FW07	Hockenheim	189.83/305.51	134.27/216.09
1980	Jacques Laffite	F	3.0 Ligier-Ford JS11/15	Hockenheim	189.83/305.51	137.22/220.83
1981	Nelson Piquet	BR	3.0 Brabham-Ford BT49C	Hockenheim	189.83/305.51	132.53/213.29
1982	Patrick Tambay	F	1.5 Ferrari 126C2 t/c	Hockenheim	190.05/305.86	130.43/209.90
1983	Rene Arnoux	F	1.5 Ferrari 126C3 t/c	Hockenheim	190.05/305.86	130.81/210.52
1984	Alain Prost	F	1.5 McLaren-TAG MP4/2 t/c	Hockenheim	185.83/299.07	131.61/211.80
1985	Michele Alboreto	I	1.5 Ferrari 156/85 t/c	New Nürburgring	189.09/304.31	118.77/191.15
1986	Nelson Piquet	BR	1.5 Williams-Honda FW11 t/c	Hockenheim	185.83/299.07	135.75/218.46

146

Lap Chart

Grid Order	1	2	3	4	5	6	7	8	9	10	11	12	13	14	15	16	17	18	19	20	21	22	23	24	25	26	27	28	29	30	31	32	33	34	35	36	37	38	39	40	41	42	43	44	
5 Nigel Mansell	12	5	5	5	5	5	5	1	1	1	1	1	1	1	1	1	1	1	1	1	5	5	5	5	5	1	1	1	1	1	1	1	1	1	1	1	1	1	1	6	6	6	6	6	1
12 Ayrton Senna	5	1	1	1	1	1	1	5	5	5	5	5	5	5	5	5	5	5	5	1	1	1	1	1	5	5	5	6	6	6	6	6	6	6	6	6	6	6	6	2	2	2	2	2	2
1 Alain Prost	1	12	6	6	6	6	6	6	6	6	6	6	6	6	6	6	6	6	6	6	12	12	6	6	6	2	2	2	2	2	2	2	2	2	2	2	2	2	2	12	12	12	12		3
6 Nelson Piquet	6	6	12	12	12	12	12	12	12	12	12	12	12	12	12	12	12	12	20	6	12	12	20	12	12	12	12	12	12	12	12	12	12	12	12	12	12	12	12	4	4	4	4		4
27 Michele Alboreto	20	27	27	20	27	27	27	27	20	20	20	20	20	20	20	20	20	20	6	20	20	20	12	20	26	26	26	26	26	26	4	4	4	4	4	4	4	3	3	3	3				5
20 Thierry Boutsen	27	20	20	27	20	20	20	20	20	2	2	2	2	2	2	2	2	28	28	2	2	2	2	2	26	4	4	4	4	4	4	3	3	3	3	3	3	3	30	30	30				6
8 Andrea de Cesaris	2	2	2	2	2	2	2	2	2	8	8	8	28	28	28	28	19	2	2	17	17	17	17	24	24	4	3	3	3	3	3	3	30	30	30	30	30	30	30						7
2 Stefan Johansson	28	28	28	28	28	28	28	28	28	28	28	28	19	19	19	19	28	26	17	24	24	24	24	26	26	3	23	30	30	30	30	30	9	9											8
19 Teo Fabi	8	8	8	8	8	8	8	8	8	8	19	19	19	26	26	26	26	26	17	26	26	26	26	26	23	23	23	30	23	9	9	9	9												9
28 Gerhard Berger	19	19	19	19	19	19	19	19	19	19	17	17	17	24	24	24	24	24	24	24	23	23	23	23	3	4	30	9	9																10
7 Riccardo Patrese	17	25	17	17	17	17	17	17	17	17	27	26	26	17	17	17	17	17	19	23	3	3	3	3	4	3	9																		11
25 Rene Arnoux	25	17	18	18	18	18	18	18	26	26	24	24	10	10	10	10	10	23	3	4	4	4	4	30	30																				12
17 Derek Warwick	18	18	11	11	11	11	11	11	24	24	10	10	23	23	23	23	10	4	30	30	30	30	9	9																					13
11 Satoru Nakajima	7	11	7	24	24	24	24	26	10	10	23	23	30	30	4	3	3	3	30	10	10	9	9																						14
18 Eddie Cheever	11	7	24	26	26	26	26	24	18	23	30	30	4	4	3	4	4	4	10	9	9																								15
24 Alessandro Nannini	24	24	26	10	10	10	10	10	23	30	4	4	3	3	30	30	30	30	9																										16
26 Piercarlo Ghinzani	26	26	10	23	23	23	23	23	30	4	3	3	21	21	21	21	21	9																											17
23 Adrian Campos	10	10	30	30	30	30	30	30	4	3	9	9	9	9	9	9	9																												18
9 Martin Brundle	4	30	23	4	4	4	4	4	3	9	21	21																																	19
10 Christian Danner	30	23	4	3	3	3	3	3	9	14																																			20
30 Philippe Alliot	3	4	3	21	21	21	21	21	14	21																																			21
4 Philippe Streiff	23	3	21	14	9	9	9	9	11																																				22
3 Jonathan Palmer	21	21	14	16	14	16	16	14	21																																				23
16 Ivan Capelli	14	14	16	9	16	14	14																																						24
14 Pascal Fabre	16	16	9	25	25	25																																							25
21 Alex Caffi	9	9	25	7	7																																								26

Championship Points

	Drivers			Constructors	
1	Nelson Piquet	39 pts	1	Williams	69 pts
2	Ayrton Senna	35 pts	2	McLaren	45 pts
3	Nigel Mansell	30 pts	3	Lotus	41 pts
4	Alain Prost	26 pts	4	Ferrari	17 pts
5	Stefan Johansson	19 pts	5	Tyrrell	8 pts
6	Gerhard Berger	9 pts	6	Arrows	6 pts
7	Michele Alboreto	8 pts	7	Benetton	5 pts
8	Satoru Nakajima	6 pts	8	Brabham	4 pts
9=	Andrea de Cesaris	4 pts	9	Zakspeed	2 pts
9=	Eddie Cheever	4 pts	10=	March	1 pt
9=	Philippe Streiff	4 pts	10=	Lola	1 pt
9=	Jonathan Palmer	4 pts	10=	Ligier	1 pt
13	Teo Fabi	3 pts			
14=	Thierry Boutsen	2 pts			
14=	Derek Warwick	2 pts			
14=	Martin Brundle	2 pts			
17=	Philippe Alliot	1 pt			
17=	Rene Arnoux	1 pt			
17=	Ivan Capelli	1 pt			

	Jim Clark Cup			Colin Chapman Cup	
1	Jonathan Palmer	48 pts	1	Tyrrell	87 pts
2	Philippe Streiff	39 pts	2	AGS	32 pts
3	Pascal Fabre	32 pts	3	Lola	19 pts
4	Philippe Alliot	19 pts	4	March	6 pts
5	Ivan Capelli	6 pts			

HUNGARIAN

GRAND PRIX

The Hungarian Grand Prix was the second successive race when Nelson Piquet suddenly found himself in the lead just when he needed to be. He was 17 seconds behind team mate Mansell nearing the close, when Mansell's lead came to an abrupt end.

Piquet was looking resigned to his sixth second place of the year, when Mansell's Williams gave a funny wriggle. The driver looked as though he might have been weaving to get more fuel into the tanks. But in fact Mansell's car had lost a wheelnut. The Williams twitched as his right rear wheel tilted over at an angle and Mansell parked the car on the grass, his race was over. The explanation of why the wheelnut came undone was a lesson to any team. The era of tyre stops is principally to blame. It was found that unless there was a little tolerance in the locating lugs, it is difficult to take a wheel off quickly at a pit stop, particularly when the wheel is hot. So a minute tolerance was built in, but this means that the wheel has room to move on its hub, and each hard and sharp acceleration loosens the wheelnut a fraction. Of course, where there are mid-race pit stops, the wheelnut is re-tightened when the new wheel is put on. But where cars don't stop for tyres – as at Hungaroring – the wheelnut just becomes looser and looser....

Piquet swooped past his team mate's stationary car and six laps later, he took the chequered flag and another nine points to extend his World Championship lead. "It's nice to have some luck sometimes", he admitted. Piquet had dominated the news off the track as much as his Williams team mate dominated it on the track. The news broke late on the Thursday evening that he had signed for Lotus for 1988. The repercussions of his signing would be far

reaching. Piquet, paid by Honda, now lined up with Nakajima. His compatriot but rival, Senna, was still negotiating with McLaren, they said, but now his bargaining power had seriously diminished. And if Williams had no Piquet, no World Champion, would they still get Honda engines in 1988? The ups and downs of the deal were discussed long and hard. What was certain was that Piquet had got just what he wanted, and had also succeeded in getting at almost all the people he wanted to.

Out on the circuit, things hadn't changed much since the previous year. The track was still very slippery and the surface still not giving much grip, although the weather was thankfully cooler than the previous year. The circuit had matured a little, there was more grass everywhere and the place didn't look as new – nor was it looking tatty. The weather was decidedly wintry on the Friday with spots of rain during the first practice session and the track only drying out by the end of the afternoon session. By then, Mansell had been on slick tyres for a while. He'd been off the track once, but set a time over two seconds faster than his nearest rival, Prost, by the end of the session. "Getting onto dry tyres early counted for a lot", he said. The next day was Mansell's 33rd birthday, and there were plenty of cakes for the driver. Out on the track, Mansell again spun a number of times, describing the circuit as a 'moving target' with the amount of grip changing every few minutes. For that reason, he never

improved, but he wasn't too worried. He would still start from pole for the seventh time out of the nine races held so far.

The pleasant surprise on that second day of qualifying was that Gerhard Berger got a Ferrari onto the front row of the grid for the first time since Stefan Johansson started from the front row at Nurburgring over two years earlier. Ferrari's aerodynamic changes after Hockenheim, plus continuous development had borne fruit. In charge of engineering at this race was Harvey Postlethwaite, dusted off, said the Italian newspapers, while John Barnard was sorting out one or two little problems at Maranello. Berger's time was achieved in spite of the fact that he wasn't at all well. But his front row grid position was great news for Austrians from over the border and the promoter of the Austrian Grand Prix scheduled a week later. Piquet started from right behind his own team mate, still 1.7 seconds slower than the other Williams-Honda and 1.2s slower than Berger. Piquet's objective was simply to get on with getting his Williams working on the slippery track, although like most others, he suffered from the odd spin and the fact that traffic can upset any lap, particularly when there is really only one overtaking place and a trip off-line could spoil several subsequent laps.

Even Alain Prost had a spin and described his car as not being right for the circuit. The problem everyone suffered from was a lack of grip, although Prost's car did improve. His time was set, like Mansell's, on the first day, although he was 2.1 seconds slower than the pole man. Berger and Piquet slotted in between them, so 2.1 seconds covered the first four. Alboreto was looking just as competitive as Berger. Indeed, he was third quickest in the warm-up, although he had a couple of spins in practice and qualifying, but didn't hit anything or anyone. Lotus were a little mystified on this billiard-smooth surface. Perhaps their active suspension wasn't working because it didn't have anything to react against. The car featured new, lower bodywork which was principally for the upcoming high speed circuits. Senna reported that the aerodynamics were OK, the engine was OK and the tyres were OK. Only problem – no grip! It sounded familiar.

Boutsen and Fabi were becoming used to their problems: lack of boost here and there, the odd spin, unpredictable handling. Fabi had a spin and nearly collected Boutsen which was certainly an unexpected dimension. Things weren't much better for Stefan Johansson, whose McLaren stuck in gear (his sister Asa was racing in the same meeting in her Autobianchi). Derek Warwick, meanwhile, was another on the sick list, with not only 'flu but conjunctivitis as well. He nearly pulled out altogether. The normally aspirated bunch thought

they might be in with a hope on this circuit, and Streiff, Alliot and Palmer formed a little breakaway group from 14th to 16th on the grid. Nowhere had the likes of Ligier, Zakspeed, Minardi and Osella looked more enviously at those nice uncomplicated normally aspirated V8s which preceded them. Nakajima, however, was also slower and nearly four seconds behind his Lotus-Honda team mate.

The organisers said they would be happy if they got a crowd of 80,000 on race day, but in the control tower excitement mounted as that figure was nearly doubled. It wasn't quite the 200,000 of the previous year, but there were absolutely no complaints and much more of the expensive seating had been taken up. Happily the weather remained sunny in the warm-up, as Mansell set a time of 1 minute 31 seconds, Berger was a second slower, Alboreto nearly another second behind and Prost 0.6s further back. If this was maintained, it would be a thoroughly boring race! Berger still didn't look well as he lay under an umbrella at the side of the track prior to the start, but he climbed into his Ferrari and briefly mixed it with the Williamses at the start. As the Williamses accelerated down the dusty right side of the track, the Ferraris lined up on the left, going round the outside of Piquet in the first corner to emerge

second and third – Berger then Alboreto – to Mansell's first at the end of the first lap. Piquet, who was knocked down to fourth, wasn't pleased. "They took some risks in the first corner", he admitted, "But then they're not Championship contenders."

The first four pulled away rapidly, never separated by much more than a second or so, but on lap 13 they were three seconds apart. Berger's CV joint had broken, leaving Alboreto second and Piquet third. Senna was fourth, challenged by Prost at first and then Boutsen. Coming through into seventh place was Johansson, even overtaking team mate Prost until he spun out with a seized gearbox bearing on lap 14. After Berger's disappearance, Mansell began to pull away from Alboreto and Piquet, although the gap between them varied enormously, such were the problems overtaking slower cars. Sometimes it would vary by as much as two seconds from one lap to the next. And then Alboreto began to pull away from Piquet too, the Williams driver finding his car varying in traffic. One battle that was consistent was that between Senna and Boutsen and it continued all the way from the start until backmarkers finally broke it up after 32 laps of the 76 lap race. Boutsen had brake problems right from the start and just couldn't get by the Lotus. Watching the two of them was

Previous page: Piquet inherited his second lucky win in two races, this time taking over the lead from team mate Nigel Mansell six laps from home

Right: The class of '87 at their Sunday morning pre-race briefing

Prost, whose engine had misfired from the warming-up lap and Patrese, who had broken free from the Arrows pair behind him, Warwick leading Cheever. De Cesaris came next, before a big gap to Capelli, already in charge of the normally aspirated class, but shadowed by Streiff.

When the Senna/Boutsen battle broke up, there wasn't a lot left in this race. Admittedly Mansell and then Piquet set fastest laps on lap 34, but they were around 14 seconds apart and Mansell set another fastest a lap later. Piquet replied with another on lap 38, but that only brought the gap down to 13.2 seconds. Alboreto, meanwhile, had been happy in third place until his engine broke on lap 44, ending another promising run. If there wasn't very much going on at the front, there was plenty happening further back. Streiff had come up to challenge Capelli's class-leading March, and from lap 40 they ran nose to tail for three laps until Streiff got by and then so did team mate Palmer, the two Tyrrells now engaging in their almost habitual battle. Palmer had been trapped in traffic at the first corner and had taken some while to recover and Streiff, meanwhile, had had a broken exhaust. After some 44 laps, the good friends in the Arrows came into conflict when the exhausted Warwick found himself under attack from Cheever as the American attempted to overtake. Cheever's nose section was damaged and Warwick had a puncture. The latter radioed in to say

that he was coming in to the pits for a new tyre, but who should appear first in the pit but Cheever, whose radio wasn't working. With the mechanics all prepared for a tyre change, Cheever was duly sent out again while Warwick's tyres were changed, and Cheever got his new nose section a lap later. Warwick didn't actually lose a place as a result of this confusion.

Soon after, Piquet made extensive inroads into Mansell's lead, lowering an 11.2 second lead on lap 49 to a 6.5 second lead on lap 52, although it got no lower and then gradually crept up to over ten seconds again by lap 57. On lap 60, the Williams pair again both set fastest laps and although the leading margin did go down to 8.9 seconds on lap 64, the trend was rapidly reversed and up it went to 12 seconds and rising by a second a lap. Piquet was suffering from tyre vibration. Mansell was suffering no such thing, and was sailing serenely to victory when suddenly his car veered one way and then the other. It was the beginning of the end which was to come seconds after. The Englishman's race was over and he could only be philosophical in retirement. Piquet was naturally delighted, even if he had been outclassed by his team mate. Being there is what it is all about, and he was in the right place at the right time. He had now won both the Hungarian Grand Prix to be held in the World Championship.

Like the previous year, Piquet was followed home by his compatriot,

Ayrton Senna. The Lotus driver had been outclassed by the two Williamses. He had suffered vibrations from half distance onwards, he was tired, he had a painful back, the car was tired and it had been jumping out of fourth gear. Under the circumstances, second place was gratefully taken. You could hear Alain Prost's engine misfire every so often, but for a while, around the two thirds mark, it cleared, and the car went superbly, catching and overtaking Boutsen's ailing Benetton. Prost even had some grip now, as well. But then back came the McLaren misfire and the World Champion had to simply cruise to what became third place.

Boutsen lost boost pressure and had more brake trouble, so fourth wasn't a bad result, although he was lapped. Patrese finished fifth and won his first two points of the year, while the unwell Warwick salvaged a point from the race in spite of his ailment. Between him and team mate Cheever was Palmer in the first of the normally aspirated Tyrrells, with Streiff behind Cheever and Capelli next up. Streiff had suffered a blistered left front tyre during the closing stages, but was still in touch with team mate Palmer in the Colin Chapman Cup, the pair being separated by 12 points. Amongst the others, Nannini brought Minardi their first finish of the year, but both Zakspeeds retired and Fabi went out early with a broken gearbox. It certainly hadn't been one of the best races of the year, but as far as Piquet was concerned, it felt fine.

Right: Cheever locks up a brake trying to avoid team mate Warwick. The two collided, causing confusion in the pits when they both appeared together. An unwell Warwick eventually finished sixth, Cheever eighth

Below left: In spite of its rural location and its huge crowd, the Hungaroring is still a tight and twisty circuit with few overtaking opportunities. Streiff confirmed Tyrrell's Colin Chapman Cup with ninth place behind Palmer

Below right: Prost and Johansson chase the leaders in the early stages, lying seventh and eighth. Prost eventually finished third

Left: If Piquet had over-taken Prost, it would have looked like this

Centre left: Piquet harries Alboreto's second placed Ferrari before overtaking and pulling away on lap 29

Below left: Early stages: Mansell leads the Ferraris, Piquet, Senna, Prost, Boutsen, Johansson and Patrese

Below right: Alessandro Nannini gave the Minardi team their first finish of the season with eleventh place

Backmarker battle: Zakspeed, Minardi and Tyrrell

Right: Piquet passes Berger: the Hungarian Grand Prix was dominated by Williams and Ferrari in the early stages but both Ferraris eventually retired

Left: Mansell called the track 'a moving target' in practice. He ended his race on the grass, having lost a wheel nut

Centre left: Brundle watches the race after retiring his Zakspeed

Centre right: Alliot off-course in the Lola

Below: Patrese picked up more World Championship points for Brabham and his first of the year with fifth place in Hungary

HUNGARIAN GRAND PRIX · August 9

Entries and Practice Times

Driver	Nat.	Car	Practice 1	Practice 2	Warm Up	Engine	Turbos	Electrics/Plugs	Fuel/Oil	Brake Discs/Calipers	Shocks
1 Alain Prost	F	Marlboro McLaren MP4/3	1m30.156s	1m30.327s	1m34.307s	1.5t TAG V6	KKK	Bosch	Shell	SEP/McL	Bil
2 Stefan Johansson	S	Marlboro McLaren MP4/3	1m31.228s	1m31.940s	1m35.012s	1.5t TAG V6	KKK	Bosch	Shell	SEP/McL	Bil
3 Jonathan Palmer	GB	Data General/Courtaulds Tyrrell DG/016	1m34.398s	1m33.895s	1m37.443s	3.5 Ford Cosworth DFZ V8		Cos/Ch	Elf	AP	Koni
4 Philippe Streiff	F	Data General/Courtaulds Tyrrell DG/016	1m33.644s	1m34.383s	1m37.760s	3.5 Ford Cosworth DFZ V8		Cos/Ch	Elf	AP	Koni
5 Nigel Mansell	GB	Canon Williams FW11B	1m28.047s	1m28.682s	1m31.719s	1.5t Honda V6	IHI	Honda/NGK	Mobil	SEP/AP	Showa
6 Nelson Piquet	BR	Canon Williams FW11B	1m30.842s	1m29.724s		1.5t Honda V6	IHI	Honda/NGK	Mobil	SEP/AP	Showa
7 Riccardo Patrese	I	Brabham BT56	1m31.586s	1.32.422s	1m36.186s	1.5t BMW S4	Garrett	Bosch/Ch	Win/Castrol	SEP/Bra	Koni
8 Andrea de Cesaris	I	Brabham BT56	1m32.628s	1m43.913s	1m35.934s	1.5t BMW S4	Garrett	Bosch/Ch	Win/Castrol	SEP/Bra	Koni
9 Martin Brundle	GB	West Zakspeed 871	1m35.754s	1m35.818s	2m06.842s	1.5t Zakspeed S4	Garrett	Bosch/Ch	Win/Castrol	AP	Sachs
10 Christian Danner	D	West Zakspeed 871	1m35.930s	1m36.371s	1m37.985s	1.5t Zakspeed S4	Garrett	Bosch/Ch	Win/Castrol	AP	Sachs
11 Satoru Nakajima	J	Camel Lotus 99T	1m34.297s	1m34.476s	1m36.459s	1.5t Honda V6	IHI	Honda/NGK	Elf	SEP/Bre	L/A
12 Ayrton Senna	BR	Camel Lotus 99T	1m31.387s	1m30.387s	1m35.096s	1.5t Honda V6	IHI	Honda/NGK	Elf	SEP/Bre	L/A
14 Pascal Fabre	F	El Charro AGS JH22C	1m38.803s	1m37.730s	1m38.863s	3.5 Ford Cosworth DFZ V8		Cos/Ch	Acto	SEP/AGS	Koni
16 Ivan Capelli	I	Leyton House March 871	1m34.950s	1m34.426s	1m37.157s	3.5 Ford Cosworth DFZ V8		Cos/Ch	BP	AP	Koni
17 Derek Warwick	GB	USF&G Arrows A10	1m31.416s	1m34.386s	1m36.470s	1.5t Megatron S4	Garrett	Bosch/Ch	Win/Castrol	AP	Koni
18 Eddie Cheever	USA	USF&G Arrows A10	1m32.336s	1m33.700s	1m38.119s	1.5t Megatron S4	Garrett	Bosch/Ch	Win/Castrol	AP	Koni
19 Teo Fabi	I	Benetton B187	1m32.452s	1m32.639s	1m36.245s	1.5t Ford V6	Garrett	Ford EED/Ch	Mobil	SEP/AP	Koni
20 Thierry Boutsen	B	Benetton B187	1m30.748s	1m30.810s	1m34.474s	1.5t Ford V6	Garrett	Ford EED/Ch	Mobil	SEP/AP	Koni
21 Alex Caffi	I	Landis & Gyr Osella FA1I	1m36.693s	1m35.594s	1m36.807s	1.5t Alfa Romeo V8	KKK	Mar/Ch	Agip	Bre	Koni
23 Adrian Campos	E	Minardi M186	1m36.067s	1m37.948s	1m39.391s	1.5t Motori Moderni V6	KKK	Mar/Ch	Agip	Bre	Koni
24 Alessandro Nannini	I	Minardi M186	1m34.796s	1m34.770s	1m38.080s	1.5t Motori Moderni V6	KKK	Mar/Ch	Agip	SEP/Bre	Koni
25 Rene Arnoux	F	Loto Ligier JS29C	1m35.346s	1m34.518s	1m36.998s	1.5t Megatron S4	Garrett	Bosch/Ch	Win/Castrol	SEP/Bre	Koni
26 Piercarlo Ghinzani	I	Loto Ligier JS29C	1m36.411s	1m36.109s	1m38.810s	1.5t Megatron S4	Garrett	Bosch/Ch	Win/Castrol	SEP/Bre	Koni
27 Michele Alboreto	I	Ferrari F187	1m30.472s	1m30.310s	1m33.750s	1.5t Ferrari V6	Garrett	Mar-Weber/Ch	Agip	SEP/Bre	Marz
28 Gerhard Berger	A	Ferrari F187	1m31.080s	1m28.549s	1m32.882s	1.5t Ferrari V6	Garrett	Mar-Weber/Ch	Agip	SEP/Bre	Marz
30 Philippe Alliot	F	Larrousse Lola LC87	1m33.777s	1m34.014s	1m36.779s	3.5 Ford Cosworth DFZ V8		Cos-Mar/Ch	BP	SEP/AP	Koni

August 7	August 8	August 9
Drying/cool	Sunny	Sunny

Starting Grid

		5	Mansell
Berger	28	6	Piquet
Prost	1	27	Alboreto
Senna	12	20	Boutsen
Johansson	2	17	Warwick
Patrese	7	18	Cheever
Fabi	19	8	de Cesaris
Streiff	4	30	Alliot
Palmer	3	11	Nakajima
Capelli	16	25	Arnoux
Nannini	24	21	Caffi
Brundle	9	10	Danner
Campos	23	26	Ghinzani
Fabre	14		

Results, Retirements and Fastest Laps

Place	Driver	Car	Laps	Time/Retirement	Fastest Lap No.	/Time
1	Nelson Piquet	1.5t Williams-Honda FW11B	76	1h59m 26.793s	63	1m30.149s
2	Ayrton Senna	1.5t Lotus-Honda 99T	76	2h00m04.520s	43	1m32.426s
3	Alain Prost	1.5t McLaren-TAG MP4/3	76	2h00m54.249s	57	1m31.602s
4	Thierry Boutsen	1.5t Benetton-Ford B187	75	2h00m08.522s	39	1m32.524s
5	Riccardo Patrese	1.5t Brabham-BMW BT56	75	2h01m00.034s	42	1m34.387s
6	Derek Warwick	1.5t Arrows-Megatron A10	74	1h59m59.527s	53	1m34.163s
7	Jonathan Palmer	3.5 Tyrrell-Ford DG/016	74	2h00m01.166s	61	1m34.824s
8	Eddie Cheever	1.5t Arrows-Megatron A10	74	2h00m09.430s	68	1m32.603s
9	Philippe Streiff	3.5 Tyrrell-Ford DG/016	74	2h00m24.789s	62	1m35.069s
10	Ivan Capelli	3.5 March-Lotus 871	74	2h00m36.164s	70	1m34.926s
11	Alessandro Nannini	1.5t Minardi-Motori Moderni M186	73	1h59m53.434s	70	1m34.519s
12	Piercarlo Ghinzani	1.5t Ligier -Megatron JS29C	73	2h00m20.411s	53	1m36.045s
13	Pascal Fabre	3.5 AGS-Ford JH22C	71	2h00m17.653s	61	1m36.043s
14	Nigel Mansell	1.5t Williams-Honda FW11B	70	1h49m22.706s lost rear wheel nut	65	1m30.298s
	Alex Caffi	1.5t Osella-Alfa Romeo FA1I	64	Electrics	18	1m37.046s
	Rene Arnoux	1.5t Ligier -Megatron JS29C	57	Electrics cut out	17	1m37.169s
	Philippe Alliot	3.5 Lola-Ford LC87	48	Accident	47	1m35.210s
	Martin Brundle	1.5t Zakspeed 871	45	Turbo	41	1m36.195s
	Michele Alboreto	1.5t Ferrari-Spa F187	43	Engine	39	1m32.679s
	Andrea de Cesaris	1.5t Brabham-BMW BT56	43	Third gear	34	1m34.039s
	Stefan Johansson	1.5t McLaren-TAG MP4/3	14	Gearbox bearing/spin	14	1m34.843s
	Teo Fabi	1.5t Benetton-Ford B187	14	Engine	14	1m35.210s
	Adrian Campos	1.5t Minardi-Motori Moderni M186	14	Accident	13	1m39.486s
	Gerhard Berger	1.5t Ferrari-Spa F187	13	C V joint	12	1m33.826s
	Christian Danner	1.5t Zakspeed 871	3	Electrics cut out	3	1m39.650s
	Satoru Nakajima	1.5t Lotus-Honda 99T	1	Driveshaft	1	2m30.651s

Average Speed of Winner: 153.239 km/h, 95.218 mph
Fastest Lap: Nelson Piquet on lap 63, 1m30.149s, 160.259 km/h, 99.603 mph (record)
Previous Lap Record: Nelson Piquet (1.5t Williams-Honda FW11), 1m31.001s, 158.794 km/h, 98.669 mph (1986)

Circuit Data

Hungarian Grand Prix, Hungaroring, Budapest, Hungary

Circuit Length: 4.014 km/2.494 miles
Race Distance: 305.064 km/189.558 miles
Race Weather: Sunny/hot

Past Winners

Year	Driver	Nat.	Car	Circuit	Distance miles/km	Speed mph/km/h
1986	Nelson Piquet	BR	1.5t Williams-Honda FW11	Hungaroring	189.56/305.06	94.33/151.80

Lap Chart

Grid Order	1	2	3	4	5	6	7	8	9	10	11	12	13	14	15	16	17	18	19	20	21	22	23	24	25	26	27	28	29	30	31	32	33	34	35	36	37	38	39	40	41	42	43	44	45	46	47	48	49	50	51	52	53	54	55	56	57	58	59	60	
5 Nigel Mansell	5	5	5	5	5	5	5	5	5	5	5	5	5	5	5	5	5	5	5	5	5	5	5	5	5	5	5	5	5	5	5	5	5	5	5	5	5	5	5	5	5	5	5	5	5	5	5	5	5	5	5	5	5	5	5	5	5	5	5	5	1
28 Gerhard Berger	28	28	28	28	28	28	28	28	28	28	28	28	27	27	27	27	27	27	27	27	27	27	27	27	27	6	6	6	6	6	6	6	6	6	6	6	6	6	6	6	6	6	6	6	6	6	6	6	6	6	6	6	6	6	6	6	6	6	6	6	2
6 Nelson Piquet	27	27	27	27	27	27	27	27	27	27	6	6	6	6	6	6	6	6	6	6	6	6	6	6	6	27	27	27	27	27	27	27	27	27	27	12	12	12	12	12	12	12	12	12	12	12	12	12	12	12	12	12	12	12	12	12	12	12	12	12	3
1 Alain Prost	6	6	6	6	6	6	6	6	6	6	6	28	12	12	12	12	12	12	12	12	12	12	12	12	12	12	12	12	12	12	12	12	12	12	12	20	20	20	20	20	20	20	20	20	20	20	20	20	20	20	20	20	20	20	20	20	20	20	1	1	4
27 Michele Alboreto	12	12	12	12	12	12	12	12	12	12	12	20	20	20	20	20	20	20	20	20	20	20	20	20	20	20	20	20	20	20	20	20	20	20	20	1	1	1	1	1	1	1	1	1	1	1	1	1	1	1	1	1	1	1	1	1	1	1	20	20	5
12 Ayrton Senna	1	1	20	20	20	20	20	20	20	20	20	20	2	1	1	1	1	1	1	1	1	1	1	1	1	1	1	1	1	1	1	1	1	1	1	1	1	1	1	7	7	7	7	7	7	7	7	7	7	7	7	7	7	7	7	7	7	7	7	7	6
20 Thierry Boutsen	20	20	1	2	2	2	2	2	2	2	2	2	2	2	1	7	7	7	7	7	7	7	7	7	7	7	7	7	7	7	7	7	7	7	7	7	7	7	7	18	18	18	18	17	17	17	17	17	17	17	17	17	17	17	17	17	17	17	17	17	7
2 Stefan Johansson	2	2	2	1	1	1	1	1	1	1	1	1	1	1	7	17	17	17	17	17	17	17	17	17	17	17	17	17	17	17	17	17	17	17	17	17	17	17	17	17	4	3	3	3	3	3	3	3	3	3	3	3	3	3	3	3	3	3	3	3	8
17 Derek Warwick	7	7	7	7	7	7	7	7	7	7	7	7	7	7	17	18	18	18	18	18	18	18	18	18	18	18	18	18	18	18	18	18	18	18	18	18	18	18	18	4	4	4	3	4	4	4	24	24	24	24	24	24	24	4	4	9					9
7 Riccardo Patrese	17	17	17	17	17	17	17	17	17	17	17	17	18	8	8	8	8	8	8	8	8	8	8	8	8	8	8	8	8	8	8	8	8	8	8	8	8	8	3	3	3	24	24	4	4	4	4	4	4	4	24	24									10
18 Eddie Cheever	18	18	18	18	18	18	18	18	18	18	18	8	16	16	16	16	16	16	16	16	16	16	16	16	16	16	16	16	16	16	16	16	16	16	16	4	16	16	24	16	16	16	16	16	16	16	16	16	16	16											11
19 Teo Fabi	8	8	8	8	8	8	8	8	8	8	8	8	19	4	4	4	4	4	4	4	4	4	4	4	4	4	4	4	4	4	4	4	4	4	4	16	24	24	16	18	18	18	18	18	18	18	18	18	18	18											12
8 Andrea de Cesaris	16	19	19	19	19	19	19	19	19	19	19	19	16	21	21	21	21	21	21	21	21	21	21	21	21	21	3	3	3	3	3	3	3	3	3	9	30	30	30	26	26	26	26	26	26	26	26	26	26	26											13
4 Phillipe Streiff	19	16	16	16	16	16	16	16	16	16	16	16	4	25	25	25	25	25	25	25	25	25	25	3	3	3	24	24	24	24	24	24	24	30	25	25	26	25	25	25	25	25	25	25	25	21	14	14													14
30 Philippe Alliot	4	4	4	4	4	4	4	4	4	4	4	4	21	9	9	9	9	9	9	9	9	9	9	9	25	25	25	25	9	9	9	9	9	9	9	25	26	26	26	25	21	21	21	21	21	21	21	14	21	21											15
3 Jonathan Palmer	30	30	30	21	21	21	21	21	21	21	21	21	25	24	24	24	24	24	24	3	3	3	3	3	24	24	24	9	25	25	25	25	25	25	30	26	9	21	21	14	14	14	14	14	14	14	14														16
11 Satoru Nakajima	21	21	21	25	25	25	25	25	25	25	25	9	9	3	3	3	3	3	3	24	24	24	24	24	9	9	9	9	21	26	26	26	26	26	26	26	26	25	21	21	14	14																			17
16 Ivan Capelli	25	25	25	9	9	9	9	9	9	9	9	9	24	26	26	26	26	26	26	26	26	26	26	26	26	26	26	30	30	30	30	30	30	30	30	26	14	14																					18
25 Rene Arnoux	3	9	9	24	24	24	24	24	24	24	24	24	3	14	30	30	30	30	30	30	30	30	30	30	30	30	30	30	21	21	21	21	21	21	21																							19
24 Alessandro Nannini	9	3	24	3	3	3	3	3	3	3	3	26	30	14	14	14	14	14	14	14	14	14	14	14	14	14	14	14	14	14																											20
21 Alex Caffi	24	24	3	23	23	23	23	23	14	14	14	14	26	14																																										21
9 Martin Brundle	10	10	10	26	26	26	14	23	26	26	14	30																																									22
10 Christian Danner	23	23	23	14	14	14	14	26	23	30	30	30	23																																								23
23 Adrian Campos	26	26	26	30	30	30	30	30	30	23	23	23																																									24
26 Piercarlo Ghinzani	14	14	14																																																			25
14 Pascal Fabre	11																																																				26

Lap Chart continued

61	62	63	64	65	66	67	68	69	70	71	72	73	74	75	76	
5	5	5	5	5	5	5	5	5	5	6	6	6	6	6	6	1
6	6	6	6	6	6	6	6	6	6	12	12	12	12	12	12	2
12	12	12	12	12	12	12	12	12	12	1	1	1	1	1	1	3
1	1	1	1	1	1	1	1	1	1	20	20	20	20	20		4
20	20	20	20	20	20	20	20	20	20	7	7	7	7	7		5
7	7	7	7	7	7	7	7	7	17	17	17	17				6
17	17	17	17	17	17	17	17	17	3	3	3	3				7
3	3	3	3	3	3	3	3	3	18	18	18					8
4	4	4	4	18	18	18	18	18	4	4	4	4				9
24	24	24	18	18	4	4	4	4	16	16	16	16				10
16	16	18	24	24	24	24	24	24	24	24	24					11
18	18	16	16	16	16	16	16	16	26	26	26					12
26	26	26	26	26	26	26	26	26	14							13
14	14	14	14	14	14	14	14	14								14
21	21	21	21													15

Championship Points

	Drivers				Constructors	
1	Nelson Piquet	48 pts	1		Williams	78 pts
2	Ayrton Senna	41 pts	2		McLaren	49 pts
3=	Nigel Mansell	30 pts	3		Lotus	47 pts
3=	Alain Prost	30 pts	4		Ferrari	17 pts
5	Stefan Johansson	19 pts	5=		Tyrrell	8 pts
6	Gerhard Berger	9 pts	5=		Benetton	8 pts
7	Michele Alboreto	8 pts	7		Arrows	7 pts
8	Satoru Nakajima	6 pts	8		Brabham	6 pts
9	Thierry Boutsen	5 pts	9		Zakspeed	2 pts
10=	Andrea de Cesaris	4 pts	10=		March	1 pt
10=	Eddie Cheever	4 pts	10=		Lola	1 pt
10=	Philippe Streiff	4 pts	10=		Ligier	1 pt
10=	Jonathan Palmer	4 pts				
14=	Teo Fabi	3 pts				
14=	Derek Warwick	3 pts				
16=	Martin Brundle	2 pts				
16=	Riccardo Patrese	2 pts				
18=	Philippe Alliot	1 pt				
18=	Rene Arnoux	1 pt				
18=	Ivan Capelli	1 pt				

	Jim Clark Cup			Colin Chapman Cup	
1	Jonathan Palmer	57 pts	1	Tyrrell	102 pts
2	Philippe Streiff	45 pts	2	AGS	35 pts
3	Pascal Fabre	35 pts	3	Lola	19 pts
4	Philippe Alliot	19 pts	4	March	10 pts
5	Ivan Capelli	10 pts			

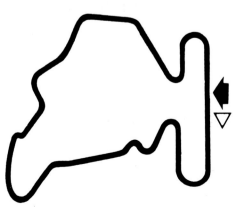

159

AUSTRIAN

GRAND PRIX

The Austrian Grand Prix was a truly extraordinary race from start to finish. In retrospect, it was almost a relief that Saturday was virtually washed out. It saved everyone from any more nasty surprises.

At the halfway mark in the 52 lap race, Nigel Mansell pulled a stunt which seemed to knock the stuffing out of his Brazilian team mate. The Williams-Honda pair were in traffic, and Mansell simply decided not to follow his team mate, but chose a different route through the slower cars. Miraculously, the road cleared ahead of him and while Piquet had to lift off, Mansell was able to charge through into the lead. Piquet seemed to settle for second place there and then. But the weekend's trials and tribulations were not yet over for Mansell, the jeep passed under the low rostrum gantry as it delivered the first three in the race and nearly knocked out the winner, Mansell, who was standing on the back of the vehicle. He nursed a large bruise on his forehead for the rest of the afternoon.

Mansell's troubles started some days previously when he began to suffer from an abscess on his wisdom tooth. It was finally decided that the offending molar had to come out the evening before practice. Another unlucky driver was Stefan Johansson. On Friday morning, a large deer suddenly appeared in the vicinity of the final corner, the Jochen Rindt Kurve, as unofficial practice was nearing completion. By rights, practice should have been stopped while the unfortunate animal was rounded up, but practice continued until the beast took to the track, where the hapless Stefan Johansson hit it as he crested the final rise. There was nothing he could do. He thumped the animal, killing it immediately and then proceeded to crash down the track, writing off his McLaren.

Thankfully Johansson wasn't hurt and a herd of venison jokes played down everyone's anxieties about what might have happened. Johansson was livid and both he and team boss Ron Dennis considered legal action. A tense Johansson commandeered the spare McLaren for the afternoon, while a monocoque was prepared back at base, ready to be flown out the next afternoon and built up overnight in the team garage for Sunday.

On Friday afternoon, Nelson Piquet went out and lapped at 159.457 mph (256.621 kph) which was fractionally quicker than the average speed of his own pole-winning lap at Silverstone. It made the Oesterreichring the fastest track in current Grand Prix use. Piquet might have been quicker, but for missing a gear due to the G-force on another lap. Mansell might have been quicker too, but for being held up by Ghinzani. They had no chance for faster times on Saturday, it poured with rain all morning. Only 21 cars made any attempt at a lap although the faithful spectators remained firmly wedged in their seats in spite of the sopping conditions. In the afternoon some drivers managed to put on slicks, but it never dried out enough for a competitive lap. The grid positions were decided by the previous afternoon's times.

It gave the grid quite an odd look. The two Williams-Hondas occupied the front row for the fourth time in the year, Piquet on pole in Austria for the third time in his career, and Mansell on the front row again, maintaining his 100 per cent record in 1987. Behind the Williamses came the Ferraris and Benettons on the next two rows. For once, we had to look beyond row three for both Ayrton Senna and Alain Prost. Neither had qualified as badly all year. But their loss was Ferrari and Benetton's gain. After the previous weekend's promise, the Ferraris were still going well in spite of the very different circuit configuration and a lack of real reliability. Berger's third spot on the grid was great news for the local promoters. The Benetton pair, sandwiched between the Italian cars, were a little more reliable and quick on the circuit than when they occupied the front row of the grid last year. However, both drivers had a nasty shock when they found Derek Warwick's spun Arrows on the racing line on their quick laps.

Ayrton Senna was only seventh and not at all happy with the handling of his Lotus, finding the car unstable on the bumps. After Patrese's Brabham, Alain Prost lined up behind Senna, again troubled by the bumpiness. That problem was at least partially cured by the warm-up, but Senna was still worried as to how his car would handle as its fuel load lessened. Behind them, some major dramas evolved. Nannini set a good 15th fastest time in the Minardi, while the normally aspirated bunch brought up the tail end of the grid as expected. Alliot was fastest from Capelli, the Tyrrell duo still trying to get their cars to handle. Pascal Fabre was five seconds down on the Tyrrells, 17 seconds slower than Nelson Piquet. One man who followed the weather forecast for Saturday was Nigel Mansell, who had heard that it

would rain on the day when most teams traditionally do their full tank race testing in the morning. Clutching an icepack to his jaw, Mansell explained how he had spent half an hour in Friday's qualifying running his race car on full tanks. That 30 minutes might have proved decisive, for virtually no one else was that far advanced when the Sunday morning warm-up began. Mansell was quickest in the warm-up, from the two Ferraris, Prost, Piquet and Senna. The two Benettons came next. Prost had briefly tried the spare car that had been built up overnight.

No one was prepared for the start line hassles on race day. It took no less than three attempts to get the race started. Not even a watching Stirling Moss could remember there being three starts to a Grand Prix before. And by then, there was a lot of damaged machinery about. First time round, the front rows got away cleanly with Fabi making a great start to take second place to Piquet halfway through the first lap, but by then, black flags were out around the circuit and the red flag was being shown at the start/finish line. Accelerating up the hill away from the grid, Martin Brundle's Zakspeed suddenly veered left and into the barrier. There was about as much reason for this as there was for Thierry

Boutsen's Arrows doing the same thing at Brands Hatch the previous year. Various theories existed: could it have bottomed on the notorious bump at that part of the circuit, or might a driveshaft have broken? There was no sure answer. Brundle's car was badly damaged, but behind him, Palmer felt his Tyrrell hit and he too veered left, collecting team mate Streiff. Both Ligiers were involved, as was Campos.

However, all drivers were back out on the grid for the second start, either in spare cars or repaired machines. On the second occasion, Nigel Mansell got away slowly from his front row grid position. He crawled away, the clutch slipping badly. "Too much welly," said team boss Frank Williams grimly as marshals cleared the aftermath. Mansell had had clutch trouble in the warm-up, and as he pointed out, these clutches aren't made to take two starts.

As he crawled away, Boutsen and Alboreto had a mild bang as they tried to avoid him, and Patrese slowed as Mansell continued to move slowly. Behind him, however, Cheever hadn't seen the reason for the blockage and thumped into the Brabham. Then all hell broke loose as virtually everyone behind them became involved, cars almost heaped on top of one another. Only the

Minardis and Palmer escaped, the latter braking hard when he saw the first puff of tyre smoke off the wall. It did not help matters that Senna had broken a driveshaft, and his car had to head for the pits. Those of Johansson, Cheever, Patrese, Capelli, Alliot, Fabre, Caffi, Brundle, Danner, Ghinzani and Streiff followed. They would all make the third start in spares or repaired cars apart from Streiff. Tyrrell had run out of cars.

The delay was considerable, but the pit lane was closed for far longer than the ten minutes laid down in the regulations. Consequently, Cheever, Fabre, Danner, Brundle and Caffi were all lined up in the pit lane ready to join in when everyone else had gone past. They were joined there by Prost, who crawled off the grid at the start of the final parade lap and parked at the pit lane exit with a battery problem. And at the end of the lap, Alboreto peeled off into the pits to have his steering wheel put on straight!

When the lights finally did turn green, the dramas weren't over. Senna's Lotus stalled, so only 17 cars got away cleanly and the use of that word is dubious: Nannini nudged Arnoux into the pit wall and the Ligier never handled the same way again. While Piquet stormed into the lead from Boutsen, Mansell, preferring to use his race car with its worn clutch rather than try Piquet's spare, got away cleanly, if not particularly quickly, in fourth place. Meanwhile there was a second start, just as busy, from the pit exit where seven cars had finally gathered. All these found Senna charging up from the grid once he had been push started, all eight of them mixing it with the ONS Porsche course cars!

Finally, the race was under way, Piquet leading Boutsen, Berger, Mansell, Fabi, Patrese, Warwick, de Cesaris, Johansson and Nakajima. Prost was 17th, followed by Senna and Alboreto, while Caffi's Osella had already stopped, a sad end for the Italian team which was celebrating its 100th Grand Prix. Within a couple of laps, Piquet, Boutsen, Berger, Mansell and Fabi had pulled away from the rest, and it would be these five who made the race. Mansell overtook Berger on lap four but two laps later, Austrian groans echoed round the hillsides as the Ferrari driver parked the car with a broken engine. Mansell quickly pulled ahead to make the leading duo into a trio although it wasn't until lap 13 that they really closed up. By this stage, Fabi was about five seconds further back. Then came an enormous gap to Patrese, then Senna and Alboreto. Warwick had de Cesaris and Prost close behind him.

Prost's tenth place wasn't McLaren's only problem. Johansson had pitted on lap two with a punctured right rear tyre, but while all four tyres were being changed, he was sent back out by team boss Ron Dennis. The mechanic doing the right front wheel was bowled over as Johansson left and he and some colleagues remonstrated with their team boss. But Johansson was in trouble. The right front wheel nut hit an Arrows mechanic when it came off as Johansson accelerated down the pit lane, and the wheel fell off later that lap. Johansson reappeared with his three-wheeled McLaren later that lap and the team tried again. It says something for the driver that he remained in the car at all. At the front, meanwhile, the Williams-Honda pair were left to fight it out when Boutsen pitted with loose gear linkage, rejoining just ahead of Piquet and Mansell, and actually drawing away from them. Mansell pressured Piquet until lap 21 when they came up on traffic and Mansell made his successful move to take the lead from his team mate.

That same lap, Piquet dashed for the pits and a relatively slow stop. Fabi made for the pits too, only to find so many people in his pit that he headed into Brabham's by accident and had to make a second stab at it a lap later. Over the next five laps, all the leaders pitted for tyres, but Mansell's was a good stop and when he re-emerged, he was over seven seconds ahead and pulling away, in spite of then losing the clutch. A resigned Piquet watched Mansell's car going away from him, happy to claim six points from yet another second place. By the end of the race he was 55 seconds behind. After his two pit stops, Fabi found himself with Alboreto, Prost and Senna close behind. Prost moved up to third place on lap 31 and Alboreto also went by. Two laps later Senna had got ahead of the Benetton driver as well, Fabi had eased up anyway in the hope of finishing. But Fabi got his third place back. Senna caught Alboreto, but so ferocious was their battle that the Brazilian damaged his nose section against the rear of the Ferrari and had to pit for new nose wings which weren't easy to fit. Fabi caught Alboreto and just as he looked as though he might challenge, the Ferrari pulled into the pits with a broken exhaust.

Prost slowed dramatically as well. The World Champion had had a miserable time, for after his battery problem, none of his instruments had worked, nor the rev counter, or the computer. And now he had lost boost, the McLaren was slowing. Fabi moved up to third on lap 43. After just one lap in fourth place, Boutsen pitted again. He thought he had a puncture, but it turned out to be a broken stay to the undertray. He'd also lost boost in one bank of cylinders due to a broken exhaust. But he rejoined and it was just a matter of whether Senna could catch Prost and Boutsen, and which was the more seriously maimed. Prost's lap times increased dramatically and on lap 46, Boutsen came by in fourth place. And just before they took the flag, Senna pipped Prost for fifth place which might have gone to Patrese, but for a late race retirement with a broken engine.

One might have thought this was a race of attrition, with the damage at the starts and long periods at high speeds. But far from it: the normally aspirated engines didn't get a look in. Sixteen cars actually crossed the finishing line. It only remained now for the winner to be brained on his way to the rostrum, to complete a remarkable Grand Prix weekend. No one would want a weekend quite like that again...

Left: Chase of the race was between Senna and Alboreto after both made late starts

163

Right: Piquet, Boutsen, Berger, Mansell and Fabi soon detached themselves from the rest in the early laps

Below: De Cesaris helps to extinguish another Brabham fire

165

166

There's no venue like
the Oesterreichring for
its spectacular scenery

Right: The normally aspirated Tyrrells scarcely got a look-in in Austria. They collided going up the hill at the first start, and Streiff didn't get a race

Left: The winner is crowned: Mansell makes contact with the rostrum

Far left: Berger and Boutsen give chase, but the race is stopped for the first time

Below left: Anything to escape the crowds: local hero Berger makes an unorthodox return to the paddock

Below right: Normally aspirated class winner, Ivan Capelli, shows off the latest in ear-wear

Right: After Brundle and the Tyrrells had crashed on the first start, Mansell got away slowly on the second start and the field piled up behind. Patrese tried to get out of the way, but Cheever, unsighted, came between him and the wall...and all hell broke loose. Johansson, Brundle, Ghinzani, Capelli, Alliot, Streiff and Caffi all become involved while Fabre tops the wreckage in the AGS

Far right: Horror in Austria: towards the end of Friday morning's session, a deer found itself out on the circuit, crossing the track just when Stefan Johansson's McLaren crested a brow at nearly 180 mph. Johansson hit the deer which was killed instantly. The McLaren slid along the track, demolishing itself against the barrier. Johansson was bruised but unhurt

Left: Another disappointing weekend for the Brabham team, with neither de Cesaris or Patrese finishing

AUSTRIAN GRAND PRIX · August 16

Entries and Practice Times

Cos=Cosworth
Ch=Champion
Win=Wintershall
McL=McLaren
Mar=Marelli
Bra=Brabham
Bre=Brembo
Bil=Bilstein
L/A=Lotus Active
Marz=Marzocchi

Driver	Nat.	Car	Practice 1	Practice 2	Warm Up	Engine	Turbos	Electrics/Plugs	Fuel/Oil	Brake Discs/ Calipers	Shocks
1 Alain Prost	F	Marlboro McLaren MP4/3	1m26.701s	1m43.132s	1m28.913s	1.5t TAG V6	KKK	Bosch	Shell	SEP/McL	Bil
2 Stefan Johansson	S	Marlboro McLaren MP4/3	1m29.003s	1m41.711s	1m31.779s	1.5t TAG V6	KKK	Bosch	Shell	SEP/McL	Bil
3 Jonathan Palmer	GB	Data General/Courtaulds Tyrrell DG/016	1m34.619s	1m49.308s	3m04.968s	3.5 Ford Cosworth DFZ V8		Cos/Ch	Elf	AP	Koni
4 Philippe Streiff	F	Data General/Courtaulds Tyrrell DG/016	1m35.338s	1m51.624s	1m37.304s	3.5 Ford Cosworth DFZ V8		Cos/Ch	Elf	AP	Koni
5 Nigel Mansell	GB	Canon Williams FW11B	1m23.459s	1m33.779s	1m28.265s	1.5t Honda V6	IHI	Honda/NGK	Mobil	SEP/AP	Showa
6 Nelson Piquet	BR	Canon Williams FW11B	1m23.357s	1m49.991s	1m29.006s	1.5t Honda V6	IHI	Honda/NGK	Mobil	SEP/AP	Showa
7 Riccardo Patrese	I	Brabham BT56	1m25.766s	1m53.119s	1m32.789s	1.5t BMW S4	Garrett	Bosch/Ch	Win/Castrol	SEP/Bra	Koni
8 Andrea de Cesaris	I	Brabham BT56	1m27.672s		1m32.589s	1.5t BMW S4	Garrett	Bosch/Ch	Win/Castrol	SEP/Bra	Koni
9 Martin Brundle	GB	West Zakspeed 871	1m29.893s	1m42.383s	1m32.035s	1.5t Zakspeed S4	Garrett	Bosch/Ch	Win/Castrol	AP	Sachs
10 Christian Danner	D	West Zakspeed 871	1m31.015s	1m48.880s	1m34.073s	1.5t Zakspeed S4	Garrett	Bosch/Ch	Win/Castrol	AP	Sachs
11 Satoru Nakajima	J	Camel Lotus 99T	1m28.786s	1m43.002s	1m31.668s	1.5t Honda V6	IHI	Honda/NGK	Elf	SEP/Bre	L/A
12 Ayrton Senna	BR	Camel Lotus 99T	1m25.492s	1m39.647s	1m29.153s	1.5t Honda V6	IHI	Honda/NGK	Elf	SEP/Bre	L/A
14 Pascal Fabre	F	El Charro AGS JH22C	1m40.633s	1m57.236s	1m42.559s	3.5 Ford Cosworth DFZ V8		Cos/Ch	Acto	SEP/AGS	Koni
16 Ivan Capelli	I	Leyton House March 871	1m34.199s	1m54.807s	1m36.582s	3.5 Ford Cosworth DFZ V8		Cos/Ch	BP	AP	Koni
17 Derek Warwick	GB	USF&G Arrows A10	1m27.762s		1m31.133s	1.5t Megatron S4	Garrett	Bosch/Ch	Win/Castrol	AP	Koni
18 Eddie Cheever	USA	USF&G Arrows A10	1m28.370s	1m37.908s	1m31.908s	1.5t Megatron S4	Garrett	Bosch/Ch	Win/Castrol	AP	Koni
19 Teo Fabi	I	Benetton B187	1m25.054s		1m29.576s	1.5t Ford V6	Garrett	Ford EED/Ch	Mobil	SEP/AP	Koni
20 Thierry Boutsen	B	Benetton B187	1m24.348s	1m48.124s	1m29.433s	1.5t Ford V6	Garrett	Ford EED/Ch	Mobil	SEP/AP	Koni
21 Alex Caffi	I	Landis & Gyr Osella FA1I	1m32.313s	1m50.273s	1m35.669s	1.5t Alfa Romeo V8	KKK	Mar/Ch	Agip	Bre	Koni
23 Adrian Campos	E	Minardi M186	1m30.797s	1m47.128s	2m29.423s	1.5t Motori Moderni V6	KKK	Mar/Ch	Agip	Bre	Koni
24 Alessandro Nannini	I	Minardi M186	1m29.435s	1m49.566s	1m35.453s	1.5t Motori Moderni V6	KKK	Mar/Ch	Agip	SEP/Bre	Koni
25 Rene Arnoux	F	Loto Ligier JS29C	1m29.733s	1m33.402s		1.5t Megatron S4	Garrett	Bosch/Ch	Win/Castrol	SEP/Bre	Koni
26 Piercarlo Ghinzani	I	Loto Ligier JS29C	1m30.682s		1m35.149s	1.5t Megatron S4	Garrett	Bosch/Ch	Win/Castrol	SEP/Bre	Koni
27 Michele Alboreto	I	Ferrari F187	1m25.077s	1m45.518s	1m28.747s	1.5t Ferrari V6	Garrett	Mar-Weber/Ch	Agip	SEP/Bre	Marz
28 Gerhard Berger	A	Ferrari F187	1m24.213s	1m38.388s	1m28.420s	1.5t Ferrari V6	Garrett	Mar-Weber/Ch	Agip	SEP/Bre	Marz
30 Philippe Alliot	F	Larrousse Lola LC87	1m33.741s	1m48.595s	1m35.659s	3.5 Lola LC87		Cos-Mar/Ch	BP	SEP/AP	Koni

August 14   August 15   August 16
Warm/sunny   Damp/drying   Dry/cloudy

Starting Grid

Mansell	5		6	Piquet
Boutsen	20		28	Berger
Alboreto	27		19	Fabi
Patrese	7		12	Senna
de Cesaris	8		1	Prost
Cheever	18		17	Warwick
Johansson	2		11	Nakajimi
Arnoux	25		24	Nannini
Ghinzani	26		9	Brundle
Danner	10		23	Campos
Alliot	30		21	Caffi
Palmer	3		16	Capelli
Fabre	14		4	Streiff

Results, Retirements and Fastest Laps

Place	Driver	Car	Laps	Time/Retirement	Fastest Lap No.	/Time
1	Nigel Mansell	1.5t Williams-Honda FW11B	52	1h18m44.898s	31	1m28.318s
2	Nelson Piquet	1.5t Williams-Honda FW11B	52	1h19m40.602s	27	1m28.358s
3	Teo Fabi	1.5t Benetton-Ford B187	51	1h18m49.003s	41	1m29.559s
4	Thierry Boutsen	1.5t Benetton-Ford B187	51	1h20m16.504s	18	1m29.111s
5	Ayrton Senna	1.5t Lotus-Honda 99T	50	1h19m02.239s	48	1m28.559s
6	Alain Prost	1.5t McLaren-TAG MP4/3	50	1h19m04.407s	32	1m29.291s
7	Stefan Johansson	1.5t McLaren-TAG MP4/3	50	1h19m57.705s	50	1m29.238s
8	Piercarlo Ghinzani	1.5t Ligier -Megatron JS29C	50	1h20m05.580s	14	1m34.372s
9	Christian Danner	1.5t Zakspeed 871	49	1h18m54.395s	28	1m32.817s
10	Rene Arnoux	1.5t Ligier -Megatron JS29C	49	1h19m46.255s	9	1m34.785s
11	Ivan Capelli	3.5 March-Ford 871	49	1h19m47.931s	42	1m35.616s
12	Philippe Alliot	3.5 Lola-Ford LC87	49	1h19m53.599s	41	1m36.027s
13	Satoru Nakajima	1.5t Lotus-Honda 99T	49	1h20m09.195s	40	1m31.685s
14	Martin Brundle	1.5t Zakspeed 871	48	1h19m18.397s	3	1m35.615s
15	Jonathan Palmer	3.5 Tyrrell-Ford DG/016	47	1h19m53.809s	17	1m38.245s
	Pascal Fabre	3.5 AGS-Ford JH22C	45	Not classified	26	1m42.844s
	Riccardo Patrese	1.5t Brabham-BMW BT56	43	Engine	30	1m30.629s
	Michele Alboreto	1.5t Ferrari-Spa F187	42	Exhaust	29	1m30.148s
	Andrea de Cesaris	1.5t Brabham-BMW BT56	35	Engine	31	1m31.960s
	Derek Warwick	1.5t Arrows-Megatron A10	35	Engine	31	1m31.783s
	Eddie Cheever	1.5t Arrows-Megatron A10	31	Blown tyre	30	1m31.814s
	Gerhard Berger	1.5t Ferrari-Spa F187	5	Engine	5	1m30.343s
	Adrian Campos	1.5t Minardi-Motori Moderni M186	3	Distributor belt	3	1m37.854s
	Alessandro Nannini	1.5t Minardi-Motori Moderni M186	1	Engine	1	2m06.843s
	Alex Caffi	1.5t Osella-Alfa Romeo FA1I	0	Electrics		
	Philippe Streiff	3.5 Tyrrell-Ford DG/016		Did not start/accident at first start		

Average Speed of Winner: 235.421 km/h, 146.284 mph
Fastest Lap: Nigel Mansell on Lap 31, 1m28.318s, 242.207 km/h, 150.500 mph (record)
Previous Lap Record: Alain Prost (1.5t McLaren-TAG MP4/2B) 1m29.241s, 239.701 km/h, 143.619 mph (1984)

Circuit Data

Austrian Grand Prix, Oesterreichring, Austria

Circuit Length: 5.942 km/ 3.692 miles
Race Distance: 52 laps, 308.984 km/191.993 miles
Race Weather: Warm/sun and cloud

Past Winners

Year	Driver	Nat.	Car	Circuit	Distance miles/km	Speed mph/km/h
1977	Alan Jones	AUS	3.0 Shadow-Ford DN8	Oesterreichring	199.39/320.89	122.98/197.91
1978	Ronnie Peterson	S	3.0 JPS/Lotus-Ford 79	Oesterreichring	199.39/320.89	118.03/189.95
1979	Alan Jones	AUS	3.0 Williams-Ford FW07	Oesterreichring	199.39/320.89	136.52/219.71
1980	Jean-Pierre Jabouille	F	1.5 Renault RS t/c	Oesterreichring	199.39/320.89	138.69/223.20
1981	Jaques Laffite	F	3.0 Ligier-Matra JS17	Oesterreichring	195.70/314.95	134.03/215.70
1982	Elio de Angelis	I	3.0 Lotus-Ford 91	Oesterreichring	195.70/314.95	138.07/222.20
1983	Alain Prost	F	1.5 Renault RE40 t/c	Oesterreichring	195.70/314.95	138.87/223.49
1984	Niki Lauda	A	1.5 McLaren MP4/2 t/c	Oesterreichring	188.31/303.06	139.11/223.88
1985	Alain Prost	F	1.5 McLaren MP4/2B t/c	Oesterreichring	191.99/308.98	143.62/231.13
1986	Alain Prost	F	1.5 McLaren-TAG MP4/2C t/c	Oesterreichring	191.99/308.98	141.56/227.82

172

Lap Chart

Grid Order	1	2	3	4	5	6	7	8	9	10	11	12	13	14	15	16	17	18	19	20	21	22	23	24	25	26	27	28	29	30	31	32	33	34	35	36	37	38	39	40	41	42	43	44	45	46	47	48	49	50	51	52	Pos
6 Nelson Piquet	6	6	6	6	6	6	6	6	6	6	6	6	6	6	6	6	6	6	6	6	6	6	6	6	6	5	5	5	5	5	5	5	5	5	5	5	5	5	5	5	5	5	5	5	5	5	5	5	5	5	5	5	1
5 Nigel Mansell	20	20	20	20	20	20	20	20	20	20	20	20	20	20	5	5	5	5	5	5	6	6	6	6	6	6	6	6	6	6	6	6	6	6	6	6	6	6	6	6	6	6	6	6	6	6	6	6	6	6	6	6	2
28 Gerhard Berger	28	28	28	5	5	5	5	5	5	5	5	5	5	5	5	19	19	19	19	19	19	19	27	27	12	12	19	19	19	19	1	1	1	1	1	1	1	1	1	1	1	19	19	19	19	19	19	19	19				3
20 Thierry Boutsen	5	5	5	28	28	19	19	19	19	19	19	19	19	19	20	7	7	7	27	27	27	12	12	27	7	27	27	27	27	27	27	27	27	27	27	27	27	19	1	20	1	20	20	20	20	20	20						4
19 Teo Fabi	19	19	19	19	19	7	7	7	7	7	7	7	7	7	7	27	27	27	7	7	12	12	7	7	7	19	1	1	1	19	19	12	12	19	19	19	19	19	19	20	20	1	20	1	1	1	1	1	12				5
27 Michele Alboreto	7	7	7	7	7	17	17	17	17	17	17	12	12	27	12	12	12	12	12	7	7	1	19	19	27	12	12	12	12	12	19	19	20	20	20	20	20	20	20	7	7	12	12	12	12	12	12	1					6
12 Ayrton Senna	17	17	17	17	17	8	8	8	8	8	8	12	27	27	12	1	1	1	1	1	1	1	1	19	1	1	1	20	20	20	20	20	20	20	20	7	7	7	7	7	7	7	27	12	26	26	26	26	26	2	2		7
7 Riccardo Patrese	8	8	8	8	8	11	12	12	12	12	8	17	17	17	17	17	17	8	17	17	17	17	20	20	7	7	7	7	7	7	7	7	8	26	26	26	26	12	12	26	2	2	2	2	2	2	26	26					8
1 Alain Prost	2	11	11	11	11	12	27	27	27	27	27	8	8	1	8	8	8	8	17	8	8	8	20	18	18	17	17	17	17	17	17	17	17	8	12	12	12	12	12	12	26	26	2	10	10	10	10	10	10				9
8 Andrea de Cesaris	11	23	12	12	12	27	1	1	1	1	1	1	1	8	18	18	18	18	18	18	18	20	18	17	17	8	8	8	8	8	8	8	17	17	25	10	10	10	10	10	2	10	25	25	25	25	25						10
17 Derek Warwick	23	16	23	27	27	1	18	18	18	18	18	18	18	18	20	20	20	20	20	20	18	8	8	8	18	18	18	18	26	26	26	10	25	25	2	2	2	10	25	16	16	16	16	16	16								11
18 Eddie Cheever	16	12	26	1	1	18	26	26	26	26	26	26	26	26	26	26	26	26	26	26	26	26	26	26	25	25	25	25	16	2	2	25	25	25	16	2	2	25	25	25	16	30	30	30	30	30	30						12
11 Satoru Nakajima	25	26	27	26	26	26	10	10	10	10	10	10	10	10	10	10	10	10	10	10	10	10	10	25	25	25	25	10	10	10	2	16	16	16	16	16	30	11	11	11	11	11											13
2 Stefan Johansson	26	25	1	18	18	10	25	25	25	25	25	25	25	25	25	25	25	25	25	25	25	25	9	9	16	16	16	16	16	30	30	30	30	30	30	30	11	9	9	9	9												14
24 Alessandro Nannini	30	1	16	16	16	25	9	9	9	9	9	9	9	9	9	9	9	9	9	9	9	9	16	16	9	30	30	10	30	30	30	9	9	9	9	11	11	9	3	3	3	3											15
25 Rene Arnoux	3	30	18	25	10	16	16	16	16	16	16	16	16	16	16	16	16	16	16	16	16	30	30	30	10	30	2	2	2	11	11	11	11	9	9	3	14	14															16
9 Martin Brundle	1	27	25	10	25	9	30	30	30	30	30	30	30	30	30	30	30	30	30	30	10	10	10	9	2	9	9	9	9	3	3	3	3	3	3	3	14																17
26 Piercarlo Ghinzani	12	18	30	30	30	30	3	3	3	3	3	3	3	3	3	3	3	3	3	3	2	2	2	3	2	2	9	3	3	11	11	14	14	14	14	14	14	14															18
23 Adrian Campos	27	3	10	9	9	3	14	14	14	14	14	14	2	2	2	2	2	2	2	2	2	3	3	3	2	3	3	3	11	11	3	3																					19
10 Christian Danner	18	10	3	3	3	14	11	2	2	2	2	2	14	14	14	11	11	11	11	11	11	11	11	11	11	11	11	11	11	14	14	14	14																				20
21 Alex Caffi	10	9	9	14	14	2	2	11	11	11	11	11	11	11	11	14	14	14	14	14	14	14	14	14	14	14	14	14	14																								21
30 Philippe Alliot	9	2	14	2	2																																																22
16 Ivan Capelli	24	14	2																																																			23
3 Jonathan Palmer	14																																																					24
4 Philippe Streiff																																																						25
14 Pascal Fabre																																																						26

Championship Points

	Drivers			Constructors	
1	Nelson Piquet	54 pts	1	Williams	93 pts
2	Ayrton Senna	43 pts	2	McLaren	50 pts
3	Nigel Mansell	39 pts	3	Lotus	49 pts
4	Alain Prost	31 pts	4	Ferrari	17 pts
5	Stefan Johansson	19 pts	5	Benetton	15 pts
6	Gerhard Berger	9 pts	6	Tyrrell	8 pts
7=	Michele Alboreto	8 pts	7	Arrows	7 pts
7=	Thierry Boutsen	8 pts	8	Brabham	6 pts
9	Teo Fabi	7 pts	9	Zakspeed	2 pts
10	Satoru Nakajima	6 pts	10=	March	1 pt
11=	Andrea de Cesaris	4 pts	10=	Lola	1 pt
11=	Eddie Cheever	4 pts	10=	Ligier	1 pt
11=	Philippe Streiff	4 pts			
11=	Jonathan Palmer	4 pts			
15	Derek Warwick	3 pts			
16=	Martin Brundle	2 pts			
16=	Riccardo Patrese	2 pts			
18=	Philippe Alliot	1 pt			
18=	Rene Arnoux	1 pt			
18=	Ivan Capelli	1 pt			

	Jim Clark Cup			Colin Chapman Cup	
1	Jonathan Palmer	61 pts	1	Tyrrell	106 pts
2	Philippe Streiff	45 pts	2	AGS	35 pts
3	Pascal Fabre	35 pts	3	Lola	25 pts
4	Philippe Alliot	25 pts	4	March	19 pts
5	Ivan Capelli	19 pts			

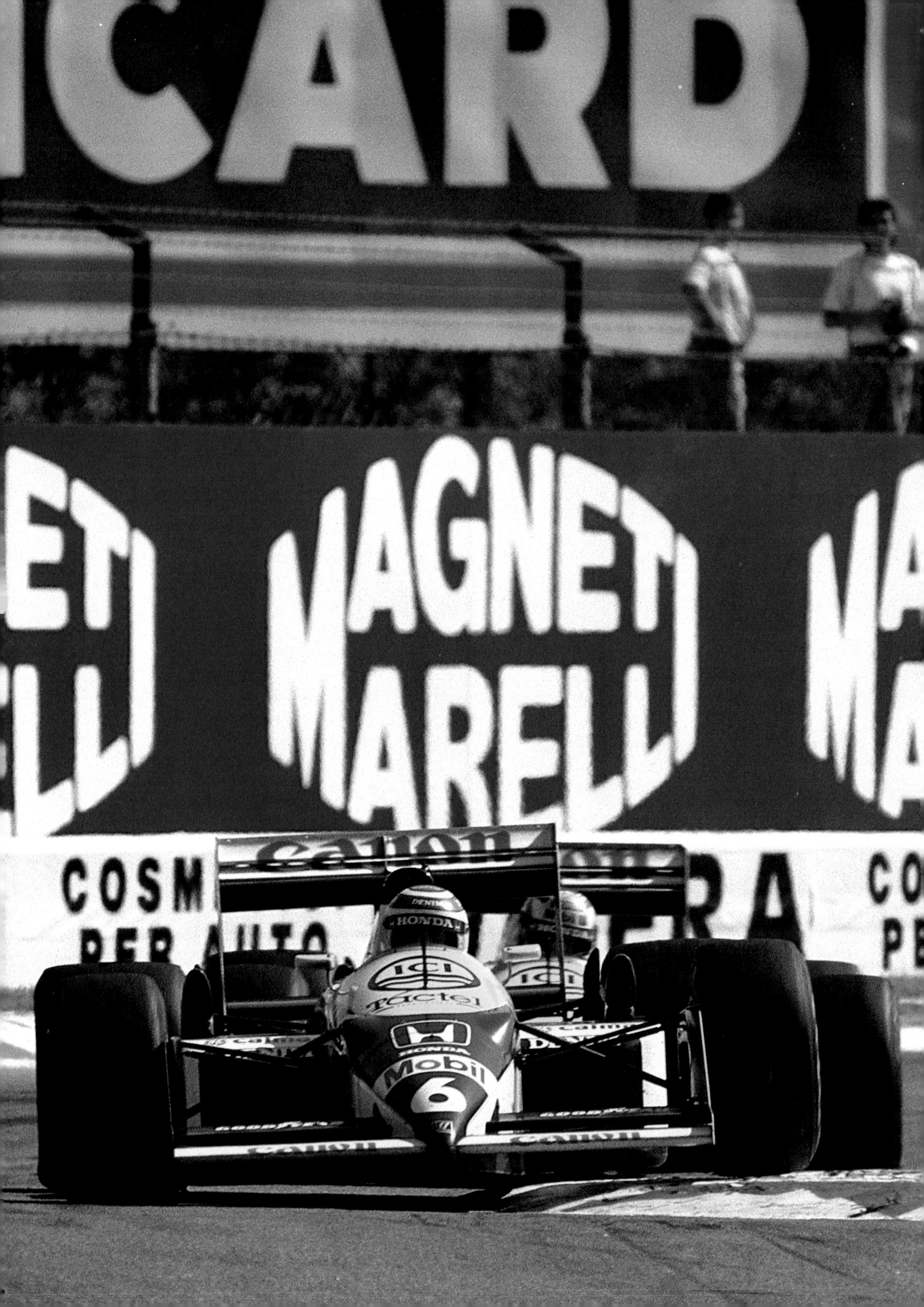
MAGNETI MARELLI
Canon
HONDA
ICI
Mobil
6

ITALIAN

GRAND PRIX

The 150,000 'tifosi' at Monza had eyes only for red, and principally red topped by a blue, yellow and white helmet – Alboreto was celebrating his 100th Grand Prix. It seemed a good reason for a special result and therefore special attendance.

For the rest of the world, there were off-track matters to be decided and then on-track matters. Honda dominated both. On this historic, outdated circuit, they claimed the front row and Nelson Piquet, giving the active suspension Williams its debut, dominated proceedings until making a scheduled pit stop for tyres. Ayrton Senna, fifth until then, didn't stop for tyres and after inheriting the lead, looked like winning until a spin seven laps from home. For the third time in four races, Nelson Piquet was in the right place to inherit a lucky win, the 20th of his career. Senna recovered for second, ahead of an unhappy and down-on-power Mansell while Berger gave the locals the flash of Ferrari red they wanted to see, at least in the top six, if not on the rostrum.

Monza had been rumoured to be the venue where Williams would announce their 1988 engine situation. And just before teams and pressmen left for Italy, a telexed invitation to a press conference on Friday afternoon came from Honda. Before Friday's qualifying even began, the Leyton House March team announced that it would be using John Judd's V8 for its two-car team in 1988. A matter of minutes later, a press release was distributed saying that Williams, too, would be using Judd engines in 1988. The divorce with Honda, it seemed, was complete. However, before Honda had a word to say on the subject, the two drivers from the rejected Williams team went out and annihilated the opposition. Nigel Mansell and Nelson Piquet were the

only two drivers to dip into the 1 minute 24 seconds bracket. Their times made that afternoon's announcement by Yoshitoshi Sakurai, Honda's managing director of Formula One, a little more difficult to understand. The split between Honda and Williams had been mutual, he said. The only remotely mutual factor in the split, said the cynics, was the pay-off.

It was especially unfortunate that Honda should have chosen Monza to announce that they were taking their eggs out of the Williams basket and putting them all into the Lotus and McLaren baskets. For Williams, after several extremely successful days' testing at Imola, decided that their active ride car was now ready for its race baptism. Mansell hadn't been interested in the active ride – until Sunday night. He claimed to have had worrying experiences with Lotus's system years previously. If someone else would like to develop it, he would race it when it was ready.

So Nelson Piquet, Jean-Louis Schlesser and R&D engineer Frank Dernie devoted themselves to the cause and some 4000 kms later, took the active Williams to Imola, where Piquet knocked three minutes off Nigel Mansell's race-winning time for the San Marino Grand Prix. Against the rest of the field, Piquet was sixth in Friday morning's session and second (0.26 seconds slower than Mansell) in that afternoon's qualifying session, in spite of a spin at the Parabolica when Capelli chopped across in front of him. On the Saturday, he was

second quickest again to Mansell in the morning and then quickest by just over a tenth of a second that afternoon in the final qualifying session – he was in pole position.

Mansell, meanwhile, was expressing his worries. Piquet was much quicker in a straightline, a phenomenon explained by the use of the active suspension, which gives a more even ride height, improved aerodynamics in the corners, which compensates for less wing, which in turn means less drag and therefore a higher straightline speed. And then he had an engine problem on Saturday afternoon. He was beginning to suspect a plot . . . But the Williams duo sat on the front row. The locals thought that was good for Piquet. They weren't very big Mansell fans. They were, of course, pleased that Berger put the Ferrari on the second row of the grid. He'd had a spin but had maintained Ferrari's recent upturn in performance with third spot on the grid.

Berger's team mate Alboreto had been a bit of a disappointment for the locals, smacking his car into the barriers when he got a wheel up on a kerb out of the first Lesmo, but no doubt the 'tifosi' reckoned that proved he was trying. In the following afternoon's qualifying session, Alboreto's engine had lost its edge, so he would start a mere eighth on the grid. Ayrton Senna was fourth, the Lotus team claiming problems with the pop-off valve and then gearbox trouble in final qualifying. Back on row three were the less happy drivers. Alain Prost complained of handling and traffic, although with better throttle response he might have bumped Senna off the second row. The Benetton men, meanwhile, had a number of varied problems. Fabi had a spin and then mysterious handling problems which disappeared with old tyres. Boutsen, meanwhile, also suffered a handling problem and then a down-on-power engine which was changed rather too late. Row five contained the two Brabham-BMWs, here sporting increased support for local sponsors Olivetti and Iceberg. De Cesaris might not have had a race if it had rained on the Saturday, for he scarcely set a time on the Friday when he damaged his gearbox on a kerb, cracking not only the casing but the engine block as well. But he qualified on Saturday, just a little slower than team mate Patrese, whose problems persisted with the lack of mechanical reliability.

Stefan Johansson was still feeling distinctly tender following his Austrian Grand Prix accident, after which it had been found that he'd broken a couple of ribs. Derek Warwick was lucky not to do more damage when he spun his Arrows into the barrier, but he only thumped two wheels and his rear wing mounting.

Relationships between Megatron and Ligier became a little strained when the team realised that they didn't have enough engines to see out the season. Neither Arnoux nor Ghinzani went out to qualify on Saturday afternoon while the two parties, plus Heini Mader, attempted to thrash out a suitable rebuild arrangement which would take them to the end of the season.

Not surprisingly, the normally aspirated cars were grouped together at the back of the grid on this high speed circuit where power out of the chicanes is so vital. Palmer was quickest ahead of Alliot and Streiff. Osella's newcomer, the Milan-based Swiss, Franco Forini, brought up the tail end of the grid, bumping off regular back row sitter Pascal Fabre. The new normally aspirated Coloni never got a look-in, with persistent clutch problems, so Nicola Larini didn't make his Formula One debut at home.

As the park began to fill out with a large crowd of enthusiastic 'tifosi', Mansell and Piquet were again quickest in the morning warm-up from Senna, Boutsen,

Prost and the two Ferraris. Fabi brought up the tail end of the field with mechanical problems. The start, always a highly charged affair at Monza, was an anti-climax. As the cars drew up in two long columns on the wide expanse of Monza's grid, flames began licking at the back of Patrese's Brabham. Starter Roland Bruynseraede had no option but to hang out the 'Start Delayed' board and the start procedure began again.

They got away cleanly for 50 laps at the second time of asking. Mansell made the best start, but was overhauled on the drag down to the first chicane by team mate Piquet followed by Berger, Boutsen, Prost and Senna over the line for the first time. The Austrian made a bid for second on lap two. Williams and Ferrari touched wheels, the Williams slid wide and as it scrabbled for grip, Boutsen went past the two of them into second place. But by the end of lap two, he was already two seconds down on Piquet. Behind them, Berger was third from Mansell, then Prost, Senna, Alboreto and Johansson, although the Ferrari shed one side pod rather publicly on pit straight after thumping over a kerb.

Boutsen briefly closed on the leader but then the gap opened up to 2.4 seconds before the Belgian began to close it

again. Berger was third, Mansell fourth and the gap to Senna was beginning to open up. Prost had slipped back, ultimately to pit with a ragged engine whose potentiometer was at fault. The electronic box was changed but it was never 100 per cent. Alboreto retired with a turbo broken, but by this stage, Mansell was threatening Berger's Ferrari, much to the chagrin of the locals. And as Berger was threatened, so he closed up on Boutsen. First of all, however, Mansell moved up to third on lap 17, and then he and Berger both caught Boutsen. Within two laps, Mansell was second: Williams in control. Senna, after a slow start, had now joined them. Even at the 20 lap mark, Piquet was still charging along, setting fastest laps on both laps 19 and 20 and opening up the gap between himself and Mansell to nearly ten seconds. Mansell still had Boutsen close behind, but the Benetton suddenly began to emit sparks which at this juncture could be taken as indicating something amiss with the underbody.

Behind these leading five came Johansson and Fabi before a largish gap to Cheever's Arrows. The Swede was the first of the leaders to pit for tyres, leading the queue in on lap 19. Fabi (lap 20), Mansell (lap 21), Berger and

Boutsen (lap 23) and Piquet (lap 24) followed. These pit stops actually resulted in a couple of immediate battles. Berger and Boutsen left the pits together, Ferrari losing a place to Benetton, even though it had been discovered that the Belgian's undertray had, indeed, come loose which was giving him oversteer. For the moment, however, the Benetton was able to remain just ahead of the Ferrari.

Piquet had a slower stop and found himself pushed by Mansell, who had now heated his tyres to working temperature having been out on them for three laps. Piquet, meanwhile, had to drive hard on his new tyres to keep ahead. He would later admit that he probably damaged his tyres by doing so. In this second half of the race, he would suffer tyre vibration and towards the end, severe blistering.

There's one name missing from all these pit stops: Senna. This was Detroit all over again, where the Brazilian Lotus driver decided that if he could, he would continue without a stop. When the team gave him the marginal signal at Monza, that was enough as far as he was concerned. He stayed out on his original tyres and found himself with a comfortable cushion over his rivals. This time the cushion was over ten seconds and even rose to 12.5s as the Williams drivers were delayed by backmarkers.

But then the chase began, and it was only Piquet who could do anything about

Senna. Both Williams drivers were hobbling in their own way. Mansell's engine was distinctly down-on-power and he could only watch, depressed, as Piquet pulled away. Subsequently, it was discovered that the engine was overheating, hence the lack of power, and for the moment Mansell would have to settle for third. "The power, the fuel economy, it was a joke", said the driver later. Piquet, meanwhile, was in fine form and chipping away at Senna's lead. From 12.5 seconds on lap 27, the gap was down to 5.2s ten laps later with 13 laps to go. It dipped to 4.5s five laps later and no one was in any doubt that Piquet would have his work cut out. But then Piquet was handed the race. Senna admitted that he had been taking risks overtaking backmarkers. Now he took a risk overtaking Piercarlo Ghinzani's Ligier. And on its worn tyres, his Lotus slewed sideways and Senna thought he was going to crash. Instead, he took to the Parabolica's sand, skittered over it and rejoined the race, but by this time, Piquet had shot by into the lead.

That was on lap 43. Senna had seven laps to get his lead back. Two laps later he had cut the gap to 5.5 seconds. Then it was 3.8s, then 2.8s and 2.6s. On lap 49, Piquet set fastest lap on his blistered tyres – a time which was promptly beaten by Senna on his worn Goodyears. But try as he might, Senna couldn't get close enough. When the chequered flag came out Piquet was just 1.8 seconds ahead of

his compatriot. There was a new spirit in his eyes. He wanted to win every race with the new suspension. He had a lead of 14 points – the Championship was within his grasp. Certainly the Constructors Championship was within his team's reach. It was Williams' sixth win in succession.

The rest were almost resigned to their positions. Mansell was certainly resigned to his, but third wasn't that bad. Berger brought a little joy to Ferrari's supporters, the red car overcoming Boutsen's Benetton on lap 34 as the Ford-engined car began to oversteer and Boutsen eased up anyway as his fuel supply dwindled. Behind him, an uncomfortable Johansson had his work cut out defending sixth from Fabi as the McLaren's rev limiter kept cutting in early while the Benetton didn't handle well and finished a lap down in seventh. Both Ligiers survived, so did Danner's Zakspeed, while Alliot had led the normally aspirated bunch from Streiff, the Lola quicker on the straight. But Streiff got a tow and found himself alongside only for the two to tangle, Alliot being sidelined while Streiff eased up to lead home Capelli and an oversteering Palmer.

And that was the Italian Grand Prix: a win for active Piquet ahead of active Senna. Prost and Mansell didn't want to talk 'Championship'. It was advantage Brazil at Monza.

Left: Piquet, Mansell, Prost, Boutsen and Senna lead the traffic jam at the first chicane on the first lap

Left: The new Coloni-DFZ made its debut, but a faulty clutch rendered it a non-qualifier

Far left: Most spectators only had eyes for things Italian

Below: Jonathan Palmer watches Alboreto in practice. In the race, the Englishman finished 14th, the Italian retired

179

Right: Boutsen, Senna
and Berger lap Nannini
at the end of the back
straight, as the Benetton
and Ferrari prepare to
stop for tyres

Left: Streiff in the Tyrrell and a Minardi driver discuss lines out of the chicane

Centre left: Some fans nearly got the winner's autograph! But then Senna spun down to second seven laps from home

Centre right: And that's just where Ferrari's English connection was . . .

Below: The normally aspirated class was as close-fought as ever. At the chequered flag, this order was reversed, Capelli beating Palmer but the two were led home by Streiff

ITALIAN GRAND PRIX · September 6

Entries and Practice Times

Cos=Cosworth
Ch=Champion
Win=Wintershall
McL=McLaren
Mar=Marelli
Bra=Brabham
Bre=Brembo
Bil=Bilstein
L/A=Lotus Active
Marz=Marzocchi

Driver	Nat.	Car	Practice 1	Practice 2	Warm Up	Engine	Turbos	Electrics/Plugs	Fuel/Oil	Brake Discs/Calipers	Shocks
1 Alain Prost	F	Marlboro McLaren MP4/3	1m25.340s	1m24.946s	1m29.747s	1.5t TAG V6	KKK	Bosch	Shell	SEP/McL	Bil
2 Stefan Johansson	S	Marlboro McLaren MP4/3	1m27.420s	1m27.031s	1m30.640s	1.5t TAG V6	KKK	Bosch	Shell	SEP/McL	Bil
3 Jonathan Palmer	GB	Data General/Courtaulds Tyrrell DG/016	1m34.218s	1m33.028s	1m35.716s	3.5 Ford Cosworth DFZ V8		Cos/Ch	Elf	AP	Koni
4 Philippe Streiff	F	Data General/Courtaulds Tyrrell DG/016	1m34.760s	1m33.264s	1m35.810s	3.5 Ford Cosworth DFZ V8		Cos/Ch	Elf	AP	Koni
5 Nigel Mansell	GB	Canon Williams FW11B	1m24.350s	1m23.559s	1m28.285s	1.5t Honda V6	IHI	Honda/NGK	Mobil	SEP/AP	Showa
6 Nelson Piquet	BR	Canon Williams FW11B	1m24.617s	1m23.460s	1m28.776s	1.5t Honda V6	IHI	Honda/NGK	Mobil	SEP/AP	Showa
7 Riccardo Patrese	I	Brabham BT56	1m26.453s	1m25.525s	1m30.336s	1.5t BMW S4	Garrett	Bosch/Ch	Win/Castrol	SEP/Bra	Koni
8 Andrea de Cesaris	I	Brabham BT56	1m40.285s	1m26.802s	1m31.707s	1.5t BMW S4	Garrett	Bosch/Ch	Win/Castrol	SEP/Bra	Koni
9 Martin Brundle	GB	West Zakspeed 871	1m30.144s	1m29.725s	1m32.643s	1.5t Zakspeed S4	Garrett	Bosch/Ch	Win/Castrol	AP	Sachs
10 Christian Danner	D	West Zakspeed 871	1m30.389s	1m29.465s	1m34.434s	1.5t Zakspeed S4	Garrett	Bosch/Ch	Win/Castrol	AP	Sachs
11 Satoru Nakajima	J	Camel Lotus 99T	1m28.463s	1m28.160s	1m32.079s	1.5t Honda V6	IHI	Honda/NGK	Elf	SEP/Bre	L/A
12 Ayrton Senna	BR	Camel Lotus 99T	1m25.535s	1m24.907s	1m29.308s	1.5t Honda V6	IHI	Honda/NGK	Elf	SEP/Bre	L/A
14 Pascal Fabre	F	El Charro AGS JH22C	1m39.393s	1m36.679s		3.5 Ford Cosworth DFZ V8		Cos/Ch	Acto	SEP/AGS	Koni
16 Ivan Capelli	I	Leyton House March 871	1m34.205s	1m33.311s	1m35.485s	3.5 Ford Cosworth DFZ V8		Cos/Ch	BP	AP	Koni
17 Derek Warwick	GB	USF&G Arrows A10	1m27.543s	1m28.083s	1m32.251s	1.5t Megatron S4	Garrett	Bosch/Ch	Win/Castrol	AP	Koni
18 Eddie Cheever	USA	USF&G Arrows A10	1m29.273s	1m28.022s	1m31.628s	1.5t Megatron S4	Garrett	Bosch/Ch	Win/Castrol	AP	Koni
19 Teo Fabi	I	Benetton B187	1m26.894s	1m25.020s	1m37.448s	1.5t Ford V6	Garrett	Ford EED/Ch	Mobil	SEP/AP	Koni
20 Thierry Boutsen	B	Benetton B187	1m25.250s	1m25.004s	1m29.496s	1.5t Ford V6	Garrett	Ford EED/Ch	Mobil	SEP/AP	Koni
21 Alex Caffi	I	Landis & Gyr Osella FA11	1m32.768s	1m31.029s	1m35.533s	1.5t Alfa Romeo V8	KKK	Mar/Ch	Agip	Bre	Koni
22 Franco Forini	SUI	Landis & Gyr Osella FA1H	1m34.467s	1m33.816s	1m37.368s	1.5t Alfa Romeo V8	KKK	Mar/Ch	Agip	Bre	Koni
23 Adrian Campos	E	Minardi M186	1m31.094s	1m30.782s	1m36.966s	1.5t Motori Moderni V6	KKK	Mar/Ch	Agip	Bre	Koni
24 Alessandro Nannini	I	Minardi M186	1m29.738s	1m31.069s	1m33.414s	1.5t Motori Moderni V6	KKK	Mar/Ch	Agip	SEP/Bre	Koni
25 Rene Arnoux	F	Loto Ligier JS29C	1m28.946s		1m33.295s	1.5t Megatron S4	Garrett	Bosch/Ch	Win/Castrol	SEP/Bre	Koni
26 Piercarlo Ghinzani	I	Loto Ligier JS29C	1m29.898s		1m32.832s	1.5t Megatron S4	Garrett	Bosch/Ch	Win/Castrol	SEP/Bre	Koni
27 Michele Alboreto	I	Ferrari F187	1m25.290s	1m25.247s	1m30.012s	1.5t Ferrari V6	Garrett	Mar-Weber/Ch	Agip	SEP/Bre	Marz
28 Gerhard Berger	A	Ferrari F187	1m25.211s	1m23.933s	1m30.125s	1.5t Ferrari V6	Garrett	Mar-Weber/Ch	Agip	SEP/Bre	Marz
30 Philippe Alliot	F	Larrousse Lola LC87	1m34.748s	1m33.170s	1m35.528s	3.5 Lola LC87		Cos-Mar/Ch	BP	SEP/AP	Koni
32 Nicola Larini	I	Coloni FC187	1m38.460s	1m35.721s		3.5 Ford Cosworth DFZ V8		Cos-Lucas/Ch	Q8	Bre	Koni

September 4 September 5 September 6
Hazy/humid Hazy/humid Sunny/warm

Starting Grid

Piquet 6			
		5	Mansell
Berger 28			
		12	Senna
Prost 1			
		20	Boutsen
Fabi 19			
		27	Alboreto
Patrese 7			
		8	de Cesaris
Johansson 2			
		17	Warwick
Cheever 18			
		11	Nakajima
Arnoux 25			
		10	Danner
Brundle 9			
		24	Nannini
Ghinzani 26			
		23	Campos
Caffi 21			
		3	Palmer
Alliot 30			
		4	Streiff
Capelli 16			
		22	Forini

Results, Retirements and Fastest Laps

Place	Driver	Car	Laps	Time/Retirement	Fastest Lap No./Time	
1	Nelson Piquet	1.5t Williams-Honda FW11B	50	1h14m47.707s	49	1m26.858s
2	Ayrton Senna	1.5t Lotus-Honda 99T	50	1h14m49.513s	49	1m26.796s
3	Nigel Mansell	1.5t Williams-Honda FW11B	50	1h15m36.743s	23	1m27.496s
4	Gerhard Berger	1.5t Ferrari-Spa F187	50	1h15m45.686s	27	1m28.519s
5	Thierry Boutsen	1.5t Benetton-Ford B187	50	1h16m09.026s	26	1m28.725s
6	Stefan Johansson	1.5t McLaren-TAG MP4/3	50	1h16m16.494s	42	1m28.468s
7	Teo Fabi	1.5t Benetton-Ford B187	49	1h14m49.112s	37	1m28.723s
8	Piercarlo Ghinzani	1.5t Ligier -Megatron JS29C	48	1h15m24.708s	35	1m32.488s
9	Christian Danner	1.5t Zakspeed 871	48	1h15m34.403s	47	1m31.636s
10	Rene Arnoux	1.5t Ligier -Megatron JS29C	48	1h15m38.453s	40	1m31.335s
11	Satoru Nakajima	1.5t Lotus-Honda 99T	47	1h15m06.492s	37	1m31.849s
12	Philippe Streiff	3.5 Tyrrell-Ford DG/016	47	1h16m00.370s	32	1m34.722s
13	Ivan Capelli	3.5 March-Lotus 871	47	1h16m04.521s	34	1m35.266s
14	Jonathan Palmer	3.5 Tyrrell-Ford DG/016	47	1h16m16.348s	37	1m35.154s
15	Alain Prost	1.5t McLaren-TAG MP4/3	46	1h15m41.433s	37	1m26.882s
16	Alessandro Nannini	1.5t Minardi-Motori Moderni M186	45	1h11m24.934s out of fuel	40	1m32.588s
	Martin Brundle	1.5t Zakspeed 871	43	Gearbox pinion bearing	24	1m32.663s
	Philippe Alliot	3.5 Lola-Ford LC87	37	Collision/Streiff	36	1m34.912s
	Adrian Campos	1.5t Minardi-Motori Moderni M186	34	Fuel filter/fire	34	1m33.629s
	Eddie Cheever	1.5t Arrows-Megatron A10	27	CV joint	18	1m32.820s
	Franco Forini	1.5t Osella-Alfa Romeo FA1H	27	Lost boost	26	1m37.964s
	Alex Caffi	1.5t Osella-Alfa Romeo FA11	16	Rear wheel bearing	15	1m34.187s
	Michele Alboreto	1.5t Ferrari-Spa F187	13	Turbo	10	1m30.124s
	Derek Warwick	1.5t Arrows-Megatron A10	9	Metering unit	7	1m33.180s
	Andrea de Cesaris	1.5t Brabham-BMW BT56	7	Front upright	4	1m31.279s
	Riccardo Patrese	1.5t Brabham-BMW BT56	5	Engine seized	4	1m31.497s
	Pascal Fabre	3.5 AGS-Ford JH22C		Did not qualify		
	Nicola Larini	3.5 Coloni-Ford FC187		Did not qualify		

Average Speed of Winner: 232.636 km/h, 144.553 mph
Fastest Lap: Ayrton Senna on Lap 49, 1m26.796s, 240.564 km/h, 149.479 mph (record)
Previous Lap Record: Teo Fabi (Benetton-BMW B186), 1m28.099s, 237.006 km/h, 147.268 mph

Circuit Data

Italian Grand Prix, Monza, Italy

Circuit Length: 5.800 km/ 3.604 miles
Race Distance: 290.00 km/ 180.197 miles
Race Weather: Sunny

Past Winners

Year	Driver	Nat.	Car	Circuit	Distance miles/km	Speed mph/km/h
1982	Rene Arnoux	F	1.5 Renault RE 30Bt/c	Monza	187.40/301.60	136.39/219.50
1983	Nelson Piquet	BR	1.5 Brabham-BMW BT52Bt/c	Monza	187.40/301.60	136.18/217.55
1984	Niki Lauda	A	1.5 McLaren-TAG MP4/2t/c	Monza	183.80/295.80	137.02/220.51
1985	Alain Prost	F	1.5 McLaren-TAG MP4/2Bt/c	Monza	183.80/295.80	141.40/227.56
1986	Nelson Piquet	BR	1.5 Williams-Honda FW11t/c	Monza	183.80/295.80	141.90/228.37

Lap·Chart

Grid Order	1	2	3	4	5	6	7	8	9	10	11	12	13	14	15	16	17	18	19	20	21	22	23	24	25	26	27	28	29	30	31	32	33	34	35	36	37	38	39	40	41	42	43	44	45	46	47	48	49	50	
6 Nelson Piquet	6	6	6	6	6	6	6	6	6	6	6	6	6	6	6	6	6	6	6	6	6	6	12	12	12	12	12	12	12	12	12	12	12	12	12	12	12	12	12	12	12	12	6	6	6	6	6	6	6	6	1
5 Nigel Mansell	5	20	20	20	20	20	20	20	20	20	20	20	20	20	20	20	5	5	20	20	12	6	6	6	6	6	6	6	6	6	6	6	6	6	6	6	6	6	6	6	6	6	12	12	12	12	12	12	12	12	2
28 Gerhard Berger	28	28	28	28	28	28	28	28	28	28	28	28	28	28	28	5	5	20	20	28	12	5	5	5	5	5	5	5	5	5	5	5	5	5	5	5	5	5	5	5	5	5	5	5	5	5	5	5	5	5	3
12 Ayrton Senna	20	5	5	5	5	5	5	5	5	5	5	5	5	5	5	5	28	28	28	12	28	28	20	20	20	20	20	20	20	20	28	28	28	28	28	28	28	28	28	28	28	28	28	28	28	28	28	28	28	28	4
1 Alain Prost	1	1	1	1	12	12	12	12	12	12	12	12	12	12	12	12	12	12	12	5	5	20	28	28	28	28	28	28	28	28	20	20	20	20	20	20	20	20	20	20	20	20	20	20	20	20	20	20	20	20	5
20 Thierry Boutsen	12	12	12	12	1	1	1	27	27	27	27	27	2	2	2	2	2	19	2	2	2	2	2	2	2	2	2	2	2	2	2	2	2	2	2	2	2	2	2	2	2	2	2	2	2	2	2	2	2	2	6
19 Teo Fabi	27	27	27	27	27	27	2	2	2	2	2	2	19	19	19	19	2	19	19	19	19	19	19	19	19	19	19	19	19	19	19	19	19	19	19	19	19	19	19	19	19	19	19	19	19	19	19	19	19		7
27 Michele Alboreto	2	2	2	2	2	2	19	19	19	19	19	19	18	18	18	18	18	18	18	18	18	18	18	18	18	9	9	9	9	9	9	9	9	9	9	26	26	26	26	26	26	26	26	26	26	26	26				8
7 Riccardo Patrese	19	19	19	19	19	19	1	1	18	18	18	18	10	10	10	10	10	10	10	10	10	10	10	10	10	26	18	10	26	26	26	26	26	9	9	9	9	10	10	10	10	10	10	10	10	10	10				9
8 Andrea de Cesaris	7	8	8	8	8	8	8	17	17	10	10	10	10	9	9	9	9	9	9	9	9	9	9	9	26	18	10	10	10	10	10	10	10	10	10	10	10	25	25	25	25	25	25	25	25	25					10
2 Stefan Johansson	8	7	7	7	7	17	17	18	18	9	9	9	9	25	25	25	25	25	25	25	25	25	26	26	26	26	26	10	24	24	24	25	25	25	25	25	25	9	9	24	24	24	24	11	11						11
17 Derek Warwick	17	17	17	17	17	18	18	10	10	25	25	25	26	26	26	26	26	26	26	26	26	26	25	24	24	24	24	25	25	24	24	24	24	24	24	24	24	24	9	9	11	11	4	4							12
18 Eddie Cheever	10	10	10	10	10	10	10	9	9	26	26	26	26	24	24	24	24	24	24	24	23	23	23	25	25	30	11	11	11	11	11	11	11	11	11	11	11	11	11	11	4	4	16	16							13
11 Satoru Nakajima	11	11	11	18	18	24	24	25	24	24	24	24	21	21	21	21	23	23	23	23	23	25	25	25	30	30	4	30	30	30	30	30	30	30	4	4	4	4	4	4	16	16	3	3							14
25 Rene Arnoux	24	18	18	24	24	9	9	25	26	21	21	21	21	23	23	23	30	30	11	11	11	30	30	30	30	4	4	11	4	4	4	4	4	4	4	16	16	16	16	16	3	3	1								15
10 Christian Danner	18	24	24	9	9	25	25	26	24	23	23	23	23	30	30	30	4	11	30	30	30	4	4	4	23	11	23	23	23	23	23	16	16	16	3	3	3	3	3	3	3	1	1								16
9 Martin Brundle	9	9	9	25	25	21	26	21	21	30	30	30	30	4	4	4	11	4	4	4	11	11	11	11	11	23	16	16	16	16	16	3	3	3	1	1	1	1	1	1											17
24 Alessandro Nannini	25	25	25	21	21	26	21	23	23	4	4	4	4	11	11	11	16	16	16	16	16	16	16	16	16	3	3	3	3	3	3	1	1	1																	18
26 Piercarlo Ghinzani	21	21	21	26	26	23	23	30	30	3	3	3	16	16	16	16	3	3	3	3	3	3	3	3	3	1	1	1	1	1	1	1																			19
23 Adrian Campos	26	26	26	23	23	30	30	4	4	16	16	16	11	3	3	3	22	22	22	22	22	22	22	22	22	22	22																								20
21 Alex Caffi	23	23	23	30	30	4	4	3	3	11	11	11	3	22	22	22	1	1	1	1	1	1	1	1	1	1	1																								21
3 Jonathan Palmer	30	30	30	4	4	3	3	16	16	22	22	22	22	1	1	1																																			22
30 Philippe Alliot	16	16	4	16	16	16	16	11	11	11	1	1	1	1																																					23
4 Philippe Streiff	4	4	16	3	3	22	22	22	22																																										24
16 Ivan Capelli	3	3	3	22	22	11	11																																												25
22 Franco Forini	22	22	22	11	11																																														26

Championship Points

Drivers			Constructors	
1	Nelson Piquet	63 pts	1	Williams	106 pts
2	Ayrton Senna	49 pts	2	Lotus	55 pts
3	Nigel Mansell	43 pts	3	McLaren	51 pts
4	Alain Prost	31 pts	4	Ferrari	20 pts
5	Stefan Johansson	20 pts	5	Benetton	17 pts
6	Gerhard Berger	12 pts	6	Tyrrell	8 pts
7	Thierry Boutsen	10 pts	7	Arrows	7 pts
8	Michele Alboreto	8 pts	8	Brabham	6 pts
9	Teo Fabi	7 pts	9	Zakspeed	2 pts
10	Satoru Nakajima	6 pts	10=	March	1 pt
11=	Andrea de Cesaris	4 pts	10=	Lola	1 pt
11=	Eddie Cheever	4 pts	10=	Ligier	1 pt
11=	Philippe Streiff	4 pts			
11=	Jonathan Palmer	4 pts			
15	Derek Warwick	3 pts			
16=	Martin Brundle	2 pts			
16=	Riccardo Patrese	2 pts			
18=	Philippe Alliot	1 pt			
18=	Rene Arnoux	1 pt			
18=	Ivan Capelli	1 pt			

Jim Clark Cup			Colin Chapman Cup	
1	Jonathan Palmer	65 pts	1	Tyrrell	119 pts
2	Philippe Streiff	54 pts	2	AGS	35 pts
3	Pascal Fabre	35 pts	3=	March	25 pts
4=	Ivan Capelli	25 pts	3=	Lola	25 pts
4=	Philippe Alliot	25 pts			

PORTUGUESE

GRAND PRIX

There were mixed emotions after the Portuguese Grand Prix. Everyone was delighted that Gerhard Berger had gained Ferrari's first pole position since Brazil in 1985. And they were delighted too that, until three laps from the end, it looked as though he might finally break Ferrari's long streak without a win. But then, on lap 68, it transpired that Prost was to be the one breaking records – for the number of Grand Prix wins.

It had been a long time coming, this final confrontation between Ferrari and McLaren, for on this day, Honda power was not in contention late in the race. There had been a second start after Alboreto, Piquet and Senna all tried to go through the first corner together. Piquet, having swerved from one side of the track to the other when the lights turned green, had been on the inside and sliding out. Alboreto tried to squeeze round the outside, two wheels on the dirt. He'd half spun and Piquet had simply pushed him off the track. The Championship leader looked out of the race. Warwick got involved too and then so did both Zakspeeds; Brundle being squeezed onto the inside by Nakajima who was avoiding Warwick. Arnoux, Campos, Ghinzani and Alliot were also involved in the crush.

The remaining cars, Berger having overtaken Mansell, streamed across the start/finish line for the first time at undiminished speed, only to be confronted by yellow flags and a circuit full of broken cars. Several drivers were standing around on the track, but the race hadn't yet been stopped. Berger eased up when he saw the chaos. Mansell drew up alongside and as they looked across their cockpit canopies at one another, they made a mutual decision to

stop. At about the same time, the red and black flags were shown around the circuit. Piquet's Williams, meanwhile, limped into the pits. A succession of broken racing cars on trucks followed him. One Ligier was destroyed, Danner's Zakspeed wouldn't be mended on time and would not start.

The lucky Piquet had been saved. He would take the restart, but the question was: in which car? His own car had been damaged: the undertray and suspension needed attention. After the Monza success, his Williams team had both an active and a conventional for each of its two drivers. Piquet's choice was simple: either change to his conventional spare (which he had scarcely driven) or get the active machine repaired quickly. He chose the latter course of action.

Mansell was, on this occasion, also in an active Williams, after admitting that this was, after all, the right way to go. Prior to the Italian Grand Prix, he had done only a few laps in the active car, preferring that Piquet and Williams' test driver, Jean-Louis Schlesser, do most of the work. But after Piquet's active success at Monza, Mansell had two days testing at Brands Hatch and spent most of practice at Estoril in the car. He did admit though, that it took some time to

feel the same trust in the active car that he felt in the conventional machine. Although he had been pipped for pole by Berger's perfectly timed lap just as the rains came on Saturday, he had at least maintained his record of front row grid positions in 1987.

At the second start, Jonathan Palmer was in the pit lane after an electrical problem, Danner was a spectator and Teo Fabi was not able to start in his own car on the grid after suffering a wheelbearing failure prior to the first start. He would abandon his spare for his repaired race car.

Again, Mansell got the better start from Berger, Piquet, Senna and Prost. But on the second lap, the Ferrari powered past Mansell, already paranoid about what he called lack of straightline speed, although there was precious little difference to Piquet's. Berger now pulled away at a remarkable rate. His lead was already 2 seconds on lap 2, 3 on lap 5. But as Berger pulled away from Mansell, so Mansell pulled away from the rest, now being led by Senna. The Lotus driver was coming under increasing pressure from Piquet now that he'd opened up a bit of a gap to Alboreto, who was being pursued by Prost and Boutsen. Then Senna suddenly lost three places on lap 12. His throttle

Previous page: Around the 40 lap mark Alain Prost and Nelson Piquet battle for second place as they lap Cheever. They finished first and third

Right: Senna and Piquet battled over third place during the early stages

sensor had ceased to work, the engine was cutting out. Two laps later, he headed for the pits at precisely the same moment that Mansell's Williams stopped out on the track. It had been fantastic, he reported, but then it misfired and then stopped altogether. Mansell was now out of the race.

As early as lap 14, the race took on a new look. Berger had a lead of more than ten seconds. Piquet was second, with Alboreto not far behind, although the Ferrari driver was being pressured by Prost in spite of tyre vibration. They had left Boutsen behind, now suffering from both fourth and fifth gears jumping out. Fabi was next, then Johansson, having overtaken the two Arrows – this group having lost Patrese early on with more engine trouble. Behind de Cesaris came an on-form Nannini before a big gap to the rest. Piquet soon began to chip away at Berger's lead. From the 11.8 seconds lead on lap 14, it dropped to 7.0s on lap 19 – although partially due to backmarkers. But then Piquet was in trouble too. His car hadn't been perfectly set up after its hurried repair and the driver was suffering oversteer. As Berger pulled away again, so the sole serious Honda representative in the race was being gained on by Alboreto and Prost.

On lap 27, Piquet's fortunes changed momentarily. He slipped back behind Alboreto, down into third place, with Prost right behind him. Berger now had a 17.2 second lead. But Piquet was back

up to second a couple of laps later as the mid-race tyre stops began. Piquet was first to stop, no doubt unhappy with his understeer. It was a relatively slow 10.3 second stop. Prost's was quick at 7.6s, Berger's a little slower at 8.3s and Alboreto didn't stop for another three laps. But once he did stop, Berger's position looked strong. At two laps after half distance, the Austrian still had a 15.7 second lead over Fabi, who had decided not to stop at all and had consequently moved up from fifth to second. But the Benetton driver was now being chased by Prost ahead of Piquet. On lap 39, it all changed. Prost came round ahead of Piquet, Fabi had dropped back to fourth. Team mate Boutsen had pitted with a misfire after 22 laps and, after the plugs and management box had been changed, was now charging along happily again, although he was well back.

Prost found himself 16.3 seconds behind Berger with 31 laps to go. He still had Piquet for company, but soon dropped him when he put his head down and began to chip away at the gap between his McLaren and the Ferrari ahead. Within three laps, he'd cut it to 11.7 seconds, but then up it went again and didn't really dip below 12 seconds again until lap 51. But then down it came in great chunks: down to 6.3 seconds on lap 54 as Berger struggled to overtake Johansson. It remained relatively stable for several laps at around 5 seconds

before Prost took another bite out of it on lap 60: down to 3.9s and then 3.1s. But Berger reacted and it climbed back to over 4 seconds with 7 laps to go. Then Prost went for it with another fastest lap: 2.7s, two laps later 2.4s.

In his cockpit, Berger was keeping a very wary eye on his pursuer. He knew where Prost was, knew that he was gaining, and knew that if he could just start the last couple of laps with a 2.5 second lead, then he would be home and dry even if his tyres were shot. Prost himself was on the limit, but perhaps more experienced at being on the limit than Berger. On this occasion the limit meant tyres, car, engine, fuel and driver. Never did Prost consider giving up however even though he would admit that catching Berger was one thing, overtaking him would be another. It was a fascinating chase. Berger decided to put in one final quick one before tackling those vital final two laps. Into the first corner he went, slid wide for the second apex and then as he came out of the corner, the car got up on the marbles and away from its driver. Prost passed the cloud of dust in a flash. At the end of lap 68, he had a 19.6 second lead before the Ferrari came by.

And that was it: victory for a delighted Prost, who admitted that he and his team were beginning to wonder if they were ever going to beat the all-time record. He hadn't been at all surprised to see Berger spin. "We were both on the limit", he said. Berger smiled in acknowledgement. He had come so close to his first win for Ferrari, but his sage acknowledgement of what had happened suggested that he'd gained valuable experience this day.

The momentous result of the Portuguese Grand Prix eclipsed many of the other events of the weekend. After his couple of days at Brands Hatch, Mansell had swapped to and from active and conventional Williams, finding the active had much more grip in slow corners. But the feel of the active car was very different. "You get kickback from the wheel of a conventional car", said Nigel, "but not from an active car. The more you slide, the more you float until you spin." Although he'd set his quick time in the conventional car, Mansell had been willing to give the active car a chance, hence his use of the car in the race. However, he'd gained his grid position with the conventional car and was preparing to go out in it again when the rain washed out final qualifying.

Benetton had looked competitive too, even if the cars eventually ended up on the fifth row – one of their worst practice performances of the year. Both drivers had complained of lack of downforce, lack of straightline speed and lack of grip. Boutsen found the car better on full

tanks and the pair had struggled into the top six by lap 14, quite an achievement for Fabi, who had been 12th early on. Fabi drove a fine race and looked to be gaining on Piquet's third placed Williams during the closing stages, but unfortunately team mate Boutsen was between them. Piquet didn't realise that his position was in jeopardy but Fabi had to overstress his tyres to get by his team mate and eventually had to settle for fourth place. Boutsen had been able to keep up their pace but he'd suffered gearbox trouble – and a long pit stop – so he was never in contention.

Johansson, as usual, seemed to be around at the end to pick up points, on this occasion two for fifth place. As usual, the engine had given problems in practice, and so had the gearbox, but in the race he'd soldiered through for two points. Arrows hadn't had a very exciting weekend, starting from row six and Cheever was actually in his spare car after being nudged by someone at the first start. Warwick's car hadn't been damaged, thankfully, but Cheever was a little uncertain of his machine. The pair were quite evenly matched and were running in close proximity behind the Benettons and Johansson when Warwick locked up a brake and spun,

leaving Cheever to wrestle with a car whose balance was totally different to his normal car – but it did result in sixth place.

Senna and Nakajima were out of the points in seventh and eighth, while the normally aspirated class belonged to Capelli on this occasion. He'd been third quickest to Alliot and Streiff in practice but had crept up on Alliot, passing him on lap 16. When the Frenchman had had an electric problem, the inseparable Tyrrell pair came into the frame, with Palmer finally getting ahead of Streiff when the Frenchman spun – although the latter had the better straightline speed which had made overtaking difficult. Once he was able to go as quickly as he liked, Palmer began to gain on Capelli, and inched closer and closer in the closing stages, eventually finishing just 0.3 seconds behind.

But the day belonged to Prost. Now, he said, he would like to relish this win, to remember it always as one of the most difficult races of his career. Jackie Stewart was there – officially to hand over the record, unofficially to heap praise on the Frenchman. And now that the record holder was beginning to consider that perhaps he still had a chance in the 1987 World Championship.

Left: Mansell has a healthy lead from Berger at the first start, but behind them, trouble is brewing with Piquet, Prost, Alboreto and Senna ranged across the track

Right: Ayrton Senna
eventually finished
seventh after a long pit
stop to cure his throttle
potentiometer

Left: Support for the Brazilians was strong, results weren't

Centre left: Warwick is facing the wrong way as Brundle gets out of his car, casualties of the first corner accident

Centre right: Stefan Johansson and Eddie Cheever, grateful recipients of points for fifth and sixth places

Below: Moment critique: Ferrari number 28 spins, Prost notches up 28 wins

189

Right: While Brabham team mate Patrese was an early retirement, de Cesaris looked to be heading for points until an injector pipe broke 16 laps from home

190

Left: Berger, Mansell, Senna, Piquet, Prost, Alboreto, Boutsen early in the race

Right: Mansell, Berger and Prost encounter crashed cars and rescue vehicles as they start lap two. Still the race is not stopped

Right: Mansell, Berger and Prost encounter crashed cars and rescue vehicles as they start lap two. Still the race is not stopped

Centre left: Happy Prost holds a post race discussion with Berger

Centre right: Alessandro Nannini finished 11th for the Minardi team, his first result of the year

Below: Berger nips inside Campos' Minardi during the drive which so nearly netted his first win for Ferrari

Left: Piquet was lucky that the race was stopped after the first corner accident. After the second start, he moved ahead of Senna on lap 11

Below: Spectator's eye view of the Portuguese Grand Prix grid, Berger starting from pole for the first time

PORTUGUESE GRAND PRIX · September 20

Entries and Practice Times

Cos=Cosworth
Ch=Champion
Win=Wintershall
McL=McLaren
Mar=Marelli
Bra=Brabham
Bre=Brembo
Bil=Bilstein
L/A=Lotus Active
Marz=Marzocchi

Driver	Nat.	Car	Practice 1	Practice 2	Warm Up	Engine	Turbos	Electrics/Plugs	Fuel/Oil	Brake Discs/Calipers	Shocks
1 Alain Prost	F	Marlboro McLaren MP4/3	1m18.404s	1m17.994s	1m21.623s	1.5t TAG V6	KKK	Bosch	Shell	SEP/McL	Bil
2 Stefan Johansson	S	Marlboro McLaren MP4/3	1m20.134s	1m20.227s	1m22.692s	1.5t TAG V6	KKK	Bosch	Shell	SEP/McL	Bil
3 Jonathan Palmer	GB	Data General/Courtaulds Tyrrell DG/016	1m24.392s	1m24.217s	1m26.480s	3.5 Ford Cosworth DFZ V8		Cos/Ch	Elf	AP	Koni
4 Philippe Streiff	F	Data General/Courtaulds Tyrrell DG/016	1m23.810s	1m24.436s	1m26.203s	3.5 Ford Cosworth DFZ V8		Cos/Ch	Elf	AP	Koni
5 Nigel Mansell	GB	Canon Williams FW11B	1m17.951s	1m18.235s	1m21.757s	1.5t Honda V6	IHI	Honda/NGK	Mobil	SEP/AP	Showa
6 Nelson Piquet	BR	Canon Williams FW11B	1m18.164s		1m22.822s	1.5t Honda V6	IHI	Honda/NGK	Mobil	SEP/AP	Showa
7 Riccardo Patrese	I	Brabham BT56	1m21.506s	1m19.965s	1m24.703s	1.5t BMW S4	Garrett	Bosch/Ch	Win/Castrol	SEP/Bra	Koni
8 Andrea de Cesaris	I	Brabham BT56	1m22.060s	1m21.725s	1m24.208s	1.5t BMW S4	Garrett	Bosch/Ch	Win/Castrol	SEP/Bra	Koni
9 Martin Brundle	GB	West Zakspeed 871	1m22.400s	1m22.794s	1m24.558s	1.5t Zakspeed S4	Garrett	Bosch/Ch	Win/Castrol	AP	Sachs
10 Christian Danner	D	West Zakspeed 871	1m22.424s	1m22.358s	1m26.111s	1.5t Zakspeed S4	Garrett	Bosch/Ch	Win/Castrol	AP	Sachs
11 Satoru Nakajima	J	Camel Lotus 99T	1m22.222s		2m36.372s	1.5t Honda V6	IHI	Honda/NGK	Elf	SEP/Bre	L/A
12 Ayrton Senna	BR	Camel Lotus 99T	1m18.382s	1m18.354s	1m22.877s	1.5t Honda V6	IHI	Honda/NGK	Elf	SEP/Bre	L/A
14 Pascal Fabre	F	El Charro AGS JH22C	1m28.756s	1m26.946s	*	3.5 Ford Cosworth DFZ V8		Cos/Ch	Acto	SEP/AGS	Koni
16 Ivan Capelli	I	Leyton House March 871	1m24.533s	1m23.905s	1m26.038s	3.5 Ford Cosworth DFZ V8		Cos/Ch	BP	AP	Koni
17 Derek Warwick	GB	USF&G Arrows A10	1m21.397s	1m21.587s	1m24.369s	1.5t Megatron S4	Garrett	Bosch/Ch	Win/Castrol	AP	Koni
18 Eddie Cheever	USA	USF&G Arrows A10	1m21.324s	1m21.207s	1m24.983s	1.5t Megatron S4	Garrett	Bosch/Ch	Win/Castrol	AP	Koni
19 Teo Fabi	I	Benetton B187	1m20.483s	1m20.548s	1m23.032s	1.5t Ford V6	Garrett	Ford EED/Ch	Mobil	SEP/AP	Koni
20 Thierry Boutsen	B	Benetton B187	1m20.305s	1m20.558s	1m22.694s	1.5t Ford V6	Garrett	Ford EED/Ch	Mobil	SEP/AP	Koni
21 Alex Caffi	I	Landis & Gyr Osella FA1I	1m24.792s	1m25.232s	1m26.906s	1.5t Alfa Romeo V8	KKK	Mar/Ch	Agip	Bre	Koni
22 Franco Forini	SUI	Landis & Gyr Osella FA1I	1m27.219s	1m26.635s	9m49.291s	1.5t Alfa Romeo V8	KKK	Mar/Ch	Agip	Bre	Koni
23 Adrian Campos	E	Minardi M186	1m24.822s	1m23.591s	1m26.977s	1.5t Motori Moderni V6	KKK	Mar/Ch	Agip	Bre	Koni
24 Alessandro Nannini	I	Minardi M186	1m21.784s	1m22.128s	1m25.899s	1.5t Motori Moderni V6	KKK	Mar/Ch	Agip	SEP/Bre	Koni
25 Rene Arnoux	F	Loto Ligier JS29C	1m23.637s	1m23.237s	1m26.053s	1.5t Megatron S4	Garrett	Bosch/Ch	Win/Castrol	SEP/Bre	Koni
26 Piercarlo Ghinzani	I	Loto Ligier JS29C	1m24.105s	1m24.979s	1m26.894s	1.5t Megatron S4	Garrett	Bosch/Ch	Win/Castrol	SEP/Bre	Koni
27 Michele Alboreto	I	Ferrari F187	1m20.069s	1m18.540s	1m22.050s	1.5t Ferrari V6	Garrett	Mar-Weber/Ch	Agip	SEP/Bre	Marz
28 Gerhard Berger	A	Ferrari F187	1m18.448s	1m17.620s	1m21.724s	1.5t Ferrari V6	Garrett	Mar-Weber/Ch	Agip	SEP/Bre	Marz
30 Philippe Alliot	F	Lola Ford LC87	1m24.181s	1m23.580s	1m25.976s	3.5 Ford Cosworth DFZ V8		Cos-Mar/Ch	BP	SEP/AP	Koni

*Pascal Fabre did not qualify in practice

September 18 Overcast/warm September 19 Overcast September 20 Cloudy

Starting Grid

Mansell	5	28	Berger
Piquet	6	1	Prost
Alboreto	27	12	Senna
Johansson	2	7	Patrese
Fabi	19	20	Boutsen
Warwick	17	18	Cheever
Nannini	24	8	de Cesaris
Danner	10	11	Nakajima
Arnoux	25	9	Brundle
Campos	23	30	Alliot
Capelli	16	4	Streiff
Palmer	3	26	Ghinzani
Forini	22	21	Caffi

Results, Retirements and Fastest Laps

Place	Driver	Car	Laps	Time/Retirement	Fastest Lap No./Time
1	Alain Prost	1.5t McLaren-TAG MP4/3	70	1h37m03.906s	65 1m19.509s
2	Gerhard Berger	1.5t Ferrari-Spa F187	70	1h37m24.399s	66 1m19.282s
3	Nelson Piquet	1.5t Williams-Honda FW11B	70	1h38m07.201s	41 1m21.191s
4	Teo Fabi	1.5t Benetton-Ford B187	69	1h36m59.290s stopped	45 1m21.821s
5	Stefan Johansson	1.5t McLaren-TAG MP4/3	69	1h37m49.676s	45 1m22.807s
6	Eddie Cheever	1.5t Arrows-Megatron A10	68	1h37m37.064s	53 1m22.682s
7	Ayrton Senna	1.5t Lotus-Honda 99T	68	1h37m41.697s	62 1m20.212s
8	Satoru Nakajima	1.5t Lotus-Honda 99T	68	1h37m56.177s	63 1m23.828s
9	Ivan Capelli	3.5 March-Ford 871	67	1h37m39.896s	64 1m25.012s
10	Jonathan Palmer	3.5 Tyrrell-Ford DG/016	67	1h37m40.151s	64 1m24.652s
11	Alessandro Nannini	1.5t Minardi-Motori Moderni M186	66	1h35m47.753s out of fuel	48 1m24.626s
12	Philippe Streiff	3.5 Tyrrell-Ford DG/016	66	1h37m10.546s	51 1m25.003s
13	Derek Warwick	1.5t Arrows-Megatron A10	66	1h38m18.782s	55 1m23.259s
14	Thierry Boutsen	1.5t Benetton-Ford B187	64	1h38m09.726s	50 1m21.535s
	Andrea de Cesaris	1.5t Brabham-BMW BT56	54	Injector pipe	52 1m22.504s
	Michele Alboreto	1.5t Ferrari-Spa F187	38	Gear linkage	33 1m25.989s
	Martin Brundle	1.5t Zakspeed 871	35	Fifth gear	28 1m25.760s
	Franco Forini	1.5t Osella-Alfa Romeo FA1H	32	Turbo	20 1m29.223s
	Philippe Alliot	3.5 Larrousse-Lola LC87	31	Electrics	22 1m27.020s
	Rene Arnoux	1.5t Ligier-Megatron JS29C	29	Holed radiator	21 1m26.131s
	Alex Caffi	1.5t Osella-Alfa Romeo FA1I	27	Turbo	23 1m26.811s
	Piercarlo Ghinzani	1.5t Ligier-Megatron JS29C	24	Ignition pick up	20 1m26.811s
	Adrian Campos	1.5t Minardi-Motori Moderni M186	24	Accident avoiding Arnoux	8 1m26.892s
	Nigel Mansell	1.5t Williams-Honda FW11B	13	Electrics cut out	12 1m22.834s
	Riccardo Patrese	1.5t Brabham-BMW BT56	13	Engine	12 1m24.433s
	Christian Danner	1.5t Zakspeed 871	0	Crash at first start	

Average Speed of Winner: 188.224 km/h, 116.957 mph
Fastest Lap: Gerhard Berger on Lap 66, 1m19.282s, 197.523 km/h, 122.735 mph (record)
Previous Lap Record: Nigel Mansell (1.5t Williams-Honda FW11), 1m20.943s, 193.469 km/h, 120.216 mph (1986)

Circuit Data

Portuguese Grand Prix, Estoril, Portugal

Circuit Length: 4.350 km/2.703 miles
Race Distance: 304.500 km/189.207 miles
Race Weather: Warm/sunny

Past Winners

Year	Driver	Nat.	Car	Circuit	Distance miles/km	Speed mph/km/h
1958	Stirling Moss	GB	2.5 Vanwall	Oporto	233.01/375.00	105.03/169.03
1959	Stirling Moss	GB	2.5 Cooper-Climax T51	Monsanto	209.00/336.35	95.32/153.40
1960	Jack Brabham	AUS	2.5 Cooper-Climax T53	Oporto	256.31/412.50	109.27/175.85
1984	Alain Prost	F	1.5 McLaren-TAG MP4/2 t/c	Estoril	189.21/304.50	112.18/180.54
1985	Ayrton Senna	BR	1.5 Lotus-Renault 97T t/c	Estoril	181.09/291.45	90.19/145.16
1986	Nigel Mansell	GB	1.5 Williams-Honda FW11 t/c	Estoril	181.21/304.50	116.60/187.64

Lap Chart

Grid Order	1	2	3	4	5	6	7	8	9	10	11	12	13	14	15	16	17	18	19	20	21	22	23	24	25	26	27	28	29	30	31	32	33	34	35	36	37	38	39	40	41	42	43	44	45	46	47	48	49	50	51	52	53	54	55	56	57	58	59	60	
28 Gerhard Berger	5	28	28	28	28	28	28	28	28	28	28	28	28	28	28	28	28	28	28	28	28	28	28	28	28	28	28	28	28	28	28	27	27	28	28	28	28	28	28	28	28	28	28	28	28	28	28	28	28	28	28	28	28	28	28	28	28	28	28	28	1
5 Nigel Mansell	28	5	5	5	5	5	5	5	5	5	5	6	6	6	6	6	6	6	6	6	6	6	6	6	6	6	27	6	27	27	28	28	28	27	19	19	1	1	1	1	1	1	1	1	1	1	1	1	1	1	1	1	1	1	1	1	1	1	1	1	2
1 Alain Prost	12	12	12	12	12	12	12	6	6	6	27	27	1	1	1	1	1	1	1	1	1	1	1	1	1	1	1	1	19	19	19	19	19	1	1	1	1	6	6	6	6	6	6	6	6	6	6	6	6	6	6	6	6	6	6	6	6	6	6	6	3
6 Nelson Piquet	6	6	6	6	6	6	6	6	6	12	27	27	1	1	1	1	1	1	1	1	1	1	1	1	1	6	19	1	1	1	1	6	6	6	6	19	19	19	19	19	19	19	19	19	19	19	19	19	19	19	19	19	19	19	19	19	19	19	19	19	4
12 Ayrton Senna	1	1	27	27	27	27	27	27	27	1	1	20	20	20	20	20	20	19	19	19	19	19	19	19	6	6	6	6	27	8	8	2	2	2	2	2	2	2	2	2	2	2	2	2	2	2	2	2	2	2	2	2	2	2	2	2	2	2	2	5	
27 Michele Alboreto	27	27	1	1	1	1	1	1	1	1	20	20	19	19	19	19	19	19	20	18	18	18	18	18	18	18	8	8	8	8	8	8	2	2	8	8	8	8	8	8	8	8	8	8	8	8	8	8	18	18	18	18	18	18	18	18	6
7 Riccardo Patrese	20	20	20	20	20	20	20	20	20	12	19	2	2	2	2	2	2	17	8	8	8	8	8	18	18	18	18	18	18	18	18	18	24	18	18	18	18	18	18	18	11	11	11	11	11	11	11	11	7
2 Stefan Johansson	7	7	7	7	7	7	19	19	19	12	18	18	18	18	18	18	24	24	24	24	24	2	2	2	2	2	24	18	24	24	24	24	24	11	11	11	11	24	24	24	12	12	12	12	24	24	24	24	8
20 Thierry Boutsen	2	2	2	19	19	19	7	7	7	7	7	17	17	17	17	17	17	8	2	2	2	2	2	2	24	24	24	24	24	11	11	11	11	11	11	11	11	11	11	11	24	24	24	12	12	12	12	12	9
19 Teo Fabi	18	18	18	19	2	2	2	2	2	2	2	8	8	8	8	8	8	29	9	9	9	9	9	9	9	11	11	11	16	16	16	16	16	16	16	16	16	12	12	12	16	16	16	16	16	16	10
18 Eddie Cheever	8	8	19	18	18	18	18	18	18	24	24	24	24	24	24	11	11	11	11	11	11	11	16	16	16	4	4	4	4	4	4	4	12	12	12	16	16	16	3	3	3	3	3	11
17 Derek Warwick	19	19	8	8	8	8	8	8	8	17	17	17	9	9	9	9	9	9	25	25	25	25	25	16	16	16	16	4	4	4	3	3	3	3	3	3	12	3	3	3	3	3	4	4	4	4	4	4	12
8 Andrea de Cesaris	17	17	17	17	17	17	17	17	8	8	8	12	11	11	11	11	11	11	16	16	16	16	16	30	30	4	4	4	3	3	3	12	12	12	12	3	4	4	4	4	4	17	17	17	17	17	13
24 Alessandro Nannini	24	24	24	24	24	24	24	24	24	11	11	25	25	25	25	25	25	30	30	30	30	30	4	4	4	3	3	3	9	12	12	12	17	17	17	17	17	17	17	17	17	17	17	20	20	20	20	20	14
11 Satoru Nakajima	9	9	9	9	9	9	9	9	9	9	25	16	16	16	16	16	16	26	26	21	21	4	4	3	3	12	12	12	17	20	20	20	20	20	20	20	20	20	20	20	20	20	15
10 Christian Danner	11	11	11	11	11	11	11	11	11	11	11	30	30	30	30	30	30	21	21	4	4	3	25	22	22	22	17	17	20	20	20	16
9 Martin Brundle	30	30	30	30	30	30	30	30	25	25	25	16	26	26	26	26	26	26	4	4	3	21	22	22	12	17	20	20	17
25 Rene Arnoux	25	25	25	25	25	25	30	30	30	26	21	21	21	21	21	21	3	3	22	22	12	17	20	18
30 Philippe Alliot	16	16	16	16	16	16	16	16	16	16	21	4	4	4	4	4	22	12	12	17	20	20	19
23 Adrian Campos	4	26	26	26	26	26	26	26	26	26	4	3	3	3	3	3	12	17	17	20	20	20
4 Philippe Streiff	26	4	21	21	21	21	21	21	21	21	22	22	22	22	22	22	17	17	20	20	21
16 Ivan Capelli	21	21	4	4	4	4	4	4	4	4	12	12	12	12	12	12	23	23	22
26 Piercarlo Ghinzani	3	3	3	3	3	3	3	3	3	3	23	23	23	23	23	23	20	20	23
3 Jonathan Palmer	22	22	22	22	22	22	22	22	22	22	22	22	24
21 Alex Caffi	23	23	23	23	23	23	23	23	23	23	25
22 Franco Forini											26

Lap Chart continued

	61	62	63	64	65	66	67	68	69	70	
	28	28	28	28	28	28	28	1	1	1	1
	1	1	1	1	1	1	1	28	28	28	2
	6	6	6	6	6	6	6	6	6	6	3
	19	19	19	19	19	19	19	19			4
	2	.	2	2	2	2	2	2	2		5
	18	18	18	18	18	18	18	18			6
	11	11	11	11	12	12	12	12			7
	12	12	12	12	11	11	11	11			8
	24	24	24	24	24	24	16				9
	16	16	16	16	16	16	3				10
	3	3	3	3	3						11
	4	4	4	4	4						12
	17	17	17	17	17						13
	20	20	20	20							14

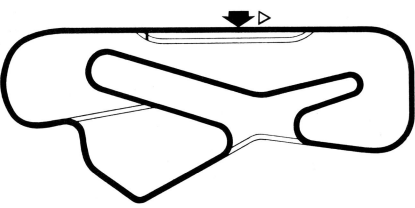

Championship Points

	Drivers			Constructors	
1	Nelson Piquet	67 pts	1	Williams	110 pts
2	Ayrton Senna	49 pts	2	McLaren	62 pts
3	Nigel Mansell	43 pts	3	Lotus	55 pts
4	Alain Prost	40 pts	4	Ferrari	26 pts
5	Stefan Johansson	22 pts	5	Benetton	20 pts
6	Gerhard Berger	18 pts	6=	Tyrrell	8 pts
7=	Teo Fabi	10 pts	6=	Arrows	8 pts
7=	Thierry Boutsen	10 pts	8	Brabham	6 pts
9	Michele Alboreto	8 pts	9	Zakspeed	2 pts
10	Satoru Nakajima	6 pts	10=	March	1 pt
11=	Eddie Cheever	5 pts	10=	Lola	1 pt
12=	Andrea de Cesaris	4 pts	10=	Ligier	1 pt
12=	Philippe Streiff	4 pts			
12=	Jonathan Palmer	4 pts			
15	Derek Warwick	3 pts			
16=	Martin Brundle	2 pts			
16=	Riccardo Patrese	2 pts			
18=	Philippe Alliot	1 pt			
18=	Rene Arnoux	1 pt			
18=	Ivan Capelli	1 pt			

	Jim Clark Cup			Colin Chapman Cup	
1	Jonathan Palmer	71 pts	1	Tyrrell	129 pts
2	Philippe Streiff	58 pts	2	AGS	35 pts
3	Pascal Fabre	35 pts	3	March	34 pts
4	Ivan Capelli	34 pts	4	Lola	25 pts
5	Philippe Alliot	25 pts			

SPANISH

GRAND PRIX

Remember the 1981 Spanish Grand Prix when winner Gilles Villeneuve managed to hold several challengers at bay? The only points scorer not involved in the exciting chase was Nigel Mansell. Six years on at the 1987 Spanish Grand Prix, Mansell was once more the only front runner not to get involved in the excitement, this time caused by Ayrton Senna driving a Lotus with similar properties to Villeneuve's Ferrari.

After the previous year's Spanish Grand Prix at Jerez where Mansell just failed to wrest victory from Senna's Lotus, the circuit has started to make a name for itself as a venue for exciting races, just as Hockenheim has a reputation for the reverse. But in the 1987 race Mansell was well out in front, and streaked home to a comfortable 22 second win. With Championship leader Nelson Piquet making plenty of mistakes and finishing fourth (his worst finishing position of the year), Mansell (1st), Prost (2nd) and Senna (5th) were all still in with a chance in the year's World Championship. And Williams were already rejoicing having won the Constructor's title for the second year running. Before the race the drivers enjoyed a FOCA-arranged, Lois-sponsored, sports competition in Marbella. Various 'celebrities' had been expected but, like all the World Championship leaders, most had failed to turn up.

Instead, the flag was flown by the enthusiastic Leo Sayer who is more like one of the lads than a celebrity. Cheever claimed to have emerged victorious overall, although he admitted he was not too hot on the golf course, and Campos claimed to have won the tennis with the help of 'a Williams of the tennis courts' – former Spanish tennis hero, Manuel Santana. After trying his hand in a

bull-ring, Riccardo Patrese attracted more headlines when as expected, he was announced as Williams' second driver for 1988, joining Nigel Mansell. Mansell, meanwhile, was still uncertain whether he wanted to use the active or conventional Williams and hoped to do back-to-back tests between the two on Saturday. He'd had problems with his active car on Friday morning and then a dramatic off-course excursion on the Friday afternoon when qualifying the conventional Williams. In spite of that, Mansell set the quickest time, even though his normal car suffered from a lack of grip. He also noted that Piquet had set third quickest time in the active car, so it had potential.

On Friday night it poured with rain, turning dry streams into torrents and washing away much of the rubber laid down during the day. According to Mansell, the track was slower, but he would continue to do his back-to-back tests. In the afternoon, he suffered from traffic, and also, he claimed, at the hands of his team, which was working with Piquet. Mansell abandoned his car, instead of having it weighed according to regulations, and set off down the pits at a jog to jump into the active car. His actions attracted the wrath of the stewards who docked his times for the

afternoon and fined him US$3000. At the end of practice, Mansell stormed off in a huff, missing the Williams briefing and only reappeared, more composed, an hour later. By then his team mate was on a comfortable pole position, having driven a superb lap around the twisty 2.6 mile circuit. It looked perfect, even to the experienced eyes of a watching Marc Surer. But Piquet himself said that the problem with the active car was that in the fast corners, it gave a little hop sideways. "You have to leave a little extra tarmac there!" said the Brazilian with a twinkle.

Piquet's time was a whole 0.6 seconds better than the time set by his team mate the previous day, and that was two tenths quicker than Mansell's best that day. But no-one should underestimate the influence traffic has on this circuit where overtaking is so difficult. Both Ferrari men were afflicted, though not by traffic. They shared the second row of the grid, which was Alboreto's best grid position of the year. But neither driver improved his time on the second day. Berger had to use a new, untested spare in official qualifying, and Alboreto was also in a spare having crashed his own Ferrari heavily in the morning. Ayrton Senna had an eventful practice, including a trip over the kerb and damaged suspension, but at least he shared row three with Teo Fabi's Benetton-Ford. The Benetton men were having an absorbing time, however. Both suffered a loss of boost, and Boutsen found his car's behaviour changing on its own without his mechanics having to do a thing – although that didn't please him particularly.

World Champion Alain Prost shared row four with Boutsen, and suffered a gearbox problem and a loss of power at high revs which rather mystified the team – although the Frenchman was beginning to get used to the feeling. Brabham occupied row five, a feat on its own given the lack of reliability in the face of some over-revving and a stuck throttle for de Cesaris. Behind Johansson, the Arrows pair and Arnoux, came the Tyrrell pair on row eight, grid positions that were on a par with normally aspirated performances in Detroit and Hungary. Right at the back, two more normally aspirated cars made it onto the grid at the expense of the two turbocharged Osellas. Pascal Fabre got his AGS onto the grid, spurred on by Roberto Moreno's testing times at Ricard in a modified car. Fabre hadn't qualified for the previous two races. Nicola Larini, meanwhile, also made it onto the grid in the Coloni's second and final race. The Osellas had their own problems anyway, Caffi had crashed, causing final qualifying to be stopped. The team also suffered from a number of broken turbos.

A healthier crowd than the previous year made Jerez's excellent stands look slightly more packed on race day. Senna sounded a warning in the warm-up. He was quickest down the straight, but only 14th fastest overall, complaining of a scarcity of grip. An intentional lack of wing seemed to be the cause. Berger, meanwhile, was quickest, with good straightline speeds too. Mansell was also quick in a straight line in the conventional Williams, which was second fastest. Thankfully the race got off to a controlled start with none of the dramas of the previous races, although Arnoux clobbered Warwick's Arrows, which needed a new nose section and Campos celebrated his home Grand Prix with an unscheduled off-track excursion which followed previous difficulties in practice and warm-up. Piquet led off the line, but Mansell was second from Senna, the

Ferraris and the Benettons. Mansell later explained that he knew from the start that he had to overtake Piquet as quickly as possible, "My conventional Williams would be better than his active car at the start, but I expected his active car to improve later in the race."

Consequently, as they came up to the final corner of the first lap, Mansell took his Williams down the inside of his team mate's car and Piquet had to give him space, falling back as they went through the corner. Mansell accelerated across the start/finish line first, with Piquet weaving around behind him, trying to find a way past. The first psychological point went to Mansell. For the next 40 laps of the 72 lap race, Mansell would steadily ease away. By ten laps, the gap was 2.9 seconds, by 20 laps it was 4.6 seconds, and by 30 laps it was just over six. Two laps later it was 7.6 seconds and then it grew in leaps and bounds. Piquet was thoroughly embroiled in the battle for tenth place between the normally aspirated cars of Palmer, Alliot and Streiff, and Nakajima's Lotus-Honda. It took him several laps to get by, and when he did, the gap between Mansell's leading Williams and Piquet's second-placed version had risen from 7 seconds to over 20 seconds. This first half duel was relatively mild in comparison with

the queue that built up behind Senna's third-placed Lotus. The Ferraris were right up with the Lotus, Berger challenging first, with Alboreto taking over at 13 laps with a similar lack of success. Boutsen and Fabi came next in their Benettons, and slowly Prost gained on them, once he'd overtaken de Cesaris. Chasing Prost through was his own team mate, Johansson, down in ninth spot.

There was no change at all after Alboreto took Berger on lap 13 up until Prost's pit stop on lap 27. No one could get by the fleet Lotus, quick on the straights, slow in the corners. Prost wasn't having much fun anyway. His McLaren doesn't like being in close proximity to other cars and was still misfiring. Prost decided to pit early on lap 27, catch up with the others and then make up places when they made their pit stops. Fabi made a slow stop for tyres on lap 29, and Boutsen did the same two laps later. Johansson stopped on lap 35 and Fabi retired on lap 41. Then Mansell stopped for 11 seconds on lap 42, re-emerging just ahead of Piquet, whom he managed to hold off. Prost meanwhile, was pushing both Ferraris and got by them. It was Piquet's turn to pit on lap 45, but his stop was twice as long as it should have been, as he didn't brake.

His rear wheels spun round and the mechanics couldn't change them until someone shouted "brake!" loud enough for Piquet to hear. When he re-emerged, he was fourth, just behind Prost, who was just behind Senna. Piquet promptly had a go at Prost but the Frenchman held his line and Piquet could only take a spin, dropping two places behind Alboreto (still to pit) and Boutsen. Berger stopped that lap.

On lap 50, with 22 laps to go, things were just as fraught for second place, 33 seconds behind Mansell. Senna still hadn't stopped for tyres, but had Prost right behind him, and he was being pushed by Alboreto, Boutsen and Piquet before a gap to Berger and Johansson. When Alboreto became the last one to stop for tyres on lap 52, Berger had all but replaced him in the queue behind Senna. On lap 55, Prost dropped two places, again thoroughly embroiled in the scrapping bunch and not impressed by the weaving of his colleagues. Now it was Boutsen's turn to challenge Senna, the Belgian pushed by Piquet, followed by Prost with Berger in hot pursuit. The World Champion found himself back at the end of the queue again by lap 57, with a misfire and lack of power hampering his challenge.

Boutsen's reign as Senna's challenger lasted five laps, until Piquet nipped into third place to challenge his compatriot. No-one else had been able to overtake the Lotus driver, but Piquet... that could be another matter. But first Berger ran wide over a kerb in the fifth-placed Ferrari and damaged the underside of his engine, which then emitted a cloud of smoke and caused his retirement four laps later. At almost the same time, Piquet got a run at Senna. The two Brazilians went side by side into the first corner. Senna was mindful that if he turned in, he would cause an accident, so he had to let Piquet through and while Senna searched for grip from his worn tyres, Boutsen and Prost also nipped by relegating him to fifth. By lap 64, it seemed as though the race might almost be settled. Mansell was way out in front, Piquet was second with Boutsen not far behind, followed by Prost. Senna in fifth, had the beginnings of a new queue behind him: Alboreto and Johansson, but Alboreto quickly got by although almost immediately his engine went sick.

Alboreto carried on, but suddenly the second-placed Piquet was off the track and onto the grass. Boutsen went spinning in sympathy. Did they go off on oil from Alboreto's engine? Whatever, Piquet continued, while Boutsen's Benetton stuck hard and fast in the gravel trap. Alboreto retired smokily.

Piquet went into the pits where his team became involved in a grass collection exercise. Prost was suddenly up to second and Johansson moved rapidly from seventh to third in just three laps. Piquet recovered and tried hard to get his place back, but had to follow the two Marlboro cars home. It was his worst placing of the year. Things weren't much better for Senna who finished fifth and lost his second place in the World Championship series to Mansell. An incident at the end of the race promoted Alliot's Lola into the points. He'd had a great battle with Jonathan Palmer's Tyrrell, the pair being shadowed by Nakajima's Lotus and Streiff in the second Tyrrell. But Arnoux, having one of his off days, knocked Palmer right out of the race – which left Alliot to claim his second World Championship point. Streiff was second in class and seventh overall. Both Arrows finished, so did Patrese and even Campos finished for the first time in the year.

The good news for Williams, of course, was that their pair had clinched the Constructors' Championship for the team. They couldn't be overtaken now. And the drivers were first and second in the Championship, with Mansell still in with a chance, as were Senna and Prost. But all Piquet needed was a win...

Right: Retirement for Berger after he ran over a kerb and split his oil tank. All the same, the engine ran for quite a while without oil

Centre left: Berger and Alboreto indulge in Ferrari infighting. Prost watches and waits

Centre right: One World Championship point and nine Jim Clark and Colin Chapman points for Alliot and Larrousse Lola

Below: Prost and Boutsen look for a way around Senna's Lotus on lap 52

After recent non-qualifications, Fabre and AGS were racing again – only for the clutch to fail

Right: Stefan Johansson enjoyed his week, playing golf at Marbella and finishing third in Jerez

Far right: Mansell inspects Williams. He finally plumped for the winning conventional chassis rather than the active model

Centre right: Luckily for Riccardo Patrese the bull was fairly tame!

Below: Arnoux, from Nannini, Prost, Patrese: only Prost would finish

204

Left: Piquet overtakes Senna on lap 63. Note the front tyre wear on both cars

Centre: Winner Mansell in amongst the back-markers – left to right: Campos, Warwick, Capelli, Brundle

Below: Mansell begins lap 2 having just got by Piquet: Senna pressures his compatriot

SPANISH GRAND PRIX · September 27

Entries and Practice Times

Cos=Cosworth
Ch=Champion
Win=Wintershall
McL=McLaren
Mar=Marelli
Bra=Brabham
Bre=Brembo
Bil=Bilstein
L/A=Lotus Active
Marz=Marzocchi

Driver	Nat.	Car	Practice 1	Practice 2	Warm Up	Engine	Turbos	Electrics/Plugs	Fuel/Oil	Brake Discs/Calipers	Shocks
1 Alain Prost	F	Marlboro McLaren MP4/3	**1m24.596s**	1m24.905s	1m29.152s	1.5t TAG V6	KKK	Bosch	Shell	SEP/McL	Bil
2 Stefan Johansson	S	Marlboro McLaren MP4/3	**1m26.147s**	1m26.147s	1m29.362s	1.5t TAG V6	KKK	Bosch	Shell	SEP/McL	Bil
3 Jonathan Palmer	GB	Data General/Courtaulds Tyrrell DG/016	**1m28.353s**	1m28.426s	1m32.413s	3.5 Ford Cosworth DFZ V8		Cos/Ch	Elf	AP	Koni
4 Philippe Streiff	F	Data General/Courtaulds Tyrrell DG/016	1m28.970s	**1m28.330s**	1m31.082s	3.5 Ford Cosworth DFZ V8		Cos/Ch	Elf	AP	Koni
5 Nigel Mansell	GB	Canon Williams FW11B	**1m23.081s**	1m23.281s‡	1m27.958s	1.5t Honda V6	IHI	Honda/NGK	Mobil	SEP/AP	Showa
6 Nelson Piquet	BR	Canon Williams FW11B	1m23.621s	**1m22.461s**	1m29.393s	1.5t Honda V6	IHI	Honda/NGK	Mobil	SEP/AP	Showa
7 Riccardo Patrese	I	Brabham BT56	1m26.639s	**1m25.335s**	1m29.587s	1.5t BMW S4	Garrett	Bosch/Ch	Win/Castrol	SEP/Bra	Koni
8 Andrea de Cesaris	I	Brabham BT56	1m31.981s	**1m25.811s**	1m31.079s	1.5t BMW S4	Garrett	Bosch/Ch	Win/Castrol	SEP/Bra	Koni
9 Martin Brundle	GB	West Zakspeed 871	1m28.876s	**1m28.597s**	1m34.581s	1.5t Zakspeed S4	Garrett	Bosch/Ch	Win/Castrol	AP	Sachs
10 Christian Danner	D	West Zakspeed 871	1m30.325s	**1m28.667s**	1m34.752s	1.5t Zakspeed S4	Garrett	Bosch/Ch	Win/Castrol	AP	Sachs
11 Satoru Nakajima	J	Camel Lotus 99T	1m28.776s	**1m28.367s**	1m30.779s	1.5t Honda V6	IHI	Honda/NGK	Elf	SEP/Bre	L/A
12 Ayrton Senna	BR	Camel Lotus 99T	1m25.162s	**1m24.320s**	1m31.170s	1.5t Honda V6	IHI	Honda/NGK	Elf	SEP/Bre	L/A
14 Pascal Fabre	F	El Charro AGS JH22C	1m32.490s	**1m30.694s**	1m35.375s	3.5 Ford Cosworth DFZ V8		Cos/Ch	Acto	SEP/AGS	Koni
16 Ivan Capelli	I	Leyton House March 871	**1m28.477s**	1m28.694s	1m31.564s	3.5 Ford Cosworth DFZ V8		Cos/Ch	BP	AP	Koni
17 Derek Warwick	GB	USF&G Arrows A10	**1m26.728s**	1m26.882s	1m32.229s	1.5t Megatron S4	Garrett	Bosch/Ch	Win/Castrol	AP	Koni
18 Eddie Cheever	USA	USF&G Arrows A10	**1m27.062s**	1m27.970s	1m31.472s	1.5t Megatron S4	Garrett	Bosch/Ch	Win/Castrol	AP	Koni
19 Teo Fabi	I	Benetton B187	1m25.263s	**1m24.523s**	1m28.342s	1.5t Ford V6	Garrett	Ford EED/Ch	Mobil	SEP/AP	Koni
20 Thierry Boutsen	B	Benetton B187	1m26.372s	**1m25.295s**	1m28.013s	1.5t Ford V6	Garrett	Ford EED/Ch	Mobil	SEP/AP	Koni
21 Alex Caffi	I	Landis & Gyr Osella FA1I	1m31.284s	**1m31.069s**	*	1.5t Alfa Romeo V8	KKK	Mar/Ch	Agip	Bre	Koni
22 Franco Forini	SUI	Landis & Gyr Osella FA1I	**1m34.723s**	1m35.572s	†	1.5t Alfa Romeo V8	KKK	Mar/Ch	Agip	Bre	Koni
23 Adrian Campos	E	Minardi M186	**1m29.538s**	1m30.204s	1m35.416s	1.5t Motori Moderni V6	KKK	Mar/Ch	Agip	Bre	Koni
24 Alessandro Nannini	I	Minardi M186	1m28.823s	**1m28.602s**	1m32.896s	1.5t Motori Moderni V6	KKK	Mar/Ch	Agip	SEP/Bre	Koni
25 Rene Arnoux	F	Loto Ligier JS29C	**1m28.241s**	1m28.362s	1m32.100s	1.5t Megatron S4	Garrett	Bosch/Ch	Win/Castrol	SEP/Bre	Koni
26 Piercarlo Ghinzani	I	Loto Ligier JS29C	1m29.663s	**1m29.066s**	1m32.746s	1.5t Megatron S4	Garrett	Bosch/Ch	Win/Castrol	SEP/Bre	Koni
27 Michele Alboreto	I	Ferrari F187	**1m24.192s**	1m24.832s	1m28.359s	1.5t Ferrari V6	Garrett	Mar-Weber/Ch	Agip	SEP/Bre	Marz
28 Gerhard Berger	A	Ferrari F187	**1m23.164s**	1m25.250s	1m27.648s	1.5t Ferrari V6	Garrett	Mar-Weber/Ch	Agip	SEP/Bre	Marz
30 Philippe Alliot	F	Larrousse-Lola LC87	1m29.147s	**1m28.361s**	1m30.591s	3.5 Ford Cosworth DFZ V8		Cos-Mar/Ch	BP	SEP/AP	Koni
32 Nicola Larini	I	Coloni FC187	1m31.319s	**1m30.982s**	1m32.765s	3.5 Ford Cosworth DFZ V8		Cos-Lucas/Ch	Q8	Bre	Koni

*†Caffi and Forini did not qualify in practice
‡Nigel Mansell was disqualified in Saturday's practice.

September 25	September 26	September 27
Overcast/warm	Overcast/warm	Overcast

Starting Grid

Mansell **5**		**6**	Piquet
Alboreto **27**		**28**	Berger
Fabi **19**		**12**	Senna
Boutsen **20**		**1**	Prost
de Cesaris **8**		**7**	Patrese
Warwick **17**		**2**	Johansson
Arnoux **25**		**18**	Cheever
Palmer **3**		**4**	Streiff
Nakajima **11**		**30**	Alliot
Brundle **9**		**16**	Capelli
Danner **10**		**24**	Nannini
Campos **23**		**26**	Ghinzani
Larini **32**		**14**	Fabre

Results, Retirements and Fastest Laps

Place	Driver	Car	Laps	Time/Retirement	Fastest Lap No./Time	
1	Nigel Mansell	1.5t Williams-Honda FW11B	72	1h49m12.692s	45	1m28.444s
2	Alain Prost	1.5t McLaren-TAG MP4/3	72	1h49m34.917s	30	1m27.459s
3	Stefan Johansson	1.5t McLaren-TAG MP4/3	72	1h49m43.510s	59	1m28.133s
4	Nelson Piquet	1.5t Williams-Honda FW11B	72	1h49m44.142s	49	1m27.108s
5	Ayrton Senna	1.5t Lotus-Honda 99T	72	1h50m26.199s	20	1m30.088s
6	Philippe Alliot	3.5 Lola-Ford LC87	71	1h49m51.179s	50	1m30.514s
7	Philippe Streiff	3.5 Tyrrell-Ford DG/016	71	1h50m30.184s	50	1m31.279s
8	Eddie Cheever	1.5t Arrows-Megatron A10	70	1h48m43.688s out of fuel	46	1m29.934s
9	Satoru Nakajima	1.5t Zakspeed 871	70	1h49m17.040s	42	1m31.228s
10	Derek Warwick	1.5t Arrows-Megatron A10	70	1h49m27.505s	41	1m31.105s
11	Martin Brundle	1.5t Zakspeed 861	70	1h49m43.353s	44	1m31.373s
12	Ivan Capelli	3.5 March-Ford 871	70	1h50m30.518s	61	1m30.407s
13	Riccardo Patrese	1.5t Brabham-BMW BT56	68	1h49m34.537s	67	1m27.150s
14	Adrian Campos	1.5t Minardi-Motori Moderni M186	68	1h49m55.599s	31	1m33.503s
15	Michele Alboreto	1.5t Ferrari-Spa F187	67	1h42m08.912s over revved engine	54	1m27.738s
16	Thierry Boutsen	1.5t Benetton-BMW B187	66	1h40m21.977s breaks/spun	65	1m28.299s
	Gerhard Berger	1.5t Ferrari-Spa F187	62	Spin damage/engine	49	1m26.986s
	Jonathan Palmer	3.5 Tyrrell-Ford DG/016	55	Collision/Arnoux	50	1m30.514s
	Rene Arnoux	1.5t Ligier-Megatron JS29C	55	Engine	50	1m32.650s
	Christian Danner	1.5t Zakspeed 861	50	Fourth gear	19	1m32.074s
	Alessandro Nannini	1.5t Minardi-Motori Moderni M186	45	Turbo	19	1m30.722s
	Teo Fabi	1.5t Benetton-BMW B187	40	Engine	32	1m29.319s
	Andrea de Cesaris	1.5t Brabham-BMW BT56	26	Gearbox	23	1m30.670s
	Piercarlo Ghinzani	1.5t Ligier-Megatron JS29C	24	Ignition pick-up	20	1m32.604s
	Pascal Fabre	3.5 AGS-Ford JH22C	10	Oil on clutch	3	1m35.672s
	Nicola Larini	3.5 Coloni-Ford FC187	8	Suspension	7	1m33.108s

Average Speed of Winner: 166.848 km/h, 103.674 mph
Fastest Lap: Gerhard Berger on lap 49, 1m26.986s, 174.566 km/h, 108.470 mph (record)
Previous Lap Record: Nigel Mansell (1.5t Williams-Honda FW11), 1m27.176s, 174.186 km/h, 108.234 mph (1986)

Circuit Data

Spanish Grand Prix, Jerez, Spain

Circuit Length: 4.218 km/2.621 miles
Race Distance: 303.696 km/188.708 miles
Race Weather: Overcast

Past Winner

Year	Driver	Nat.	Car	Circuit	Distance miles/km	Speed mph/km/h
1986	Ayrton Senna	BR	1.5t Lotus-Renault 98T	Jerez	188.71/303.70	104.07/167.49

Lap Chart

Grid Order	1	2	3	4	5	6	7	8	9	10	11	12	13	14	15	16	17	18	19	20	21	22	23	24	25	26	27	28	29	30	31	32	33	34	35	36	37	38	39	40	41	42	43	44	45	46	47	48	49	50	51	52	53	54	55	56	57	58	59	60	61	
6 Nelson Piquet	5	5	5	5	5	5	5	5	5	5	5	5	5	5	5	5	5	5	5	5	5	5	5	5	5	5	5	5	5	5	5	5	5	5	5	5	5	5	5	5	5	5	5	5	5	5	5	5	5	5	5	5	5	5	5	5	5	5	5	5	5	1
6 Nigel Mansell	6	6	6	6	6	6	6	6	6	6	6	6	6	6	6	6	6	6	6	6	6	6	6	6	6	6	6	6	6	6	6	6	6	6	6	6	6	6	6	6	6	6	6	6	6	12	12	12	12	12	12	12	12	12	12	12	12	12	12	12	12	2
28 Gerhard Berger	12	12	12	12	12	12	12	12	12	12	12	12	12	12	12	12	12	12	12	12	12	12	12	12	12	12	12	12	12	12	12	12	12	12	12	12	12	12	12	12	12	12	12	12	1	1	1	1	1	1	1	1	20	20	20	20	20	6	6			3
27 Michele Alboreto	28	28	28	28	28	28	28	28	28	28	28	27	27	27	27	27	27	27	27	27	27	27	27	27	27	27	27	27	27	27	27	27	27	27	27	27	27	27	1	1	6	27	27	20	20	20	20	6	6	6	6	6	20	20								4
12 Ayrton Senna	27	27	27	27	27	27	27	27	27	27	28	28	28	28	28	28	28	28	28	28	28	28	28	28	28	28	28	28	28	28	28	28	28	28	28	28	27	20	20	20	6	6	6	1	1	28	28	28	1	1	5											5
19 Teo Fabi	20	20	20	20	20	20	20	20	20	20	20	20	20	20	20	20	20	20	20	20	2	2	2	1	1	1	1	1	1	1	1	27	27	20	6	6	6	28	28	28	28	1	1	28	28																	6
1 Alain Prost	19	19	19	19	19	19	19	19	19	19	19	19	19	19	19	19	19	19	19	2	2	1	1	20	20	20	20	20	20	20	20	20	28	28	28	28	2	2	2	2	2	2	2	2	27																	7
20 Thierry Boutsen	8	8	8	8	8	8	1	1	1	1	1	1	1	1	1	1	1	1	1	1	1	2	2	1	19	19	19	2	2	2	2	2	2	2	2	2	2	27	27	27	27	27	2	8																		8
7 Riccardo Patrese	1	1	1	1	1	1	8	8	8	8	8	8	8	8	8	8	2	2	2	2	2	2	2	2	1	19	19	19	19	19	19	2	2	2	19	3	3	3	3	3	3	3	3	3	3	3	3	30	30	30	30	30	9									9
8 Andrea de Cesaris	18	18	18	18	18	18	18	18	18	2	2	2	2	2	2	8	8	8	8	8	8	8	3	3	3	3	3	3	3	3	3	3	30	30	30	30	30	30	30	30	30	30	30	18	18	18	18	18	18	10												10
2 Stefan Johansson	7	7	7	2	2	2	2	2	2	2	18	18	18	18	18	18	18	3	3	3	3	30	30	30	30	30	30	30	30	30	30	11	11	11	11	11	11	11	11	11	11	18	11	4	4	4	4	11													11
17 Derek Warwick	3	2	2	7	7	7	7	7	7	7	7	7	7	7	3	3	3	3	30	30	30	30	11	11	11	11	11	11	11	11	4	4	4	4	4	4	4	4	4	18	11	11	4	11	11	11	11	12													12
18 Eddie Cheever	2	3	3	3	3	3	3	3	3	3	3	3	30	30	30	30	11	11	11	11	11	4	4	4	4	4	4	4	18	18	18	18	18	18	18	18	18	4	4	17	17	17	17	13																	13
25 Rene Arnoux	30	30	30	30	30	30	30	30	30	30	30	30	7	11	11	11	11	4	4	4	4	16	9	9	9	9	9	18	18	18	25	25	25	25	25	25	17	17	17	9	9	9	9	9	14																14
4 Philippe Streiff	11	11	11	11	11	11	11	11	11	11	11	11	11	11	4	4	4	16	16	16	16	9	18	18	18	18	18	9	9	25	24	24	24	9	9	9	9	17	25	25	9	9	16	16	16	16	15															15
3 Jonathan Palmer	4	24	24	24	24	24	24	24	24	24	24	24	16	16	16	9	9	9	18	25	25	17	17	17	17	25	24	16	16	16	16	17	17	9	9	9	25	16	7	7	7	23	23	16																	16
30 Philippe Alliot	24	4	4	4	4	4	4	4	4	4	4	9	9	9	18	18	18	18	25	17	17	25	25	25	24	16	9	9	9	24	17	16	16	16	16	16	16	25	23	23	23	7	7	17																	17
11 Satoru Nakajima	9	9	9	9	9	9	9	9	9	9	9	9	25	25	25	25	25	25	17	24	24	24	24	24	16	9	17	17	17	17	23	23	23	23	23	7	7	7	7	18																				18
16 Ivan Capelli	10	10	16	16	16	16	16	16	16	16	16	16	17	17	17	17	17	17	24	16	16	16	16	16	17	17	23	23	23	23	7	7	7	7	23	23	23	23	19																						19
9 Martin Brundle	16	16	10	10	10	10	10	25	25	25	25	25	25	26	26	26	26	24	24	24	24	23	23	23	23	23	23	23	23	7	7	7	7	10	10	10	10	20																							20
24 Alessandro Nannini	14	25	25	25	25	25	10	10	10	10	26	26	26	26	24	24	24	24	26	26	26	7	7	7	7	7	7	7	7	10	10	10	10	21																											21
10 Christian Danner	25	14	32	32	32	32	32	26	26	11	17	17	17	17	23	23	23	23	23	23	23	3	7	7	10	10	10	10	10	10	22																													22
26 Piercarlo Ghinzani	32	32	14	26	26	26	26	26	14	17	17	23	23	23	23	7	7	7	7	7	7	7	10	10	23																																		23
23 Adrian Campos	26	26	26	14	14	14	14	14	17	23	23	10	10	10	10	10	10	10	10	10	10	10	24																																					24
14 Pascal Fabre	23	23	23	23	23	23	23	17	23	14	25																																																	25
32 Nicola Larini	17	17	17	17	17	17	17	23	26																																																			26

Lap Chart continued

62	63	64	65	66	67	68	69	70	71	72	
5	5	5	5	5	5	5	5	5	5	5	1
12	6	6	6	6	6	1	1	1	1	1	2
6	20	20	20	20	1	6	2	2	2	2	3
20	1	1	1	27	2	6	6	6	6		4
1	12	12	27	27	2	12	12	12	12	12	5
28	27	27	12	12	30	30	30	30			6
27	2	2	2	30	18	18	18	4			7
2	30	30	30	30	18	4	4	4			8
30	18	18	18	4	11	11	11	11			9
18	4	4	4	11	17	17	17				10
4	11	11	11	11	17	9	9	9			11
11	17	17	17	17	9	16	16	16			12
17	9	9	9	9	16	7					13
9	16	16	16	16	7	23					14
16	7	7	7	7	23						15
23	23	23	23	23							16
7											17

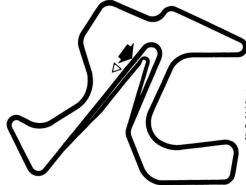

Championship Points

	Drivers				Constructors	
1	Nelson Piquet	70 pts	1		Williams	122 pts
2	Nigel Mansell	52 pts	2		McLaren	72 pts
3	Ayrton Senna	51 pts	3		Lotus	57 pts
4	Alain Prost	46 pts	4		Ferrari	26 pts
5	Stefan Johansson	26 pts	5		Benetton	20 pts
6	Gerhard Berger	18 pts	6=		Tyrrell	8 pts
7=	Teo Fabi	10 pts	6=		Arrows	8 pts
7=	Thierry Boutsen	10 pts	8		Brabham	6 pts
9	Michele Alboreto	8 pts	9=		Zakspeed	2 pts
10	Satoru Nakajima	6 pts	9=		Lola	2 pts
11	Eddie Cheever	5 pts	11=		March	1 pt
12=	Andrea de Cesaris	4 pts	11=		Ligier	1 pt
12=	Philippe Streiff	4 pts				
12=	Jonathan Palmer	4 pts				
15	Derek Warwick	3 pts				
16=	Martin Brundle	2 pts				
16=	Riccardo Patrese	2 pts				
16=	Philippe Alliot	2 pts				
19=	Rene Arnoux	1 pt				
19=	Ivan Capelli	1 pt				

	Jim Clark Cup			Colin Chapman Cup	
1	Jonathan Palmer	71 pts	1	Tyrrell	135 pts
2	Philippe Streiff	64 pts	2	March	38 pts
3	Ivan Capelli	38 pts	3	AGS	35 pts
4	Pascal Fabre	35 pts	4	Lola	34 pts
5	Philippe Alliot	34 pts			

MEXICAN

The 1987 Mexican Grand Prix will probably be remembered for all the wrong reasons. The race was a messy, two-part affair, unfortunately stopped mid-way when Derek Warwick had an accident. When the race was re-started, Nigel Mansell finally emerged as the winner.

With his win, Mansell closed within 12 points of team mate Piquet on the Championship table. Piquet finished second for the seventh time of the year. Earlier, Mansell had landed pole position, and broke the record for the number of consecutive front row starts by a driver. At 15, he had just pipped Alberto Ascari's record which had stood since the 1952/3 seasons.

The Autodromo Hermanos Rodriguez circuit had been resurfaced and its bumps ironed out since the previous year. But the resurfacing work left the track very dusty and dirty. It turned out to be one of those circuits which gradually becomes faster during the weekend's racing. Such were the worries about the track and its surface that Goodyear not only decided to supply teams with 15 instead of the usual 10 sets of tyres per car, but they also provided two different compounds of tyre. Recollections of the previous year when some drivers had to stop three times for new tyres were strong – the slippery surface increased the risk of blistering.

The field assembled in Mexico, was still 27 strong. Osella were down to one car – driven by Alex Caffi, (now sponsored by Stievani, an electrical merchant). Yannick Dalmas arrived fresh from his F3000 win at Jarama to make his Grand Prix racing debut at the beginning of a three-race campaign in the second Larrousse Lola. An agreement had been signed by all but Benetton for 27 cars to

start, but because it wasn't unanimous, it was decided to stick to the regulation 26. Therefore the slowest in qualifying would not race.

After the previous year's generally overcast race, the hot sun was welcome. And it wasn't just warm, it was baking – pale faces turned red in Mexico City. Those who were staying out to go on to Japan via Honolulu would look positively glowing by Christmas! Points of interest in Mexico included pondering which engine manufacturer had best coped with the increase of altitude to Mexico City's 7200 feet. Could Ferrari's chassis remain competitive? Would the normally aspirated runners really be as slow as Ken Tyrrell feared? He thought that they might not be classified even if they finished. Some of these questions were answered by the end of qualifying. Altitude is a great leveller, it seems. The first seven cars in practice were covered by just 0.7 seconds. The closest margin covering the first seven had been 1.6s in Italy – but it had been 4.2 seconds in Brazil. Furthermore, the conditions allowed the likes of Minardi and Zakspeed to close up with the front runners. Martin Brundle gave the German team their best-ever grid position with 13th at their 30th Grand Prix. The normally aspirated runners weren't that slow either, Capelli was only 6.3 seconds behind Mansell. In Austria, by contrast, the fastest normally aspirated runner, Alliot, had been

10.4 seconds behind pole man Piquet.

Despite achieving pole position yet again, Mansell found little joy in his record-breaking accomplishment. After all, he took a spin in first qualifying, then his suspension collapsed and he had a 'big moment' after he set pole position. The first spin was out of the very quick, slightly banked final corner, when the car hit a bump, jumped sideways and spun around, going backwards down the start/finish straight. It crossed the finishing line and was timed at 1 minute 24.7 seconds for the lap, before hitting the pit wall, lightly twisting the front of the car and causing slight injury to one of Nigel's ankles. Next day, the Williams' front suspension collapsed going through the penultimate corner. In the ensuing drama, the rear suspension was damaged and so too was the monocoque, as the car slid along on its belly. Further inspection revealed that the damage was so great that a new monocoque would have to be built up. Eight hours later it was complete. Nigel Mansell would, in effect, race a new car. That wasn't the end of the Williams team's dramas. The next morning Piquet was knocked off the track by Arnoux at the end of the warm-up and there was more damage to repair before the car took to the grid. Given these setbacks, the Williams team performed particularly well to finish first and second.

There were dramas too for McLaren, whose cars both suffered engine problems. Even so, Alain Prost was fifth quickest and pleased to be less than half-a-second off pole position. His tyres made him one of the favourites, while the man himself thought that Ferrari's chassis and the Honda engine was probably the best combination. Prost's team mate, Stefan Johansson, however, was way back in 15th position – his engine problems all came at the wrong moments. Gerhard Berger proved that Ferrari was still competitive and backed up Prost's feeling that the Ferrari chassis was good, while he confirmed that there was still work to do on the engine. His team mate Alboreto was celebrating the birth of Alice, his first child, with a modest ninth on the grid – in the all-important final qualifying session, both he and Berger had slid off the track at the first corner.

Ayrton Senna, competing in his 60th Grand Prix, was another who made the headlines for the wrong reasons. After a spin in first qualifying and then an attack from de Cesaris in the Brabham on Saturday morning, it all went wrong, when Senna bottomed in the middle of the final corner during qualifying. The car settled down on its suspension and skidded off into the tyre barrier. Although Senna was very shaken, the barrier saved both him and the car. After a period of observation in the medical centre, he was allowed to leave and turned up the next day to drive his regular car. Unfortunately, it suffered an electrical failure, the active suspension failed to work and Senna had to opt for the repaired car for the race. He started from a mere seventh on the grid, his equal lowest for the year. The Brabham pair had a trouble-free practice, although they did have a number of spins, including one where the pair tangled and were caught spinning in tandem by the TV cameras. However, Patrese started eighth, and de Cesaris (who had rather more spins), tenth.

Eddie Cheever was another celebrating an anniversary, his 100th Grand Prix. He and team mate Derek Warwick ended up on the sixth row of the grid. Of the rest, Ligier suffered a series of gearbox casing breakages, while Capelli was the quickest of the normally aspirated runners, and newcomer Dalmas was faster than team mate Alliot, although the latter had a catalogue of disasters. Out of the race went Pascal Fabre – the

slowest qualifier – a bitter pill after so many teams had agreed on 27 runners.

When the red light turned green on race day, Mansell got away fastest but he fell away with too much wheelspin, and it was Berger who led into the first corner, from Boutsen, Piquet, Prost and Mansell. Halfway round that first lap, Prost noticed that Piquet, on the harder B Compound tyres, was relatively slow, and thought that he might try and get by the Williams driver. He tried down the inside of the corner, got on to the marbles, and, unable to control the car, slid into the side of Piquet. The pair of them spun, and Prost went out there and then with damaged front suspension. While the field streamed by, Piquet was pushed away from his dangerous position and managed to get his car restarted in the process, rejoining last.

At the end of lap one, Berger and Boutsen came by in tight formation, while Mansell was third, already 6.7 seconds behind and pushed by Alboreto, Fabi and Senna, with a gap to the Brabham-BMW duo. Behind Nannini came the two Arrows. On lap two, Boutsen moved up into the lead. By now the leading pair had pulled a further 1.9 seconds away from Mansell, who had Senna behind him from Alboreto, Fabi, de Cesaris and his team mate Patrese. But Warwick now came trickling into the pits without a rear wing. Going down into the first corner, Warwick had turned the Arrows a little bit sideways – as had happened quite frequently in

practice – and Nakajima who was following, missed his braking. To the surprise of the TV viewers throughout the world, the cameraman thumped into the back of the Arrows. The Lotus lost its right front wheel, Warwick got back to the pits to spend six minutes having a new rear wing fitted. Johansson missed the original accident, but on rejoining the circuit, tangled with Danner, and went out there and then as well.

The race now settled into a pattern. Boutsen and Berger gradually pulling further away: 12.2 seconds ahead of Mansell on lap five, 14.0s on lap ten, 15.8s on lap 16. By that stage, Berger was on his own. Boutsen had led from lap two, but the Austrian had been in close attendance throughout. On lap 15, Boutsen slid wide, the engine cutting out and two laps later, the Ferrari came around on its own. The Benetton's electrics had failed. Things were looking bleak for Benetton when Fabi pitted from eighth position for a tyre change. Berger continued to pull away from Mansell until lap 21, when the Ferrari began to smoke. And on lap 22, Mansell's Williams-Honda came around on its own, now nearly 25 seconds ahead of the second-placed group. For several laps, de Cesaris had carefully tried to pressurise Senna into making a mistake

The Italian Brabham driver followed the Lotus-Honda religiously, attempting sensible overtaking manoeuvres. But on lap 23, Senna missed a gear. De Cesaris attempted to overtake, but Senna restarted, cut across him and sent him off into a gravel trap. One of the Italian's best drives to date had come to an end.

Now Mansell's lead was nearly 30 seconds over Senna. Patrese wasn't far behind in third. Piquet had made phenomenal progress to reach fourth place ahead of Cheever, who was now being pressed by the recovered Fabi. Behind them came the two Ligiers. At the back of the field, Warwick had rejoined and was making good progress as the race approached half distance. But suddenly, Warwick's Arrows left the track at the end of the final corner, sliding straight off into the tyre wall at high speed. The car hit it hard and bounced out again, but not too far. It had clearly lost two wheels and the two on the other side were half off as well. The driver sat in the car for several worrying seconds. Finally, Warwick began to heave himself out of his car. There were still no marshals present, although already they were preparing to crane the car out of the way. Then suddenly black flags appeared around the circuit, and a red flag at the start/finish line. The race was halted.

Warwick limped across the road back to the pits. The cars came to rest on the finishing line and began to take up grid positions for a restart. The organisers had stopped the race quickly and

efficiently, but their ability to restart it wasn't so expert. There was confusion about the distance to be completed, whether tyre changing was allowed and it was even rumoured that a team topped up with fuel. Finally, after about 30 minutes, the race restarted – the two Williams-Hondas racing down into the first corner and into a controversy. Mansell accused his team mate of carving him up, although in fact, Mansell only had to shadow his team mate to the chequered flag and make sure that he still had some of his 40 second first race margin in hand. He settled on doing that as Piquet eased away slightly. Mansell always had at least 20 seconds in hand.

Piquet overtook Senna early into the second half. The Lotus driver was having considerable trouble with his clutch, and while he trailed the Williams pair, he lost it altogether and had a spin. Senna wanted a push-start, just as Piquet had received one earlier in the race, but he didn't get one and promptly took his ire out on a marshal. That cost him $15,000 and to make matters worse, he was no longer in Championship contention. Behind the Williams pair now came Patrese into third. The Brabham driver had followed Cheever throughout the second half, but knew that he had the first race margin to rely on. Such races are always tactical: Patrese third, Cheever fourth and Fabi, after yet

another pit stop, (to clear grass from a radiator) was fifth. The normally aspirated battle had been led early on by Ivan Capelli until he had a spin and then Alliot and Palmer had come through. Palmer admitted that his car's balance had never been as good as the Lola driver's, but remarkably, the reliability not only allowed Alliot to be classified ahead of Palmer, Streiff and Dalmas – against the predictions of various team managers – but also put him in the points for the second race running.

The atmosphere after the race was strained. Now only the Williams-Honda pair were in contention for the World Championship. Mansell was unhappy with his team mate's tactics at the start of the second half of the race, and unhappy with one or two other things besides. The two argued somewhat publicly back at the paddock. With two races remaining, Mansell was 12 points behind Piquet. He was still in with a chance...

Right: Derek Warwick
was lucky to walk away
from his horrendous
accident on lap 27

Left: Another fine race by Eddie Cheever who finished fourth

Centre left: Mansell in jovial mood with Marco Piccinini, Jean-Marie Balestre and Bernie Ecclestone

Centre right: Piquet, talking here to FIA president Jean-Marie Balestre, earned a controversial second place, after being push started, following a collision with Alain Prost

Below: Patrese's third place was his best finish of the season

Right: Yannick Dalmas, here pursuing Philippe Streiff, produced an impressive performance on his Grand Prix debut

Below: Nelson Piquet leading Berger, Johansson, Prost and Senna during the disrupted Grand Prix

214

Entries and Practice Times

Cos=Cosworth
Ch=Champion
Win=Wintershall
McL=McLaren
Mar=Marelli
Bra=Brabham
Bre=Brembo
Bil=Bilstein
L/A=Lotus Active
Marz=Marzocchi

Driver	Nat.	Car	Practice 1	Practice 2	Warm Up	Engine	Turbos	Electrics/Plugs	Fuel/Oil	Brake Discs/ Calipers	Shocks
1 Alain Prost	F	Marlboro McLaren MP4/3	1m20.572s	1m18.742s	1m21.384s	1.5t TAG V6	KKK	Bosch	Shell	SEP/McL	Bil
2 Stefan Johansson	S	Marlboro McLaren MP4/3	1m22.185s	1m22.382s	1m23.063s	1.5t TAG V6	KKK	Bosch	Shell	SEP/McL	Bil
3 Jonathan Palmer	GB	Data General/Courtaulds Tyrrell DG/016	1m27.306s	1m24.723s	1m27.451s	3.5 Ford Cosworth DFZ V8		Cos/Ch	Elf	AP	Koni
4 Philippe Streiff	F	Data General/Courtaulds Tyrrell DG/016	1m27.011s	1m26.305s	1m27.362s	3.5 Ford Cosworth DFZ V8		Cos/Ch	Elf	AP	Koni
5 Nigel Mansell	GB	Canon Williams FW11B	1m20.696s	1m18.383s	1m21.273s	1.5t Honda V6	IHI	Honda/NGK	Mobil	SEP/AP	Showa
6 Nelson Piquet	BR	Canon Williams FW11B	1m20.701s	1m18.463s	1m22.655s	1.5t Honda V6	IHI	Honda/NGK	Mobil	SEP/AP	Showa
7 Riccardo Patrese	I	Brabham BT56	1m21.720s	1m19.889s	1m22.164s	1.5t BMW S4	Garrett	Bosch/Ch	Win/Castrol	SEP/Bra	Koni
8 Andrea de Cesaris	I	Brabham BT56	1m22.930s	1m20.141s	1m21.491s	1.5t BMW S4	Garrett	Bosch/Ch	Win/Castrol	SEP/Bra	Koni
9 Martin Brundle	GB	West Zakspeed 871	1m25.184s	1m21.711s	1m24.150s	1.5t Zakspeed S4	Garrett	Bosch/Ch	Win/Castrol	AP	Sachs
10 Christian Danner	D	West Zakspeed 871	1m23.992s	1m22.593s	1m25.134s	1.5t Zakspeed S4	Garrett	Bosch/Ch	Win/Castrol	AP	Sachs
11 Satoru Nakajima	J	Camel Lotus 99T	1m23.750s	1m22.214s	1m24.073s	1.5t Honda V6	IHI	Honda/NGK	Elf	SEP/Bre	L/A
12 Ayrton Senna	BR	Camel Lotus 99T	1m21.361s	1m19.089s	1m25.367s	1.5t Honda V6	IHI	Honda/NGK	Elf	SEP/Bre	L/A
14 Pascal Fabre	F	El Charro AGS JH22C	1m30.285s	1m28.655s	*	3.5 Ford Cosworth DFZ V8		Cos/Ch	Acto	SEP/AGS	Koni
16 Ivan Capelli	I	Leyton House March 871	1m27.161s	1m24.404s	1m26.217s	3.5 Ford Cosworth DFZ V8		Cos/Ch	BP	AP	Koni
17 Derek Warwick	GB	USF&G Arrows A10	1m23.347s	1m21.664s	1m22.516s	1.5t Megatron S4	Garrett	Bosch/Ch	Win/Castrol	AP	Koni
18 Eddie Cheever	USA	USF&G Arrows A10	1m24.445s	1m21.705s	1m23.117s	1.5t Megatron S4	Garrett	Bosch/Ch	Win/Castrol	AP	Koni
19 Teo Fabi	I	Benetton B187	1m22.666s	1m18.992s	1m21.443s	1.5t Ford V6	Garrett	Ford EED/Ch	Mobil	SEP/AP	Koni
20 Thierry Boutsen	B	Benetton B187	1m20.766s	1m18.691s	1m20.666s	1.5t Ford V6	Garrett	Ford EED/Ch	Mobil	SEP/AP	Koni
21 Alex Caffi	I	Stievani Osella FA11	1m27.670s	1m30.010s	1m29.772s	1.5t Alfa Romeo V8	KKK	Mar/Ch	Agip	Bre	Koni
23 Adrian Campos	E	Minardi M186	1m27.798s	1m23.955s	1m27.338s	1.5t Motori Moderni V6	KKK	Mar/Ch	Agip	Bre	Koni
24 Alessandro Nannini	I	Minardi M186	1m26.055s	1m22.035s	1m24.631s	1.5t Motori Moderni V6	KKK	Mar/Ch	Agip	SEP/Bre	Koni
25 Rene Arnoux	F	Loto Ligier JS29C	1m24.299s	1m23.053s	1m27.276s	1.5t Megatron S4	Garrett	Bosch/Ch	Win/Castrol	SEP/Bre	Koni
26 Piercarlo Ghinzani	I	Loto Ligier JS29C	1m27.059s	1m24.553s	1m24.850s	1.5t Megatron S4	Garrett	Bosch/Ch	Win/Castrol	SEP/Bre	Koni
27 Michele Alboreto	I	Ferrari F187	1m21.290s	1m29.967s	1m22.599s	1.5t Ferrari V6	Garrett	Mar-Weber/Ch	Agip	SEP/Bre	Marz
28 Gerhard Berger	A	Ferrari F187	1m19.992s	1m18.426s	1m20.863s	1.5t Ferrari V6	Garrett	Mar-Weber/Ch	Agip	SEP/Bre	Marz
29 Yannick Dalmas	F	Larrousse Lola LC87	1m28.156s	1m24.745s	1m26.893s	3.5 Ford Cosworth DFZ V8		Cos-Mar/Ch	BP	SEP/AP	Koni
30 Philippe Alliot	F	Larrousse Lola LC87	1m27.184s	1m25.096s	1m25.917s	3.5 Ford Cosworth DFZ V8		Cos-Mar/Ch	BP	SEP/AP	Koni

*Pascal Fabre did not qualify in practice

October 16 October 17 October 18
Hot/sunny Hot/sunny Warm/sunny

Starting Grid

Berger **28**	**5** Mansell
Boutsen **20**	**6** Piquet
Fabi **19**	**1** Prost
Patrese **7**	**12** Senna
de Cesaris **8**	**27** Alboreto
Cheever **18**	**17** Warwick
Nannini **24**	**9** Brundle
Nakajima **11**	**2** Johansson
Arnoux **25**	**10** Danner
Capelli **16**	**23** Campos
Palmer **3**	**26** Ghinzani
Alliot **30**	**29** Dalmas
Caffi **21**	**4** Streiff

Results, Retirements and Fastest Laps

Place	Driver	Car	Laps	Time/Retirement	Fastest Lap No./Time
1	**Nigel Mansell**	1.5t Williams-Honda FW11B	63	1h26m24.207s	59 1m19.527s
2	**Nelson Piquet**	1.5t Williams-Honda FW11B	63	1h26m50.383s	57 1m19.132s
3	**Riccardo Patrese**	1.5t Brabham-BMW BT56	63	1h27m51.086s	57 1m21.057s
4	**Eddie Cheever**	1.5t Arrows-Megatron A10	63	1h28m05.559s	54 1m20.934s
5	**Teo Fabi**	1.5t Benetton-Ford B187	61	1h27m31.973s	38 1m20.829s
6	**Philippe Alliot**	3.5 Lola-Ford LC87	60	1h26m42.504s	39 1m24.320s
7	**Jonathan Palmer**	3.5 Tyrrell-Ford DG/016	60	1h27m02.721s	39 1m24.657s
8	**Philippe Streiff**	3.5 Tyrrell-Ford DG/016	60	1h28m26.436s	28 1m26.039s
9	**Yannick Dalmas**	3.5 Lola-Ford LC87	59	1h27m30.697s	39 1m24.405s
	Ayrton Senna	1.5t Lotus-Honda 99T	54	Spin	44 1m20.586s
	Ivan Capelli	3.5 March-Ford 871	51	Engine	36 1m24.274s
	Alex Caffi	1.5t Osella-Alfa Romeo FA11	50	Engine	49 1m23.628s
	Piercarlo Ghinzani	1.5t Ligier-Megatron JS29C	43	Engine overheating	39 1m23.659s
	Adrian Campos	1.5t Minardi-Motori Moderni M186	32	Gear linkage	31 1m25.734s
	Rene Arnoux	1.5t Ligier-Megatron JS29C	29	Ignition pick-up overheated	19 1m23.887s
	Derek Warwick	1.5t Arrows-Megatron A10	26	Accident	15 1m23.124s
	Andrea de Cesaris	1.5t Brabham-BMW BT56	22	Spin	17 1m22.535s
	Gerhard Berger	1.5t Ferrari-Spa F187	20	Engine	19 1m21.520s
	Thierry Boutsen	1.5t Benetton-Ford B187	15	Electrics	9 1m22.170s
	Alessandro Nannini	1.5t Minardi-Motori Moderni M186	13	Turbo	12 1m24.668s
	Michele Alboreto	1.5t Ferrari-Spa F187	12	Engine	9 1m23.273s
	Martin Brundle	1.5t Zakspeed 871	3	Engine	2 1m28.816s
	Stefan Johansson	1.5t McLaren-TAG MP4/3	1	Collision/Danner	1 1m43.361s
	Satoru Nakajima	1.5t Lotus-Honda 99T	1	Collision/Warwick	1 1m43.533s
	Christian Danner	1.5t Zakspeed 871	1	Collision/Johansson	1 1m44.266s
	Alain Prost	1.5t McLaren-TAG MP4/3	0	Collision/Piquet	

Average Speed of Winner: 193.411 km/h, 120.179 mph

Fastest Lap: Nelson Piquet on lap 57, 1m19.132s, 201.127 km/h, 124.974 mph (record)

Previous Lap Record: Nelson Piquet (1.5t Williams-Honda FW11), 1m19.360s, 200.549 km/h, 124.615 mph (1986)

Circuit Data

Mexican Grand Prix, Mexico City, Mexico

Circuit Length: 4.421 km/ 2.747 miles
Race Distance: 278.523 km/ 173.066 miles
Race Weather: Hot/Sunny

Past Winners

Year	Driver	Nat.	Car	Circuit	Distance miles/km	Speed mph/km/h
1963	**Jim Clark**	GB	1.5 Lotus-Climax 25	Mexico City	201.95/325	93.24/150.13
1964	**Dan Gurney**	USA	1.5 Brabham-Climax BT7	Mexico City	201.95/325	93.28/150.19
1965	**Richie Ginther**	USA	1.5 Honda RA272	Mexico City	201.95/325	94.22/151.70
1966	**John Surtees**	GB	3.0 Cooper-Maserati T81	Mexico City	201.95/325	95.67/154.04
1967	**Jim Clark**	GB	3.0 Lotus-Ford 49	Mexico City	201.95/325	101.37/163.22
1968	**Graham Hill**	GB	3.0 Lotus-Ford 49B	Mexico City	201.95/325	103.75/167.05
1969	**Denny Hulme**	NZ	3.0 McLaren-Ford M7A	Mexico City	201.95/325	106.11/170.84
1970	**Jackie Ickx**	B	Ferrari 312B	Mexico City	201.95/325	108.44/174.60
1986	**Gerhard Berger**	A	1.5 Benetton-BMW B186 t/c	Mexico City	186.80/300.63	120.12/193.31

Lap Chart

Grid Order	1	2	3	4	5	6	7	8	9	10	11	12	13	14	15	16	17	18	19	20	21	22	23	24	25	26	27	28	29	30	31	32	33	34	35	36	37	38	39	40	41	42	43	44	45	46	47	48	49	50	51	52	53	
5 Nigel Mansell	28	20	20	20	20	20	20	20	20	20	20	20	20	20	28	28	28	28	28	28	5	5	5	5	5	5	5	5	5	5	5	5	5	5	5	5	5	5	5	5	5	5	5	5	5	5	5	5	5	5	5	5	5	1
28 Gerhard Berger	20	28	28	28	28	28	28	28	28	28	28	28	28	28	20	5	5	5	5	5	12	12	12	12	12	12	12	12	12	12	12	12	12	12	12	12	12	12	6	6	6	6	6	6	6	6	6	6	6	6	6	6	6	2
6 Nelson Piquet	5	5	5	5	5	5	5	5	5	5	5	5	5	5	5	12	12	12	12	12	8	7	7	7	7	7	7	7	7	7	7	7	6	6	6	6	12	12	12	12	12	12	12	12	12	12	12	12	12	12	12	12	12	3
20 Thierry Boutsen	27	12	12	12	12	12	12	12	12	12	12	12	12	12	12	8	8	8	8	8	7	6	6	6	6	6	6	6	6	6	7	7	7	7	7	7	7	7	7	7	7	7	7	7	7	7	7	7	7	7	7	7	7	4
1 Alain Prost	19	27	27	27	27	8	8	8	8	8	8	8	8	8	7	7	7	7	18	18	18	18	18	18	18	18	18	18	18	18	18	18	18	18	18	18	18	18	18	18	18	18	18	18	18	18	18	18	18	18	18	18		5
19 Teo Fabi	12	19	19	8	8	27	27	27	27	27	27	19	19	7	7	18	18	18	18	6	19	19	19	19	19	19	19	19	19	19	19	19	19	26	26	26	26	26	26	26	19	19	19	19	19	19	19	19	19	19	19	19	19	6
12 Ayrton Senna	7	8	8	19	19	19	19	19	19	19	19	19	7	7	18	6	6	6	6	6	19	25	25	25	25	25	26	26	26	26	26	19	19	19	19	19	19	19	21	21	21	21	21	21	21	30	30	30						7
7 Riccardo Patrese	8	7	7	7	7	7	7	7	7	7	7	7	18	18	19	19	19	19	19	19	25	25	26	26	26	26	30	30	30	21	21	21	21	21	21	21	21	30	30	30	30	30	3	3	3									8
27 Michele Alboreto	24	24	24	24	24	24	24	24	24	24	24	24	6	19	25	25	25	25	26	26	21	21	21	21	30	30	21	21	30	30	30	30	30	30	30	30	30	30	3	3	3	3	3	3	3	29	29	4						9
8 Andrea de Cesaris	18	9	18	18	18	18	18	18	18	18	18	18	25	25	25	26	26	26	26	21	21	30	30	30	30	30	3	3	3	3	3	3	3	3	3	3	3	3	29	29	29	29	29	29	29	4	4	29						10
17 Derek Warwick	17	18	25	25	25	25	25	25	25	25	25	6	26	26	21	21	21	21	30	30	3	3	3	3	3	21	29	29	29	29	29	29	29	29	29	29	29	29	4	4	4	4	4	4	4	16								11
18 Eddie Cheever	9	21	21	21	21	21	21	21	26	26	26	26	21	21	30	30	30	30	30	3	3	29	29	29	29	29	21	4	4	4	4	4	4	4	4	4	4	16	16	16	16	16	16	16										12
9 Martin Brundle	2	25	9	23	26	26	26	26	26	21	21	6	21	30	30	3	3	3	3	3	29	29	4	4	4	4	4	4	16	16	16	16	16	16	16	16	16	16	16	16	16													13
24 Alessandro Nannini	11	23	23	26	23	23	23	23	23	6	6	21	30	3	3	29	29	29	29	4	4	16	16	16	16	16	16	16	16	23	23	23	23																					14
2 Stefan Johansson	10	16	16	16	16	16	16	16	6	30	30	30	3	29	29	4	4	4	4	4	16	16	17	17	17	17	23	23	23																										15
11 Satoru Nakajima	21	26	30	30	30	30	30	30	16	16	16	3	29	4	4	16	16	16	16	16	17	17	23	23	23	23																													16
10 Christian Danner	25	30	30	3	3	3	3	3	30	3	3	29	4	16	16	23	23	23	23	17	23	23																																	17
25 Rene Arnoux	16	3	3	4	4	4	29	6	3	29	29	4	16	23	23	17	17	17	17	23																																			18
23 Adrian Campos	23	4	4	29	29	29	6	29	29	4	4	16	23	17	17																																								19
16 Ivan Capelli	26	29	29	6	6	6	4	4	4	23	23	23	17																																										20
26 Piercarlo Ghinzani	30	6	6	17	17	17	17	17	17	17	17	17																																											21
3 Jonathan Palmer	3	17	17																																																				22
29 Yannick Dalmas	4																																																						23
30 Philippe Alliot	29																																																						24
4 Philippe Streiff	6																																																						25
21 Alex Caffi																																																							26

Lap Chart continued

54	55	56	57	58	59	60	61	62	63	
5	5	5	5	5	5	5	5	5	5	1
6	6	6	6	6	6	6	6	6		2
12	7	7	7	7	7	7	7	7		3
7	18	18	18	18	18	18	18	18		4
18	19	19	19	19	19	19	19			5
19	30	30	30	30	30	30				6
30	3	3	3	3	3	3				7
3	4	4	4	4	4	4				8
4	29	29	29	29	29					9
29										10

Championship Points

Drivers			Constructors	
1	Nelson Piquet	pts	1 Williams	137 pts
2	Nigel Mansell	pts	2 McLaren	72 pts
3	Ayrton Senna	pts	3 Lotus	57 pts
4	Alain Prost	pts	4 Ferrari	26 pts
5	Stefan Johansson	pts	5 Benetton	22 pts
6	Gerhard Berger	pts	6 Arrows	11 pts
7	Teo Fabi	pts	7 Brabham	10 pts
8	Thierry Boutsen	pts	8 Tyrrell	8 pts
9=	Michele Alboreto	pts	9 Lola	3 pts
9=	Eddie Cheever	pts	10 Zakspeed	2 pts
11=	Riccardo Patrese	pts	11= March	1 pt
11=	Satoru Nakajima	pts	11= Ligier	1 pt
13=	Andrea de Cesaris	pts		
13=	Philippe Streiff	pts		
13=	Jonathan Palmer	pts		
16=	Derek Warwick	pts		
16=	Philippe Alliot	pts		
18	Martin Brundle	pts		
19=	Rene Arnoux	pt		
19=	Ivan Capelli	pt		

Jim Clark Cup			Colin Chapman Cup	
1	Jonathan Palmer	77 pts	1 Tyrrell	145 pts
2	Philippe Streiff	68 pts	2 Lola	46 pts
3	Philippe Alliot	43 pts	3 March	38 pts
4	Ivan Capelli	38 pts	4 AGS	35 pts
5	Pascal Fabre	35 pts		
6	Yannick Dalmas	3 pts		

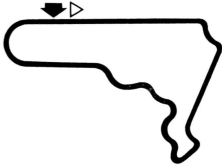

JAPANESE

GRAND PRIX

The victor in the 1987 World Championship became obvious at around 2.40 pm on the Friday before the Japanese Grand Prix. Nigel Mansell's Williams-Honda rode up on a newly painted kerb, the rear end got away from the driver and the car spun. Mansell's challenge of Piquet was over.

At almost any other circuit, anywhere else in the world, it would have been an innocuous accident. Mansell was negotiating the series of corners known as the S-Bend. Although initially it was considered that they should be taken in third gear, some drivers were in fourth negotiating this series of five corners. On the left, small hills had been shifted back to create a larger run-off area, but that wasn't the problem. It was on the right, where the ground fell away steeply to two lakes. There the barrier was backed by debris fencing and faced with tyres, and it was obviously close to the track.

Nelson Piquet had just set the fastest time of the session and his name had scarcely flickered up onto the screen in front of Mansell's Williams, when Mansell's arm shot into the air, asking his mechanics to apply the air starter. A few minutes later, Mansell's car was spinning towards the barrier. It was probably only doing around 120 mph when Mansell lost control of it, and certainly quite a lot of speed had been scrubbed off when he hit the tyres. The car went in backwards, damaging the right rear corner and then rising up on the tyres, spinning round as the front end went into the tyres before it bounced back, crashing down into the right front wheel, and then coming to rest just off the track on the inside of the next corner.

The car was in one piece and, apart from one rear corner, seemed to be undamaged. But Mansell was obviously in

agony. In fact, he was badly winded, seeing stars and desperately afraid that he'd broken his back. He managed to heave himself up in the car slightly, but it was several long minutes before he was extricated from the car, laid on a stretcher and taken by ambulance to the medical centre. There it was confirmed that he hadn't broken anything, but he was still in considerable pain. From the centre, Mansell was taken to the University Hospital in nearby Nagoya, where he remained for the night. What did trouble doctors was that he was in so much pain. It transpired that he had suffered severe bruising and muscular damage to his back. Frank Williams said that a decision as to whether he would be racing would be made the following day. But the already confused media reports were aggravated further when a team spokesman said that night that Mansell would not be racing.

He was right, and indeed, Frank Williams had, at last, to make his decision, for FISA's medical officer Syd Watkins visited Mansell early the next morning and decreed that he was medically unfit to race. It wasn't until after morning practice was over that Nelson Piquet heard that his chief rival would not be racing, and that he was now unbeatable in the World Championship. The race therefore became a little academic. Or did it? Would the pressure now be off Piquet who could go all out and show Honda why they pay him so

much – apart from the fact that he was now a three time World Champion? Some said that this popular circuit had Prost's name written all over it. Could he score win number 29 here where he so hoped that the TAG engine would beat McLaren's future engine supplier Honda on home ground? And surely a win for Gerhard Berger and Ferrari was overdue. Could the pair finally end Ferrari's 26-month spell without a Grand Prix victory.

On Sunday afternoon those questions were answered. Prost was relegated from second place within minutes when a cut tyre resulted in a slow crawl to the pits for a new one. Piquet never really looked in the hunt, but had a lively battle with Senna until he retired to the pits with oil spurting from the rear end of the car. When Prost slowed, Berger already had such a comfortable lead that he turned down the boost within minutes of the start. It was only after the mid-race tyre stops that Berger found Johansson close behind, but he was still able to draw away. On this fuel consuming circuit, his economy engine allowed him to do that, whereas Johansson fell back and was pipped for second place on the last lap by Senna's Lotus-Honda.

The Suzuka circuit was extremely well received by the visiting drivers when they first took a look at the track from their cockpits on Thursday afternoon. They liked the high speed corners and the S-Bend series. But early feelings not only pointed to a circuit demanding of fuel, but also quite a tiring circuit in spite of the high average speed. There was little time to relax: it was one corner after another, said the drivers. Fuel consumption turned out to be a worry, it was true, but the race wasn't nearly as tiring as some feared. The track was pleasantly clean and not too slippery. The only criticism was that there were only two passing places and that the track was a little narrow in parts. Mansell's was the only serious incident in practice. Ivan Capelli plus Michele Alboreto and Ayrton Senna all slid off harmlessly into gravel traps, but without the spectacular consequences of Mansell's accident. Without Mansell, a heavy burden rested on the shoulders of the remaining Honda-powered trio in qualifying. There had, after all, been a Honda-powered car on every front row of the grid since the Italian Grand Prix in 1986 – but there wouldn't be at Suzuka.

Piquet wasn't in good form and he and the team made several mistakes preparing themselves for qualifying. He didn't change springs after running full tanks in the morning, which upset the handling and they upset the brake balance by taking off brake scoops. Furthermore, one of the body screws was left undone briefly. Piquet was only on the third row of the grid, and Senna wasn't much help. He was on the fourth row in seventh spot, his equal worst grid position of the year. He made a visit to the sand trap and then ran out of fuel at the end of the session. Like one or two others, he found the track getting quicker the later you stayed out. If there was any delight for the locals, it was in Nakajima's best grid position of the year, 11th, although even he admitted that he found the track very different in comparison to previous visits. Berger later explained that when Mansell withdrew, he lost two strong rivals. "For the last seven races I've been fighting both Nelson and Nigel. But with Nigel going home, Nelson hasn't had to take any risks and has been more careful, which has meant that he hasn't fought so hard. He didn't want to break his legs. He wants to win the World Championship again next year. So in fact I had two guys less to fight here."

It was Berger who started from pole, having captured his second pole position of the year. The Ferrari chassis was, by now, almost consistently good. The

engine had been his biggest problem in recent races, but that, too, was good on this occasion. The lap was almost perfect apart from a wheel on the grass in a quick corner. Of all the drivers, Berger seemed the least worried by fuel consumption. For only the second time in the year, Prost would start from the front row after a traffic-free lap. The engine wasn't playing up, and Prost had been happy with his chassis almost throughout qualifying – when it was not on full tanks. Thierry Boutsen had been on pole until ten minutes before the end, but the track got quicker and he was bumped down to third. Even so, it was his best grid position ever and he knew that he couldn't have gone as quickly as Berger. Michele Alboreto was putting a brave face on the fact that he was now being regularly out-qualified by his team mate. But then he had his excuses for starting fourth. There was a problem with the engine at the end of his lap and he had taken a spin. Behind the leading Honda runner, Teo Fabi completed the top six, and found that his tyres were at their best early in the session.

The rest were pretty much where you would expect to find them. By now there was a fairly statutory order of position: the Brabham boys and Johansson, then the two Arrows, Nannini and the

Zakspeeds before the first of the normally aspirated drivers, and on this occasion, Philippe Alliot one second behind Arnoux. Noteworthy amongst this bunch was Danner, who was as close to team mate Brundle as he had ever been and Roberto Moreno was now in the AGS after Pascal Fabre's recent non-qualifications. Moreno was only half-a-second slower than the rest (the gap had been five seconds in Austria) but even Moreno wouldn't have made the grade but for Mansell's withdrawal. From the point of view of spectators, the race had been a success right from the word go. The organisers were so inundated with applications for tickets, that they conducted a lottery for the right to buy tickets and even then there were some tickets that were only good for practice days. There had been 36,000 spectators on the Friday, 60,000 on Saturday and on race day the neighbouring funfair and amusement park was packed with racegoers all surging through the tunnel under the main road towards the track. Unlike so many other venues, however, this is a circuit used to huge numbers of spectators and there were never queues at the gates. An official 112,000 spectators packed themselves into the track for race day and those who got there early enough saw Prost set fastest time in the warm-up, although Alboreto, Piquet, Berger and Johansson were all within 0.7 seconds of the outgoing World Champion. Zakspeed's weekend of engine problems continued with two engine failures, and Senna had to switch to the spare for the rest of the day when his active suspension computer's warning light came on to signal impending failure.

There hadn't been any organisational hiccups so far and the record remained right the way to the start. But there things went a little wrong. There were several problems. Warwick, for instance, thought he saw a yellow flag being waved (probably in the pit lane) and thinking that the start would be delayed, took his Arrows out of gear. Not surprisingly, when the lights turned green, it took a moment or two to get under way. In the meantime, Arnoux took avoiding action and spun Alliot round and into the wall. The normally aspirated poleman's run ended there and then. At the front, meanwhile, Alboreto's clutch jammed and he couldn't get his car into gear at all. As he didn't raise his hand immediately, the start was given anyway and Piquet and Senna complained of one another's tactics after they had to take action to avoid the stationary Ferrari, which finally got going at the back of the field.

Berger led from Prost, followed by Boutsen, Senna, Piquet, Fabi and Johansson. Even at the end of lap one, Berger had a 2 second lead. When Prost suffered a cut tyre which promptly deflated and then disintegrated, Berger was left with a 6.3 second lead ahead of second man Boutsen who was being pushed hard by the Brazilian duo, Senna leading Piquet. And Berger just eased away from the rest. Boutsen managed to pull away from the Brazilians for a time, but by lap 11 they'd caught him and they brought Johansson up with them as well. But then Boutsen lost his clutch and slipped back behind the Lotus/Williams/McLaren trio and just ahead of team mate Fabi. Then came Patrese and Nakajima, about to be overtaken by the swift Alboreto. Leading the normally aspirated class was Capelli, but suddenly he, Danner and Arnoux were all in trouble. The Zakspeed's engine blew up and Danner slid off into the barrier on his own oil. And Arnoux, after his earlier efforts, continued his campaign against the unfortunate normally aspi-

rated runners. He knocked off Capelli, damaging his nose section, which then folded under the March, lifting the front wheels off the ground which caused him to crash. The Frenchman headed for the pits for minor temporary repairs.

Before the mid-race tyre stops, Berger had a 13.5 second lead. When everyone had stopped by lap 27, that lead was down to 4.6 seconds and who should now be in second place but Johansson, comfortably ahead of the Brazilian duo who had stopped in unison on lap 25. Berger, however, had the measure of Johansson and steadily eased away. The Swede just didn't have the fuel to play with. The two Brazilians continued their battle for many more laps however, and slowly the 20-second-plus gap between Johansson and the Honda pair began to shrink. On lap 40, however, Senna came by with his biggest margin yet over Piquet. The Williams driver's engine had begun to overheat. He eased up before attacking again three laps later but the engine lasted only another two laps and with five to go, Piquet retired for only the second time in 1987, oil spurting out of the back of the Williams. Rubber was found to have clogged the radiator ducts, causing the overheating.

Berger cruised in to his second Grand Prix win, once again in the penultimate race of the season. More importantly, he ended that long run without a win for Ferrari. Behind him, Senna, once free of Piquet, closed right up on the hobbled Johansson and pinched second place on the very last lap. The Swede was unable to do anything about it. Alboreto was

happy to finish – his third finish of the year – and even fourth was quite an achievement after his clutch problem. Fifth was Boutsen, also troubled by fuel consumption, and sixth was Nakajima, delighted to have scored a point at home. Prost came seventh after a great charge through the field which netted him fastest lap – 1.7 seconds quicker than anyone else's. After Capelli was removed from the track right in front of him, Palmer inherited the normally aspirated lead and held it all the way to the chequered flag, Arnoux having removed both of his principal rivals as Streiff had been troubled all weekend by a lack of straightline speed. His class win meant that Palmer clinched the Jim Clark Cup. In ninth and tenth came the two Arrows, not a particularly happy pair as Cheever claimed to have misread Warwick's stop for tyres as being his own and came in. In spite of being waved out again, he insisted on stopping while Warwick was sent out for another two laps before he pitted. The team was not happy with its ninth and tenth places, particularly as Cheever had been sixth two laps from the end, but ran out of fuel. Patrese was another unhappy driver, having been seventh until his engine blew four laps from home.

Formula One's visit to Japan sadly resulted in a rather flat end to the Championship, although as Piquet said, the series was decided over the previous 14 races, not just this one. It meant, however, that there was nothing to race for in Australia: only a relaxed atmosphere in which one lucky driver could win as he pleased – perhaps.

Left: Stefan Johansson drove a superb race, only to be pipped at the finish by Ayrton Senna. Third place and four points was his reward in his last but one race for McLaren

Right: Suzuka's hairpin, with extensive run off areas

Below: Satoru Nakajima delighted his home crowd by finishing in the points

222

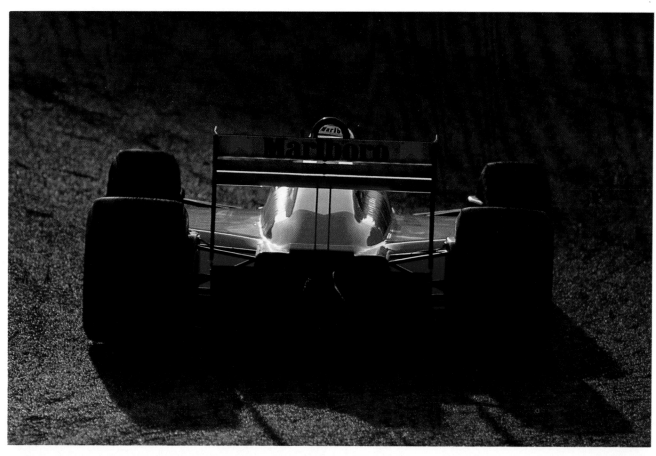

Left: Racing under an oriental sunset

Below: The excitement of a fast pit stop

Right: Gerhard Berger put Ferrari back on the winners' rostrum, with a brilliant win

Centre left: Jubilant Ferrari mechanics respond to their first victory for over two years

Centre right: Nelson Piquet hounded Ayrton Senna for much of the race, with the Lotus driver holding off his fellow countryman until the Williams engine expired

Below: Jonathan Palmer clinched the Jim Clark championship, finishing first in his class and eighth overall

Left: Ayrton Senna kept Honda's honour intact with a fine second place

Left: Ayrton Senna kept Honda's honour intact with a fine second place

Below: After failing to qualify for three of the previous four Grand Prix, AGS's new driver, Roberto Moreno, put in an excellent perform-ance, before engine problems ended his race on lap 38

The accident which ended Nigel Mansell's championship hopes for the second year running. The title has eluded him due to dramatic incidents at the last hurdle

JAPANESE GRAND PRIX · November 1

Entries and Practice Times

Cos=Cosworth
Ch=Champion
Win=Wintershall
McL=McLaren
Mar=Marelli
Bra=Brabham
Bre=Brembo
Bil=Bilstein
L/A=Lotus Active
Marz=Marzocchi

Driver	Nat.	Car	Practice 1	Practice 2	Warm Up	Engine	Turbos	Electrics/Plugs	Fuel/Oil	Brake Discs/ Calipers	Shocks
1 Alain Prost	F	Marlboro McLaren MP4/3	1m42.496s	1m40.652s	1m46.113s	1.5t TAG V6	KKK	Bosch	Shell	SEP/McL	Bil
2 Stefan Johansson	S	Marlboro McLaren MP4/3	1m43.612s	1m43.371s	1m46.890s	1.5t TAG V6	KKK	Bosch	Shell	SEP/McL	Bil
3 Jonathan Palmer	GB	Data General/Courtaulds Tyrrell DG/016	1m48.902s	1m47.775s	1m52.573s	3.5 Ford Cosworth DFZ V8		Cos/Ch	Elf	AP	Koni
4 Philippe Streiff	F	Data General/Courtaulds Tyrrell DG/016	1m50.896s	1m49.741s	1m53.944s	3.5 Ford Cosworth DFZ V8		Cos/Ch	Elf	AP	Koni
6 Nelson Piquet	BR	Canon Williams FW11B	1m41.423s	1m41.144s	1m46.590s	1.5t Honda V6	IHI	Honda/NGK	Mobil	SEP/AP	Showa
7 Riccardo Patrese	I	Brabham BT56	1m44.767s	1m43.304s	1m49.781s	1.5t BMW S4	Garrett	Bosch/Ch	Win/Castrol	SEP/Bra	Koni
8 Andrea de Cesaris	I	Brabham BT56	1m46.399s	1m43.618s	1m50.114s	1.5t BMW S4	Garrett	Bosch/Ch	Win/Castrol	SEP/Bra	Koni
9 Martin Brundle	GB	West Zakspeed 871	1m46.715s	1m46.023s	1m50.604s	1.5t Zakspeed S4	Garrett	Bosch/Ch	Win/Castrol	AP	Sachs
10 Christian Danner	D	West Zakspeed 871	1m49.337s	1m46.116s	1m52.661s	1.5t Zakspeed S4	Garrett	Bosch/Ch	Win/Castrol	AP	Sachs
11 Satoru Nakajima	J	Camel Lotus 99T	1m45.898s	1m43.685s	1m48.607s	1.5t Honda V6	IHI	Honda/NGK	Elf	SEP/Bre	L/A
12 Ayrton Senna	BR	Camel Lotus 99T	1m44.026s	1m42.723s	1m47.740s	1.5t Honda V6	IHI	Honda/NGK	Elf	SEP/Bre	L/A
14 Roberto Moreno	BR	El Charro AGS JH22C	1m51.835s	1m50.212s	1m56.362s	3.5 Ford Cosworth DFZ V8		Cos/Ch	Acto	SEP/AGS	Koni
16 Ivan Capelli	I	Leyton House March 871	1m49.814s	1m48.212s	1m51.687s	3.5 Ford Cosworth DFZ V8		Cos/Ch	BP	AP	Koni
17 Derek Warwick	GB	USF&G Arrows A10	1m44.768s	1m44.626s	1m49.794s	1.5t Megatron S4	Garrett	Bosch/Ch	Win/Castrol	AP	Koni
18 Eddie Cheever	USA	USF&G Arrows A10	1m45.427s	1m44.277s	1m49.834s	1.5t Megatron S4	Garrett	Bosch/Ch	Win/Castrol	AP	Koni
19 Teo Fabi	I	Benetton B187	1m43.351s	1m41.679s	1m50.986s	1.5t Ford V6	Garrett	Ford EED/Ch	Mobil	SEP/AP	Koni
20 Thierry Boutsen	B	Benetton B187	1m43.130s	1m40.850s	1m47.802s	1.5t Ford V6	Garrett	Ford EED/Ch	Mobil	SEP/AP	Koni
21 Alex Caffi	I	Stievani Osella FA1I	1m49.017s	1m50.902s	1m53.218s	1.5t Alfa Romeo V8	KKK	Mar/Ch	Agip	Bre	Koni
23 Adrian Campos	E	Minardi M186	1m53.455s	1m48.337s	1m57.255s	1.5t Motori Moderni V6	KKK	Mar/Ch	Agip	Bre	Koni
24 Alessandro Nannini	I	Minardi M186	1m48.948s	1m45.612s	1m51.514s	1.5t Motori Moderni V6	KKK	Mar/Ch	Agip	SEP/Bre	Koni
25 Rene Arnoux	F	Loto Ligier JS29B	1m50.542s	1m46.200s	1m52.262s	1.5t Megatron S4	Garrett	Bosch/Ch	Win/Castrol	SEP/Bre	Koni
26 Piercarlo Ghinzani	I	Loto Ligier JS29C	1m51.554s	1m49.641s	1m52.821s	1.5t Megatron S4	Garrett	Bosch/Ch	Win/Castrol	SEP/Bre	Koni
27 Michele Alboreto	I	Ferrari F187	1m42.416s	1m40.984s	1m46.201s	1.5t Ferrari V6	Garrett	Mar-Weber/Ch	Agip	SEP/Bre	Marz
28 Gerhard Berger	A	Ferrari F187	1m42.160s	1m40.042s	1m46.590s	1.5t Ferrari V6	Garrett	Mar-Weber/Ch	Agip	SEP/Bre	Marz
29 Yannick Dalmas	F	Larrousse Lola LC87	1m51.230s	1m48.887s	1m52.816s	3.5 Ford Cosworth DFZ V8		Cos-Mar/Ch	BP	SEP/AP	Koni
30 Philippe Alliot	F	Larrousse Lola LC87	1m49.470s	1m47.395s	1m51.230s	3.5 Ford Cosworth DFZ V8		Cos-Mar/Ch	BP	SEP/AP	Koni

October 30   October 31   November 1
Hazy/warm   Cloudy/warm   Cloudy

Starting Grid

		28	Berger
Prost	1		
		20	Boutsen
Alboreto	27		
		6	Piquet
Fabi	19		
		12	Senna
Patrese	7		
		2	Johansson
de Cesaris	8		
		11	Nakajima
Cheever	18		
		17	Warwick
Nannini	24		
		9	Brundle
Danner	10		
		25	Arnoux
Alliot	30		
		3	Palmer
Capelli	16		
		23	Campos
Dalmas	29		
		21	Caffi
Ghinzani	26		
		4	Streiff
Moreno	14		

Results, Retirements and Fastest Laps

Place	Driver	Car	Laps	Time/Retirement	Fastest Lap No./Time	
1	Gerhard Berger	1.5t Ferrari-Spa F187	51	1h32m58.072s	34	1m45.540s
2	Ayrton Senna	1.5t Lotus-Honda 99T	51	1h33m15.456s	49	1m45.805s
3	Stefan Johansson	1.5t McLaren-TAG MP4/3	51	1h33m15.766s	34	1m46.323s
4	Michele Alboreto	1.5t Ferrari-Spa F187	51	1h34m18.513s	28	1m46.534s
5	Thierry Boutsen	1.5t Benetton-Ford B187	51	1h34m23.648s	41	1m47.182s
6	Satoru Nakajima	1.5t Lotus-Honda 99T	51	1h34m34.551s	27	1m48.206s
7	Alain Prost	1.5t McLaren-TAG MP4/3	50	1h32m59.440s	35	1m43.844s
8	Jonathan Palmer	3.5 Tyrrell-Ford DG/016	50	1h33m45.706s	34	1m50.111s
9	Eddie Cheever	1.5t Arrows-Megatron A10	50	1h33m57.583s	41	1m47.421s
10	Derek Warwick	1.5t Arrows-Megatron A10	50	1h34m42.270s	33	1m49.221s
11	Riccardo Patrese	1.5t Brabham-BMW BT56	49	1h32m03.706s Engine	24	1m48.581s
12	Philippe Streiff	3.5 Tyrrell-Ford DG/016	49	1h33m24.919s	44	1m51.236s
13	Piercarlo Ghinzani	1.5t Ligier-Megatron JS29C	48	1h31m21.914s Fuel	29	1m49.915s
14	Yannick Dalmas	3.5 Lola-Ford LC87	47	1h32m54.028s Electrics	40	1m52.080s
15	Nelson Piquet	1.5t Williams-Honda FW11B	46	1h24m44.283s Engine	41	1m46.706s
	Rene Arnoux	1.5t Ligier-Megatron JS29B	44	Fuel	28	1m49.384s
	Alex Caffi	1.5t Osella-Alfa Romeo FA1I	43	Fuel	35	1m51.917s
	Roberto Moreno	3.5 AGS-Ford JH22C	38	Injection box	15	1m54.015s
	Alessandro Nannini	1.5t Minardi-Motori Moderni M186	35	Engine	32	1m51.848s
	Martin Brundle	1.5t Zakspeed 871	32	Overheated engine	28	1m50.367s
	Andrea de Cesaris	1.5t Brabham-BMW BT56	26	Engine	18	1m50.422s
	Teo Fabi	1.5t Benetton-Ford B187	16	Engine	9	1m49.170s
	Christian Danner	1.5t Zakspeed 871	13	Engine/crashed	7	1m52.813s
	Ivan Capelli	3.5 March-Ford 871	13	Collision/Arnoux	13	1m52.213s
	Adrian Campos	1.5t Minardi-Motori Moderni M186	2	Engine	2	1m49.121s
	Philippe Alliot	3.5 Lola-Ford LC87	0	Collision/Arnoux		

Average Speed of Winner: 192.847 km/h, 119.758 mph
Fastest Lap: Alain Prost on lap 35, 1m43.844s, 203.116 km/h, 126.135 mph (record)
Circuit configuration not previously used

Circuit Data

Japanese Grand Prix, Ino-Cho Suzuka-City, Mic-Ken, Japan

Circuit Length: 5.913 km/ 3.499 miles
Race Distance: 298.089 km/ 185.560 miles
Race Weather: Cloudy

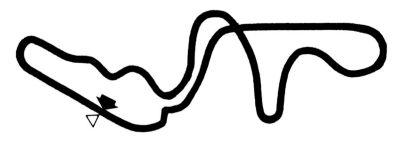

Lap Chart

Grid Order	1	2	3	4	5	6	7	8	9	10	11	12	13	14	15	16	17	18	19	20	21	22	23	24	25	26	27	28	29	30	31	32	33	34	35	36	37	38	39	40	41	42	43	44	45	46	47	48	49	50	51	
28 Gerhard Berger	28	28	28	28	28	28	28	28	28	28	28	28	28	28	28	28	28	28	28	28	28	28	28	12	28	28	28	28	28	28	20	28	28	28	28	28	28	28	28	28	28	28	28	28	28	28	28	28	28	28	28	1
1 Alain Prost	1	20	20	20	20	20	20	20	20	20	20	20	12	12	12	12	12	12	12	12	12	12	12	12	12	12	6	2	2	2	2	2	2	2	2	2	2	2	2	2	2	2	2	2	2	2	2	2	2	2	12	2
20 Thierry Boutsen	20	12	12	12	12	12	12	12	12	12	12	12	6	6	6	6	6	6	6	6	6	6	6	28	12	12	12	12	12	12	12	12	6	12	12	12	12	12	12	12	12	12	12	12	12	12	12	12	12	2	3	3
27 Michele Alboreto	12	6	6	6	6	6	6	6	6	6	6	6	20	2	2	2	2	2	2	2	20	27	27	27	27	12	6	6	6	6	6	6	6	6	6	6	6	6	6	6	6	6	6	6	6	6	6	27	27	27	27	4
6 Nelson Piquet	6	19	19	19	19	19	2	2	2	2	2	2	20	20	20	20	20	20	20	20	27	2	2	2	2	6	27	27	27	27	27	27	27	27	27	27	27	27	27	27	27	27	27	27	27	27	20	20	20	20	20	5
19 Teo Fabi	19	2	2	2	2	2	19	19	19	19	19	19	19	19	7	27	27	27	27	2	11	20	20	20	20	20	20	20	20	20	20	11	11	11	11	11	11	11	11	11	11	11	11	11	11	11	18	18	11	11		6
12 Ayrton Senna	2	7	7	7	7	7	7	7	7	7	7	7	7	7	7	11	7	7	11	11	11	20	8	8	11	11	11	11	11	11	11	11	20	20	20	20	20	20	20	20	20	20	20	20	20	18	11	11	1			7
7 Riccardo Patrese	7	8	8	8	8	11	11	11	11	11	11	11	11	11	11	11	27	11	11	7	7	18	11	7	7	7	7	7	7	7	7	18	18	18	18	18	18	18	18	18	18	18	18	7	7	1	3					8
2 Stefan Johansson	8	11	11	11	11	8	8	8	18	18	18	18	27	27	19	18	18	18	18	8	18	7	7	18	18	18	18	18	18	18	18	7	7	7	7	7	7	7	7	7	7	7	7	1	1	1	3	18				9
8 Andrea de Cesaris	11	18	18	18	18	18	18	18	8	8	8	27	27	18	18	18	8	8	8	8	7	17	17	18	8	3	3	3	3	3	3	3	3	3	3	3	3	3	3	3	1	1	1	3	3	7	17					10
11 Satoru Nakajima	18	17	17	17	17	17	17	17	17	17	27	8	8	8	8	17	17	17	17	17	17	7	18	17	3	3	29	17	17	17	17	17	17	17	17	17	17	1	1	1	3	3	3	17	17	17						11
18 Eddie Cheever	17	24	24	24	24	24	24	27	27	17	17	17	17	17	17	17	24	24	24	24	24	24	24	29	17	29	29	29	9	9	29	1	1	1	1	1	1	1	17	17	17	17	17	26	26	4						12
17 Derek Warwick	24	9	9	9	9	9	27	24	24	24	24	24	24	24	9	9	9	9	9	9	3	3	29	17	9	9	9	9	29	29	1	29	29	29	29	29	29	26	26	26	26	26	4	4								13
24 Alessandro Nannini	9	10	10	10	10	27	9	9	9	9	9	9	9	9	9	3	3	3	3	3	3	9	29	17	9	24	24	24	24	24	24	24	21	21	21	26	26	29	29	29	4	4	29									14
9 Martin Brundle	10	25	25	27	27	10	10	10	10	10	10	10	3	3	3	26	26	26	26	26	9	24	21	21	21	21	21	1	21	26	26	26	21	4	4	4	4	4	29	29												15
10 Christian Danner	25	16	16	25	25	25	25	25	25	25	25	25	26	26	26	29	29	29	29	29	29	21	21	4	4	4	1	21	26	26	4	4	4	21	21	21	25	25	25													16
25 Rene Arnoux	16	3	27	16	16	16	16	16	16	16	16	16	29	29	29	21	21	21	21	21	4	4	26	26	26	4	4	4	4	24	25	25	25	25	25	21	21															17
30 Philippe Alliot	3	23	3	3	3	3	3	3	3	3	3	3	21	21	21	4	4	4	4	4	26	26	1	1	1	1	26	26	14	25	25	14	14	14																		18
3 Jonathan Palmer	23	26	26	26	26	26	26	26	26	26	26	4	4	4	14	14	14	14	14	1	1	14	14	14	14	14	14	14	25	14	14																					19
16 Ivan Capelli	26	27	29	29	29	29	29	29	29	29	29	29	14	14	14	1	1	1	1	1	14	14	1	1	25	25	25	25	25																							20
23 Adrian Campos	29	29	21	21	21	21	21	21	21	21	21	21	25	1	1	25	25	25	25	25	25	25	25																													21
29 Yannick Dalmas	14	21	14	14	14	14	14	4	4	4	4	4	1	25	25																																					22
21 Alex Caffi	21	14	4	4	4	4	4	14	14	14	14	14	14																																							23
26 Piercarlo Ghinzani	27	4	1	1	1	1	1	1	1	1	1	1	1																																							24
4 Philippe Streiff	4	1																																																		25
14 Roberto Moreno																																																				26

Championship Points

	Drivers			Constructors	
1	Nelson Piquet	73 pts	1	Williams	137 pts
2	Nigel Mansell	61 pts	2	McLaren	76 pts
3	Ayrton Senna	57 pts	3	Lotus	64 pts
4	Alain Prost	46 pts	4	Ferrari	38 pts
5	Stefan Johansson	30 pts	5	Benetton	24 pts
6	Gerhard Berger	27 pts	6	Arrows	11 pts
7=	Teo Fabi	12 pts	7	Brabham	10 pts
7=	Thierry Boutsen	12 pts	8	Tyrrell	8 pts
9	Michele Alboreto	11 pts	9	Lola	3 pts
10	Eddie Cheever	8 pts	10	Zakspeed	2 pts
11	Satoru Nakajima	7 pts	11=	March	1 pt
12	Riccardo Patrese	6 pts	11=	Ligier	1 pt
13=	Andrea de Cesaris	4 pts			
13=	Philippe Streiff	4 pts			
13=	Jonathan Palmer	4 pts			
16=	Derek Warwick	3 pts			
16=	Philippe Alliot	3 pts			
18	Martin Brundle	2 pts			
19=	Rene Arnoux	1 pt			
19=	Ivan Capelli	1 pt			

	Jim Clark Cup			Colin Chapman Cup	
1	Jonathan Palmer	86 pts	1	Tyrrell	160 pts
2	Philippe Streiff	74 pts	2	Lola	50 pts
3	Philippe Alliot	43 pts	3	March	38 pts
4	Ivan Capelli	38 pts	4	AGS	35 pts
5	Pascal Fabre	35 pts			
6	Yannick Dalmas	7 pts			

AUSTRALIAN

GRAND PRIX

Until the race itself, there was a distinct end-of-term feeling about the Australian Grand Prix. Then Gerhard Berger showed complete domination, during what he called the hardest race of his life. But, just as he had in Japan, he started from pole position and led every lap of the race, usually with a comfortable margin.

The race brought a nasty sting in the tail for Brazil's Ayrton Senna who finished second. On this circuit, which is so hard on brakes, extra ducting had been added to his car in the shape of two hoses positioned around the outside of the existing brake duct. Unfortunately, these hoses meant that the width of the ducting was now 2.5 centimetres over-width. As the Lotus mechanics duly doused the second-placed Senna in a pit water fight, the stewards of the meeting dampened his spirits by excluding the Lotus from the meeting, elevating Michele Alboreto in his brake-troubled Ferrari to second – making it a Ferrari double – and Thierry Boutsen's Benetton-Ford to the team's equal best result of the season, third.

The other three points-winners were all driving normally aspirated cars in a race of abnormally high attrition, although that was almost to be expected. Brakes rapidly became the talking point of the weekend as drivers realised that they could be in dire trouble. In the past, drivers have switched to steel brake discs for this one race, but only one top team, Benetton, did so on this occasion and their cars were still in trouble. Fuel was also tight, and as the weather got hotter and hotter throughout the weekend, the prospect of nearly two hours rushing around a tight street circuit became a daunting one. The only things that weren't taxed were tyres, and by Sunday morning, nearly everyone had decided not to change tyres mid-race. On this occasion, it wasn't a circuit that got quicker over the weekend. On the contrary, the quickest times were set on Friday, since the rising temperatures impeded engine efficiency.

As drivers and teams assembled in Adelaide, there were some very healthy and bronzed faces to be seen, since drivers had spent ten days in such exotic locations as Bali, Singapore, the Great Barrier Reef and even surfing in Sydney. Only a few, such as Boutsen, Nannini and Campos had returned to Europe. Mechanics meanwhile, had almost become honorary burgers of Adelaide, so long had some of them been there, and most had thoroughly enjoyed the usual Aussie hospitality. One of the less healthy drivers in Adelaide was Gerhard Berger. He had contracted some kind of virus between Singapore and Adelaide which was to affect his throat and ears during the weekend, although by Sunday he felt much better. However, he still wasn't completely fit, and the combination of having been ill and losing an ear plug early in the race meant that he was utterly exhausted by the end of the race. Unfortunately, Berger was very much in demand as his photograph is on the front cover of the current Adelaide telephone directory! And he made himself even more in demand by setting a time 1.2 seconds quicker than Nigel Mansell's pole-winning time in 1986, with what was a nearly perfect lap on the Friday. He scarcely bothered to go out at all the next day in qualifying. After the Japanese performance, however, no one was in any doubt that the Ferraris were a very real threat, and Berger reinforced that by playing down any potential fuel problem. It was his third pole position of the year.

Once again, there was no Honda on the front row of the grid, although it was very much touch and go, for it was only in the final seconds of the last qualifying session that Alain Prost set second quickest time. But the team already knew that it was in considerable brake trouble on this circuit and Prost had reinforced that with at least five spins in practice, one of which caused him considerable back pain. The out-going World Champion had pushed his successor back to row two, although Nelson Piquet had had a difficult weekend. In Mexico, he had pleaded with Frank Williams to allow him to drive the hydro-pneumatic suspension car again this season, even offering to pay for its transport costs himself, and suddenly, here it was in the Adelaide pit lane. He also had a conventional car to use, and as the weekend progressed, he used the latter more than the former.

Ayrton Senna had been a frequent spinner in the streets of Adelaide in the past, but he was also one of the first to recognise the potential brake problem. He started fourth alongside Piquet after

231

two mainly trouble-free days. After just a couple of days in Bali with Senna and others, Thierry Boutsen had managed to get a bit of a tan, and he was inside the top ten in qualifying as usual, but this was a brave effort, for his car's handling was decidely strange. The Benetton was pulling to the left and locking wheels and Boutsen also found traffic unfavourable. Michele Alboreto completed the top six although he had a spin on both days and didn't improve on Saturday.

If Berger was in demand with Australia's eager media, so too was Riccardo Patrese. This was because he was joining the Williams team one race early, as Nigel Mansell had decided not to make the journey to Australia, since he was still suffering pain from his back. So Bernie Ecclestone had kindly released Patrese from the Brabham team so that he could join Williams. It wasn't, however, the first time that Patrese had driven a Williams; he'd done an extensive test at Imola earlier in the year. This time, however, he had handling problems, finding the car difficult in the warm-up and he also had trouble with tyres and clutch.

Stefan Johansson was eighth, discovering McLaren's brake problems and also having a spin, while Teo Fabi came ninth in his last Grand Prix drive for Benetton before opting for another season in CART. Fabi had both an engine and turbo failure on Friday and failed to improve the next day when his car understeered and locked its brakes. Completing the top ten was Andrea de Cesaris in the Brabham which had a trouble-free day on the Friday, but on Saturday problems returned, with an engine blow-up in the morning. His new team mate was none other than the young F3000 champion, Stefano Modena who had never even seen a Grand Prix live before. He did a sensible job, quietly breaking himself in over the two

Previous page: New recruit, Riccardo Patrese, discusses the Williams FW11B with Patrick Head

Above: Another short race for Satoru Nakajima, sidelined with suspension problems

Right: Racing through the streets of Adelaide

days in spite of a spin. He suffered a blown engine on the Saturday which was changed in a record 63 minutes, qualified 15th and then set fifth fastest time in the warm-up. Fastest of the normally aspirated runners was Philippe Alliot ahead of Philippe Streiff, while Roberto Moreno was 25th, one place ahead of Adrian Campos. The unfortunate non-qualifier was poor Alex Caffi who had had a turbo fire which stopped practice on Friday morning. He then suffered a damaged engine and was down to his last power unit by Saturday morning. A broken turbo put paid to his chances that afternoon and the car was ready to go back to Europe by Sunday.

As usual, the Australian Grand Prix was magnificently promoted and there had been big crowds on both Friday and Saturday with the streets full of partygoers every evening. There was also a fine variety of entertainment, both in the air and on the ground, and by the time the cars came out to take up their grid positions, there were around 123,000 spectators in the brightly coloured stands, enjoying a hot but hazy sun. In the warm-up, Berger and Prost had set the quickest times with Alboreto third, ahead of the two Brabhams. It was rather a strange session, with Piquet seventh and opting for the standard Williams, while Patrese was only 22nd and already in brake trouble. Boutsen was only 11th and Fabi was last, having to change to the spare Benetton when his own suffered electrical problems. Every stand seat was full and Australians packed the perimeter fences as the cars

formed up on the grid, and in front of the Australian Prime Minister, Mr Hawke, starter Roland Bruynseraede switched the lights from red to green.

Berger had been glad that Piquet's powerful Honda had been relegated to row two by Prost, but still the Williams driver came powering through down the inside of Berger and for a second, it looked as though the two cars touched. Piquet led briefly, but very soon Berger was back in front and when he crossed the start/finish line at the end of lap one, he was already over one second ahead of Piquet who was in second place. Senna was another 1.4 seconds behind in third and then came Prost, Alboreto, Patrese, Boutsen, Johansson, de Cesaris, Cheever and Fabi, before a gap to Warwick who had made contact with both Nannini who crashed and Palmer who then complained of bent suspension. Within three laps, Berger had a 4-second lead, but the rest behind him were all bunched up, although not for long. By lap six, Berger's lead was 5.8 seconds over Piquet who had Prost in close attendance. Two seconds behind came Alboreto leading Senna, Patrese, Boutsen, Johansson, de Cesaris and Cheever before a small gap to Fabi and Modena.

Now that Alboreto had overtaken Senna, he was able to move himself up to the Piquet/Prost battle. And Prost was really looking determined, although the medium speed corners certainly favoured his car more than the slow speed corners. Senna, meanwhile, was dropping back to Patrese and Johansson. Boutsen's steel brakes were not proving to be the answer and he also dropped back. For lap after lap, Piquet, Prost and Alboreto circulated within meters of one another, the gaps varying but only fractionally. But for much of the time, they were losing ground to Berger. Behind them, Senna became more confident in his machinery and began to push a little harder. That took him away from the Patrese/Johansson battle and by lap 28, he was back in touch with the Piquet/Prost/Alboreto trio. Johansson, in the meantime, had got past Patrese after the Williams' rear brakes overheated and the new driver spun. Boutsen was eighth and there was now a gap to the rest. Fabi had already had a pit stop and dropped back, eventually to retire with a lack of brakes.

By lap 30, Berger's lead over Piquet was more than 13 seconds, but Piquet was soon to change tyres. Nearly everyone else had decided not to, but Piquet was suffering a tyre vibration and decided he couldn't bear it any longer. Pitting for a new set on lap 35 dropped him back to sixth place. Interestingly, his lap times didn't improve with new tyres. But his stop made no statistical difference to the race: there was still a three-way fight for second place, this time comprising Prost, Alboreto and now Senna. Johansson was fifth, ahead of Piquet. Then came Boutsen and Patrese. The rest were lapped. Finding himself second, with no one ahead, Prost was able to chip away at Berger's lead. It had risen to over 17 seconds but now Prost was able to cut it back to 11.6 seconds by lap 40 – and that wasn't even half distance!

But then Prost came up behind Arnoux, who had Cheever just ahead of him and Danner closing up from behind. Obviously keen not to lose time, Arnoux cost his compatriot and former team mate 4 seconds instead, which of course allowed Alboreto and Senna to close up. The trio flashed across the line as one for the 41st time, at half distance. Prost was close behind Arnoux, Alboreto had pulled out alongside, and Senna was lining up to flash down the inside of them both. It was quite a dangerous moment, as Prost later confirmed, but all of a sudden, he had slipped from second to fourth, with Senna now leading him, and Alboreto between the two. Berger's lead, meanwhile, had stretched out to 18.8 seconds.

Prost's time was limited, however. The first cause for alarm came when Johansson's carbon fibre brake disc exploded quite suddenly on lap 49, while the Swede was in fifth place. And just five laps later, fourth-placed Prost suffered exactly the same problem. "We've never had anything like that happen before," he commented ruefully. Both the McLarens were out. Senna, meanwhile, had taken up where Prost left off, slowly chipping away at Berger's lead. He got the lead down to 10.6 seconds but that was enough for Berger who promptly put in a fastest lap and the gap began to rise again. Senna couldn't respond. While the brakes weren't giving trouble, the tyres were. But Berger's Ferrari was obviously in trouble too, although the driver wasn't aware of it. It was emitting sparks from the rear right corner of the underbody, which was dragging. But he did appear to ease up again and Senna closed the gap to 7.2 seconds on lap 64, but that's as far as it went and then Berger turned in more fastest laps. By the end, he was more than 30 seconds ahead of Senna. The Brazilian had been able to throw off the attentions of Alboreto as the Ferrari driver was having brake trouble, but Alboreto was delighted to get back on the rostrum. After Senna had been disqualified, he climbed another step to confirm that Ferrari was well and truly back in business. Piquet might have finished an eventual third, but 23 laps from the end his gearshift broke. He'd been having brake trouble and as he came into the pits, a brake disc exploded.

Patrese had led Boutsen earlier, but then came in for tyres and dropped back behind the Benetton again. However, with 20 laps to go, he caught the Belgian again as the car improved with a lighter fuel load. But it had been sending out little puffs of smoke with every gear change and six laps from the end, the engine expired in a huge cloud of oil smoke and Patrese spun off on his own oil. So Boutsen came in third, equal best placing for Benetton in 1987. Cheever might have been fourth, but much earlier he had had a puncture, had done one slow lap and although the engine was still in one piece, he had retired with overheating. He'd been caught by the flying Danner but then the Zakspeed driver's brakes began to disappear and he was overtaken by a remarkable series of normally aspirated cars which claimed the rest of the top six positions.

The class had been led by Capelli, but he was being caught when he spun off 23 laps from the end. And who should find himself in the lead but Palmer. After his touch from Warwick, Palmer's Tyrrell understeered one way and oversteered the other. And a few laps later, he'd had to pit for a new tyre. But he'd battled through the field, overtaken both Larrousse Lolas having their own tussle and then overtaken Danner. He'd even overtaken Boutsen, and gone a lap ahead of him, briefly. So Ken Tyrrell got the 11 points he'd promised his sponsors at the beginning of the year. Yannick Dalmas should have taken two points, but his car hadn't been entered for the full championship. Moreno got and deserved his point for sixth in the bulky AGS which, with its driver, had proved consistently competitive during the race. So Adelaide had proved to be a special circuit again with an unpleasant turn of events for Senna. But what was Mansell thinking back at his home on the Isle of Man, as he watched Piquet retire for the second race running...

Left: Nelson Piquet pushes past Gerhard Berger at the start, only to be overtaken by the Ferrari before the end of the first lap

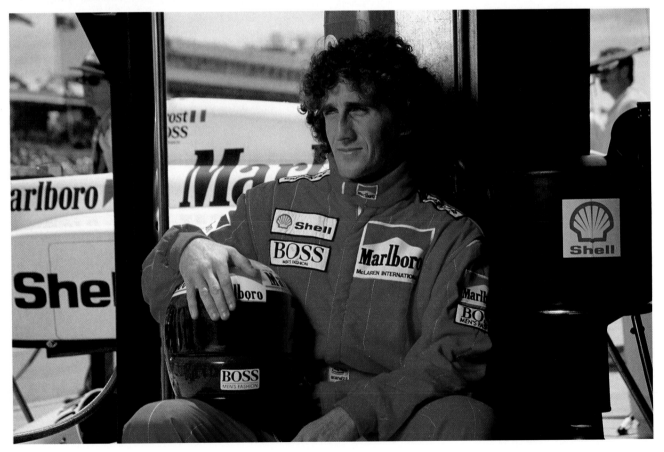

234

Left: A disappointing last
McLaren Grand Prix
for Stefan Johansson

Below: Thierry Boutsen
again in the points with
a superb third place

Right: The second win
on the trot for Gerhard
Berger

Left: A fine 1-2 for Ferrari, with Michele Alboreto following Gerhard Berger over the line for 2nd place

Far left: Roberto Moreno in the points in only his second Grand Prix

Centre: The start of the third Australian Grand Prix with Stefan Johansson leading the latter portion of the grid

Below left: Stefano Modena qualified an excellent 15th on his Grand Prix debut

Below right: Jonathan Palmer drove brilliantly, and despite a pit stop, finished a credible fourth

Entries and Practice Times

Cos=Cosworth
Ch=Champion
Win=Wintershall
McL=McLaren
Mar=Marelli
Bra=Brabham
Bre=Brembo
Bil=Bilstein
L/A=Lotus Active
Marz=Marzocchi

Driver	Nat.	Car	Practice 1	Practice 2	Warm Up	Engine	Turbos	Electrics/Plugs	Fuel/Oil	Brake Discs/Calipers	Shocks
1 Alain Prost	F	Marlboro McLaren MP4/3	1m18.200s	**1m17.967s**	1m21.953s	1.5t TAG V6	KKK	Bosch	Shell	SEP/McL	Bil
2 Stefan Johansson	S	Marlboro McLaren MP4/3	1m19.761s	1m18.826s	1m23.529s	1.5t TAG V6	KKK	Bosch	Shell	SEP/McL	Bil
3 Jonathan Palmer	GB	Data General/Courtaulds Tyrrell DG/016	1m22.315s	1m22.087s	1m25.328s	3.5 Ford Cosworth DFZ V8		Cos/Ch	Elf	AP	Koni
4 Philippe Streiff	F	Data General/Courtaulds Tyrrell DG/016	**1m21.971s**	1m22.434s	1m25.622s	3.5 Ford Cosworth DFZ V8		Cos/Ch	Elf	AP	Koni
5 Riccardo Patrese	I	Canon Williams FW11B	1m19.507s	1m18.813s	1m26.193s	1.5t Honda V6	IHI	Honda/NGK	Mobil	SEP/AP	Showa
6 Nelson Piquet	BR	Canon Williams FW11B	**1m18.017s**	1m18.176s	1m23.628s	1.5t Honda V6	IHI	Honda/NGK	Mobil	SEP/AP	Showa
7 Stefano Modena	I	Brabham BT56	1m21.887s	1m21.014s	1m23.332s	1.5t BMW S4	Garrett	Bosch/Ch	Win/Castrol	SEP/Bra	Koni
8 Andrea de Cesaris	I	Brabham BT56	1m19.768s	1m19.590s	1m23.184s	1.5t BMW S4	Garrett	Bosch/Ch	Win/Castrol	SEP/Bra	Koni
9 Martin Brundle	GB	West Zakspeed 871	1m22.224s	1m21.483s	1m25.296s	1.5t Zakspeed S4	Garrett	Bosch/Ch	Win/Castrol	AP	Sachs
10 Christian Danner	D	West Zakspeed 871	1m23.046s	1m22.736s	1m24.526s	1.5t Zakspeed S4	Garrett	Bosch/Ch	Win/Castrol	AP	Sachs
11 Satoru Nakajima	J	Camel Lotus 99T	1m21.708s	1m20.891s	1m25.141s	1.5t Honda V6	IHI	Honda/NGK	Elf	SEP/Bre	L/A
12 Ayrton Senna	BR	Camel Lotus 99T	1m18.508s	1m18.488s	1m23.701s	1.5t Honda V6	IHI	Honda/NGK	Elf	SEP/Bre	L/A
14 Roberto Moreno	BR	El Charro AGS JH22C	**1m23.659s**	1m24.149s	1m26.354s	3.5 Ford Cosworth DFZ V8		Cos/Ch	Acto	SEP/AGS	Koni
16 Ivan Capelli	I	Leyton House March 871	**1m22.698s**	1m22.704s	1m24.690s	3.5 Ford Cosworth DFZ V8		Cos/Ch	BP	AP	Koni
17 Derek Warwick	GB	USF&G Arrows A10	**1m20.638s**	1m20.837s	1m24.820s	1.5t Megatron S4	Garrett	Bosch/Ch	Win/Castrol	AP	Koni
18 Eddie Cheever	USA	USF&G Arrows A10	**1m20.187s**	1m21.592s	1m25.593s	1.5t Megatron S4	Garrett	Bosch/Ch	Win/Castrol	AP	Koni
19 Teo Fabi	I	Benetton B187	1m19.461s	1m20.301s	1m28.918s	1.5t Ford V6	Garrett	Ford EED/Ch	Mobil	SEP/AP	Koni
20 Thierry Boutsen	B	Benetton B187	1m18.943s	**1m18.523s**	1m24.551s	1.5t Ford V6	Garrett	Ford EED/Ch	Mobil	SEP/AP	Koni
21 Alex Caffi	I	Stievani Osella FA1I	**1m25.872s**	1m27.331s*		1.5t Alfa Romeo V8	KKK	Mar/Ch	Agip	Bre	Koni
23 Adrian Campos	E	Minardi M186	1m25.760s	**1m24.121s**	1m27.761s	1.5t Motori Moderni V6	KKK	Mar/Ch	Agip	Bre	Koni
24 Alessandro Nannini	I	Minardi M186	**1m20.701s**	1m21.523s	1m25.506s	1.5t Motori Moderni V6	KKK	Mar/Ch	Agip	SEP/Bre	Koni
25 Rene Arnoux	F	Loto Ligier JS29B	1m24.833s	**1m22.303s**	1m28.074s	1.5t Megatron S4	Garrett	Bosch/Ch	Win/Castrol	SEP/Bre	Koni
26 Piercarlo Ghinzani	I	Loto Ligier JS29C	**1m22.689s**	1m24.652s	1m24.413s	1.5t Megatron S4	Garrett	Bosch/Ch	Win/Castrol	SEP/Bre	Koni
27 Michele Alboreto	I	Ferrari F187	**1m18.578s**	1m19.612s	1m22.274s	1.5t Ferrari V6	Garrett	Mar-Weber/Ch	Agip	SEP/Bre	Marz
28 Gerhard Berger	A	Ferrari F187	**1m17.267s**	1m18.142s	1m21.738s	1.5t Ferrari V6	Garrett	Mar-Weber/Ch	Agip	SEP/Bre	Marz
29 Yannick Dalmas	F	Larrousse Lola LC87	1m25.021s	**1m22.650s**	1m25.713s	3.5 Ford Cosworth DFZ V8		Cos-Mar/Ch	BP	SEP/AP	Koni
30 Philippe Alliot	F	Larrousse Lola LC87	**1m21.888s**	1m22.846s	1m25.922s	3.5 Ford Cosworth DFZ V8		Cos-Mar/Ch	BP	SEP/AP	Koni

*Alex Caffi did not qualify in practice

November 13 — Warm/sunny
November 14 — Warmer sunny
November 15 — Hot/sunny

Starting Grid

Berger 28		1 Prost	
Piquet 6		12 Senna	
Boutsen 20		27 Alboreto	
Patrese 5		2 Johansson	
Fabi 19		8 de Cesaris	
Cheever 18		17 Warwick	
Nannini 24		11 Nakajima	
Modena 7		9 Brundle	
Alliot 30		4 Streiff	
Palmer 3		25 Arnoux	
Dalmas 29		26 Ghinzani	
Capelli 16		10 Danner	
Moreno 14		23 Campos	

Results, Retirements and Fastest Laps

Place	Driver	Car	Laps	Time/Retirement	Fastest Lap No./Time
1	Gerhard Berger	1.5t Ferrari-Spa F187	82	1h52m56.144s	72 1m20.416s
2	Michele Alboreto	1.5t Ferrari-Spa F187	82	1h54m04.028s	48 1m21.124s
3	Thierry Boutsen	1.5t Benetton-Ford B187	81	1h54m16.070s	45 1m22.769s
4	Jonathan Palmer	3.5 Tyrrell-Ford DG/016	80	1h54m16.400s	59 1m23.197s
5	Yannick Dalmas	3.5 Lola-Ford LC87	79	1h53m04.456s	55 1m23.207s
6	Roberto Moreno	3.5 AGS-Ford JH22C	79	1h53m44.855s	62 1m24.488s
7	Christian Danner	1.5t Zakspeed 871	79	1h53m55.483s	35 1m24.119s
8	Andrea de Cesaris	1.5t Brabham-BMW BT56	78	1h52m47.682s	65 1m20.917s
9	Riccardo Patrese	1.5t Williams-Honda FW11B	76	1h46m57.436s	52 1m21.491s
	Nelson Piquet	1.5t Williams-Honda FW11B	58	Broken gear shift	40 1m21.981s
	Ivan Capelli	3.5 March-Ford 871	58	Spin	55 1m23.296s
	Alain Prost	1.5t McLaren-TAG MP4/3	53	Brake disc exploded/spin	47 1m21.381s
	Eddie Cheever	1.5t Arrows-Megatron A10	53	Overheating	18 1m23.390s
	Stefan Johansson	1.5t McLaren-TAG MP4/3	48	Brake disc exploded	38 1m22.232s
	Teo Fabi	1.5t Benetton-Ford B187	46	Brakes	44 1m22.246s
	Adrian Campos	1.5t Minardi-Motori Moderni M186	46	Gearbox	35 1m27.676s
	Philippe Alliot	3.5 Lola-Ford LC87	45	Electrics	39 1m24.834s
	Rene Arnoux	1.5t Ligier-Megatron JS29B	41	Electrics	30 1m23.999s
	Stefano Modena	1.5t Brabham-BMW BT56	31	Driver exhaustion	4 1m24.294s
	Piercarlo Ghinzani	1.5t Ligier-Megatron JS29C	26	Turbo	24 1m25.196s
	Satoru Nakajima	1.5t Lotus-Honda 99T	22	Suspension	18 1m24.926s
	Derek Warwick	1.5t Arrows-Megatron A10	19	Final drive	18 1m24.478s
	Martin Brundle	1.5t Zakspeed 871	18	Broken gear lever/turbo	11 1m25.554s
	Philippe Streiff	3.5 Tyrrell-Ford DG/016	6	Spin	6 1m26.823s
	Alessandro Nannini	1.5t Minardi-Motori Moderni M186	0	Accident/Warwick	– –

Note: Ayrton Senna was disqualified for oversize brake cooling intakes
Average Speed of Winner: 164.631 km/h, 102.298 mph
Fastest Lap: Gerhard Berger (1.5t Ferrari-Spa F187) on lap 72, 1m20.416s, 169.175 km/h, 105.120 mph (record)
Previous Lap Record: Nelson Piquet (1.5t Williams-Honda FW11) 1m20.787s, 168.398 km/h 104.637 mph (1986).

Circuit Data

Australian Grand Prix, Adelaide, South Australia

Circuit Length: 3.778 km/2.348 miles
Race Distance: 309.878 km/192.549 miles
Race Weather: Hot/hazy

Past Winners

Year	Driver	Nat.	Car	Circuit	Distance miles/km	Speed mph/km/h
1985	Keke Rosberg	SF	1.5 Williams-Honda FW10 t/c	Adelaide	2.347/3.778	95.71/154.032
1986	Alain Prost	F	1.5 McLaren-TAG MP4/2C t/c	Adelaide	2.347/3.778	101.040/162.609

Lap Chart

Grid Order	Laps 1–61	Pos
28 Gerhard Berger	28 28 28 28 28 28 28 28 28 28 28 28 28 28 28 28 28 28 28 28 28 28 28 28 28 28 28 28 28 28 28 28 28 28 28 28 28 28 28 28 28 28 28 28 28 28 28 28 28 28 28 28 28 28 28 28 28 28 28 28 28	1
27 Michele Alboreto	6 6 6 6 6 6 6 6 6 6 6 6 6 6 6 6 6 6 6 6 6 6 6 6 6 6 6 6 6 6 6 6 6 6 6 6 6 6 6 6 1 1 1 1 1 1 1 1 12 12 12 12 12 12 12 12 12 12 12 12 12	2
20 Thierry Boutsen	12 1 1 1 1 1 1 1 1 1 1 1 1 1 1 1 1 1 1 1 1 1 1 1 1 1 1 1 1 1 1 1 1 1 1 1 1 1 1 1 27 27 27 27 27 27 27 27 27 27 27 27 27 27 27 27 27 27 27 27 27	3
3 Jonathan Palmer	1 12 12 12 27 27 27 27 27 27 27 27 27 27 27 27 27 27 27 27 27 27 27 27 27 27 27 27 27 27 12 12 12 12 12 12 12 1 1 1 1 1 1 1 1 1 1 1 1 6 6 6 6 20 20 20 20	4
29 Yannick Dalmas	27 27 27 12 12 12 12 12 12 12 12 12 12 12 12 12 12 12 12 12 12 2 2 2 2 2 2 2 2 2 2 2 2 2 2 6 6 6 6 6 20 20 20 20 20 5 5 5	5
14 Roberto Moreno	5 5 5 5 5 5 5 5 5 5 5 5 5 5 5 5 5 5 5 5 5 5 2 2 2 2 2 2 6 6 6 6 6 6 6 6 6 6 20 20 20 20 5 5 5 5 3 3 3	6
10 Christian Danner	20 20 20 20 20 2 2 2 2 2 2 2 2 2 2 2 2 2 2 5 5 5 5 5 5 5 5 20 20 20 20 20 20 20 5 5 5 16 16 16 16 10 10 10	7
8 Andrea de Cesaris	2 2 2 2 2 20 20 20 20 20 20 20 20 20 20 20 20 20 20 5 5 5 5 5 5 5 5 5 5 5 5 5 5 10 10 10 10 10 10 3 29 29	8
5 Riccardo Patrese	8 8 8 8 8 8 8 8 18 18 18 18 18 18 18 18 18 18 18 18 18 18 18 18 18 18 18 18 18 18 18 18 18 18 10 16 16 16 16 3 3 3 3 10 14 14 14	9
6 Nelson Piquet	18 18 18 18 18 18 18 8 19 19 19 25 25 25 25 25 25 25 25 25 25 25 25 25 25 25 25 25 10 10 10 10 10 18 8 8 8 8 29 29 29 29 8 8 8	10
16 Ivan Capelli	19 19 19 19 19 19 19 19 8 8 25 17 17 17 19 19 19 10 10 10 8 8 8 8 10 10 10 10 16 16 16 8 16 3 3 3 3 14 14 14 14	11
1 Alain Prost	17 7 7 7 7 7 7 7 25 17 9 9 9 19 10 10 10 10 8 8 8 10 10 10 10 8 16 16 16 8 8 8 16 16 8 29 29 29 29 8 8 8 8	12
18 Eddie Cheever	7 17 17 17 17 17 17 25 25 7 9 19 19 9 10 11 8 8 8 8 16 16 16 16 16 16 8 8 8 3 3 3 3 3 14 14 14 14	13
2 Stefan Johansson	3 9 25 25 25 25 25 17 17 17 7 7 10 10 11 11 16 30 30 30 30 30 30 30 3 3 3 19 19 19 19 29 29 18 18 18 18	14
19 Teo Fabi	9 3 25 9 9 9 9 9 9 16 10 7 11 11 16 16 29 29 29 29 29 29 29 29 29 3 30 30 30 19 30 29 29 29 14 14	15
23 Adrian Campos	11 25 3 3 11 11 11 11 11 10 16 16 16 8 29 29 30 30 14 14 14 14 14 3 3 29 29 29 19 30 29 30 14 14	16
30 Philippe Alliot	25 11 11 11 3 16 16 16 16 11 11 11 8 8 29 30 30 14 14 19 3 3 3 3 14 14 19 19 29 14 14 30 23	17
25 Rene Arnoux	16 16 16 16 16 30 30 10 10 10 30 30 29 29 30 14 3 3 3 19 19 19 19 19 19 14 14 14 14 23 23 23	18
7 Stefano Modena	4 4 4 4 4 30 29 10 30 30 30 30 29 8 30 14 3 3 7 7 7 7 23 23 23 23 23 23 23 23 23 23 23	19
26 Piercarlo Ghinzani	30 30 30 30 30 29 10 29 29 29 29 8 8 30 14 3 7 7 7 23 23 23 7 7 7 7	20
11 Satoru Nakajima	29 29 29 29 29 10 14 14 14 14 14 14 14 3 7 23 23 26 26 26 26	21
17 Derek Warwick	26 26 14 10 14 26 26 26 26 26 26 26 7 7 23 26 26 26	22
9 Martin Brundle	14 10 10 10 14 26 3 3 3 3 3 3 3 23 23 26	23
4 Philippe Streiff	10 14 14 26 26 26 23 23 23 23 23 23 23 23 26 26	24
24 Alessandro Nannini	23 23 23 23 23 23	25

Lap Chart continued

Laps 62–82	Pos
28 28 28 28 28 28 28 28 28 28 28 28 28 28 28 28 28 28 28 28 28	1
12 12 12 12 12 12 12 12 12 12 12 12 12 12 12 12 12 12 12 12 12	2
27 27 27 27 27 27 27 27 27 27 27 27 27 27 27 27 27 27 27 27 27	3
5 5 5 5 5 5 5 5 5 5 5 5 5 5 5 20 20 20 20 20	4
20 20 20 20 20 20 20 20 20 20 20 20 20 20 3 3 3 3	5
3 3 3 3 3 3 3 3 3 3 3 3 3 3 29 29 29	6
10 10 29 29 29 29 29 29 29 29 29 29 29 29 14 14 14	7
29 29 10 10 10 10 10 8 10 10 10 10 10 10 10 10'10 10	8
14 8 8 8 8 8 8 10 14 14 14 14 14 14 8 8	9
8 14 14 14 14 14 14 14 8 8 8 8 8	10

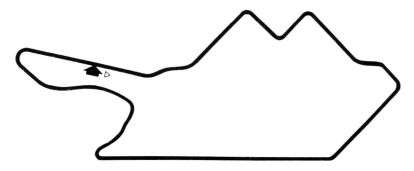

Championship Points

	Drivers			Constructors	
1	Nelson Piquet	73 pts	1	Williams	137 pts
2	Nigel Mansell	61 pts	2	McLaren	76 pts
3	Ayrton Senna	57 pts	3	Lotus	64 pts
4	Alain Prost	46 pts	4	Ferrari	53 pts
5	Gerhard Berger	36 pts	5	Benetton	28 pts
6	Stefan Johansson	30 pts	6=	Tyrrell	11 pts
6	Michele Alboreto	17 pts	6=	Arrows	11 pts
8	Thierry Boutsen	16 pts	8	Brabham	10 pts
9	Teo Fabi	12 pts	9	Lola	3 pts
10	Eddie Cheever	8 pts	10	Zakspeed	2 pts
11=	Jonathan Palmer	7 pts	11=	March	1 pt
11=	Satoru Nakajima	7 pts	11=	Ligier	1 pt
13	Riccardo Patrese	6 pts	11=	AGS	1 pt
14=	Andrea de Cesaris	4 pts			
14=	Philippe Streiff	4 pts			
16=	Derek Warwick	3 pts			
16=	Philippe Alliot	3 pts			
18	Martin Brundle	2 pts			
19=	Rene Arnoux	1 pt			
19=	Ivan Capelli	1 pt			
19=	Roberto Moreno	1 pt			

	Jim Clark Cup			Colin Chapman Cup	
1	Jonathan Palmer	95 pts	1	Tyrrell	169 pts
2	Philippe Streiff	74 pts	2	Lola	56 pts
3	Philippe Alliot	43 pts	3	AGS	39 pts
4	Ivan Capelli	38 pts	4	March	38 pts
5	Pascal Fabre	35 pts			
6	Yannick Dalmas	13 pts			
7	Roberto Moreno	4 pts			

PHOTOGRAPHIC CREDITS

Page 1 : ST
Page 2 : KS
Page 3 : LG
Page 4 : ST
Page 5 : Z
Page 6 : Z
Page 8 : Z
Page 10 : MN, PB
Page 11 : LG
Page 12 : KS
Page 14 : CBK
Page 15 : KS, ST
Page 16 : BA
Page 18 : FK
Page 19 : Z, Z
Page 20 : Z
Page 22 : Z, BA
Page 23 : BA
Page 24 : ZZ
Page 25 : Z
Page 26 : LG, PB
Page 27 : KS
Page 28 : Z, DK
Page 29 : ST
Page 30 : ST, Z
Page 31 : Z, LG, Z
Page 32 : DK
Page 33 : Z
Page 34 : Z, C, BK, Z
Page 35 : Z, Z
Page 36 : MN, Z
Page 37 : Z, ST
Page 38 : Z
Page 40 : Z
Page 41 : DW
Page 42 : Z
Page 43 : PB, ST
Page 44 : JPF
Page 46 : Z
Page 47 : Z
Page 48 : Z
Page 50 : Z, BA
Page 51 : BA
Page 52 : FK, Z, JPF, ST, Z
Page 53 : Z
Page 54 : CBK
Page 56 : BA
Page 57 : PP, DK, FK, LG
Page 59 : BA
Page 60 : ST
Page 62 : DK
Page 63 : LG
Page 64 : Z
Page 65 : LG, KS, PN, FK
Page 66 : ST
Page 68 : LG, CBK, ST, PB
Page 69 : DK
Page 71 : CBK
Page 72 : ST
Page 74 : MN
Page 75 : KS
Page 76 : GU

Page 78 : CBK
Page 79 : CBK, ST, BA, DM
Page 80 : CBK
Page 82 : Z, ST, Z
Page 83 : ST
Page 85 : RS
Page 86 : ST
Page 88 : CBK
Page 89 : LG
Page 90 : RS, MN, CBK
Page 91 : CBK
Page 92 : PB
Page 94 : Z
Page 95 : CBK, CBK, CBK,
     CBK, DM
Page 96 : JB
Page 97 : PB
Page 99 : Z
Page 100 : BA
Page 102 : BA
Page 103 : CBK, PG
Page 104 : LG
Page 105 : ZZ, KS, LG
Page 106 : BA
Page 108 : B
Page 109 : B, Z, Z, KS
Page 111 : RS
Page 112 : PP
Page 114 : FK
Page 115 : DK
Page 116 : KS
Page 117 : EC, Z, JB, PN
Page 118 : Z
Page 120 : PB, GP, FK
Page 121 : Z, LG, ST
Page 123 : RS
Page 124 : JB
Page 126 : JB
Page 127 : LG
Page 128 : KS
Page 129 : Z, LG, Z, DK, SD
Page 130 : RS
Page 132 : ST, DK, DK, Z
Page 133 : ST, EC
Page 135 : Z
Page 136 : Z
Page 138 : ST
Page 139 : RS
Page 140 : PN, PN, LG, PN,
     Z, PN
Page 141 : Z
Page 142 : GS
Page 144 : Z
Page 145 : ST, DK, ST, JPF
Page 147 : RS
Page 148 : KS
Page 150 : Z
Page 151 : PP
Page 152 : KS, Z, KS
Page 153 : ST, Z, Z, FK
Page 154 : RS
Page 156 : KS

Page 157 : KS, PN, FK, PN
Page 159 : Z
Page 160 : DK
Page 162 : BA
Page 163 : DK
Page 164 : DK, LG
Page 165 : KS, LG
Page 166 : Z
Page 168 : BA
Page 169 : ST, LG, LG, SD
Page 170 : BA, LG, ST, ST, LG,
     BA, BA, BA
Page 171 : Z
Page 173 : KS
Page 174 : DK
Page 176 : LG
Page 177 : CBK
Page 178 : Z, CBK
Page 179 : LG, CBK, ST
Page 180 : Z
Page 181 : DK, LG, PN, Z
Page 183 : PN
Page 184 : KS
Page 186 : KS
Page 187 : PP
Page 188 : DK
Page 189 : ST, KS, DK, MN
Page 190 : B
Page 191 : B
Page 192 : B, B, B, FK
Page 193 : DK, KS
Page 195 : FK
Page 196 : DK
Page 198 : LG
Page 199 : LG
Page 200 : Z, Z, LG, LG
Page 201 : KS, DK
Page 202 : K
Page 204 : KS, Z, LG, Z
Page 205 : KS, Z, DK
Page 207 : Z
Page 208 : Z
Page 210 : Z
Page 211 : PP, Z
Page 212 : Z
Page 213 : ST, Z, Z, ST
Page 214 : ST, Z
Page 215 : KS, Z, ST
Page 217 : Z
Page 218 : Z
Page 220 : KS
Page 221 : KS
Page 222 : ST, KS
Page 223 : ST, DK
Page 224 : Z, Z, Z, Z
Page 225 : Z, ST
Page 226 : TK, TK, TK, TK
Page 227 : TK
Page 229 : ST
Page 230 : DK
Page 232 : ST, KS
Page 233 : ST

Page 234 : KS, KS
Page 235 : Z, KS
Page 236 : Z
Page 237 : Z, Z, Z, Z, LG
Page 239 : Z
Page 240 : Z

Z	:	Zooom Photographic
BA	:	Bernard Asset
FK	:	Ferdi Kraling
ST	:	Stephen Tee
KS	:	Keith Sutton
PP	:	David Phipps
LG	:	Lukas Gorys
DK	:	Dave Kennard
RS	:	Rainer Schlegelmilch
EC	:	Ercole Colombo
GS	:	Graham Smith
PB	:	Patrick Behar
PN	:	Peter Nygaard
JPF	:	J P Froidevaux
CBK	:	Charles Briscoe-Knight
MN	:	Mark Newcombe
SD	:	Stephen Davis
JB	:	Jeff Bloxham
DM	:	David Martin
B	:	John Blakemore
PG	:	Peter Gurr
TK	:	Toshiyuki Kita
GP	:	Gerard Petitsean
GU	:	Gustavo Ugueto
DW	:	David Winter